About the Author

Educated at King Edward's High School, Birmingham, and St Catharine's College, Cambridge University, Peter Dawkins practised as an architect for ten years in both England and Scotland before devoting himself full-time to research and educational work in connection with the world's wisdom traditions, mythology, geomancy and landscape cosmology. One specialised area of research has been into Bacon, Shakespeare, the Rosicrucians and other philosophers of the Renaissance. To this end, the Francis Bacon Research Trust was founded in 1979, and Peter is its founder-director. Since then Peter has been giving seminars, lectures, workshops and summer schools throughout Europe, and occasionally the USA, and leading many Wisdom tours and geomantic pilgrimages world-wide. He has given special Shakespeare seminars and workshops for over twenty years, and is an adviser to actors and directors, including the acclaimed 'Shakespeare's Globe' theatre in London where, since 1997, he has been giving Wisdom of Shakespeare seminars with Mark Rylance. Peter is also founder-director of Zoence Academy, which provides a training course in a synthesis of the western wisdom traditions, sacred architecture, landscape cosmology and geomancy. Peter is the author of many books, and is married to Sarah who shares his passion for this work. They have three children.

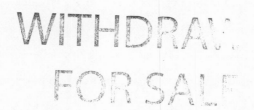

Other Publications by Peter Dawkins

Building Paradise (FBRT, 2001).

Herald of the New Age (FBRT, 1997).

The Pattern of Initiation in the Evolution of Human Consciousness (FBRT Journal 1/1, 1981).

The Virgin Ideal (FBRT Journal 1/2, 1982).

Dedication to the Light (FBRT Journal 1/3, 1985).

The Great Vision (FBRT Journal 1/4, 1985).

Arcadia (FBRT Journal 1/5, 1988).

The Wisdom of Shakespeare in As You Like It (I.C.Media Productions, 1998).

The Wisdom of Shakespeare in The Merchant of Venice (I.C.Media Productions, 1998).

The Wisdom of Shakespeare in Julius Caesar (I.C.Media Productions, 1999).

The Wisdom of Shakespeare in The Tempest (I.C.Media Productions, 2000).

The Wisdom of Shakespeare in Twelfth Night (I.C.Media Productions, 2002).

Zoence: the Science of Life (Samuel Weiser Inc., 1998).

PETER DAWKINS

THE

SHAKESPEARE

ENIGMA

POLAIR PUBLISHING · LONDON · 2004

Published 2004 by Polair Publishing
London, United Kingdom

ISBN 0-9545389-4-3

British Library Cataloguing-in-Publication Data:

A Catlaogue Record for this book is available from the British Library

Printed in Great Britain by
Cambridge University Press

Contents

Dedication

To Hope, who started me off on this extraordinary treasure trail.

When you play characters in a play, it is natural to assume that when they use images and ideas with any authority, or relate an experience with any authenticity, they know what they are saying through learning or experience. It was Samuel Johnson who said, 'Nature gives no man knowledge and when images are collected by study and experience, can only assist in combining or applying them. Shakespeare, however favoured by nature, could only impart what he had learnt'. Though all the alternative authorship societies have many questions to answer in regard to their candidates, so too do those who believe that Shakespeare, the Stratford actor, wrote the plays. The most intriguing question is how to reconcile the actor Shakespeare's extremely limited access to learning with the huge amount of apparent and submerged learning in the plays of Shakespeare; learning which appears immediately and most scholastically in his first plays. The amount of learning in the plays has been downplayed and the opportunities that the actor Shakespeare had to learn have been played up, but ironically the fantastic research in this last century of Stratfordians—those who believe the actor wrote the plays—has unearthed ever more proof of the author Shakespeare's learning, and widened the evidential gulf between the actor's life and writing.

I don't mean to criticize any Stratfordian for his or her belief. I welcome and love to hear all views. Actually, it is an enormous blessing that so many Stratfordian scholars have not focused on the question of the authorship. There is so little to study about Shakespeare the actor that they have moved quickly through the few facts in order to get to the plays and their special area of interest, yielding more and more detail to the picture. I do argue that there is cause for reasonable doubt that Shakespeare the actor wrote the Shakespeare plays and poems, and alternative theories should be weighed fairly without resort to slander of the individual proposing the theory—an all too common occurrence in the media.

Whoever wrote the plays, they wanted us to believe that Shakespeare from Stratford was responsible. Even in the case of the actor, he must have hidden himself away to be so little known as a writer in his own life and left so little evidence of writing in the memorabilia gathered after his life. This is an important point for those of us who question the Shakespeare authorship. What was the purpose of such disguise and concealment? Was the purpose confined to the author's life? If so, why did no friends unmask the author after death? There is so much hiding and revealing in the plays, so much use of disguise to reveal, that we should take care to consider the purpose of disguise when our author seems to wish to conceal himself.

Peter Dawkins and I have discussed Sir Francis Bacon's relationship to the plays primarily, but fascinating research is also being done by the Stratfordians, Oxfordians and Marlovians, not to mention a Russian scholar, Professor Gillilov, who is writing with great insight about the Earl of Derby, and an American scholar, Ms Robin Williams, who is writing about Mary Sidney with similar insight.

In the nineties my work with Peter Dawkins led me and my wife to mount a production of *The Tempest* in the Rollright Stone Circle on the Oxfordshire–Warwickshire border. That led to performances on the concrete site of Shakespeare's Globe Theatre. In 1996 I became the Artistic Director and had to take great care not to alarm with my authorship questions. Even so, Mr Bernard Levin of *The Times* newspaper had his fun with 'A Heretic at the Globe'. It is a great sign of the times that the discussion is now much less offensive. And indeed my fellows at the Globe, who all hold their own personal views about the authorship, have agreed we are an institution that welcomes all forms of interest in Shakespeare, and hopes to refine and develop the questions about the authorship in the same way that we have refined and developed the questions about his amphitheatre. In the exhibition below the Globe we have a terrific panel introducing all the alternative candidates and questions, as well as all the known knowledge of the actor Shakespeare's life in London. Peter and I hold three Wisdom of Shakespeare weekends every summer, where we explore the esoteric meanings of the plays being performed at the Globe.

I like encouraging communication, enquiry and enjoyment in the wide field of authorship studies and societies, so this book, gathering together over twenty years of enquiry by Peter and the many people who have contributed at FBRT weekends, is a great joy to me. Peter and I serve with our good friends as trustees of the Shakespearean Authorship Trust. There we have in our care one of the oldest collections of books on the authorship, and we work to bring together representatives from all the different viewpoints in open enquiry.

When something truly beautiful is made by an inspired human being like Shakespeare, I can't help wondering how he did it and how he wanted it shared. The marriage of heaven and earth, spirit and matter; the soul and psyche of the characters; these are all aspects of Shakespeare's wisdom. In these areas Peter has always been a unique and profound friend and teacher. I have not approached a Shakespeare play since meeting Peter without his thoughts in my mind. He is a gentle-spoken gentleman who loves to laugh at himself and possesses the patient curiosity of a wise man.

If you are new to the subject of Shakespeare's authorship, I hope you enjoy your first enquiries. I always think the enigma of the subject is worthy of Shakespeare's genius, as he so loved to test the intuition of his imagined characters. He may well be doing so with ours. He was a master of disguise and revelation. If one thing is certain in his plays, it is that nothing is as it appears. Perhaps this is true also of his life.

M.R.

Introduction

In Sonnet 83 Shakespeare refers to 'both your poets'. What does this mean? Who is the other poet, if there is one? Moreover, why is it so difficult to discover anything in Shakespeare's life to equate him with the author of the immortal works ascribed to him? This book unravels this double mystery, following each clue to wherever it leads and finally uncovering a whole team of 'Spear-shakers' or 'Shake-speares' led by their chief poet, a master artist, and his 'twin'. Yet the discovery of this literary studio and the genius who led it is not the end of the story. The clues lead on much further, right up to the eighteenth century and maybe beyond, even to the present day, suggesting a coherent plan and profound knowledge passed on to future generations for a purpose yet to be fully revealed.

All in all, this Shakespeare enigma is a treasure trail, the treasure being truth itself and also the sheer delight of self-education and discovery. The concealment, the false trails and the clues have been deliberately created for us. Searching out and following the clues is an exercise and training in the art of discovery, which is probably one of the main reasons for the concealment of the truth in the first place. Moreover, this treasure trail is indeed a mystery, in the classical sense of an allegorical play in which truth is hidden in such a way that it can be discovered, with effort. It could be considered to be Shakespeare's last play—a 'living' play, comprehending all the others, in which each of us is a principal actor, a detective on the trail of elusive truth or a Theseus in the labyrinth of concealed wisdom.

It has taken me the best part of thirty years to follow the treasure trail thus far, and the fact that I am able to have come this far and written this book is thanks not only to my own researches, discoveries and insights, but also to the many others who have followed the trail and shared their discoveries. In the course of this journey many sidetracks or false trails have been followed, by myself as well as others, which have led to many dead ends and misconceptions. But part of the magic of this treasure trail is that it allows for mistakes and, as in solving a crossword puzzle, the solution of other clues eventually brings about a reappraisal and correction of each misconception.

Despite the many clues it is, or has been, a rigorous journey. It demands rigour. It demands attention to detail. It demands accuracy, as far as that is humanly possible. It demands open-mindedness and humility as well as a willingness to question everything, taking notice especially of the paradoxes, ambiguities and allusions. It also demands a wide-ranging research into all kinds of subjects—history, geography, art, literature, drama, architecture, language, mythology, Neoplatonism, alchemy or Hermeticism, Cabala, and even the landscape—and visits to the various places where such knowledge can be found. Finally and most importantly, as in everything, a strong intuition and good inspiration are two things much to be hoped and prayed for, just as Shakespeare acknowledged and prayed for inspiration from his Muse, Pallas Athena.

Of course, to do all this perfectly would require someone almost super-human. Naturally, I am not, but I have done my best in the circumstances and I offer you, the reader, this book, which combines, condenses and synthesises the results of my own researches and discoveries together with those of others, in the hope that they will be interesting, useful and inspiring. In this matter one can only be the dwarf who, because he is seated on the shoulders of a giant, can see a little bit further—the giant being the sum total of all those who have researched and discovered so many fascinating and useful things, and who have been generous enough to share their findings and thoughts.

Much of my time has been spent in sifting through such discoveries and speculations, checking primary sources and trying to weed out the more spurious or abstruse so as to capture what I would call the 'golden egg' or heart of the matter. In addition to this I have made many discoveries of my own, to add to the pool of research, which has enabled a greater synthesis and understanding of the enigma to be made than was available before—or so I believe and hope. To do all this I have been nourished, supported, helped, advised and encouraged, emotionally and otherwise, by many good friends, including my wife Sarah, my children (when they were old enough to see what their Dad was up to), and my parents (even though they could never understand why), without which I am sure I would have fallen by the wayside long ago.

I personally find the whole thing extraordinarily inspiring—not just the wonderful drama and poetry of Shakespeare but the whole Shakespeare mystery, of which the discovery of two master poets and their Shakespeare team is, in fact, but a beginning. It is by no means just an academic or historical exercise. If you follow this treasure trail yourself, you will, I hope, see what I mean. This book is offered as a guide, to perhaps make the path a little bit easier and to enable you the readers, and others, to go far further.

P.D.

Easter 2004

Chapter 1

The Star of Poets

Sweet Swan of Avon! what a sight it were
　　To see thee in our waters yet appeare,
And make those flights upon the bankes of Thames,
　　That so did take Eliza, and our James!
But stay, I see thee in the Hemisphere
　　Advanc'd, and made a Constellation there!
Shine forth, thou Starre of Poets....

Ben Jonson, Eulogy in Shakespeare First Folio (1623)

To begin this book with these adulatory words of Ben Jonson, Shakespeare's friend and associate, seems to me most fitting. A great many people the world over would probably agree with Jonson's sentiments: that Shakespeare was and in many ways still is the star of poets, at least in terms of the English language, and some would say more than that. His light still blazes strongly today and, indeed, even seems to increase. More than any other poet–playwright, Shakespeare has made an enduring mark upon the minds and culture of nations all around the world—even upon those whose languages are vastly different from Shakespeare's English. Shakespeare's works are seen as the creations of one of the most gifted geniuses the world has ever known and are often considered by some people as a complement to the Scriptures. There was a time, for instance, when no well-educated Englishman would travel without two particular books—a Bible and a copy of the Shakespeare plays.

The Shakespeare plays are now translated into every major language on earth and acted in countries the world over. They have been made into award-winning films, and presented time and again on television networks. They have spawned all kinds of creations, from cartoons to operas, and provided inspiration for a host of later dramatists and film writers. Directors have found them extraordinarily adaptable and have been able to extract from them a pertinent message or challenging question for every generation and type of society in which they are performed. They have given vast numbers of people great opportunities to excel.

In England the well-established and well-patronised Royal Shakespeare Company regularly presents high-quality productions of Shakespeare's plays at their group of theatres in Stratford-upon-Avon and other theatres in London, as well as on tour. A recently-built reconstruction of Shakespeare's original Globe Theatre occupies a prime site on the south bank of the Thames, close to the site of the original Globe, complete with its own thriving Globe Theatre Company and Globe Education department. The United States of America boast several fine centres and theatres devoted almost exclusively to Shakespeare. Libraries are packed with books by or about Shakespeare. Schools teach Shakespeare, universities study Shakespeare and a great number of doctorates are obtained because of Shakespeare. A huge Shakespeare industry exists involving the theatre, television, film, literature, publishing, scholarship, art, schools, universities, historical properties, tourism, and trade generally. More time and expense has been devoted to researching, writing and talking about Shakespeare and his works than any other poet or playwright who has ever lived.

Shakespeare's works are astounding, not only in their exquisite poetry and in the power of the spoken word in them, but also in their construction, variety and depth of meaning. The plays are superb studies of human nature and psychology, ranging from the depths to the heights of emotion and thought, and encompassing all walks of life—but with particular emphasis on the rich, famous and politically powerful. Shakespeare is a wonderful storyteller, drawing on both old and contemporary stories and weaving them into new tales to suit his purpose, dramatised for the stage. Except for the three plays that appear to have no other sources but his own invention (*Love's Labour's Lost, Midsummer Night's Dream* and *The Tempest*), he manages, like an alchemist, to turn all his source-material into gold. He uses and invents a whole range of styles and tones, and shows himself a master of both oratory and poetry as well as of drama and storytelling. Moreover, he knows the importance of music and uses it accordingly. It has an almost mystical significance for him, a meaning to which he refers many times in the plays as relating to the unseen spirit that is able not only to set or express the mood but also inspire and heal.

The Shakespeare plays are a remarkable mixture and synthesis of classical, medieval and Renaissance influences; of historical, romantic, pastoral and mythological themes; and of both comedy and tragedy in varying proportions. Moreover, Shakespeare combines all this with contemporary issues of his day, both political and social, with each of his characters seemingly drawn from life. This he seems to have achieved by means of emphasising or fusing together various characteristics of contemporaries whom he had met, observed or studied in some way. In this sense, he uses the plays to mirror society—not only his own but also ours, since so many of the issues and characteristics portrayed are still true today. From this point of view, he can be understood as an ethical Hamlet, holding the mirror up to his 'mother'—our world of human kind.

Even more remarkable is the sheer depth of knowledge and breadth of experience displayed in the plays. Although not necessarily to be noticed at once, this knowledge and experience is quite breathtaking when one begins to study the plays and Shakespeare's sources in any depth. It is remarkable not just because it is the attribute of one man, as is supposed, but also because this impressive phenomenon tends to be all too swiftly played down, ignored or dismissed as the result purely of genius. However, as Samuel Johnson so aptly pointed out a century and a half after Shakespeare, 'Nature gives no man knowledge, and Shakespeare, however favoured by nature, could only impart what he had learned'. His namesake, Ben Jonson, playwright, poet laureate and friend of Shakespeare, likewise emphasises this point in his eulogy in the Shakespeare Folio of plays: 'For a good poet's made, as well as born. And such wert thou'. Natural genius and knowledge are two distinct things, and the author of the Shakespeare works had both to a high degree.

Shakespeare draws upon a whole wealth of literary sources for his plays, both classical and modern, and from various countries and in several different languages. His favourite poets seem to have been Ovid and Chaucer, but the extent of his reading included well over one hundred different classical authors alone.[1] Ovid, Virgil and Homer were favourites, but others included Apuleius, Aesop, Caesar, Cicero, Heliodorus, Herodotus, Homer, Josephus, Livy, Lucan, Marianus, Plato, Plautus, Pliny, Plutarch and Seneca, for instance. Some of the works of some of these authors were published in English translation by the time that Shakespeare used them, but by no means all, which means that Shakespeare could read the Latin or Greek originals with sufficient scholarly ease, even though some of the matter was abstruse. Moreover, besides being a classical scholar and reading his Latin and Greek source material in the original versions, evidence shows that Shakespeare also read source material in French, Italian and Spanish, either because no English translations were present at the time he wrote each play or because he chose to do so. He also borrowed from poems and other stories written by French and Italian authors, such as Aretino, Ariosto, Bandello, du Bellay, Belleforest, Boccaccio, Cinthio, Desportes, Fiorentino, Jodell, Montemayor, Petrarch, Rabelais, the essayist Montaigne, and the prince of French Renaissance poets, Ronsard.[2]

Closer to home, Shakespeare was influenced and perhaps even helped by his contemporaries. These included Thomas Kyd and Christopher Marlowe in tragedy, John Lyly, George Peele and Robert Greene in comedy, and Thomas Lodge for his *Rosalynde*. Then there were Arthur Brooke, Samuel Daniel, Edmund Spenser, Thomas Watson, Sir Philip Sidney, George Whetstone, Samuel Rowley, George Gascoigne, Thomas Preston, Francis Bacon and Ben Jonson. Francis Beaumont and Thomas Middleton possibly collaborated with Shakespeare on some of his plays, and John Fletcher was a definite collaborator for the final Shakespeare plays. This alone shows an active interest and participation in the literary world of his day by Shakespeare, as well as of a kind of fraternity of poets who assisted each other when required. Some of them were also not shy of criticising each other in public, or satirising each other. Ben Jonson was famed for this, with his biting but perceptive wit—and yet he seems to have been a good friend of Shakespeare.

English history was of particular concern to Shakespeare, although the Shakespeare history plays are not strictly historical but dramatised stories based on history and forged in the fire of Shakespeare's creative imagination. His main historical sources were the *Chronicles* of Raphael Holinshed and Edward Hall, and the *Histories* of Sir Thomas More, which were considered suitable by the Tudor monarchy. This was obviously a wise choice by Shakespeare in those days of official torture, burnings, mutilation and beheadings! What is particularly fascinating is that Shakespeare's history plays have performed a major role in interesting people in English history, despite Shakespeare's poetic licence in terms of historical veracity—which only goes to prove the importance of a good storyteller in the life of a nation. To create a whole cycle of history plays, spanning hundreds of years in one epic sequence, is a major achievement. As for Shakespeare's Celtic and Roman historical tragedies, they are a *tour de force*!

However, it was not just history that interested Shakespeare but also his modern world. The plays contain many political references and topical stories derived from both public and private sources. Indeed, it is remarkable how much Shakespeare knew about the politics of his day—especially about the private lives, activities and policies of not just the English but also the French and Italian aristocracy and governing class. It is remarkable how he was allowed to get away with his sometimes very pointed allusions to and criticisms of those in power. He seems, indeed, to have led either a very charmed or else a very protected life in this respect. This throws up some interesting questions. He seems to have been privy to various matters of state that were not known or discussed beyond a certain small circle of courtiers and officials. Moreover, he displays a thorough knowledge of aristocratic and courtly pursuits such as hunting, hawking and riding, and of the forests, parks and gardens enjoyed by the privileged classes. His detailed descriptions and

Chapter 2

The Actor

The Enigma

Leaving aside for the moment the question of what the reference to 'both your poets' might really mean, something which we will gradually address as the book progresses, it is really greatly to be remarked on that there seems to be such a gulf between the life of William Shakespeare of Stratford-upon-Avon and the life-experience of the author that can be gleaned from the Shakespeare poems and plays. In fact, the answer to the one question might help resolve the other point. It might also help to answer why contemporary references to Shakespeare seem on the one hand to acclaim him as a poet and on the other hand to suggest that he was not a poet, and why his principal memorials, the Folio of plays and the monument at Stratford-upon-Avon, have such enigmatic features.

A poet is usually to be seen in his writings, which are expressions of his knowledge and experience as well as his inspiration. The disconcerting fact is that the vast breadth and depth of knowledge, learning and experience of life exhibited by the Shakespeare poems and plays, as well as the literary skills, contacts and activity required, appear to have almost nothing whatsoever to do with the actor William Shakespeare from Stratford-upon-Avon. Moreover, this is not because we do not know much about the Stratford man. On the contrary, quite a lot is known about him, and the more we discover the greater the dichotomy becomes; for the records of William Shakespeare's life show him to have been a busy actor and joint owner–manager of a theatre, and (later in life) a businessman dealing in corn and other commodities, a land-owner, money-lender and property-dealer, but not a literary man—not a well-travelled and highly cultured, educated poet, writer and playwright, which the author of the Shakespeare poems, plays and sonnets clearly was.

The knowledge of Shakespeare's life that we possess has been gradually and painstakingly gleaned by historians and Shakespeare scholars from various authentic documents of the time, each containing some record of William

Shakespeare and his family, friends, colleagues and acquaintances. The 1623 First Folio of Shakespeare plays provided no biographical observations, even though the Folio was published as a lasting memorial to the author by his colleagues. Moreover, even though original manuscripts of the plays—either the author's original manuscripts or the actors' promptbook copies— were painstakingly collected for the purpose of publishing the First Folio, none has ever been found. This is strange, because manuscripts of plays by other leading dramatists, such as Marlowe, Jonson, Fletcher, Beaumont, Greene, Heywood, Dekker and Middleton, are still in existence, whereas every single original Shakespeare manuscript, whether of a play, poem or sonnet, seems to have vanished into thin air! Whether such evidence would help establish the author of the plays, though, would depend on whether or not the manuscripts were the author's original 'foul papers', penned in his own handwriting or, even better, contained his signature.

That the name 'William Shakespeare' is printed on the title pages of the published plays, sonnets and poems is in itself no proof that the actor William Shakespeare of Stratford-upon-Avon was the author, since the name could refer to someone else known by that name or be the pseudonym of a secret author. However, the reference to William Shakespeare in the 1623 Shakespeare Folio that links him with the Shakespeare Monument at Stratford-upon-Avon, as well as the inscription on the monument itself, would appear to point to the actor William Shakespeare from Stratford-upon-Avon as the author of the Shakespeare works. For most people this clinches the matter.

If this surmise were true, then there should be a match between the author that is to be found in the Shakespeare works and the actor from Stratford-upon-Avon; but therein lies the problem and the enigma. There is no real match, even though many Shakespeare scholars and writers have tried their hardest to create one—sometimes with a seriously over-liberal use of assumption and imaginative speculation.

For instance, there is no factual evidence that William Shakespeare ever received a day's formal schooling in his life: it is merely assumed that he must have attended Stratford's grammar school and that the school must have been a good one. There is no evidence that either of these assumptions is true, although of course they could be. Even assuming that William attended the Stratford grammar school, there is no evidence that he later went to university, since the well-kept university archives of Oxford and Cambridge have no record of his doing so; yet the Shakespeare poems and plays—especially the earlier ones—are full of academic learning and university matters. Neither is there the slightest evidence that William of Stratford ever studied law, hobnobbed with the aristocracy, travelled abroad, had access to any good libraries or was in a position to know intimate matters of Court life and politics.

Other than acting and trading in commodities, nothing associates William Shakespeare with literary or intellectual pursuits of any kind. No letters written by him have ever been found, and there are no references whatsoever to any letters having been written by him. One letter penned to William by his friend, Richard Quiney, which was never sent, still exists, but that is all. For the more ordinary person the non-survival of private letters is not unusual, but for a well-known and well-connected literary man in London, which the author Shakespeare certainly was, it is somewhat remarkable.

Moreover, although some would like to disagree, there is no definite evidence nor even any mention of Shakespeare ever buying, borrowing, possessing or even reading any of the hundreds of books, written in many different languages, classical and modern, which the true author of the plays clearly read, studied and noted with great care. Those who would disagree with this base their viewpoint on the surmise that one or two books have been discovered with marginal notes that might be in Shakespeare's handwriting. The problem with this is that all guesses as to what Shakespeare's handwriting actually looked like are based on an analysis of the six very different and somewhat crude signatures of William Shakespeare that exist on legal documents. Since there is still an ongoing debate as to whether these signatures were actually penned by Shakespeare or signed by a clerk on his behalf, and since assessing someone's handwriting accurately on the basis of such signatures is fraught with difficulty and the possibility of self-deception, this provides no solid ground to support the contentions.

Also strange is that William Shakespeare never gave his daughters any education, yet they were not alienated from him.[1] Shakespeare's eldest daughter Susanna, who married a doctor, learnt to sign her name; but there is no evidence for her ever being able to do more than that, but rather to the contrary. Shakespeare's youngest daughter Judith signed her name with a mark. For a relatively wealthy Stratford man and a supposed author to whom ignorance was 'the curse of God' and knowledge 'the wing wherewith we fly to heaven',[2] and whose heroines were all well-educated women, this seems an extraordinary oversight!

The Actor and Businessman

The church records, in Latin, show that William was baptised *Gulielmus filius Johannes Shakspere* on 26 April 1564 in Holy Trinity Church, Stratford-upon-Avon.[3] He was born the first son of John Shakespeare, a glover and wool trader of Stratford-upon-Avon. His mother, John's wife, was Mary Arden, the daughter of a yeoman farmer of Wilmcote. Nothing else is known of William until his marriage in November 1582 to 'Anne Hathwey of Stratford',[4] assumed to be the daughter of Richard Hathaway of Shottery. Seven months later a daughter was born to them, who was baptised Susanna on 26 May 1583 in Holy Trinity Church, Stratford-upon-Avon. Two years after this Anne gave birth to twins, a son and a daughter, who were baptised Hamnet and Judith on 2 February 1585 in the same parish church of Stratford-upon-Avon.

Either then or in one of the following years, William left Stratford for reasons unknown. His name is not mentioned again until 15 March 1595, when he is recorded as having been one of the players in plays presented before the Queen the previous December by the acting company known as the Lord Chamberlain's Men. This company of players, which operated under the patronage of the Queen's Lord Chamberlain, Lord Hunsdon, was run by the famous tragic actor Richard Burbage, one of the two sons of James Burbage. James was the actor–manager and builder of The Theatre, the first permanent theatre to be built in London, which was located on the north side of the city.

By the spring of 1597 William had, surprisingly, a sufficient sum of money to enable him to buy New Place, one of the largest and finest houses in Stratford-upon-Avon, together with a few other properties. Although he moved into it with his family, he was also resident in Chapel Street ward in London. He divided his time so that while in Stratford he was a businessman dealing in corn and malt, and when in London he continued his acting. In 1598 he was listed in Ben Jonson's 1616 Folio edition of poetry and plays as having performed in Jonson's *Every Man in his Humour*.

In December 1598, the Lord Chamberlain's Men pulled down the Theatre and, in the following month, transported the materials across the Thames to build a new theatre on Bankside, on the south side of the Thames. They named this re-situated and rebuilt theatre 'The Globe'. In February 1599 William was named with Cuthbert and Richard Burbage, John Heminges, William Kempe, Augustine Phillips and Thomas Pope as a lessee/shareholder in land for the new Globe Theatre, thereby becoming one of the actor-managers of the theatre company. The Globe was opened for performances a few months later, probably in May 1599. That same year the Heralds' College granted a Coat of Arms to William's father and his posterity, enabling them to be referred to as 'gentlemen'. John Shakespeare did not enjoy this for long, however, for he died in September 1601, leaving William as his heir.

1603 was a major year of changes for the whole country. Queen Elizabeth died on 24 March and the Stuart king, James VI of Scotland, acceded to the throne of England as James I. James Stuart was greatly interested in the theatre, and within ten days of arriving in London he took over the patronage of the Lord Chamberlain's Men, which by then had become the most popular

quently, most of the later (post-1594) plays. At some time between the formation of the Lord Chamberlain's Men in 1594 and December that year William
Shakespeare either joined or became involved with the company as an actor.

The earliest surviving mention of the Lord Chamberlain's Men is in June
1594, when they are recorded as playing at Newington Butts; but they soon
moved to the Theatre in Shoreditch, until at the end of 1598 they dismantled
the building, moved it south across the river and re-erected it on Bankside as
the Globe. This then became their principal home for the rest of Queen Elizabeth's reign and throughout the following reigns, until the closure of the
theatres in 1642. Even though the Globe was burnt down in June 1613 the company, which had been renamed the King's Men when James I came to the
throne of England, immediately rebuilt it as the second Globe, which lasted
until it was demolished in 1644. Besides the public performances at the Globe,
the company performed an average of four times a year at Queen Elizabeth's
court and twelve times a year at King James'. In 1608 they took over Blackfriars
Theatre as their winter home.

Even during the height of William's career several Shakespeare plays were
seemingly owned and staged by Philip Henslowe, the owner and manager of
the Rose and other theatres: plays such as *Titus Andronicus, Henry V, Henry VI,
King Lear, Hamlet* and *The Taming of the Shrew*, all of which were later included in
the Shakespeare Folio. Henslowe kept good records, but he made no acknowledgment of Shakespeare as the author of these. It seems very strange that
Shakespeare should write plays for performance by a rival company and yet
receive no payment for them! It further adds to the mystery that for *Troilus
and Cressida* Henslowe records in his diary two part-payments to Thomas
Dekker and Henry Chettle; presumably because he thought they were co-
authors of the work.

The Burbages' Letter to the Earl of Pembroke

In 1635 Cuthbert Burbage, in conjunction with his nephew William, son of
Cuthbert's deceased brother Richard, presented a petition to the Earl of
Pembroke, the Lord Chamberlain to Charles I, asking for consideration in a
quarrel about certain theatres and requesting that their rights in the Globe be
respected. (The Lord Chamberlain was in charge of the Revels Office, organising court entertainments, overseeing all plays and representing the King's interests in all playing matters.)

The Earl of Pembroke at that time was Philip Herbert, the 4th Earl of
Pembroke and Earl of Montgomery. He was the survivor of the 'Incomparable pair of Brethren' to whom the First Folio of Shakespeare plays had been

dedicated nine years previously. His elder brother William, 3rd Earl of Pembroke, had previously been Lord Chamberlain to James I from 1615 to 1626. Philip succeeded his brother as Lord Chamberlain when Charles I came to the throne in 1626, while William became Lord Steward of the Royal Household until his death in 1630.

The mother of Philip and William was Mary, Countess of Pembroke. Mary was the sister of the renowned Sir Philip Sidney, who led the group of English writers known as the Areopagites until his untimely death in 1586. Hailed by the diarist John Aubrey as 'the greatest patroness of wit and learning of any lady of her time', Mary and her husband patronised the stage and literature—so much so that 'in her time Wilton House [the Pembrokes' country seat] was like a college, there were so many learned and ingenious persons'.[10] These persons—poets, writers, philosophers, musicians and dramatists—included the group that was directly associated with the author Shakespeare, and it is reputed that at least one Shakespeare play, *Twelfth Night*, was first performed at Wilton. Philip and William continued this patronage long after the death of their father in January 1601 and their mother in 1609.

The father of William and Philip, and Mary's husband, was Henry Herbert, 2nd Earl of Pembroke, a Knight of the Garter and member of the Privy Council, who held many high offices under Elizabeth I. He was the patron of the Lord Pembroke's Men from 1577, when he married Mary Sidney, until its final break-up in 1597.

In the letter to Philip, 4th Earl of Pembroke, setting out a full account of the Globe Theatre and the connection of the Burbage family with it, Cuthbert and Richard Burbage wrote: 'To ourselves we joined the deserving men Shakespeare, Hemings, Condell, and others.' They also stated that at Blackfriars (which the Burbage consortium leased) they had 'men players which were

3 (far left). William Herbert, 3rd Earl of Pembroke. Portrait by Daniel Mytens

4. Philip Herbert, Earl of Montgomery, 4th Earl of Pembroke Portrait (c.1635) by Daniel Mytens

THE SHAKESPEARE ENIGMA

Hemings, Condell, Shakespeare, etc....'

It is certainly strange that, if the Shakespeare mentioned in this letter had been the 'Star of Poets' and author of the famous plays that had been dedicated to Philip and his brother William Herbert, the Burbages did not refer to this. Instead they simply referred to Shakespeare as a player, an actor of no more importance than Heminges and Condell.

The Quandary

So what do all these facts suggest? We are presented with plays, poems and sonnets published under the name of 'William Shakespeare', but what is in serious doubt is whether it was the actor William Shakespeare from Stratford-upon-Avon who was the author. What we know of the actor's life and character simply does not match with the knowledge, experience, education, schol-

5. Henry Herbert, 2nd Earl of Pembroke. Line drawing by Simon Passe, engraved for Holland's Herwologia (1620)

6 (far right). Mary Sidney, Countess of Pembroke: 'Swan portrait'. Engraving (1618) by Simon van de Pass

arship and character of the author as is evidenced in the Shakespeare works themselves. On the contrary, every aspect of the life of the actor William Shakespeare that is known to us shows him to have been a non-literary man: an actor and businessman, yes, but not the scholarly author of the Shakespeare plays and poems. It is not a question of class that is the issue, as some would have it; it is purely a matter of observation and facts.

It is entirely possible that William Shakespeare the actor was a mask for the real author. Such a device is not unknown or, indeed, uncommon, as we shall see. The fact that his name, or a name similar to his, is to be found on the Shakespeare plays and poems is not proof in itself of authorship. Many times authors have published under pseudonyms or even other people's names, living or dead. Even the fact that others have referred to the author of the plays as Shakespeare is not sufficient, for the same reasons, unless they specifically make clear who they mean. They might, for instance, be using the name 'Shakespeare' knowingly as a pseudonymous reference, or they may not know who the author of the plays really is and be using the Shakespeare name unwittingly. More than this is required to prove authorship, and this is where the quandary lies—especially when the actor Shakespeare's own contemporaries seem to indicate, as we shall see, that he was definitely not the author of the plays ascribed to him.

Chapter 3

Two Shakespeares?

Ben Jonson, Shakespeare's Witness

Of all Shakespeare's contemporaries, the only one who came anywhere near matching Shakespeare's abilities and fame as a playwright was Ben Jonson. He loved good company, was popular at Court and knew most of the interesting and notable people of his time. According to his own accounts and reputation from others, Jonson knew William Shakespeare of Stratford-upon-Avon well, along with the other actors and playwrights, and was probably the fittest person to write about Shakespeare.

7. Ben Jonson Aged 44, crowned with bays as poet laureate. From engraving of Jonson by Robert Vaughan on title page of the First Folio of Jonson's Works (1616)

Born in London in 1572, the son of a minister who died a month before he was born, Jonson was educated at Westminster School, one of the best schools in London. His stepfather was a master-bricklayer from Westminster, whom his mother had married soon after the death of Ben's father. Ben became a formidable scholar and all his life remained proud of his classical learning. After completing his schooling he was apprenticed to his stepfather and became a master-bricklayer in his turn; but he did not enjoy the work and ran away to fight the Spanish in the wars in the Low Countries. There he became an expert swordsman and gained some renown. Returning to England in 1592, he married in 1594 and sired several children, towards whom he seems to have been very affectionate. Two of them died young and Ben commemorated them with moving epitaphs.

Sometime in the mid-1590s Ben became an actor, at first as a travelling player. By 1597 he was a journeyman player acting and writing for the Earl of Pembroke's Company at the recently-opened Swan Theatre. In that year he experienced with two other members of Pembroke's Men the ever-present danger for actors and dramatists alike. He was thrown into gaol for performing the 'seditious and slanderous' *Isle of Dogs,* a play originated by Thomas Nashe, but which he himself helped to complete.

Jonson and his colleagues were eventually released after two months in the Marshalsea Prison, but the episode had severe repercussions on the London theatres and acting companies. From then on, only two adult companies were granted a licence to play in London—the Lord Admiral's Men at the Rose and the Lord Chamberlain's Men at the Curtain. But Jonson had a success with his first surviving full-length play, *The Case Is Altered*, performed by the Children of the Chapel; and Philip Henslowe, owner of the Rose Theatre and manager of the Lord Admiral's Men, had spotted his talent.

While in prison, Jonson had been lent money by Henslowe, and after his release he went to work at the Rose for Henslowe's company, as a playwright. He soon became a well-established member of the mixed but talented group of Elizabethan dramatists, who collaborated with each other, argued with, criticised and satirised each other, and often co-authored the plays that were performed at Court and in the London theatres. These comprised 'tradesmen' playwrights such as Anthony Munday, Henry Chettle, Thomas Dekker, Michael Drayton and George Chapman, and 'university wits' like John Marston, Thomas Nashe, John Lyly, Samuel Daniel, Thomas Watson and Thomas Lodge—and Shakespeare.

In 1598 Jonson wrote his first major play, *Every Man in his Humour*, which was performed in September by the Lord Chamberlain's Men, with William Shakespeare of Stratford-upon-Avon taking a part.[1] It was a great success. Yet in the same month it was staged, Ben again tasted the lash of the law when he slew one of his fellow actors in a duel. Gaoled in Newgate Prison, he only escaped the death penalty by pleading 'benefit of clergy'. This was accomplished by successfully reading the 'neck verse' (the first verse of Psalm 51) in Latin, thereby satisfying the authorities that he had 'read like a clerk' and was therefore exempt from punishment. (According to this archaic law clergymen were defined as all those who were capable of reading the Bible in Latin!) Jonson was released, but he was branded with a Tyburn 'T' on his left thumb and all his goods were confiscated.

Jonson, however, had the ability to turn tragedy into triumph and went

In this 'biography' Jonson begins by referring to Heminges and Condell's letter, 'To the great Variety of Readers', in the 1623 Shakespeare Folio, which remarks that they 'scarce received from him [Shakespeare] a blot in his papers':

His mind and hand went together: And what he thought, he uttered with that easinesse, that wee have scarce received from him a blot in his papers.

Heminges and Condell, 'To the Great Variety of Readers',
Shakespeare Folio (1623)

Ben Jonson appears to mock this reputation that the players had given Shakespeare. As written, Heminges and Condell's meaning of 'blot' refers to ink spots or stains on the paper, the sense of which Jonson reiterates in his words, 'blotted out'. Jonson replies to this that he regrets that Shakespeare had not blotted a thousand lines. The players naturally thought that what he said was 'a malevolent speech'. His statement could have two possible interpretations. It could, of course, mean that Jonson disliked many of the lines written by Shakespeare and wished he had blotted them all out. The alternative meaning, which seems to me the more likely in the context of what follows, and which would be entirely in character with the learned, sharp satirical wit of Jonson, is that by turning around the meaning of 'blotted' (and deliberately omitting the word 'out') Jonson implies that Shakespeare had in fact written so little that he wished that Shakespeare had indeed blotted (i.e., finished)[5] a thousand lines. But Jonson could not have been speaking of the author Shakespeare, who wrote many thousands of lines: he could only have been speaking of the actor Shakespeare, whom the players may well have believed, or wanted to believe, or wanted us to believe, was the author of the plays.

That he is speaking of the actor as distinct from the author is made clearer in the lines that follow. Jonson gives his reason for having made his statement as being to put the record straight, for the other players had chosen 'that circumstance to commend their friend by, wherein he most faulted'; and this, when discovered by others, would do Shakespeare's reputation no good. Ben seems to wish, instead, that his actor friend William be remembered not as he might be considered, a fraud, but for what he really was—'a man of an open and free nature', with an 'excellent phantasy, brave notions and gentle expressions'.

Jonson follows this up, though, by comparing his actor friend to the Roman orator Haterius, who had the unfortunate reputation of being often so impetuous and carried away with his words that he would muddle them, burst into tears, speak *ex tempore* and become so profuse in his language that he had to be stopped. The example that Jonson gives is taken from the Shakespeare play, *Julius Caesar*, wherein Caesar says: 'Know, Caesar doth not wrong, nor without cause will he be satisfied'.[6] Jonson infers that William Shakespeare acted the part of Caesar and got his words muddled up in a ridiculous way— a mistake that no author of such a play, with its major focus on good oratory, would have made. In fact, from what Jonson says, both Shakespeare and the other actor got their words muddled.

This description, which is by no means complimentary to Shakespeare, is mostly a literal translation from Book 4 of *Controversia* by the Roman philosopher and playwright, Seneca the Elder, concerning Haterius. To use such translated quotations in his writing was a normal habit of Jonson's, and he used them succinctly. He concludes his comment on Shakespeare by saying: 'But he redeemed his vices with his virtues. There was ever more in him to be praised than to be pardoned.' This sounds very friendly on Jonson's part—and perhaps it is; but in fact, by saying this, Jonson actually emphasises his analogy of the actor Shakespeare with Haterius, as these last two sentences are a further quotation of Seneca concerning Haterius.

Mellifluous & Honey-Tongued

All this is in contrast to the published author Shakespeare, for it is apparent from the plays that the latter was not only in full control of his wit but also a great orator, or at least could write great orations, as witness the abundance of magnificent speeches in the plays and the emotive reactions of audiences to them. It is not by chance, for instance, that Francis Meres referred to Shakespeare as 'mellifluous & honey-tongued' in his *Palladis Tamia* of 1598. The Shakespeare speeches can move people, which is the mark of every good orator. Moreover, a great orator will know the rules of good oration, as well as have tested them out to see how they work. That this is so in respect of the author Shakespeare is demonstrated clearly in the two famous speeches addressed to the general populace of Rome in *Julius Caesar* (III, ii), one speech being made by Marcus Brutus and the other by Mark Antony, each being the antithesis of the other.

Brutus's speech is an example of a more intellectual or academic approach, being carefully organised and constructed with parallelism and antithesis, and having a mathematical sequence with a set beginning, middle and ending. It is the sort of speech that is carefully prepared and cannot be changed, and so Brutus gives his speech regardless of how his audience feels, standing aloof in his honour and hiding his own feelings. He is in fact so removed from his audience in feeling that he ends up by being shocked at the result of his speech.

Mark Antony, by contrast, gives a highly theatrical and emotional speech, adapting his words to suit the mood of the plebeians as it changes and as he changes it for them. By being fully engaged with his audience Antony is able to lead them to where he wants them to go, whipping them up into a frenzy against Brutus and the other assassins of Caesar. Although not academic, Antony's speech is no less clever than Brutus' oration. Indeed, it is far more clever: for always Antony knows exactly what he is doing and wants to do, appealing to the emotions and adeptly using theatrical props and gestures to help him (e.g.,, reading Caesar's will, descending from the pulpit, getting the plebeians to make a ring around Caesar's body, then picking up Caesar's mantle and weeping over it).

Brutus' speech is a good speech, but is one belonging to the universities and academies. Antony's speech, by contrast, is a speech that belongs to a real master of oratory and the stage. It is the speech of a great playwright, performed by a great actor; or of a great politician and statesman. It also demonstrates how malleable a crowd of people can be, especially the under-privileged and under-educated populace, and how easily a callous orator can turn them into a bloodthirsty murdering mob. From this point of view, it is a warning. Other Shakespeare speeches in other plays show the positive side of such orations, when the orator has better motives.

Altogether, from this example, we can see how the author Shakespeare knows the secret that the emotions are the key to motivating people and either helping or making them think in certain ways. The Shakespeare plays are, above all, a study in human emotion and the results of such emotion, good or bad. In these orations this is made abundantly clear. It is also clear that the author Shakespeare was a great orator; whereas, according to Ben Jonson, the actor Shakespeare was not.

Upstart Crow

The description by Ben Jonson of the actor Shakespeare as being like Haterius, and being presented by the players as the author of the Shakespeare plays, matches what is thought to be the very first mention in writing of the actor Shakespeare. This was a warning concerning the actor given by the Elizabethan scholar and playwright Robert Greene to his fellow playwrights.

Robert Greene (1558–92), a graduate of Cambridge University, was the author of the prose romance *Pandosto, the Triumph of Time* (c.1588), which provided the main plot and idea of Shakespeare's *Winter's Tale*. As a dramatist, Greene wrote the romantic comedies *Friar Bacon and Friar Bungay* (c.1589–92) and *James IV* (c.1590–1), influences from which can also be found in the Shakespeare plays. In addition, he was responsible for a number of autobiographical pamphlets. His criticism of the actor Shakespeare is to be found in the last of these pamphlets, which was published a few weeks after his death, which came on 3 September 1592. They formed his confessions and were edited by his friend, the playwright and printer Henry Chettle,[7] who published the pamphlet under the title Greene's Groats-worth of Witte, bought with a Million of Repentance. The passage in question is in the epistle addressed To those Gentlemen his Quondam acquaintance that spend their wits in making plays.

In his confessions, the demoralised and poverty-stricken Greene tried to warn three of his fellow playwrights not to trust actors—those 'puppets', 'burrs' and 'anticks garnished in our colours'—and refers to a particular actor, whom scholars generally assume to be Shakespeare, as an 'upstart Crow' beautified with the 'feathers' of the playwrights, who not only believes that he is able to bombast out a blank verse as well as the best of the playwrights but also, being an 'absolute Iohannes fac totum', is conceited enough to imagine that he is the only 'Shake-scene' in a country. Greene urges his fellow playwrights to follow more profitable courses of action by allowing these 'Apes' (i.e., the actors) to imitate their 'past excellence' (i.e., poetry or drama already published or performed on stage) but not to make them privy to their 'admired inventions' (i.e., those new ideas and poetic creations of the playwrights of the sort that the actors admire):

> Base-minded men all three of you, if by my miserie you be not warnd: for unto none of you (like mee) sought those burres to cleave: those Puppets (I meane) that spake from our mouths, those Anticks garnisht in our colours. Is it not strange, that I, to whom they all have beene beholding: is it not like that you, to whom they all have been beholding, shall (were yee in that case as I am now) bee both at once of them forsaken? Yes trust them not: for there is an upstart Crow, beautified with our feathers, that with his *Tyger's hart wrapped in a Player's* hyde, supposes he is as well able to bombast out a blanke verse as the best of you: and beeing an absolute *Iohannes fac totum*, is in his owne conceit the onely Shake-scene in a countrey. O that I might entreate your rare wits to be employed in more profitable courses: & let these Apes imitate your past excellence, and never more acquaint them with your admired inventions.
>
> Robert Greene, *A Groats-worth of Wit* (1592)

'Iohannes fac totum' was a term of abuse used mainly by university wits and meaning 'Jack-of-all-trades, master of none'. The qualifying 'absolute' emphasises Greene's contempt, ironically declaring the 'upstart Crow' to be a perfect Jack-of-all-trades, who is conceited enough to think he can do anything well.

The crow is famous for mimicry but not for invention. It also croaks bombastically. Furthermore, the crow in classical fables is associated with stealing whatever it finds beautiful or attractive, even the finer plumes of other birds. For this reason, in Renaissance symbolism the crow is associated with plagiarism, particularly literary plagiarism. In this instance the actor who is the 'upstart Crow' is accused of beautifying himself with the words that come from the 'feathers' (*i.e.*, the quill pens) of the playwrights.

The meaning of this is made even clearer in the speech by Juliet in *Romeo and Juliet*, which not only has the same sense but also uses the same imagery of the feathers that beautify the crow or the raven, the latter being traditionally confused with the crow. In this play, the feathers which the black raven uses to beautify itself are those of a white dove, symbol of all that is good, beautiful, inspiring and peaceful:

> O serpent heart, hid with a flowering face…
> Dove-feather'd raven…
> Just opposite to what thou justly seem'st!

Shakespeare, Romeo and Juliet, III, ii, 73–78

Related in meaning to this whole quotation, the 'Tyger's hart wrapped in a Player's hyde' is a parody of a line in the Shakespeare play of *Henry VI*, Part 3, spoken by Richard Plantagenet, Duke of York, to Queen Margaret, who has captured York and is about to have him beheaded. In his final condemnation of the 'proud queen', the 'she-wolf of France', York refers to the murder of his young son Rutland and the offering to him by the queen of a handkerchief soaked in his son's blood:

> Oh tiger's heart wrapp'd in a woman's hide!
> How could'st thou drain the life-blood of the child,
> To bid the father wipe his eyes withal,
> And yet be seen to bear a woman's face?

Shakespeare, 3 Henry VI, I, iv, 137–40

This Shakespearean reference makes it clear that the 'Shake-scene' is to do with Shakespeare and the Shakespeare plays, thereby identifying the 'upstart Crow' as the actor William Shakespeare. But Greene is accusing this actor, William Shakespeare, of possessing a tiger's heart, which in the symbolism of the sixteenth century meant having a dangerous, proud, lustful, hypocritical, duplicitous, deceitful, ferocious, ruthless, destructive and downright evil nature. Whether Greene associated the actor Shakespeare with all these qualities is unclear, but he must have meant many of them because of his analogy with the 'ruthless' Queen Margaret, the 'she-wolf of France, but worse than wolves of France',[8] who was determined to have the throne of England for herself and her son.

Greene clearly not only felt angry and betrayed by the actors, who took the playwrights' plays as if they were their own and made a lot of money and fame out of them while the playwrights received little of either, but he was also clearly annoyed that the actor Shakespeare, in his own conceit, thought that he was the only 'Shake-scene' in a country. In saying this Greene acknowledges that the actor is a 'Shake-scene', but at the same time points out that he is not by any means the only 'Shake-scene' in England or any other country for that matter. More than this, Greene identifies the actor's 'Shake-scene' with what might be thought a fraud, wherein the actor Shakespeare was not only stealing or plagiarising the writings of others but also passing himself off as the only poet Shakespeare. Indeed, the inference of Greene's statement is that the other 'Shake-scene' is not only the truer one in terms of poetic invention but also is made up of Greene and his fellow playwrights, whose 'feathers' are beautifying the 'upstart Crow'.

Elsewhere in his *Groats-worth of Witte* Greene makes a clear distinction between the university-educated 'Gentlemen' who 'spend their wits in making plays' and the common actors among whom the 'upstart Crow' is counted. The gentlemen playwrights to whom Greene refers were the 'University Wits', of whom Greene himself was one. They were the university-educated poets of the 1580s who revolutionised the stage. These included Thomas Nashe, Christopher Marlowe and Robert Greene of Cambridge University, George Peele, John Lyly and Thomas Lodge of Oxford University, plus some others. Of all these, the three friends to whom Greene's confessions were specifically addressed, and who were named by him, were Peele, Nashe and Marlowe.

Several of the playwrights apparently took offence at Greene's *Groats-worth of Wit,* and it was even suspected that Greene's name had been used as a cover for someone else. Both Nashe and Chettle were accused. Nashe immediately published a denial, followed soon after by Chettle, who published his own pamphlet, *Kind-Harts Dreame,* in reply. Chettle claimed that he and Nashe were being wrongly accused by one or two of the other 'play-makers' of having written Greene's pamphlet posthumously; but, having denied his and Nashe's authorship of *Groats-worth of Wit*, Chettle accepted that he had been the editor of it and apologised for the fault. He then went on to describe one of these playwrights as being civil, honest, and having a witty grace in writing:

I am sorry, as if the original fault had been my fault, because myselfe

THE SHAKESPEARE ENIGMA

have seene his demeanor no lesse civill, than he exelent in the qualitie he professes;—besides, divers of worship have reported his uprightnes of dealing, which argues his honesty, and his facetious grace in writting, that aprooves his Art.

Henry Chettle, Kind-Harts Dreame (1592)

Generally it has been assumed that Chettle was describing the actor Shakespeare, although this is highly unlikely, indeed impossible, as the *Groats-worth of Wit* was not addressed to the Shake-scene actor in the first place: it was addressed to gentlemen playwrights, among whom the 'upstart Crow' was not counted. Chettle was apologising to these playwrights, not to the actors, and his description of the 'play-maker' was of one of these university-educated authors.

The phrase 'divers of worship', who reported this unnamed playwright's characteristics to Chettle, refers to lords and gentlemen, particularly men of high rank, not actors, and Chettle made a clear distinction between the two. Strictly speaking, *gentleman* was the term for a man of gentle birth (*i.e.,* noble, or well-born), belonging to a family that had both land and position and was entitled to bear arms—in other words, the landed gentry. It also applied as the complimentary designation of a member of certain societies or professions, such as the gentlemen lawyers of the Inns of Court, and of certain privileged students (*i.e.,* the gentlemen-commoners) of the two universities, Oxford and Cambridge. The actor William Shakespeare only became a gentleman in 1599, upon the occasion of his father being awarded a grant of Arms (which William inherited in 1601 as his father's eldest son and heir). Greene's *Groats-worth of Witte* was written seven years earlier, in 1592.

Some scholars think that Chettle, who wrote or helped to write forty-eight plays for the Admiral's Company, indeed wrote both the pamphlets, *Groats-worth of Wit* and *Kind-heart's Dream,* in order to stir up controversy and convey a message.[9] Others think it was Nashe, because of the style. Whatever the answer to this, the message itself is clear: the 'Shake-scene' actor was not the author Shakespeare, despite his passing himself off as the author, and the true playwrights, who were university-educated gentlemen, were not receiving their due.

Mouthing words that better wits have framed

A series of Christmas plays put on by the students of St John's College, Cambridge, in the years 1598–1601, is likewise concerned with this theme of university-educated playwrights versus common actors. These plays, three satirical comedies entitled *The Return from Parnassus,*[10] are full of references to the 'War of the Theatres' or war of poets that started at the end of 1599 with the production of Jonson's *Every Man Out of His Humour* by the Lord Chamberlain's Men at the newly-built Globe theatre on Bankside, and carried on to the staging of Dekker's *Satiromastix, or the Untrussing of the Humorous Poet,* in the late summer of 1601. This two-year contest of increasingly bitter and defamatory satire took place principally between Ben Jonson on the one hand and John Marston and Thomas Dekker on the other, although other poets and actors are mentioned and satirised by them as well.[11]

A large part of *The Return from Parnassus* is concerned with the adventures of two graduates who are learning from bitter experience how little is to be gained in the outside world by a university education. Living in poverty and desperately searching for a means of earning a livelihood, they try one profession after another. Finally they consider acting and approach the Lord Chamberlain's company (*i.e.,* Shakespeare's company).

In considering their applications to join the company, Burbage is shown as being friendly towards the two graduates. He remarks that it is certainly possible that scholars, after a little teaching in humility, may be able to help the company by writing plays. By contrast, Kempe (*i.e.,* William Kempe, a comic actor and jig-artist in the company who at one time contributed a 'merriment' or short passages of repartee to an anonymous play, *A Knack to Know a Knave*) is shown taking up a more critical attitude. He pours scorn on university-educated playwrights generally, including Ben Jonson, who did not go to a university but was known for his classical learning nonetheless. Kempe puts forward his opinion that few of the university men can write plays well, and that they are all (Jonson included) far outshone by Shakespeare:

> Few of the university men pen plays well. They smell too much of that writer Ovid, and that writer Metamorphosis, and talk too much of Proserpina and Jupiter. Why! here's our fellow Shakspeare puts them all down; aye, and Ben Jonson too. O that Ben Jonson's a pestilent fellow; he brought up Horace giving the poet's a pill, but our fellow Shakspeare hath given him a purge that made him bewray his credit.
>
> *The Return from Parnassus,* Pt 2

Although Shakespeare's poems and plays are highly influenced by Ovid's *Metamorphoses,* it is true that they do not contain many open references to Jupiter and Proserpina compared with some of the other Elizabethan poets.[12] It would seem, therefore, that the character Kempe is not blind to what is in the Shakespeare plays but is saying that his fellow actor, Shakespeare, is far and away the best of the playwrights, one who doesn't blatantly overemphasise his use of Ovid or overindulge his portrayal of the classical divinities—

Loues labors lost was the first of Shakespeare's plays to be printed with the name, 'W. Shakespere', on its title page, while *Palladis Tamia: Wits Treasury* was a volume of apophthegms on philosophy and the arts by Francis Meres. In the sixteen-page section of his book labelled 'Comparative discourse of our English Poets, with the Greeke, Latine, and Italian Poets', Meres gives the first reference to Shakespeare as being the author of four of the earlier published plays, and goes on to list eight others plus the two narrative poems, *Venus and Adonis* and *The Rape of Lucrece.*

Meres praises Shakespeare together with Sidney, Spenser, Daniel, Drayton, Warner, Marlowe and Chapman for 'mightily' enriching and 'gorgeouslie' investing the English language 'in rare ornaments and resplendent abiliments', just as 'the Greeke tongue is made famous and eloquent by Homer ... and the Latine tongue by Virgill'. He writes that 'The Muses would speak Shakespeare's

11. Title page,
Love's Labour's
Lost (1598).

fine filed phrase if they could speak English', and proclaims Shakespeare as being one of the best poets for lyric poetry, comedy and tragedy, as well as one of 'the most passionate among us to bewail and bemoan the perplexities of love':

> As the soul of Euphorbus was thought to live in Pythagoras: so the sweete wittie soule of Ovid lives in mellifluous & honey-tongued *Shakespeare,* witness his *Venus and Adonis,* his *Lucrece,* his sugared Sonnets among his private friends...

VENVS
AND ADONIS

Vilia miretur vulgus: mihi flauus Apollo
Pocula Castalia plena ministret aqua.

LONDON.

Imprinted by Richard Field, and are to be fold at
the figne of the white Greyhound in
Paules Church-yard.
1594.

LVCRECE.

LONDON.

Printed by Richard Field, for Iohn Harrifon, and are
to be fold at the figne of the white Greyhound
in Paules Churh-yard. **1594.**

12. *Title page, Venus and Adonis*
(1593)

14. *Title-page, Lucrece (1594)*

TO THE RIGHT HONORABLE
Henrie VVriothefly , Earle of Southampton,
and Baron of Titchfield.

 *Ight Honourable , I know not how I shall offend in
dedicating my vnpolisht lines to your Lordship,
nor how the vvorld vvill cenfure me for choosing
so strong a proppe to support so vveake a burthen,
onely if your Honour feeme but pleafed, I account
my felfe highlie prayfed, and vow to take aduantage of all idle
houres , till I haue honoured you vvith fome grauer labour . But
if the firft heyre of my inuention proue deformed, I shall be fory it
had fo noble a god-father : and neuer after eare fo barren a land,
for feare it yeeld me still fo bad a harueft , I leaue it to your Honourable furuey,and your Honor to your hearts content,vvhich I wish
may alwayes anfwere your owne vvish, and the vvorlds hopefull
expectation.*

Your Honors in all dutie,

William Shakefpeare.

TO THE RIGHT
HONOVRABLE, HENRY
VVriothefley, Earle of Southhampton,
and Baron ot Titchfield.

 HE loue I dedicate to your
Lordfhip is without end:wher-
of this Pamphlet without beginning is but a fuperfluous
Moity. The warrant I haue of
your Honourable difpofition,
not the worth of my vntutord
Lines makes it affured of acceptance. VVhat I haue
done is yours, what I haue to doe is yours, being
part in all I haue, deuoted yours . VVere my worth
greater,my duety would fhew greater, meane time,
as it is,it is bound to your Lordfhip; To whom I wifh
long life still lengthned with all happineffe.

Your Lordfhips in all duety.

William Shakefpeare.

A 2

13. *Dedication page, Venus and*
Adonis (1594)

15. *Dedication page, Lucrece (1594)*

Chapter 4

The Shakespeare Trail

The Memorials

So where do we start, if we want to solve this conundrum? Let us begin where others have begun, at the only real beginning for this purpose—the First Folio of Shakespeare plays and the Shakespeare Monument at Stratford-upon-Avon.

The assumption that the actor Shakespeare might be the author Shakespeare is based upon certain evidence presented to us by Shakespeare's colleagues and friends. This evidence is contained in the two original seventeenth-century memorials to Shakespeare—the First Folio of Shakespeare plays that was published in 1623, seven years after the actor's death, and the Shakespeare Monument that was probably erected only a year or two earlier (*c.*1620–2) in Holy Trinity Church, Stratford-upon-Avon. These two memorials, the one literary and the other architectural, are linked together, with the Folio providing clues that lead us to the Monument.

The Shakespeare Folio

Although the name of William Shakespeare, variously spelt, had appeared on the title pages of some published plays before, each one printed individually in cheap quarto editions, comparable with the paperback of today, the 1623 Folio of *Mr. William Shakespeares Comedies, Histories, & Tragedies* was the first time all of Shakespeare's plays (except for *Pericles* and two lost plays)[1] were collected together, authenticated as being Shakespeare's by his colleagues, and published in one single volume. Moreover, the 1623 Folio included eighteen plays previously not published, fourteen of which had not even been registered with the Stationers' Company.[2] If the Folio had not been published, these eighteen plays, virtually half of Shakespeare's canon, would have been unknown to us and the true greatness of Shakespeare would have remained hidden.

The printed folios of plays, thirty-six plays in all, were bound together with and prefaced by a number of pages containing preliminary matter. The very first page of these contains a twelve-line verse 'To the Reader' by 'B.I.', who is understood to be Ben Jonson. The verse describes a portrait of Shakespeare that is to be found on the next page, the title page. After the title page comes a two-page dedicatory letter to William, Earl of Pembroke, and his brother Philip, Earl of Montgomery, signed by Heminge and Condell. This is followed by an 'Address to the great Variety of Readers', also signed by Heminge and Condell, a 'Catalogue' of the plays, a two-page poem in the author's memory by Ben Jonson, a sonnet in tribute by Hugh Holland, two further eulogies by Leonard Digges and 'I.M.', and finally a page containing the 'Names of the Principal Actors'.

These preliminary pages were seemingly organised and compiled by Ben Jonson. John Heminges and Henry Condell were the last surviving members

To the Reader.

This Figure, that thou here seest put,
　　It vvas for gentle Shakespeare cut;
Wherein the Grauer had a strife
　　with Nature, to out-doo the life :
O, could he but haue dravvne his wit
　　As well in brasse, as he hath hit
His face ; the Print vvould then surpasse
　　All, that vvas euer vvrit in brasse.
But, since he cannot, Reader, looke
　　Not on his Picture, but his Booke.

　　　　　　　　　　　　　B. I.

17. Portrait Verse, Shakespeare Folio (1623)

MR. WILLIAM
SHAKESPEARES
COMEDIES,
HISTORIES, and
TRAGEDIES.

Publifhed according to the True Originall Copies.

LONDON
Printed by Ifaac Iaggard, and Ed. Blount. 1623.

*18. Title page
and Portrait,
Shakespeare
Folio (1623)*

TO THE MOST NOBLE

A n d

INCOMPARABLE PAIRE

OF BRETHREN.

William

Earle of Pembroke, &c. Lord Chamberlaine to the
Kings most Excellent Maiesty.

AND

Philip

Earle of Montgomery, &c. Gentleman of his Maiesties
Bed-Chamber. Both Knights of the most Noble Order
of the Garter, and our singular good
LORDS.

Right Honourable,

Hilst we studie to be thankful in our particular, for
the many fauors we haue receiued from your L.L
we are falne vpon the ill fortune, to mingle
two the most diuerse things that can bee, feare,
and rashnesse ; rashnesse in the enterprize, and
feare of the successe. For, when we valew the places your H.H.
sustaine, we cannot but know their dignity greater, then to descend to
the reading of these trifles:and, vvhile we name them trifles, we haue
depriu'd our selues of the defence of our Dedication. But since your
L.L. haue beene pleas'd to thinke these trifles some-thing, heereto-
fore ; and haue prosequuted both them, and their Authour liuing,
vvith so much fauour : we hope, that (they out-liuing him, and he not
hauing the fate, common with some, to be exequutor to his owne writings) you will vse the like indulgence toward them, you haue done

A 2   vnto

19. First page of
Dedicatory
Letter,
Shakespeare
Folio (1623)

The Epistle Dedicatorie.

vnto their parent. There is a great difference, vvhether any Booke choose his Patrones, or finde them : This hath done both. For, so much were your L L. likings of the seuerall parts, vvhen they were acted, as before they vvere published, the Volume ask'd to be yours. We haue but collected them, and done an office to the dead, to procure his Orphanes, Guardians; vvithout ambition either of selfe-profit, or fame: onely to keepe the memory of so worthy a Friend, & Fellow aliue, as was our SHAKESPEARE, *by humble offer of his playes, to your most noble patronage. Wherein, as we haue iustly obserued, no man to come neere your L.L. but vvith a kind of religious addresse; it hath bin the height of our care, vvho are the Presenters, to make the present worthy of your H.H. by the perfection. But, there we must also craue our abilities to be considerd, my Lords. We cannot go beyond our owne powers. Country hands reach foorth milke, creame, fruites, or what they haue : and many Nations (we haue heard) that had not gummes & incense, obtained their requests with a leauened Cake. It vvas no fault to approch their Gods, by what meanes they could: And the most, though meanest, of things are made more precious, when they are dedicated to Temples. In that name therefore, we most humbly consecrate to your H.H. these remaines of your seruant* Shakespeare; *that what delight is in them, may be euer your L.L. the reputation his, & the faults ours, if any be committed, by a payre so carefull to shew their gratitude both to the liuing, and the dead, as is*

Your Lordshippes most bounden,

IOHN HEMINGE.
HENRY CONDELL.

20. Second page of Dedicatory Letter, Shakespeare Folio (1623)

To the great *Variety* of *Readers.*

 Rom the moſt **able**, to him that can but ſpell: There you are number'd. We had rather you were weighd. Eſpecially, when the fate of all Bookes depends vpon your capacities : and not of your heads alone, but of your purſes. Well ! It is now publique, & you wil ſtand for your priuiledges wee know : to read, and cenſure. Do ſo, but buy it firſt. That doth beſt commend a Booke, the Stationer ſaies. Then, how odde ſoeuer your braines be, or your wiſedomes, make your licence the ſame, and ſpare not. Iudge your ſixe-pen'orth, your ſhillings worth, your fiue ſhillings worth at a time, or higher, ſo you riſe to the iuſt rates, and welcome. But, what euer you do, Buy. Cenſure will not driue a Trade, or make the Iacke go. And though you be a Magiſtrate of wit, and ſit on the Stage at *Black-Friers*, or the *Cock-pit*, to arraigne Playes dailie, know, theſe Playes haue had their triall alreadie, and ſtood out all Appeales ; and do now come forth quitted rather by a Decree of Court, then any purchas'd Letters of commendation.

It had bene a thing, we confeſſe, worthie to haue bene wiſhed, that the Author himſelfe had liu'd to haue ſet forth, and ouerſeen his owne writings ; But ſince it hath bin ordain'd otherwiſe, and he by death departed from that right, we pray you do not envie his Friends, the office of their care, and paine, to haue collected & publiſh'd them ; and ſo to haue publiſh'd them, as where (before) you were abus'd with diuerſe ſtolne, and ſurreptitious copies, maimed, and deformed by the frauds and ſtealthes of iniurious impoſtors, that expos'd them : euen thoſe, are now offer'd to your view cur'd, and perfect of their limbes ; and all the reſt, abſolute in their numbers, as he conceiued thē. Who, as he was a happie imitator of Nature, was a moſt gentle expreſſer of it. His mind and hand went together : And what he thought, he vttered with that eaſineſſe, that wee haue ſcarſe receiued from him a blot in his papers. But it is not our prouince, who onely gather his works, and giue them you, to praiſe him. It is yours that reade him. And there we hope, to your diuers capacities, you will finde enough, both to draw, and hold you : for his wit can no more lie hid, then it could be loſt. Reade him, therefore ; and againe, and againe : And if then you doe not like him, ſurely you are in ſome manifeſt danger, not to vnderſtand him. And ſo we leaue you to other of his Friends, whom if you need, can bee your guides : if you neede them not, you can leade your ſelues, and others. And ſuch Readers we wiſh him.

A 3   *Iohn Heminge.*
                    Henrie Condell.

21. *Address to the Reader, Shakespeare Folio (1623)*

THE SHAKESPEARE ENIGMA

A CATALOGVE

of the feuerall Comedies, Hiftories, and Tragedies contained in this Volume.

COMEDIES.

He Tempeft.	Folio 1.
The two Gentlemen of Verona.	20
The Merry Wiues of Windfor.	38
Meafure for Meafure.	61
The Comedy of Errours.	85
Much adoo about Nothing.	101
Loues Labour loft.	122
Midfommer Nights Dreame.	145
The Merchant of Venice.	163
As you Like it.	185
The Taming of the Shrew.	208
All is well, that Ends well.	230
Twelfe-Night, or what you will.	255
The Winters Tale.	304

HISTORIES.

The Life and Death of King John.	Fol. 1.
The Life & death of Richard the fecond.	23
The Firft part of King Henry the fourth.	46
The Second part of K. Henry the fourth.	74
The Life of King Henry the Fift.	69
The Firft part of King Henry the Sixt.	96
The Second part of King Hen. the Sixt.	120
The Third part of King Henry the Sixt.	147
The Life & Death of Richard the Third.	173
The Life of King Henry the Eight.	205

TRAGEDIES.

The Tragedy of Coriolanus.	Fol. 1.
Titus Andronicus.	31
Romeo and Juliet.	53
Timon of Athens.	80
The Life and death of Julius Cæfar.	109
The Tragedy of Macbeth.	131
The Tragedy of Hamlet.	152
King Lear.	283
Othello, the Moore of Venice.	310
Anthony and Cleopater.	346
Cymbeline King of Britaine.	369

22. Catalogue,
Shakespeare
Folio (1623)

To the memory of my beloued,
The AVTHOR
Mr. WILLIAM SHAKESPEARE:
AND
what he hath left vs.

> *O draw no enuy* (Shake∫peare) *on thy name,*
>   *Am I thus ample to thy Booke. and Fame :*
> *While I confe∫∫e thy writings to be ∫uch,*
>   *As neither* Man, *nor* Mu∫e, *can prai∫e too much.*
> *'Tis true, and all mens ∫uffrage. But the∫e wayes*
>   *Were not the paths I meant vnto thy prai∫e :*
> *For ∫eelie∫t Ignorance on the∫e may light,*
>   *Which, when it ∫ounds at be∫t, but eccho's right ;*
> *Or blinde Affection, which doth ne're aduance*
>   *The truth, but gropes, and vrgeth all by chance ;*
> *Or cra∫ty Malice, might pretend this prai∫e,*
>   *And thinke to ruine, where it ∫eem'd to rai∫e.*
> *The∫e are, as ∫ome infamous Baud, or whore,*
>   *Should prai∫e a Matron. What could hurt her more ?*
> *But thou art proofe again∫t them, and indeed*
>   *Aboue th'ill fortune of them, or the need.*
> *I, therefore will begin. Soule of the Age !*
>   *The applau∫e ! delight ! the wonder of our Stage !*
> *My* Shake∫peare, *ri∫e ; I will not lodge thee by*
>   Chaucer, *or* Spen∫er, *or bid* Beaumont *lye*
> *A little further, to make thee a roome :*
>   *Thou art a Moniment, without a tombe,*
> *And art aliue ∫till, while thy Booke doth liue,*
>   *And we haue wits to read, and prai∫e to giue.*
> *That I not mixe thee ∫o, my braine excu∫es ;*
>   *I meane with great, but di∫proportion'd* Mu∫es :
> *For, if I thought my iudgement were of yeeres,*
>   *I should commit thee ∫urely with thy peeres,*
> *And tell, how farre thou did∫t∫ our* Lily *out-∫hine,*
>   *Or ∫porting* Kid, *or* Marlowes *mighty line.*
> *And though thou had∫t ∫mall* Latine, *and le∫∫e* Greeke,
>   *From thence to honour thee, I would not ∫eeke*
> *For names; but call forth thund'ring* Æschilus,
>   Euripides, *and* Sophocles *to vs,*
> Paccuuius, Accius, *him of* Cordoua *dead,*
>   *To life againe, to heare thy Buskin treed,*
> *And ∫hake a Stage : Or, when thy Sockes were on,*
>   *Leaue thee alone, for the compari∫on*

of

23. First page of Ben Jonson's eulogy, Shakespeare Folio (1623)

Of all, that insolent Greece, or haughtie Rome
   sent forth, or since did from their ashes come.
Triumph, my Britaine, thou hast one to showe,
   To whom all Scenes of Europe homage owe.
He was not of an age, but for all time!
   And all the Muses still were in their prime,
When like Apollo he came forth to warme
   Our eares, or like a Mercury to charme!
Nature her selfe was proud of his designes,
   And ioy'd to weare the dressing of his lines!
Which were so richly spun, and wouen so fit,
   As, since, she will vouchsafe no other Wit.
The merry Greeke, tart Aristophanes,
   Neat Terence, witty Plautus, now not please;
But antiquated, and deserted lye
   As they were not of Natures family.
Yet must I not giue Nature all: Thy Art,
   My gentle Shakespeare, must enioy a part.
For though the Poets matter, Nature be,
   His Art doth giue the fashion.   And, that he,
Who casts to write a liuing line, must sweat,
   (such as thine are) and strike the second heat
Vpon the Muses anuile: turne the same,
   (And himselfe with it) that he thinkes to frame;
Or for the lawrell, he may gaine a scorne,
   For a good Poet's made, as well as borne.
And such wert thou. Looke how the fathers face
   Liues in his issue, euen so, the race
Of Shakespeares minde, and manners brightly shines
   In his well torned, and true filed lines:
In each of which, he seemes to shake a Lance,
   As brandish't at the eyes of Ignorance.
Sweet Swan of Auon! what a sight it were
   To see thee in our waters yet appeare,
And make those flights vpon the bankes of Thames,
   That so did take Eliza, and our Iames!
But stay, I see thee in the Hemisphere
   Aduanc'd, and made a Constellation there!
Shine forth, thou Starre of Poets, and with rage,
   Or influence, chide, or cheere the drooping Stage;
Which, since thy flight frō hence, hath mourn'd like night,
   And despaires day, but for thy Volumes light.

BEN: IONSON.

24. Second page of Ben Jonson's eulogy, Shakespeare Folio (1623)

Vpon the Lines and Life of the Famous
Scenicke Poet, Maſter WILLIAM
SHAKESPEARE.

Hoſe hands, which you ſo clapt, go now, and wring
You *Britaines* braue; for done are *Shakeſpeares* dayes :
His dayes are done, that made the dainty Playes,
Which made the Globe of heau'n and earth to ring.
  Dry'de is that veine, dry'd is the *Theſpian* Spring,
Turn'd all to teares, and *Phœbus* clouds his rayes :
That corp's, that coffin now beſticke thoſe bayes,
Which crown'd him *Poet* firſt, then *Poets* King.
If *Tragedies* might any *Prologue* haue,
All thoſe he made, would ſcarſe make one to this :
Where *Fame*, now that he gone is to the graue
(Deaths publique tyring-houſe) the *Nuncius* is.
    For though his line of life went ſoone about,
    The life yet of his lines ſhall neuer out.

HVGH HOLLAND.

25. *Hugh Holland's sonnet, Shakespeare Folio (1623)*

28. Shakespeare Monument Bust and Inscription, Holy Trinity Church, Stratford-upon-Avon.

This is a strange inscription, blatantly enigmatic, asking us a personal question (where else, on monument inscriptions, is there usually even a question?) and challenging us to read if we can.

Of the ten incised lines, the first two and last two are in Latin, while the six middle ones are in English. The initial two lines are the ones that confirm that this monument is indeed the memorial to the renowned author of the Shakespeare plays mentioned by Digges, as no-one else warranted such a tribute as is given in these lines—a tribute which is confirmed by the plays themselves. The Latin translates as:

> A Pylus in judgement, a Socrates in genius, a Maro in art:
> The Earth encloses, the people mourn, Olympus holds him.

The middle part of the inscription—the six lines in rhyming English—contains a riddle that we are challenged to solve:

READ IF THOV CANST, WHOM ENVIOVS DEATH HATH PLAST,
WITH IN THIS MONVMENT SHAKSPEARE

[i.e., 'Read, if thou canst, whom envious Death hath placed within this Shakspeare monument.']

But what are we supposed to read? And why should it be difficult for us to do so? It sounds as if we are challenged to read the name of the person whom envious death has placed within the monument, and whose 'name doth deck this tombe'. However, at first glance this appears to be not much of a challenge, for the name 'Shakspeare' is clearly given, followed by the date, in abbreviated Latin, of the death and age of the actor William Shakespeare of Stratford-upon-Avon:

OBIIT AÑO DO¹ 1616
ÆTATIS • 53 DIE 23 AP^R.

[*i.e., Obiit Anno Domine 1616, ætatis 53 die 23 Aprilis,* which translates: 'He died AD 1616 aged 53 on the 23rd day of April.']

According to the monument Shakespeare died on St George's Day, 23 April 1616, in his 53rd year (*i.e.,* aged 52). He was buried on 25 April 1616 in Holy Trinity Church, as the Stratford Parish Register records:

> *Aprill 25   Will. Shakspear gent.*

The body of William Shakespeare, who had been a lay rector of the church since 1605, was buried beneath the chancel floor of the church, where later the bodies of his wife and eldest daughter were also interred, adjacent to his. A small roughly-inscribed stone slab set into one of the steps of the chancel is reputed to mark his resting-place, over which the Shakespeare monument on the north wall of the chancel looks. The reference on the monument, together with the positioning of the monument relative to the grave, therefore tallies with the death and burial of the actor in the parish church of his home town. Moreover, at the top of the monument is carved the coat of arms of the Shakespeare family that was first granted to William's father, John Shakespeare, and which William inherited on his father's death in 1601.

This would seem to clinch the matter. Here is a monument to the author Shakespeare which refers to the actor Shakespeare and bears Shakespeare's coat of arms and date of death, and which is erected in the actor's parish church overlooking where he was buried. Furthermore, it is known from records that an actor called William Shakespeare belonged to the company of players that owned and performed the Shakespeare plays, and who is recorded as having acted in several of them and who heads the list of 'Principall Actors in all these Playes' in the Shakespeare Folio.

Quod erat demonstrandum. It must be so. The actor William Shakespeare of Stratford-upon-Avon is the author William Shakespeare.

But is this correct?

Stay Passenger

Like Portia's interjection to Shylock in *The Merchant of Venice* ('Tarry a little, there is something else'),[3] the inscription warns us:

STAY PASSENGER, WHY GOEST THOV BY SO FAST?

Have we, the passenger or traveller, indeed read the inscription and the inferences too quickly? Have we jumped to some hasty conclusion based on too little knowledge and some false assumptions? Let us look again.

The inscription really is a riddle, and yet the whole design demonstrates that it was not made by idiots. In fact, nothing about the author Shakespeare is idiotic, unless it be the fact that the monument's bust shows him with a vacant expression and writing on a cushion! A cushion is comfortable but it would be the last thing to choose to write on with a quill pen: it is far too soft a surface and would only cause the pen to blot the paper, or puncture it, or at the best produce a scrawl.

Then how, for instance, can Shakespeare (presumably his body) be placed within the monument?

READ IF THOV CANST, WHOM ENVIOVS DEATH HATH PLAST,
WITH IN THIS MONVMENT SHAKSPEARE

The body of the actor William Shakespeare was buried in a grave beneath the chancel of Holy Trinity Church and not in the monument, which was erected high up on the chancel wall several years after Shakespeare's death and burial. The monument was never designed to hold a corpse: so, if we take this strictly and literally, the inscription is not, it seems, referring to the actor, unless it be his ghost. So who, we might ask, has been placed by envious Death within the Shakespeare monument, and how?

In an inference that is clearly linked with the suggestion that Death has placed 'someone' within the monument, the inscription goes on to state that that someone's name 'doth deck' (*i.e.,* decorate or cover) this tomb:

> WHOSE NAME DOTH DECK YS TOMBE,
> FAR MORE THEN COST: SIEH ALL, YT HE HATH WRITT,
> LEAVES LIVING ART, BVT PAGE, TO SERVE HIS WITT.

[i.e., 'Whose name doth deck this tomb far more than cost: since all that he hath writ leaves living art but page to serve his wit.']

The tombstone of the actor Shakespeare lies in the chancel floor, marking his reputed burial-place or tomb and overlooked by the monument. However, there is no name on the tombstone, just a roughly-worded common curse on anyone who might dare to disturb his bones:

> Good frend for Iesus sake forbeare,
> to digg the dust enclosed heare:
> Blese be ye man yt spares thes stones.
> And cvrst be he yt moves my bones.

This crude verse is something vastly different from the beautifully-crafted,

29. Will Shakespeare's Gravestone, Holy Trinity Church, Stratford-upon-Avon

THE SHAKESPEARE ENIGMA

the moon, and hence with the mind and all things secret or veiled. Since the mind is illumined by and reflects the wisdom of the heart, as the moon reflects the light of the sun, so the knowledge that the mind acquires in this way is the *cabala* or received wisdom. This knowledge is associated with seeing the truth, while wisdom, which is the truth, is associated with being and the Word of God:

> And God said, 'Let there be light:' and there was light.
> And God saw the light, that it was good: and God divided the light from the darkness.
>
> Genesis 1 : 3–4

As an apt illustration of the use of this symbolism, there was a cabalistic cipher method adopted in Italy in 1621, known as the Latin Cabala, which was said to have been established on the occasion of the left arm of the blessed Conrad, a famous hermit of his time, being brought with ceremony from Netina to Placentia.[8] This cipher substitutes numbers for letters in a simple format (A = 1, B = 2, etc.), just as suggested by the initial sentence of the Address to the great Variety of Readers in the Shakespeare Folio:

> From the most able, to him that can but spell: There you are number'd.

The Anatomy of Melancholy

An interesting comparison can be made between the description and picture of Shakespeare in the Shakespeare Folio and that of the author of *The Anatomy of Melancholy*. *The Anatomy of Melancholy* was published in 1621, just prior to the printing of the Shakespeare Folio. Its frontispiece contains a little portrait of the book's author, similar to but much smaller than the portrait of Shakespeare in the Shakespeare Folio. Under this portrait the author's name is inscribed as Democritus Junior, an obvious pseudonym. The real author is believed to have been the Oxford scholar, Robert Burton.

An elaborate poem describing the frontispiece, called 'The Argument of the Frontispiece', contains a verse that refers to the picture of the author. This verse is very similar in tone and meaning to Ben Jonson's portrait verse fronting the Shakespeare Folio:

> Now last of all to fill a place
> Presented is the Author's face;
> And in that habit which he wears,
> His image to the world appears.

His mind no art can well express,
That by his writings you may guess.
It was not pride, nor yet vain glory,

> (Though others do it commonly)
> Made him do this: if you must know,
> The Printer would needs have it so.

The similarities and proximity of publishing dates of *The Anatomy of Melancholy* and the Shakespeare Folio should alert us to the possibility that the name of 'William Shakespeare' as author of the Shakespeare plays might be just as much a pseudonym as 'Democritus Junior' is as author of *The Anatomy of Melancholy*.

Judge—Philosopher—Poet

So here we have a wonderful enigma—or is it a carefully-laid treasure trail with clever signposts and clues to follow? The two authenticated portraits that we have of Shakespeare are both masks. The Stratford Monument portrays Shakespeare's death mask, whereas the Folio picture, which supposedly shows the face of Shakespeare when he was younger and still alive, is a mask in a different sense, hiding the face of the true author behind it. The inference from these two portrayals of Shakespeare, it would seem, is that the actor Shakespeare, who wrote nothing, was a mask for the author Shakespeare, who wrote all.

But then, who was the author Shakespeare? In respect of this there is the top two-line Latin inscription on the monument. This can too easily be forgotten or overlooked in our haste or ignorance—either because it is in Latin, which few people nowadays are able to read, or because of what it is actually saying, which requires some knowledge and thought:

> A Pylus in judgement, a Socrates in genius, a Maro in art:
> The Earth encloses, the people mourn, Olympus holds him.

Pylus was the appellation of Nestor, King of Pylus, one of the Argonauts who went in search of the Golden Fleece and the most perfect of Homer's heroes in the Trojan War. As a statesman, ruler and judge, Pylus was renowned for his eloquence, address, wisdom, justice and prudence of mind.

Socrates, on the other hand, was the most celebrated philosopher of Greece and a renowned orator. He can be regarded as the principal instigator of the great philosophies that have constituted the major traditions of Western civilisation ever since, and the advocate of clarity and the inductive procedure, for which he was particularly famed. He was said to have drawn down philosophy from heaven to earth by deriding the more abstruse enquiries and ungrounded metaphysical researches of his predecessors, and encouraging his countrymen to learn from experience. By introducing moral philosophy he induced humankind to consider themselves, their passions, their opinions, their duties, faculties and actions. Socrates' aim was the happiness and good of his countrymen, and the reformation of their corrupted morals. The tragedies of his pupil Euripides are said to have been at least partly composed by him, although he remained hidden as a playwright behind the mask of his pupil. He was attended by a number of illustrious pupils, whom he instructed by his exemplary life as well as by his doctrines.

Maro, by contrast, was the surname of Virgil,[9] the greatest of the Roman poets, known as the prince of poets and Homer's successor. He was not only a highly learned scholar and refined writer but also an initiate of the Orphic Mysteries as practised at Cumae, near Naples, where he lived for the last part of his life. His *Æneid* was based upon the Mysteries and Homer's epic tales, the *Iliad* and *Odyssey*. In his early years he was forced to live in an impoverished state, but later he managed to reach Rome where he formed an acquaintance with the celebrated Roman knight, Maecenas, the favourite of Augustus, who recommended Virgil to the Emperor. From then on the Emperor patronised the poet, restoring his lands, and Virgil in return dedicated many of his poems to Augustus. Maecenas was himself a liberal patron of men of learning, and Virgil dedicated his *Georgics* to him. According to the English poet Edmund Spenser, Virgil also wrote pseudonymously under the name of Tityrus.

That is to say, in a carefully-designed and prominently-placed inscription, carved as a tribute on the first monument to Shakespeare, the author Shakespeare is declared by his own contemporaries to be a renowned statesman and judge, a celebrated orator and philosopher, and a supreme poet, scholar and initiate—a triple analogy that invites comparison with Hermes Trismegistus ('Thrice Greatest') who had 'the power and fortune of a king, the knowledge and illumination of a priest, and the learning and universality of a philosopher'.[10] Moreover, he wrote plays and poetry pseudonymously, masked by one of his pupils.

The Challenge

Here in the Shakespeare monument, therefore, I believe, we are presented with two Shakespeares—the actor Shakespeare and the author Shakespeare—and we are challenged to discover this.

It appears to me that the first two lines of the inscription uniquely describe the author, while the last two lines refer to the actor, with both sets of lines being in Latin. The six lines in English that contain the challenging words not only works of poesie, which include drama as well as poetry (epic and otherwise), were published anonymously by certain notable gentlemen in the Court, but seems to imply further that they were published under pseudonyms to mask the true authorship.

The university wit, Robert Greene, in his *Farewell to Folly,* also mentions the practice among writers of publishing under someone else's name in order to remain incognito. Pointedly, he refers to the 'ass' who, because he masks an author of higher social standing and professional calling, is 'made proud' by the 'underhand brokery' (*i.e.,* secret dealing in deception in return for a fee), this pride making him by necessity pretend he is the 'father of interludes' (*i.e.,* author of stage-plays),[2] even though he needs the help of clerks of parish churches to write true English:

> Others … if they come to write or publish anything in print, it is either distilled out of ballets [ballads] or borrowed of theological poets which, for their calling and gravity, being loth to have any profane pamphlets pass under their hand, get some other Batillus to set his name to their verses. Thus is the ass made proud by this underhand brokery. And he that cannot write true English without the aid of clerks of parish churches will need make himself the father of interludes.
>
> Robert Greene, *Farewell to Folly* (1591)

John Taylor, commonly known as 'the water poet', likewise refers to this practice of 'underhand brokery' or masking. In his poem, Taylor picks out one actor in particular (whom he addresses), who brags to eight Knights of the Garter that the writings in his possession are his own creation, whereas in fact they were written by someone else, a 'learned brain':

> Thou brag' st what fame thou got'st upon the stage
> Upon St. George's day last, sir; you gave
> To eight Knights of the Garter (like a knave)
> Eight manuscripts (or books) all fairly writ,
> Informing them they were your mother wit
> And you compil'd them; then you were regarded.
> All this is true and this I dare maintain
> The matter came from out a learned brain.[3]

The employment of another person to mask an author was not an unusual practice, having been done many times before, during and since those days of the English Renaissance. For instance, Sir Thomas More, Lord Chancellor to King Henry VIII, used the name of Guilielmus Rosseus ('William Ross') to mask his vituperative work, *Responsio ad convitia Martini Lutheri* (published in

1523). William Ross was in fact a living person at that time, who went on a pilgrimage and died in Rome.

Not only was masking a well-used practice in England but it was also so on the continent. The name of Molière, for instance, the greatest of the seventeenth-century French comic dramatists, was a nom-de-plume, the author's real name being Jean Baptiste Poquelin. Pseudonyms were often chosen for their descriptive allusion or symbolism. For instance, in Elizabethan England Martin Marprelate was the pseudonym of an anti-clerical pamphleteer; Cuthbert Curryknave and Pierce Penniless were two of the noms-de-plume of the writer and dramatist Thomas Nashe; W. Kinsayder was a nom-de-plume used by the poet–dramatist John Marsden;[4] and Immerito ('the blameless one') was the pseudonym of the poet Edmund Spenser. These were all contemporaries of Shakespeare.

There was one particularly good reason in Elizabethan days for a playwright, especially a courtier or a nobleman, to remain anonymous or, if this was impossible, to either use a pseudonym or employ another living person to act as a mask. The reason was the attitude of the authorities, local and national, civil and religious, to the theatres. The power of the theatre was feared. It was thought to be not only a hotbed of immorality but also a seedbed for political or religious subversion and the spreading of radical ideas, which of course it often was. Moreover, although enjoyed, the public theatre was still considered to be a low occupation, and the playwright, if known, tended to share the same opprobrium as the actors. For a courtier or nobleman, or for anyone desiring to hold office in the sovereign's government, to be thus stigmatised could sound his social and political death-knell. This is clearly stated in the play *Sir Thomas More* (c.1600), wherein the Earl of Surrey says: 'Poets were ever thought unfit for state'.[5]

Nevertheless, Queen Elizabeth loved drama, and she was surrounded by councillors and courtiers who supported and often encouraged it, many of them being patrons of acting companies. The Queen's Court type of drama was grandiose, with pageantry, masquing and revelling on a gorgeous scale, giving full scope to all kinds of writers, poets, playwrights, actors, painters, musicians, craftsmen and the like. The lengthy Christmas Revels at Court and the Queen's Accession Day Tournament were particularly important events of each year, the former giving opportunities to the professional players to stage their plays at Court as part of the entertainments, and the latter providing the opportunity *par excellence* for the courtiers to play the major heroic roles and ingratiate themselves with the Queen. There was also the annual royal progress, in which the Queen moved around her realm, complete with her Court, staying and being entertained at the great country houses of her ministers of State, noblemen and other wealthy courtiers.

miral's Men in 1587.[10] Moreover, *Edward II*, the title-page of which was inscribed as being by Marlowe only after his death (like all his works), was the precursor of the early Shakespeare history plays, such as *Henry VI.* In *As You Like It*, seemingly written between 1593 and 1599, Shakespeare even quotes directly from Marlowe's narrative poem, *Hero and Leander*, this being the only time that he ever quotes directly from a contemporary work.[11] Shakespeare prefaces the quotation, which is spoken by Phebe, by attributing it to a 'dead shepherd' (*i.e.*, Marlowe, who died on 30 May 1593).

Intriguingly, Marlowe's *Dr Faustus*, first published in 1604 and again in 1609 and 1611 with some minor changes, was greatly enlarged and rewritten for its 1616 publication, yet nevertheless the text reads as if written by Marlowe, even though Marlowe died twenty-three years earlier. One suggestion here is that perhaps it was Shakespeare who made the alterations, using the style of Marlowe that he knew so well, although there is a certain school of thought that believes Marlowe never died in 1593 but lived on in secret and even wrote all the Shakespeare plays.

George Peele has often been proposed as a possible part-author of Shakespeare's *Henry VI*, Part 1, and *Titus Andronicus*, the latter being an expansion of a Peele work that survives chiefly in Act 1. Likewise it has been suggested that Robert Greene was partly responsible for some of *Titus Andronicus* and *Henry VI*, Parts 1 & 2, and also contributed to *The Comedy of Errors* and *The Two Gentlemen of Verona*. Greene's *Friar Bacon and Friar Bungay* (1590–1) has a number of elements pointing to his and Shakespeare's collaboration on the play, and his *Pandosto* (1588) was the source for the plot of Shakespeare's *Winter's Tale*.

Thomas Middleton is considered to have been a collaborator on Shakespeare's *Timon of Athens* and *Macbeth.* For instance, there are signs of the Hecate scenes in *Macbeth* having been written by Middleton, and two songs are included which are also to be found in Middleton's play, *The Witch* (*c.* 1610–20).

None of this is strange by any means. Collaboration of this kind was the norm rather than the exception in the Elizabethan and early Jacobean period, with some Elizabethan plays being written by as many as five or six different authors. However, it doesn't in any way diminish the role of the Bard, whose works the Shakespeare plays truly are. His is the primary inspiration and the art, both recognisable throughout. The fact that he was able to utilise and integrate the creative abilities of others in such ways shows yet another skill.

From this point of view, therefore, 'Shakespeare' can be understood to be the company name for a group of writers working in collaboration with or under the direction of a master poet, as well as being the personal pseudonym of the master himself. Such a practice follows Medieval and Renaissance practice: aspiring artists, for instance, being accustomed to work in the studio of a master, with the name of the master being used as the name of the studio, covering the work done by all the artists in collaboration and according to the master's inspiration and instruction. The comments made by Ben Jonson and Robert Greene about the author Shakespeare (see chapter 3) all point to there having been such a Shakespeare group of writers, poets and playwrights—a 'Shake-scene' led by their 'chief', their master, 'Shakespeare'.

Moreover, as I have already mentioned (see chapter 3), the use of the 'Shakespeare' name by contemporary publishers under which to publish various works by various authors implies an understanding that it could be used as a group name. It is possible that there was still the same understanding when the Shakespeare Third Folio of plays was published in 1664, which added six other plays to the canon—plays which, it is generally acknowledged, were not written by Shakespeare.

The Pseudonymous Shakespeare

There exist several strong hints or indications by Shakespeare's contemporaries that the author Shakespeare is disguised under a pseudonym. One of them is the allusion to Virgil on the Shakespeare monument in Holy Trinity church in Stratford, wherein Shakespeare is directly associated with Virgil, rather than any other poet, by being likened to him in art ('a Maro in art'). Not only was Virgil one of the major inspirations for most of the English Renaissance poets, including Shakespeare, but also, according to the English poet Edmund Spenser, Virgil sometimes used the pseudonym of Tityrus. Spenser points this out in his epic romance, *The Shepheard's Calendar,* adding that the use of pseudonyms or masks had always been common practice for poets, the French poet Marot having veiled himself under the name of Colin, and Spenser himself using the pseudonyms of Colin Clout and Immerito:

> Now I think no man doubteth but by Colin is meant the Authour selfe.....
>
> Spenser, *The Shepheard's Calendar,* Æclogue IX

> *Colin Clout* is a name not greatly used, and yet I have sene a Poesie of M. Skeltons under that title. But indeede the word Colin is French, and used of the French Poete Marot (if he be worthy of the name of a Poete) in a certain Æglogue. Under which name this Poete secretly shadoweth himself, as sometimes did Virgil under the name of Tityrus, thinking it much fitter then such Latin names, for the great unlikelyhoode of the language.
>
> Spenser, *The Shepheard's Calendar,* Æclogue I

An earlier and perhaps stronger hint as to Shakespeare being a mask was given by John Davies of Hereford. Davies, who was famed as a poet, writing master and an instructor of Prince Henry at the Court of King James I, wrote a book of epigrams addressed to the great writers of his time whom he knew well. This book, *The Scourge of Folly,* published around the year 1610, includes an epigram addressed to 'Mr. Will Shake-speare', referring to Shakespeare as 'our English Terence':

To our English Terence, Mr Will
Shake-speare
Epig. 159

Some say (good Will), which I, in sport, do sing
Had'st thou not plaid some kingly parts in sport,
Thou hadst bin a companion for a King;
And, beene a King among the meaner sort.
Some others raile; but raile as they thinke fit,
Thou hast no rayling, but a raigning Wit:
And honesty thou sow'st, which they do reape;
So, to increase their Stocke which they do keepe.

John Davies of Hereford, *The Scourge of Folly* (1610)

Davies chose his analogy very carefully and aptly to describe the actor Will Shakespeare. Terence was a Roman slave, famous because he was assisted by and was alleged to have been used as a mask for the writings of great men, such as the Roman senators, Scipio the younger and Laelius, who wished to keep the fact of their authorship concealed. One of the clearest inferences we might take from Davies is that the actor Mr Will Shakespeare was a mask for the true author or authors just as Terence was for Scipio and Laelius.

Twelve years before Davies' analogy of Shakespeare to Terence, Joseph Hall and John Marston had already indicated that Shakespeare was a mask for the true author of the Shakespeare poems. They begin their exchange of satires by referring to a certain poet as 'Labeo'. In Hall's second book of *Satires* he reproves Labeo for the licentious tone of his writing and implies that Labeo was writing in conjunction with someone else:

For shame write better Labeo, or write none,
Or better write, or *Labeo* write alone.

Joseph Hall, *Satires Virgidemiarum* (1597), Bk 2, p.25

In Satire I of his fourth book of *Satires*, Hall links Labeo with Shakespeare, satirising Labeo for his use of 'But' and 'Oh' with which he began his stanzas

('While bit But OHs each stanze can begin') and his use of hyphenated words as epithets ('In Epithets to join two words as one, / Forsooth for Adjectives cannot stand alone'). These lines refer respectively to Shakespeare's poem *Lucrece,* where it is noticeable how many stanzas commence with 'But' or 'Oh', and to both *Lucrece* and *Venus and Adonis* in which hyphenated words are employed as epithets. Hall goes on further to imply that Labeo is writing under another person's name (we might say, Shakespeare's name):

> Labeo is whip't and laughs me in the face....
> Who list complaine of wronged faith or fame
> When hee may shift it on to anothers name?

Joseph Hall, Satires Virgidemiarum (1597), Bk 4, Satire I

The following year John Marston joined the game in his *Metamorphosis of Pygmalion's Image*, confirming that Labeo was the author Shakespeare:

> So Labeo did complaine his loue was stone,
> Obdurate, flinty, so relentless none;
> Yet Lynceus knows, that in the end of this
> He wrought as strange a metamorphosis.
> Ends not my poem thus surprising ill?
> Come, come, Augustus, crowne my laureat quill.

John Marston, The Metamorphosis of Pygmalion's Image (1598), p. 25

The first two lines of this passage allude to lines 200 and 201 of *Venus and Adonis* ('Art thou obdurate, flintie, hard as steele? / Nay more then flint, for stone at raine relenteth'), while in the remaining lines Marston compares the metamorphosis of Pygmalion as described in his own work to that of Adonis as described in *Venus and Adonis.*

Marston, who was a member of Middle Temple, was in a good position to know the truth, since he was a close friend of Thomas Greene of Warwickshire, also a member of Middle Temple, who claimed to be the cousin of William Shakespeare of Stratford (and possibly was by marriage). Greene had stood surety for John Marston's entry to the Middle Temple Inn of Court in 1594, and Marston had stood surety for Greene's entry in 1595. Greene named his children, Anne and William, after the Shakespeares, and in 1609 rented the rooms in New Place, Stratford-upon-Avon, from the actor. His brother, John Greene, who had been a student at Clement's Inn, also settled in Stratford.

So we have both Hall and Marston referring to the concealed author, whom the actor Shakespeare masked, as Labeo. Marston himself was no stranger to the use of pseudonyms and masks. He had hidden himself under the pseudonym of W. Kinsayder for both his poems, *The Metamorphosis of*

Pygmalion's Image and *The Scourge of Villainy*. But why choose Labeo as a pseudonym for the author of the Shakespeare poems? It is a pointed allusion, in fact, for Antistius Labeo was a celebrated lawyer in the time of the Roman Emperor Augustus, who lost favour with the Emperor for opposing the Emperor's views.

The Spear-shaker

As I have set out in chapter 3, it is significant that the name of Shakespeare is more often than not printed as *Shake-speare*, which points to its being a pseudonym. Ben Jonson makes use of a play on words with the name *Shake-speare* in his dedicatory poem to the 'beloved Author' in the Shakespeare First Folio. After the passage about a good poet being made as well as born, Jonson goes on to imply that Shakespeare had a very great knowledge, which he seems to shake like a lance of light at minds that are dark with ignorance:

> For a good Poet's made, as well as borne.
> And such wert thou. Looke how the father's face
> Lives in his issue, even so, the race
> Of Shakespeares minde, and manners brightly shines
> In his well torned, and true filed lines:
> In each of which, he seemes to shake a Lance,
> As brandish't at the eyes of Ignorance.
>
> Ben Jonson, Eulogy, Shakespeare Folio (1623)

In other words, Shakespeare is a lance- or spear-shaker, which is the strict interpretation of his name. The link between a poet and a Spear-shaker or spearman has a direct association with the founding of Rome and Roman civilisation, although it has earlier origins. The laurel wreath or sprig of bay leaves that is the attribute of a great poet is associated with the spear of Romulus who, when founding Rome, hurled his spear of laurel wood into the ground on the Quirinal Hill, where it took root and became a laurel tree. Romulus took the name of Quirinus, meaning 'Spearman', as his surname, in honour of his reputed father, the god Mars, who was known as Quirinus.[12] In this way Mars was acknowledged as the special god and protector of Rome and the Roman people, with his temple on the Quirinal Hill marking the spot where the laurel spear had pierced the ground and become a tree.[13] Before a Roman consul embarked upon any expedition, it was usual for him to visit the temple of Mars. There he offered prayers and, in a solemn ritual, shook the laurel spear which was in the hand of the statue of the god and at the same time exclaimed, 'Mars vigila! Watch over the welfare and safety of this city.'

The laurel of the Romans is the fragrant Mediterranean laurel, *Laurus nobilis,* known also as the bay. In classical times a wreath of this fragrant laurel was worn on the head as an emblem either of heroic victory in war or of honour and fame in the arts and sciences. The laurel wreath became especially the emblem of a great writer or poet, hence the title of poet laureate.

The spear of the Spear-shaker thus has a classical association with the laurel or bay tree, the tree of the great poet-philosophers and artists. To hold a sprig of bay leaves is equivalent to holding the laurel-wood spear, and he who holds either is a 'Spear-shaker', a great and honoured poet who shakes his spear of light at the dragon of ignorance. This is, in fact, how Shakespeare is depicted in the 1640 edition of *Shakespeare's Poems*, which shows another delib-erately-drawn 'left-handed' portrait of Shakespeare (see illustration 32, p.90). The face of Shakespeare looks like a mask, as in the 1623 Folio of Shakespeare plays. He is shown facing towards the left of the picture, rather than to the right as in the Folio. A light is behind his head, not a shadow. His right shoul-der and arm are cloaked, whereas his left shoulder and arm are visible, with the left hand (not right hand) holding a sprig of bay leaves.

A relevant example of a poet actually holding a laurel spear can be seen in the picture fronting *Hermetes the Heremyte*, a manuscript presented to Queen Elizabeth I in 1575. This picture shows a poet-knight in the Arcadian romantic tradition offering a book to the Queen with his right hand while grasping an upright spear in his left. The text at the foot of the page reads, 'Beholde (good Queene) a poett with a spear,' while the motto reads, *'Tam Marti quam Mercurio',* meaning 'As much by Mars as by Mercury'. Whereas the book is associated with Mercury, the spear in the poet's left hand represents Mars, being the lau-rel spear of Mars Quirinus, the Spearman.

According to the story told in the manuscript, this poet is a knight who has become a wise hermit, one who associates himself with Hermes Trismegistus, the great writer, educator and sage of Egypt, whom the Romans called Mercury. This theme of the poet-knight who becomes a great sage was the major theme of Elizabethan pageantry, developed year by year through-out Elizabeth's reign.

St George, the Red Cross Knight

In England the Spear-shaker or poet-knight was in particular associated with St George, the Red Cross knight and patron saint of England who shakes his founded a similar institution in Rome under the patronage of the same goddess, known to them as Minerva. This has been the custom in nearly all literary communities throughout Europe ever since.

Both Apollo and Athena, god and goddess of wisdom and illumination, are known as Spear-shakers. In particular the Greek name *Pallas Athena* literally means 'Spear Shaker' or 'Shake Spear'. The signature of the author on the Shakespeare poems and plays could just as well have been 'Apollo' or 'Pallas Athena'—the significance is the same; which helps to explain why both Ben Jonson and John Weever hailed Shakespeare as an Apollo, and why in his sonnets Shakespeare claims his Muse or genius to be Pallas Athena, the Tenth Muse:

> He was not of an age, but for all time!
> When all the Muses still were in their prime,
> When like Apollo he came forth to warme
> Our eares, or like a Mercury to charme!
>
> Ben Jonson, Eulogy, Shakespeare First Folio (1623)

> Honie-tong'd Shakespeare, when I saw thine issue,
> I swore Apollo got them and none other,
> Their rosie tainted features clothed in tissue
> Some heaven-born goddess said to be their mother.
>
> John Weever, Epig. 22, *Epigrams in the Oldest Cut and Newest Fashion* (c 1599)

The 'heaven-born goddess' referred to by Weever is none other than Pallas Athena, who in the older versions of the myths was considered to be the spouse of Apollo. In his verse Weever is equating 'honey-tongued Shakespeare' with both Apollo and Athena, the divine parents of Shakespeare's verse.

This idea is not just Weever's fancy. In Shakespeare's thirty-eighth Sonnet, the poet declares his Muse to be the Tenth Muse, Pallas Athena. A Muse is equated with genius; hence to speak of one's Muse is to speak of one's genius or higher, divine self—that aspect or portion of Divinity that is one's own personal source of inspiration:

> How can my Muse want subject to invent
> While thou dost breath that poor'st into my verse,
> Thine owne sweet argument, to excellent,
> For every vulgar paper to rehearse:
> Oh give thy selfe the thankes if ought in me,
> Worthy perusal stand against thy sight,
> For who's so dumbe that cannot write to thee,
> When thou thy selfe dost give invention light?

Be thou the tenth Muse, ten times more in worth
Then those old nine which rimers invocate,
And he that calls on thee, let him bring forth
Eternal numbers to out-live long date.
    If my slight Muse doe please these curious daies,
    The paine be mine, but thine shall be the praise.

Shakespeare, Sonnet 38

Shakespeare was not alone in this self-conceit. The Muse of Shakespeare's famous predecessor, the poet Edmund Spenser, is likewise the Tenth Muse, whom Spenser proclaims in the Prologue to his epic poem, *The Faerie Queen*:

Help then, O holy Virgin, chief of nine,
    Thy weaker Novice to perform thy will....
O help thou my weak wit, and sharpen my dull tongue.

Spenser, *The Faerie Queene*, Bk 1, Prologue

Pallas Athena, the Tenth Muse, was a very important and powerful archetype to the Elizabethans. The whole Elizabethan Age was seen as ruled by her. Spenser called her Gloriana and Belphoebe, and from the verse quoted above it is possible to see how this goddess of light was deliberately equated on earth with Queen Elizabeth. The poets likened the fiery, redheaded, witty and learned Tudor queen of England to this virgin sun-goddess Athena, as also to the virgin moon-goddess Diana or Cynthia (the Greek Artemis, sister of Apollo). She, the Faerie Queen, was the patroness of all poets, writers and artists, and of all arts and sciences. She presided on her throne over the culture of England. In her reign the English Renaissance was firmly established and brought to its glorious climax.

Traditionally, the queen represents the soul of her country. She and her land are inseparable. The old Roman image of Britannia, with her spear and shield, was Athena's British counterpart, and Elizabeth, as queen of ancient Britain (i.e., England and Wales), was Britannia. Moreover she was a redheaded Tudor sovereign with the blood of the Celts coursing through her veins. As such she was the very picture of the redheaded Bride or Bridget, the Celtic virgin goddess and protector of the land.

With her own explicit encouragement, Elizabeth Tudor was built up into a glamorous model of the Virgin Queen. Not only was this expedient for her politically, but also in this way she was honoured by her subjects and given tribute by the poets for patronising poetry and all the creative arts, as well as for being queen of ancient Britain, the country that Caesar dubbed the land of Apollo. The effect was to build up a national cult with the Queen as the fig-

36. *Queen Elizabeth I as 'Diana'. Miniature (c.1586–7) by Nicholas Hilliard*

urehead, in order to combat the power struggles that were constantly occurring and thereby to unite the people of the land, inspire them, increase learning and raise their consciousness.

It is therefore most interesting that research by a computer-graphics expert, Dr Lillian F Schwartz, using computer-aided art analysis, has shown that the mask-like face of the portrait of Shakespeare in the Shakespeare Folio appears to be based upon Queen Elizabeth I's official portrait—a kind of mask of perpetual youth and beauty on which every other painting of the Queen had to be based, whatever age the Queen happened to be at the time.[27]

This is surely a clever jest! The face is that of a man, the actor Shakespeare, who is masking the author Shakespeare; but the actor's face is based on that of Queen Elizabeth who, as a royal actress on the stage of the world, is personifying the goddess Athena. Since a persona is a mask (the literal meaning of the word *persona*), so the face of the Queen is the mask of the goddess. In one design, therefore, a double paradox seems to be offered. First, the actor Shakespeare is the mask for the author Shakespeare, but that author can be understood as either the human author or his Muse, the spear-shaking goddess Athena; or, second, is it saying that the Queen was the real author Shakespeare? The answer to this last question is, in my opinion, no, as there is abundant evidence to indicate another person as the author; but in one way or another the Queen was certainly involved.

The symbolism of Shakespeare as a pseudonym is given even further weight by the additional forename 'William'. Since this was the Stratford actor's actual Christian name, it is certainly fortuitous that it could also be used as part of the spear-shaking symbolism; but, as the Bard fully appreciated, fortune is full of surprises, wonders and hidden designs of her own ('Yet doth this accident and flood of fortune / So far exceed all instance, all discourse…'),[28] and it is up to us to make the most of the opportunities when they occur.

The name *William* is derived from *Hwyll*, the name in Welsh of the god of light, called Apollo by the Greeks, and *helm*, meaning helmet. In other words, *William* is a reference to Apollo's golden helmet of light, for which both Apollo and his feminine counterpart, Athena, were particularly noted, along with their 'shaking' spears. Whereas their spears symbolise the light of wisdom radiating out into the darkness, their helmets are representative of salvation or illumination. Athena in particular is said to present her golden helmet to any knight–hero who attains mastery of the liberal arts and sciences. It is equivalent to the poet's crown of bay leaves. Moreover, Athena's helmet is known as the helmet of invisibility, since it is reputed to bestow an invisible protection upon the wearer. Like the rose, it implies discretion, secrecy, concealment and anonymity. Freemasonic tradition explains it as such, pointing out that the root word of *helmet* is *hell*, meaning 'the covered place' or 'concealed world'. Its related word, *hele*, derived from Anglo-Saxon *helan*, meaning 'to cover and conceal', is used in the candidate's oath: 'I will always hele, conceal and never reveal.'[29]

The Gemini Spear-shakers

All this symbolism is also associated with the Rosicrucians, who have now been mentioned in a number of comments, and who were known as the 'Invisible Brethren'. Wearing symbolic helmets of light and led by their Apollo, they were dedicated to renewing and reducing all arts to perfection so that man might thereby understand his own nobleness and worth.[30] They were associated not only with St George and the Knights of the Round Table, the British equivalent of the knight–heroes of Apollo and Athena, but also with the Gemini, the 'Heavenly Twins'. The Gemini—Castor and Pollux—were known as Spear-shakers. Another name for them was the Dioscuri, meaning the sons of Jupiter. They were often symbolised as two swans.

In the classical myth of their origin, Jupiter took the form of a swan in order to woo Leda, the wife of Tyndareus of Sparta. As a result, Leda gave birth to two eggs. From one issued Pollux and Helen, who were regarded as the children of Jupiter, while from the other came Castor and Clytemnestra, who were reputed to be the children of Tyndareus. The brothers Castor and Pollux became inseparable in their friendship, despite the one twin being born mortal and the other immortal. In their youth they joined the Argonauts' expedition in search of the Golden Fleece, during which a great storm assailed the ship Argo in the sea of Colchis. While Orpheus called upon the gods to

The earth can yield me but a common grave,
When you entombèd in men's eyes shall lie:
Your monument shall be my gentle verse
Which eyes not yet created shall o'er-read;
And tongues to be your being shall rehearse,
When all the breathers of this world are dead,
    You still shall live—such virtue hath my Pen—
    Where breath most breathes, even in the mouths of men.

Shakespeare, Sonnet 81

The poet saw himself, his human personality, as being too unworthy to be remembered with his Muse, lest his human frailties and imperfections should mar the glory of the higher being. Being mortal and humble, he wished his personality to be forgotten, so that his divine self could be remembered untarnished:

O, lest the world should task you to recite
What merit lived in me that you should love,
After my death, dear love, forget me quite;
For you in me can nothing worthy prove,
Unless you would devise some virtuous lie
To do more for me than mine own desert,
And hang more praise upon deceasèd I
Than niggard truth would willingly impart:
O, lest your true love may seem false in this,
That you for love speak well of me untrue,
My name be buried where my body is
And live no more to shame nor me nor you:
    For I am shamed by that which I bring forth,
    And so should you, to love things nothing worth.

Shakespeare, Sonnet 72

But be contented when that fell arrest
Without all bail shall carry me away:
My life hath in this line some interest
Which for memorial still with thee shall stay.
When thou reviewest this, thou dost review
The very part was consecrate to thee.
The earth can have but earth, which is his due;
My spirit is thine, the better part of me.
So then thou hast but lost the dregs of life,
The prey of worms, my body being dead,
The coward conquest of a wretch's knife,

Too base of thee to be rememberèd.
   The worth of that is that which it contains,
   And that is this, and this with thee remains.

Shakespeare, Sonnet 74

In all this, Shakespeare echoes Ovid and Horace:

And now I have completed a work which neither the anger of Jove, nor fire, nor sword, nor devouring Time will be able to destroy.

Let that day, which has no power but over my body put an end to my uncertain life when it will.

Yet in the better part of me I shall be raised immortal above the lofty stars, and indelible shall be my name.

Ovid, Metamorphoses, XV

Then when this body falls in funeral fire,
My name shall live, and my best part aspire.

Ovid, Amores, translated by Ben Jonson in Poetaster

I shall not wholly die;
For the better part of me shall escape Libertina [Death];
And I shall ever be renewed in the praise of posterity.

Horace, Odes, translated by Ben Jonson

Shakespeare was not alone in focussing on this idea. The Elizabethan poets Daniel, Drayton and Peele, besides Ben Jonson who translated the *Odes* of Horace into English, all refer to their better part which is equated with their mind, name or genius:

And look how much the Mind, the better part,
Doth overpass the body in desert.

Peele, The Arraignment of Paris

Ensuing ages yet my rhymes shall cherish
Where I entombed my better part shall save;
And though this earthly body fade and die,
My name shall mount upon eternity.

Drayton, Idea, Sonnet 44

The nom-de-plume 'Shakespeare', therefore, seems in this context to refer to the poet's higher immortal self—his genius or spirit—which in his philosophy is the true poet, partaking of the divine nature. His name as a person is purposely omitted so as not to detract from the honour due to the higher self, or to tarnish its glory by linking it with the weaknesses and failings of the mortal self.

To search then for the person whose genius is the immortal 'Shakespeare' could be accounted a fault and not what the poet desires in his idealistic philosophy. Yet he has left (or his friends have left) signs by which we may discover his identity if we want to. It is a quandary as to what is best to do—honour his poetic wishes or follow the treasure trail? Once again the person, whoever he is, has left us two seemingly contrary choices.

This book pursues the treasure-trail option, since honour is surely due to the person who has laboured, as well as to the immortal who has inspired. Moreover, by discovering the person much of great value may be learnt, while at the same time we can be adult enough to recognise and respect what he meant in his sonnets. Perhaps, with the help of Jupiter, we can be to him as Pollux was to his slain brother Castor.[33]

Chapter 6

The Authorship Evidence of the Plays

Scholar–Poet

Besides all the hints as to who the author Shakespeare might actually be, such as are provided by the inscription on the Shakespeare Monument and the statements of his friends and contemporaries, there is also much that can be discovered from the evidence of the plays themselves. All of this evidence, taken together, is capable not only of revealing the true author but much more besides. This is something we shall discover as we continue, for the question of authorship is only the beginning of a great voyage of discovery and self-education in some of the profoundest matters of life.

As I have already said, an outstanding feature of the Shakespeare plays is their underlying scholarship as well as poetic skill. Shakespeare's knowledge of classical philosophy and mythology, and of literature generally, is both encyclopaedic and outstandingly detailed. This was recognised by Shakespeare's contemporaries and has been equally well-demonstrated by modern Shakespeare scholars. We have already looked at the tribute by Ben Jonson and the inscription on the Shakespeare Monument, in which Shakespeare is likened to the renowned statesman and judge Nestor, the celebrated orator and philosopher Socrates, and the great poet and scholar–initiate Virgil. In addition there is the testimony of Francis Meres, a parson, schoolmaster and Master of Arts of both Oxford and Cambridge, who not only bears witness to Shakespeare's great scholarship and learning in his book *Palladis Tamia,* published in 1598, but also provides some further subtle clues as to the identity of the author that are in complete harmony with the claims of the Shakespeare Monument:

> As the soul of Euphorbus was thought to live in Pythagorus: so the sweete wittie soule of Ovid lives in mellifluous & honey-tongued Shakespeare.…
> As Plautus and Seneca are accounted the best for comedy and trag-

the illustrious university men of William Clerke's own day and age, and takes the form of a 'Letter' written by 'England' to her 'Three Daughters'—namely, the Universities of Oxford, Cambridge and the Inns of Court in London (the latter being considered as the third university). Cambridge is addressed as the

three Daughters.

mongſt men, to gaine pardon of the *Wanton Adonis.*
ſinne to *Roſemond*, pittie to diſtreſſed *Watſons*
Cleopatra, and euerliuing praiſe to her *heyre.*
louing *Delia:* Regiſter your childrens *So well gra-*
petegree in Fames forehead, ſo may *ced Autho-*
you fill volumes with *Chauſers* praiſe, *ueth immor-*
with *Lydgate,* the Scottiſh Knight, and *tall praiſe &*
ſuch like, whoſe vnrefined tongues *of that di-*
farre ſhorte of the excellencie of this *uine Lady*
age, wrote ſimplie and purelie as the *rinna conte-*
times weare. And when baſe and in- *ding with*
iurious trades, the ſworne enemies to *Pindarus*
Learnings eternitie (a thing vſuall) *ctorious.*
ſhall haue deuoured them, either with *Sir Dauid*
the fretting cancker worme of mouldie *Matilda ho-*
time : with *Arabian* ſpicerie: with eng- *norably ho-*
liſh honnie : with outlandiſh butter *ſweet a Poe.*
(matters of imployment for the aged *Diana.*
dayes of our late authors) yet that then
ſuch (if you thinke them worthie) in
deſpite of baſe Groſers, (whome I *Procul hinc,*
charge vpon paine of learnings curſe, *procul ire*
not to handle a leafe of mine) may liue *profani.*
by your meanes, canonized in lear-
R 3 ning

42. Page 23, 'England to her Three Daughters', Polimanteia, Pt 2 (1595)

eldest daughter, Oxford as the second eldest, and the Inns of Court as the youngest.

Throughout the text and printed margins of this Letter appear the names of twenty-nine of 'England's Grandchildren', as they are called, whose *Alma Mater* was one or other of the three 'Daughters'.[5] The majority of them are contemporaries of William Clerke. Also mentioned are some learned foreign or classical poets, to whom the English alumni are compared or above whom they are exalted,[6] plus some founders of universities.[7] In the margin adjacent to some text that names Spenser (Cambridge) and Daniel (Oxford), Shakespeare is listed as one of the illustrious English university men. His name appears in such a way that it compares him with Thomas Watson (?1557–92), an Oxford alumnus and poet, one of the 'university wits' literary set in London in the 1580s (see illustrations 41–42):

> All praise worthy. Lucretia Sweet Shakspeare. Eloquent Gaveston. Wanton Adonis. Watsons heyre. So well graced Anthonie deserveth immortall praise from the hand of that divine Lady who like Corrina contending with Pindarus was oft victorious.

'Lucretia' refers to the second of Shakespeare's narrative poems, *The Rape of Lucrece*, published in 1594, while 'Wanton Adonis' refers to Shakespeare's first narrative poem, *Venus and Adonis*, published the previous year and referred to by him as the 'first heyre of my invention'. Gaveston is a character in *Edward II*, a play attributed to Marlowe two years after Marlowe's death but which is, arguably, Shakespearean in character. 'So well graced Anthonie' would seem to allude to Shakespeare's *Anthony and Cleopatra*, which is pointed at by the sense of the corresponding main text and the preceding marginal notes, Anthony being well graced and praised by his 'divine Lady' Cleopatra, who was beautiful and talented like the poetess Corrina.[8] But if this is the case, then Clerke must be referring to an earlier version of the play, or perhaps one of Watson's lost plays,[9] for Shakespeare's *Antony and Cleopatra* is normally dated 1606–7.

'Watson's heir' seems to imply that Clerke saw Shakespeare as Watson's heir—or, contrariwise, that Watson himself wrote *Venus and Adonis*, the first heir of his invention. Since Watson died in 1592 and went to Oxford, not Cambridge University, and since Clerke mentions Shakespeare as a separate person who wrote *Lucrece*, it is highly unlikely, if not impossible, that Watson was the poet 'Shakespeare', author of the immortal plays; but it poses an interesting thought concerning the person whom scholars call 'the rival poet', referred to in Shakespeare's Sonnet 83 ('both your poets') and the sonnet sequence to which that particular sonnet belongs (see chapter 14). It also opens up the possibility that 'Shakespeare' was more than one person, since the dedication of *Venus and Adonis* was signed 'William Shakespeare', which, if Clerke's marginal note does in fact point to Watson being the author of the poem, implies that Watson was the Shakespeare who wrote the Shakespeare poem, *Venus and Adonis*. The third possibility is that the author Shakespeare simply 'stole' Watson's poem and published it under his own pseudonym for some reason we can, at the moment, only guess at.

Whichever way one takes it, William Clerke's note is important, as Thomas Watson, who died in 1592, just five years before the publication of *Polimanteia*, was one of the most learned and accomplished of the English poets and classical scholars, writing Greek, Latin and English verse with equal facility. Clerke compares Shakespeare to Watson, identifying Shakespeare as a noted classical scholar and an alumnus of one of the 'three universities', which the evidence of the plays would suggest is Cambridge University (and also Gray's Inn, as we shall see). Yet no person by the name of Shakespeare is registered as having been at Cambridge University at that time—or, for that matter, at either of the other two universities eulogised, Oxford or the Inns of Court. Putting aside for the moment the group inference (*i.e.*, that 'Shakespeare' was the pseudonym of two poets or more), the most obvious conclusion to be drawn from this is that 'Shakspeare' or 'Shakespeare' was the pseudonym of someone who was educated at Cambridge University, was a noted classical scholar and was the author of the Shakespeare poems and plays.

Private Tuition and Libraries

The author Shakespeare was not only a classical scholar who often read his Latin and Greek source material in their original versions but he also read some of his source material in French, Italian and Spanish. The ability to read all these untranslated works could only have come from private tuition or extensive experience in a foreign country, or both, as neither French nor Italian nor Spanish were taught in the grammar schools or at university.

Shakespeare's linguistic skill in Latin, Greek, French, Italian and Spanish is not the only thing that is remarkable. Also remarkable are all the sources Shakespeare used for his vast assortment of passing remarks and allusions, with some of the sources being quite abstruse. All in all, it reveals an author who was exceptionally well-read and who clearly loved reading and researching in books and manuscripts—and who must have spent a good deal of time doing so.

To have read so widely and in such a variety of languages, classical and modern, Shakespeare must have accessed books in libraries other than at Cambridge, for the University Library at Cambridge was very limited in those days, numbering only about 450 books and manuscripts in 1581, and devoted to the classics. The Inns of Court had better libraries, but the principal libraries containing many of the books that Shakespeare used can only have been private libraries. Among such libraries were that of Dr John Dee, the Queen's astrologer and sage, who had the largest collection of books and manuscripts in England (nearly 4,000 by 1583) at his house in Mortlake-on-Thames, and those of the nobility, such as Lord Lumley, whose collection was the second largest in the country (about 3,000 by the end of the sixteenth century), and Lord Arundel, whose fine collection of books and art treasures was housed in Arundel House, on the Strand, next to Leicester (later Essex) House. Some books may have been found in foreign libraries. Indeed, some information could only be found abroad, and some of that was privileged information, such as the letter written by Joan of Arc, dated 17 July 1429 and addressed to the Duke of Burgundy, which Shakespeare used as source-material for the parley between the Duke and Joan in *Henry VI*, Part 1 (III, iii).

In the play the Duke of Burgundy, who is the ally of the English and marching towards Paris at the head of the English army, asks for the parley, while the 'Maid', Joan of Arc, speaks for the King of France, Charles VII. Joan makes an extraordinary speech, which moves Burgundy to abandon the English cause. This parley is Shakespeare's invention, as historically none actually took place. Burgundy did change sides, but only in 1435, four years after the death of Joan. This whole episode would appear to be entirely fabricated by Shakespeare, except that in 1780 there was published for the first time a letter written by Joan of Arc, dated 17 July 1429 and addressed to the Duke of Burgundy. The letter contains an impassioned appeal to the Duke to cease warring on France and to make peace with the French king. It in fact began the series of negotiations that resulted in the peace treaty of 1435, as represented in the play. The Duke did march his forces across the plain of Rouen towards Paris in the summer of 1429, and did agree to a truce soon after receiving Joan's letter.

This letter remained buried among the ducal papers at Lisle, the capital of Burgundy, until its discovery and publication three hundred and fifty years after it was written. The only way anyone could have read this letter was by visiting the Duke's palace at Lisle and being given access to the ducal papers.

Gray's Inn Lawyer

The Shakespeare plays and many of the sonnets are filled with legal terminology, some of it most abstruse. Moreover, this legal knowledge is not just applied to one sonnet or play but is to be found permeating all the author's

the most abstruse proceedings in English jurisprudence.'[15] Not only does Lord Campbell's analysis suggest that Shakespeare was actually well-trained in law, it also disposes of the oft-mooted idea that he (meaning here the actor Shakespeare) was probably able to acquire sufficient legal knowledge casually over a long period: for the *Comedy of Errors* is one of the early plays, its first known performance having been in 1594, as part of Gray's Inn Christmas Revels.

Sir James Wilde, K.C., afterwards Lord Penzance, another highly-eminent lawyer and leading legal authority of the nineteenth century, Baron of the Exchequer in 1860 and Judge of the Courts of Probate and Divorce in 1863, echoes Lord Campbell's observations. He noted Shakespeare's 'perfect familiarity with not only the principles, axioms, and maxims, but the technicalities of English law, a knowledge so perfect and intimate that he was never incorrect and never at fault.... At every turn and point at which the author required a metaphor, his mind ever turned to the law. He seems almost to have thought in legal phrases—the commonest of legal expressions were ever at the end of his pen in description or illustration.'[16] Lord Penzance also notes that: 'Without the regular training of a lawyer he could not express himself after the fashion in which the writer of Shakespeare's plays uniformly does.'[17]

Such a conclusion—that Shakespeare was a lawyer—is supported by Francis Meres' analogy of Shakespeare with the eminent lawyer Seneca (see chapter 3, p.59), and Joseph Hall's similar analogy of Shakespeare with the celebrated lawyer Antistius Labeo (see chapter 5, p.101).

One can go further than this, moreover, for the Shakespeare plays indicate not only the author's expert acquaintance with the law in general but also the source of his learning and practice. From the evidence of the plays, Shakespeare was well acquainted with the language, rules, circumstances and even the most trivial aspects of Gray's Inn and its twin establishment, the Inner Temple; and yet, like the Colleges of Oxford and Cambridge Universities, the Inns of Court were sacred precincts. The public knew very little of their internal affairs, for guests were seldom admitted behind the doors. They were the home of lawyers and judges, and acted as a university for the training of young noblemen and gentlemen in the intricacies of English law and the requirements of the royal Court.

For instance, one of the scenes in Part 1 of *Henry VI* is laid in the garden of the Inner Temple. It is in this scene and in this garden and by four hot-headed young aristocrats, students of law, that the Wars of the Roses were begun, according to Shakespeare! This is not history but the dramatist's invention, coined in his imagination from his own crucible of experience. Richard Plantagenet plucks a white rose, Somerset a red rose, supported respectively by Warwick (white rose) and Suffolk (red rose). In addition two other lawyers, who are also present, support Richard Plantagenet:

Plantagenet. Great lords and gentlemen, what means this silence?
 Dare no man answer in a case of truth?
Suffolk. Within the Temple hall we were too loud;
 The garden here is more convenient....
 [*Argument develops*]
Plantagenet. Let him that is a true-born gentleman
 And stands upon the honour of his birth,
 If he suppose that I have pleaded truth,
 From off this brier pluck a white rose with me.
Suffolk. Let him that is no coward nor no flatterer
 But dare maintain the party of the truth,
 Pluck a red rose from off this thorn with me....
 [*Argument continues. Somerset and Suffolk exit.*]
Plantagenet. [*To Warwick and the two other lawyers*] Thanks, gentlemen.
 Come, let us four to dinner. I dare say
 This quarrel will drink blood another day.

Shakespeare, 1 *Henry VI*, II, iv

One of the Inner Temple rules, as also at Gray's Inn, was silence at meals. Only if absolutely necessary were low tones or whispers allowed, otherwise all wants were made known by gestures, as in some monastic establishments. In addition, members of both Inns of Court sat at table in 'messes' or groups of four, each table accommodating three messes.

 The expression 'mess of four' is used twice in *Love's Labour's Lost.* The first time is by Berowne, when the men's loves are discovered:

Berowne. Ah! you whoreson loggerhead, you were born to do me shame.
 Guilty, my lord, guilty! I confess, I confess.
King. What?
Berowne. That you three fools lack'd me, fool, to make up the mess;
 He, he, and you, and you, my liege, and I,
 Are pick-purses in love, and we deserve to die.
 O! Dismiss this audience, and I shall tell you more.
Dumaine. Now the number is even.
Berowne. True, true, we are four.

Shakespeare, *Love's Labour's Lost*, IV, iii, 204

The phrase is later used by the French Princess who refers to the disguised King of Navarre and his three friends as 'a mess of Russians'.[18]

In *The Comedy of Errors,* the action turns on a misunderstanding with a goldsmith about a gold chain, yet this has no place in the original play of Plautus on which the *Comedy* was based. As the Rt. Hon. Sir D. Plunket Barton, a Judge of the High Court of Justice in Ireland and a Bencher of Gray's Inn, once pointed out, 'This was evidently a skit on a dispute between Chief Baron Manswood and a goldsmith over a gold chain, which caused much merriment at Gray's Inn and afterwards became a Privy Council affair'.[19]

Both *The Comedy of Errors* and *Love's Labour's Lost* are so scholarly and specialised, with their Gray's Inn jargon and references to the Gray's Inn Revels and other in-jokes, that they could have been written by and for the lawyers of that Inn. Furthermore, many of the characters mentioned in other Shakespeare plays were associated with Gray's Inn. To give another example, Peter Phesant, a great advocate and Gray's Inn man, was well known to the lawyers of that time, and he is brought very neatly into a witty legal repartee in *The Winter's Tale*:

> *Shepherd.* My Business, Sir, is to the King.
> *Autolycus.* What Advocate ha'st thou to him?
> *Shepherd.* I know not (and't like you.)
> *Clown.* Advocate's the Court-word for a Pheazant.
>
> Shakespeare, The Winter's Tale, IV, iv, 740–744

Peter Phesant, or Fesant, or Pheasant, as his name was variably spelled, was called to the bar at Gray's Inn in 1608 and later became a judge of Common Pleas. His father, also called Peter, was elected Reader of Gray's Inn in 1581. The Phesants were a well-known legal family, all connected with Gray's Inn.

The Inns of Court, like the Universities, were run in a somewhat similar manner to Navarre's Academy in *Love's Labour's Lost*, with the one major exception that in Queen Elizabeth's time the student lawyers of the Inns of Court were not only allowed but also expected to hold revels each year in which masques and other entertainments took place. These were all designed and enacted by the members and student lawyers and intended to provide training for the royal Court as well as the courts of law and offices of government.

The 1594/5 Christmas/New Year Revels at Gray's Inn, entitled *The Prince of Purpoole and the Order of the Knights of the Helmet*, were exceptionally lavish. These extended revels, which acted out the reign of a mock prince, the Lord of Misrule, complete with imitation Privy Council and officers of State, continued intermittently from the winter solstice, 20 December 1594, until Shrove Tuesday, 4 March 1595. During them certain Grand Nights were set aside for special entertainments to which honoured guests were invited.

One of the Grand Nights was on Innocent's Day, 28 December, at night, and its entertainment included a performance of 'a *Comedy of Errors* (like to Plautus his *Menechmus*)' played by 'Players'.[20] Shakespeare scholars generally agree that this was the first recorded performance of Shakespeare's *Comedy of*

Errors, because of the way it is described in the *Gesta Grayorum* recording the event. However, the usual assumption that the company of players were the Lord Chamberlain's Men, to which the actor Shakespeare belonged, is open to serious question, as the company is recorded as performing at Greenwich before the Queen that very same St Innocent's Day. This in fact means at night on St Innocent's Day, since the Queen always saw performances of plays at Court at night, beginning about 10.00 pm and ending about 1.00 am.[21] If this is so, then the players at Gray's Inn must have either been student members of Gray's Inn or another company of professional actors hired for the purpose, with the play as usual having been written by a member of the Inn (*i.e.,* the author Shakespeare). The play itself, as stated, is based on a classical play by Plautus called *Menaechmi*, but the theme of mistaken identities is almost certainly derived from *Supposes*, a play written by George Gascoigne, a member of Gray's Inn,[22] which was acted at the Inn in 1566 (but never on the public stage) and published in 1573, 1575 and 1587.

To this Grand Night entertainment were invited lords, ladies and members of the Privy Council, and dancing with ladies took place as part of the entertainment. However, such allowed pleasures with ladies were the exception, not the rule, and Gray's Inn, like the other Inns of Court and the Universities, were strictly-governed all-male preserves. Relating to this, Berowne's speech in *Love's Labour's Lost* echoes that of the Sixth Counsellor in the ensuing Grand Night masque, *The Order of the Knights of the Helmet,* which was enacted a few days later, on 3 January 1595, to make up for the 'errors' that had occurred during the first Grand Night, which was nicknamed 'the Night of Errors'. When addressing the Prince of Purpoole, the Counsellor gave a heartfelt plea for some feasting, comedies, love and ladies:

> *Sixth Counsellor.* They would make you a king in a play...
>   What! nothing but tasks? Nothing but working days?
>   No feasting, no comedies, no love, no ladies?
>   Let other men's lives be as pilgrimages,
>   But Prince's lives are as Progresses
>   Dedicated only to variety and solace.

In *Love's Labour's Lost* Berowne objects to the strictures ordered by the King of Navarre in a similar vein:

> *Berowne.* Oh, these are barren tasks, too hard to keep,
>   Not to see ladies; study, fast, not sleep.
>
> Shakespeare, *Love's Labour's Lost,* I, i, 47—8

In Act V, scene 2, of *Love's Labour's Lost,* the masque of Russians with their 'Black moores' is derived from the procession up the Thames and through the streets of London made by the Prince of Purpoole and his Knights of the Helmet on 1 February as part of the Revels. This processional masque was done in pretence of the Prince and his knights returning from a campaign in Russia against Negro-Tartars—the blackamoors of *Love's Labour's Lost.* Moreover, Rosaline's jibe in the same scene, 'Sea-sick, I think, coming from Muscovy,'[23] echoes the excuse made by the Prince of Purpoole who, on his return from the mock visit to Russia, wrote a letter to Sir Thomas Heneage, the Queen's Vice-Chamberlain, to excuse himself from attending on her Majesty that day because of his exhaustion 'by length of my journey, and my sickness at sea'.

The conclusion of these Revels took place a month later, on Shrove Tuesday, at the start of Lent, with a performance by the lawyers before the Queen at Whitehall of a masque entitled *The Masque of Proteus.* (Shakespeare also took the fascinating and profoundly-philosophical Greek myth of Proteus as the underlying subject for his comedy, *The Two Gentlemen of Verona,* in which the two gentlemen are Valentine and Proteus.) The Revels were in fact curtailed from what was originally planned, by order of the Readers and Ancients of the House, with two Grand Nights cut out, and *Love's Labour's Lost* has all the hallmarks of having been written specifically for the Grand Night ending that was originally intended.[24]

With respect to *The Comedy of Errors,* the indications are that it was written for the 1594/5 Gray's Inn Revels, whose theme was built around the idea of errors being committed, a trial being held of the 'sorcerer' responsible, and then the errors being made good and the sorcerer redeeming himself with something better. *The Comedy of Errors* is not alone in this, for *Twelfth Night,* performed at the Middle Temple on Candlemas, 2 February 1602, is another example of a Shakespeare play written for and first performed at an Inn of Court. Shakespeare's highly intellectual and 'legal' play, *Troilus and Cressida,* is another one.[25]

The first recorded performance of *Twelfth Night* was on Candlemas, 2 February 1602, at the Middle Temple Inn of Court in London. The performance would have taken place in the large, beautiful and well-illuminated Elizabethan hall, with its clerestory of sparkling glazed windows on both north and south walls, two bay windows at the west end, a finely-carved screen at its east end, and a magnificent double hammer-beam roof, the finest domestic example in existence at the time it was built. Queen Elizabeth I opened it in 1572 and it still exists today. Sir John Shurley was the Treasurer and head of the Inn at that time, and thus the person who was responsible for the Revels and commissioning the play.

Buried in the text of *Twelfth Night* are two allusions to John Shurley's family.

The references are to Sir Anthony and Sir Robert Sherley (Shurley), brothers-in-law to the Treasurer's nephew, who was also named John Shurley and a member of Middle Temple. These two brothers, Anthony and Robert, were educated at the Inns of Court, became followers of the Earl of Essex and, under Essex's patronage, went on an expedition to visit the Shah of Persia, arriving at the Shah's court in 1599. Between November 1599 and April 1601 Sir Anthony Sherley made visits to Moscow, Prague and Rome, purportedly as the Shah's ambassador, while his brother Robert remained in Persia both as a hostage and a military adviser.[26] Sir Anthony returned to England in a ship named *The Sophie*. Two accounts of his journeys and exploits were published in England: *A True Report of Sir Anthonie Shierlies Journey* (September 1600) and *A New and Large Discourse of the Travels of Sir Anthony Shirley* (late 1601).

'The Sophie' was the name by which the Shah was known, and there are two jokes in *Twelfth Night* about him that allude to the Sherley brothers and their expedition. Fabian's remark in the play as he watches Malvolio being tricked by Maria's forged letter refers to Sir Anthony Sherley, who claimed the Shah gave him a pension of 30,000 crowns. Sir Tobie's attempt to frighten Sir Andrew by presenting Cesario as a swordsman to be feared refers to Sir Robert Sherley, the Shah's military adviser.

> *Fabian.* I will not give my part of this sport for a pension of thousands
>   to be paid from the Sophie.
>
> Shakespeare, *Twelfth Night*, II, v, 180

> *Sir Tobie.* ...They say he has been fencer to the Sophie.
>
> Shakespeare, *Twelfth Night*, III, iv, 283

Fabian is a character in the play who appears to have been added late into the plot by the author, together with another character called Curio. Both these names are new to the Shakespeare canon and unique to *Twelfth Night*. They happen to be the nicknames of two students of the Inns of Court and are the commonest of the various nicknames used in the many satires and epigrams written by the young lawyers around that time. It is quite possible that Shakespeare, by request, wrote the parts of Fabian and Curio into the play both as an Inns of Court in-joke and also to enable the two student lawyers known as Fabian and Curio to act the parts themselves at this first Middle Temple performance of *Twelfth Night*.

Fabian (according to the playwright and student member of Middle Temple, John Marston) was a 'silken dancer' and 'had some doings with the Prince D'Amour / And play'd a noble man's part in a play'.[27] This refers to the playing of an actor's part in a play performed at one of the Middle Temple's Christmas Revels, which were presided over by a Lord of Misrule known in the Middle Temple as the Prince D'Amour (*i.e.,* Prince of Love).

Curio was particularly associated with lovemaking, since the satires speak of him in this way. A whole satire is dedicated to Curio under the title of *Curio Inamorato*—the point of the satire being a jest at Curio and other young men who make themselves ridiculous when it comes to lovemaking. In *Twelfth Night*, Curio's first (and almost his only) lines of speech are, suitably and cryptically, related to the heart:

> *Curio.* Will you go hunt, my lord?
> *Orsino.* What Curio?
> *Curio.* The hart.

Shakespeare, Twelfth Night, I, i, 16–17

Not only are exploits and names of members of the Middle Temple built into the play, but there are also references to the Middle Temple Hall itself, such as in the scene when Malvolio is imprisoned in darkness and questioned by the clown, Feste, in disguise as Sir Topas the curate:

> *Clown.* Sayst thou that house is dark?
> *Malvolio.* As hell, Sir Topas.
> *Clown.* Why, it hath bay windows transparent as barricades, and the clerestories toward the south-north are as lustrous as ebony: and yet complainest thou of obstruction?

Shakespeare, Twelfth Night, IV, ii, 35–40

There are also allusions to and in-jokes about the affairs of certain Inns of Court lawyers, such as William Strachey's connection with the Yeoman of the Wardrobe. Strachey was a member of Gray's Inn and, as a result, had direct communion and friendly relationships with members of the Middle Temple. He was also a partner in Blackfriar's Theatre, a co-partner of his being Edward Kirkham, who was Yeoman of the Royal Wardrobe.

> *Malvolio.* There is example for't. The Lady of the Strachy married the yeoman of the wardrobe.

Shakespeare, Twelfth Night, II, v, 39–40

Besides these in-jokes, the general setting of *Twelfth Night* is one of revelry in a puritanical environment, which echoes the setting of the Middle Temple's Christmas Revels that, like those of Gray's Inn and the other Inns of Court, included dancing, masques, play-acting, feasting and drinking. Sir Tobie

Belch and Sir Andrew Aguecheek are excellent parodies of certain gentlemen—students of the Inns of Court in Shakespeare's day and almost certainly would have drawn a good laugh of recognition! By way of contrast, Malvolio's character is a parody of puritanical attitudes that were at odds with the revelling of the Inns of Court, or indeed of revels, feasts, plays or entertainments of any kind anywhere. There are hints in the play suggesting that Malvolio, the Countess Olivia's steward, is partly modelled on a fusion of two notable Elizabethans, Sir William Knollys and Sir Posthumus Hoby.

Sir William Knollys was the Comptroller of the Queen's Household. His father, Sir Francis Knollys, had been a Privy Councillor and Treasurer of the Royal Household, and a renowned puritan who had proposed expelling all recusants (*i.e.,* Roman Catholics) from England. Sir Francis had died in 1596, before *Twelfth Night* was written, but his reputation lived on. Sir William Knollys, his son, ruled the Queen's household with some severity, frowning upon sporting and revelling—an attitude which was in direct contrast to that of the Queen herself, who loved dancing, entertainment and plays, although she kept it all within a certain control.

In *Twelfth Night,* when Malvolio rebukes Sir Tobie, saying that he will quench his familiar smile with an 'austere regard of control' (II, v, 66–67), the phrase is very possibly a pun on Sir William's office, as suggested by Leslie Hotson in his book, *The First Night of Twelfth Night.*[28] Part of Sir William's responsibilities was to look after the Queen's Maids of Honour, one of whom was Mary Fitton, who had been placed in Sir William's care by her father when she was aged seventeen (in 1595). Knollys was married to Dorothy Brydges, Lady Chandos, a widow older than himself, but he became infatuated with his young, beautiful protégé and wrote her extravagant love letters. He even dyed his beard for her. Mary herself was in love with William Lord Herbert (later the Earl of Pembroke, to whom the Shakespeare Folio is dedicated) and, in 1601, bore a child by him. A widely-circulated lampoon of that period suggests that this love triangle was well-known.

At that time yellow symbolised love (also jealousy), and in a popular ballad called *Peg a Ramsey* reference is made to a married man who is troubled with a wife and who asks for his yellow hose:

> When I was a bachelor I led a merry life;
> But now I am a married man, and troubled with a wife...
> Give me my yellow hose again, give me my yellow hose.
> For now my wife she watcheth me; see yonder where she goes.[29]

In *Twelfth Night* Sir Tobie refers to Malvolio as a 'Peg a Ramsey', and the jest played on Malvolio by Maria and Sir Tobie is to persuade Malvolio to dress up

matic fall and death, in all of which she was an unwitting but key player. R. H. Case, in his introduction to the first Arden edition of *Coriolanus,* puts it succinctly: 'She [Volumnia] is skilled in what the Bastard of the earlier play [*King John*] calls "commodity", and behind her fashioning it is possible to detect Shakespeare's mastery of the politics of English history'.[48]

Other contemporaries of Shakespeare had also taken Plutarch's *Life of Coriolanus* as a basis for an open discussion of politics,[49] as did Shakespeare for his play, but none show such a comprehensive grasp of the issues involved as does Shakespeare.

Philosopher

The Shakespeare plays and poems are saturated with philosophical concepts, most of which are still relevant and many still challenge us today. The plays show that the author had a profound understanding and knowledge of human nature and psychology as well as of the Bible, the Cabala, the works of Hermes and the Platonic and Neoplatonic writers, and of the classical myths and their meanings. Furthermore, in the plays the author makes it abundantly clear that he considers knowledge—real knowledge, not imagined or assumed or untested—to be of vital importance to the human being. He is also somewhat of a revolutionary in his philosophy concerning women and marriage. Not only are his heroines highly-educated and cultured women, but arranged marriages for money, or any marriage in which the bride is treated as her husband's chattel, are satirised over and over again. Love, practised as mercy, is the playwright's great teaching.

To give but a few examples of Shakespeare's range and depth of philosophical thought and learning, the following four quotations from the plays provide plentiful food for thought. First, let us consider Hamlet's anguished question:

> *Hamlet.* To be or not to be, that is the question:
>   Whether 'tis nobler in the mind to suffer
>   The slings and arrows of outrageous fortune,
>   Or to take arms against a sea of troubles
>   And by opposing end them....
>
> Shakespeare, *Hamlet*, III, i, 56–60

This philosophical debate voiced by Hamlet deals with the deepest of matters. The question as to whether being proceeds from non-being or from itself (*i.e.,* being) was the focus of passionate argument by the Greek philosophers for centuries. Hamlet's words and thoughts concerning this are derived from Plato and also from what is known as the *Eleatic Fragment*. This *Fragment* originates from Simplicius' Greek commentary on the works of Aristotle,[50] which deals with Parmenides' identification of being with thought, and his conclusion that the source of being is and can only be itself:

> Never do thou learn to fancy that not-being is; but keep thy mind from this path of enquiry; nor let custom force thee to pursue that beaten way, to use blind eyes and sounding ear and tongue, but judge by reason the knotty argument which I declare. One only way of reasoning is left— that being is. Wherein are many signs that it is uncreate and indestructible, whole in itself, unique in kind.... For neither birth nor beginning belongs to being. Wherefore either to be or not to be is the unconditioned alternative. Nor will the might of proof allow us to believe that anything can spring from being but itself.... This then is the point for decision: it is, or it is not.[51]

From this point of view, there can never be any death of being, but only changes of form and circumstance; and even this is illusion, since all phenomena are but the result of thoughts or dreams, as thought and being are one. Hamlet thinks and dreams, and in this he is afraid of the nightmare, the bad dream, in which he has perceived his father to be:

> *Hamlet.* To die, to sleep;
> To sleep, perchance to dream—ay, there's the rub:
> For in that sleep of death what dreams may come,
> When we have shuffled off this mortal coil,
> Must give us pause.
>
> Shakespeare, *Hamlet*, III, i, 60–68

The second of Hamlet's questions, which follows the first, is: what should he do about his vision or dream of his father, who still exists in the cosmic realm of thought. Should he forgive, or take revenge? Which is the just course of action? Through the character of Prince Hamlet the author presents to us the great question we each have to answer when wrong confronts us, particularly a great wrong: do we take up the sword or turn the other cheek? Moreover, is it merciful to turn the other cheek, or is this simply weakness or irresponsibility that allows the wrong to propagate and do worse things? What therefore is justice, and how do we apply it with mercy?

Probably the finest and best-known of Shakespeare's speeches on this subject is that of Portia in *The Merchant of Venice*:

> Portia. The quality of mercy is not strain'd,

It droppeth as the gentle rain from heaven
Upon the place beneath: it is twice blest,
It blesseth him that gives, and him that takes,
'Tis mightiest in the mightiest, it becomes
The thronèd monarch better than his crown.
His sceptre shows the force of temporal power,
The attribute to awe and majesty,
Wherein doth sit the dread and fear of kings:
But mercy is above this sceptred sway,
It is enthronèd in the hearts of kings,
It is an attribute to God himself;
And earthly power doth then show likest God's
When mercy seasons justice: therefore Jew,
Though justice be thy plea, consider this,
That in the course of justice, none of us
Should see salvation: we do pray for mercy,
And that same prayer, doth teach us all to render
The deeds of mercy.

Shakespeare, *Merchant of Venice,* IV, i, 180–198

As a lawyer dealing with the law, Shakespeare makes a clear distinction between the law that Shylock demands, of so-called justice without mercy, and divine law which includes mercy. He further reminds us of the ancient teaching that mercy is what makes a true king, and that mercy is the grace which anoints and crowns the merciful, of which the fragrant unguent and crown of gold is but an image. Hamlet is shown striving in his mind to find a just and possibly merciful solution to the situation, but slips into revenge when he makes his decision to kill his uncle, the usurping king, not while the king is at prayer but when immersed in debauchery, so that he would go to hell, not heaven.

Others who are like Hamlet include the conspirators in *Julius Caesar*, particularly Brutus, whom Shakespeare shows as rejecting love, rejecting mercy, and thinking to right wrong by the murder of a tyrant. Likewise, Caesar is shown murdered because he refuses to show mercy, whereas if he had pardoned Publius Cimber the assassination might never have been carried out and the civil war that followed might never have taken place. Equally vividly, Mark Antony is shown as choosing the path of revenge instead of working out a more peaceful, loving and just solution to the injustices that have been committed.

Hamlet and *Julius Caesar* both show a solution that is more to do with revenge than either justice or mercy, although both Hamlet and Brutus set out to do what they believe is just, until circumstances that they themselves precipitate take things out of control. Hamlet is a study of a person who might have naturally followed a path of justice and mercy had it not been that the ghost of his father urged him to revenge. Brutus, by contrast, is a study of a person who seems to be unaware of the revenge motive behind the thoughts of his fellow-conspirators. Both characters are fundamentally good at heart but are manipulated and used by others—Hamlet by his father's ghost and Brutus by his friends. So these plays of Shakespeare are a study in character-weakness, emotional blackmail and blinded perception, as well as in the problems of understanding and applying justice and mercy.

The Merchant of Venice shows how justice can be brought about in a court of law with the help of a skilful barrister, and equally how mercy can be given once the injustice is pinpointed and the perpetrator of the injustice brought under the power of the law. *The Tempest* deals with the same idea, but presents it in terms of a magus who is both ruler and judge on his island, assisted and prompted by a spirit (Ariel) just as the Doge is assisted and prompted by the 'lawyer' Portia in *The Merchant of Venice*. Shakespeare makes it very clear that whereas a judge deals with justice, a king or ruler is in a position to bestow mercy, and that the one has to precede the other up to the point where mercy can be offered. Then, if the mercy is accepted (which itself depends on repentance), it can transmute both the situation and the persons involved into something better and more blessed.

Equally challenging to this justice–mercy question is Shakespeare's perception of truth, especially considering the age in which he lived, in which, despite there being a queen on the throne of England, male chauvinism and religious bigotry was at its height, and a woman was not only deemed to be of less value than a man but also associated with the 'original sin' as the temptress of Adam. Through the character of Berowne in *Love's Labour's Lost,* Shakespeare throws down the gauntlet to both Church and State, as well as to all places of learning and society in general, challenging some precious tenets, supposedly ordained by God, upon which society was based—and upon which to some extent it still is based today:

> *Berowne.* Have at you then, affection's men-at-arms:
>   Consider what you first did swear unto,
>   To fast, to study, and to see no woman;
>   Flat treason 'gainst the kingly state of youth.
>   Say, can you fast? Your stomachs are too young,
>   And abstinence engenders maladies.
>   And where that you have vow'd to study, lords,
>   In that each of you have foresworn his book,

Chapter 7

The Author

The Probable Candidate

The description of the author Shakespeare, as summarised at the end of the previous chapter, sounds almost impossible to match to any one person. There have been many attempts to do so, however, and various possible candidates for the Shakespeare authorship have been put forward over the years by people who came to the conclusion that the author could not have been the actor William Shakespeare of Stratford-upon-Avon.

In order to fit the criteria laid out in the previous chapter, the author Shakespeare could not have been the actor Will Shakespeare, for reasons already given; nor could he have been Christopher Marlowe, or Edward de Vere, 17th Earl of Oxford, or William Stanley, 6th Earl of Derby, or Mary Sidney, Countess of Pembroke, all of whom have been put forward as possible candidates for the authorship. For one thing, none of them were lawyers, parliamentarians or renowned philosophers. Moreover, Marlowe attended Cambridge University but never went to an Inn of Court. Stanley attended Oxford and not Cambridge University. Edward de Vere was entered on the matriculation role of Queen's College, Cambridge University, at the age of nine, but, except for a short period when he lodged at St John's College, there is no evidence that he ever took up this place as a full-time resident student. Most of his education and residence was first with his parents at Castle Hedingham and later with the Cecils at their London and country houses, and the degrees he received from Cambridge and Oxford were honorary. Mary Sidney, as a woman, was unable to go to university or any Inn of Court, which were then the preserve of men. Stanley lived until 1642 and Will Shakespeare until 1616, but both Oxford and Marlowe died too early to have written all of the plays—Oxford in 1604, when some of the finest Shakespeare plays were still to be written, and Marlowe in 1593, when the vast majority of the Shakespeare plays were not even conceived. The Oxfordian case depends on the proposition that the Shakespeare plays were written many years earlier than is generally accepted, despite the internal and external evidence of the plays that has been so comprehensively researched. The Marlovian case rests on the proposition that Marlowe did not die in 1593, but lived on in disguise, secretly writing the Shakespeare plays—but no real evidence is forthcoming in support of this contention.

There was one man, however, who fits the delineation of the author Shakespeare completely, and that person was Francis Bacon. Moreover, there is strong evidence that goes a long way towards confirming that Bacon was the author Shakespeare, with some of that evidence being purposefully and carefully left to posterity in such a way that we might, with effort, discover the true author, as in a treasure hunt or game of hide and seek. First, though, let us begin with a brief summary of Bacon's life, so that we might know the person about whom we are talking, check the summary against the criteria, and see the context in which he could have written the plays. In the ensuing sections and chapters we will go into more detail, unfolding layer upon layer of evidence for his authorship of the poems and plays, and much more besides.

Francis Bacon was born in 1561 and died in 1626. He was an alumnus of Cambridge University, a classical scholar in Latin, Greek and Hebrew, a multi-linguist fluent in French, Italian and Spanish, an international traveller, a courtier, intelligencer and cryptologist, a celebrated philosopher and writer, a musician, a mystic, a naturalist and horticulturist, a lawyer and barrister. He became in his lifetime a Reader and Treasurer of Gray's Inn, a Member of Parliament, a statesman and, ultimately, as Lord Chancellor, a judge. As we shall see, he was in addition a renowned orator, poet and playwright who was the acknowledged leader of the poets and wits of his time, and who ran a scrivenery of writers, poets, translators, cryptanalysts and secretaries to assist him. He had a powerful motive for writing the Shakespeare plays as well as being fully capable of doing so. He had the time in which to write them, and the necessary assistance. Moreover, he was alive and of writing age throughout the whole 'Shakespeare' period, from the first appearance of the plays to their final compilation in the 1623 Shakespeare Folio, in which are certain additions and alterations that could not have been made earlier. He also had more than one good reason to keep his name secret as the author of the Shakespeare poems and plays, and at one time mused with the idea of using another pseudonym to conceal the authorship of his philosophical works as well (see chapter 8, p. 218).

Francis Bacon grew up with his elder brother Anthony[1] in a milieu which demonstrated the highest culture and learning in the country, as well as in the midst of Court politics and life. His father was Sir Nicholas Bacon, the Queen's Lord Keeper of the Great Seal, one of the wisest as well as most pow-

THE SHAKESPEARE ENIGMA

43. Francis Bacon (b.1561, d.1626) Aged 18 years. 'If only a picture deserving of his mind could be made.' Miniature (1578/9) by Nicholas Hilliard

erful men in the land.[2] His mother, as we have seen, was Lady Ann Bacon, the second daughter of the great scholar Sir Anthony Cooke,[3] a tutor to the royal family, who had a magnificent library at his family seat, Gidea Hall in Essex, and whose five daughters were among the most highly educated and scholastically talented women in the country. His mother's eldest sister, Mildred, was the wife of Sir William Cecil, the Queen's Principal Secretary of State, who later became Lord Burghley and the Queen's Lord Treasurer. Both Sir Nicholas and Sir William, besides holding the highest political offices under Queen Elizabeth, were patrons of the arts and sciences.

The two families, the Cecils and the Bacons, maintained close contact with each other. This meant, for instance, that the Earl of Oxford, Edward de Vere, who lived with the Cecil family as a ward of Burghley until he came of age in 1571 and married Burghley's daughter Anne, was well known to Francis and his brother Anthony. The Earl's estrangement from and harsh treatment of his wife became a matter of great concern to the two families and their friends, as well as to the Queen, and between them they contrived an eventual reunion of the couple. Anne eventually died in 1588 and Oxford remarried in 1591, his new wife being Elizabeth Trentham. Much of *All's Well That Ends Well*, which scholars surmise was first written *c.*1597-8 and revised *c.*1603–1604, appears to be largely based upon Oxford's marriage to Anne. The play's title was first recorded in Francis Bacon's private notebook in 1594.[4]

Francis was given a special upbringing with the best private tutors, and was acclaimed as a child prodigy. In April 1573, at the age of twelve, he went up with his brother Anthony to Trinity College, Cambridge, where their contemporaries and friends included John Lyly, William Clerke, Edmund Spenser, Philemon Holland and Gabriel Harvey—the latter being their tutor in rhetoric and poetry as well as later being a member of the English Areopagus of philosopher–poets, led by Sir Philip Sidney. After leaving Cambridge University, in September 1576 Francis was sent abroad to attend the French Court for three years, where he saw the Italian *Commedia dell'Arte* perform and where the French culture and the *Pléiade*[5] of French poets were a great inspiration to him.

When Francis returned to England in 1579, on the death of Sir Nicholas, his uncle Lord Burghley sent him to Gray's Inn, where he commenced a mighty programme for the advancement of learning and renewal of the arts and sciences, ostensibly with the encouragement of Burghley and the Queen. Some of the inspiration for this almost certainly came from his father Sir Nicholas, who had been an earnest promoter of a special scheme for the education of the wealthier crown wards. This scheme involved a means of educating the young gentlemen in French, Latin, Greek, civil and common law, music and dancing, together with overseas experience accompanying ambassadors, as preparation for royal service. Sir Nicholas' proposal for the establishment of a special academy in London for this purpose was seemingly ignored, but the Inns of Court, and especially Gray's Inn (Sir Nicholas' own Inn), appear to have incorporated many of his proposals during Elizabeth's reign. Francis' visit to France in the company of Sir Amyas Paulett, the English ambassador to the French Court, may have been part of this scheme. Francis' ideas, however, went much further than his father's and were much more universal in their scope. In his own words, he 'rang the bell that called the wits together', and a group of poets, writers, philosophers and other talented people soon began gathering around him. He started writing masques and plays, and speeches for pageants and entertainments, as an important part of his great scheme (which he later came to call 'The Great Instauration').

In 1581–2, Francis made a specially-prepared twelve-month journey to France, Spain, Italy, Germany and Denmark, to observe life and gather information. The journey was at his own request but was made use of by the Queen, who commissioned him, via Sir Thomas Bodley,[6] to make report and compile notes of observations respecting the 'laws, religion, military strength and whatsoever concerneth pleasure or profit' in the countries of Europe. Francis' brother Anthony, who had become one of the Queen's chief intelligencers working on the continent, helped Francis by advising, arranging contacts and preparing a route. Anthony returned briefly from the continent to England in

net sequence, *Astrophel and Stella,* plus other poems and a masque entertainment, *Lady of May,* written for the Queen. He was the reputed leader of the English Areopagus of philosopher–poets[27] in the exciting years preceding the Spanish Armada, when the English Renaissance was at last truly underway.

> Not but that I may defend the attempt I have made upon Poetry by the examples, not to trouble you with history, of many wise and worthy persons of our times; as Sir Philip Sidney, Sir Fra. Bacon, Cardinal Perron, the ablest of his countrymen, and the former Pope who, they say, instead of the triple crown wore sometimes the poet's ivy as an ornament perhaps of lesser weight and trouble. But Madam, these Nightingales sung only in the Spring, it was the diversion of their youth.
>
> Preface to Waller's Poems (1645)

'Diversion' is a good summing-up for how poetry was perceived. For although poetry was greatly loved and enjoyed in the Court, it was nevertheless regarded as a pastime, a recreation, and not to be taken seriously. To be a serious or professed poet was not conducive to achieving any office or position of standing in the State. Sir Philip Sidney, for instance, kept his poetic works private during his life and asked for them all to be destroyed after his death. Fortunately for us, his wish was not observed, and the publication of his poetry after his death has provided England with a great legacy and has made Sidney's name famous to later ages.

As she did with Philip Sidney, Queen Elizabeth knew that Francis Bacon was a poet, but it was important for him that she and, later, King James, and their respective ministers, should believe that he was reasonably serious about the law as a profession and that poetry was for him a pastime. Therefore, referring to a particular sonnet that he once wrote to the Queen, when she was due to dine with him at his Lodge at Twickenham, Francis states:

> At which time I had, though I profess myself not to be a poet, prepared a sonnet directly tending and alluding to draw on her Majesty's reconcilement to my Lord [Essex].
>
> Francis Bacon, Apology in Certain Imputations Concerning the late Earl of Essex (1604)[28]

That is to say, Francis wrote a sonnet to the Queen, who must have known by this and other poetic devices written by Francis for Essex for performance at the royal Court, that he was a poet; but Francis emphasises in the *Apology* that he did not profess to be a poet. 'Profess' means openly to confess or claim to be or do something; it doesn't mean that the person either is not or does not do that something privately or secretly. Ben Jonson uses the word in the same sense and in a similar situation in his *Silent Woman* (1609), where there is an argument as to the advisability or otherwise of Sir John Daw publishing verses under his own name. Daw says that he does not 'profess' to be a poet. Another character, Clerimont, declares in response that 'Sir John Daw has more caution; he'll not hinder his rising in the State.'

However, Francis Bacon was, in certain circles, too well-known as a poet and too serious about his literary pursuits for it to go unheeded. Despite his undisputed genius, wide knowledge and great abilities, he was never appointed to any suitably influential and remunerative position in Queen Elizabeth's reign, even though asking for such a position so as to have 'commandment of more wits than of man's own', as he put it, to assist him in carrying out his Herculean programme of renovating the arts and sciences and placing them on firmer foundations than before. Although the Queen and Burghley had clearly made such a promise to Francis, they never fulfilled it. For fifteen years they kept Francis on a string concerning his 'rare and unaccustomed suit', until in 1591 he wrote in exasperation to his uncle Burghley, threatening that if his Lordship would not 'carry him on' he would sell the small inheritance he had in order to become some sorry bookmaker or a true pioneer in that mine of truth which Anaxagoras said lay so deep:

> And if your lordship will not carry me on, I will not do as Anaxagoras did, who reduced himself with contemplation unto voluntary poverty: but this I will do; I will sell the inheritance that I have, and purchase some lease of quick revenue, or some office of gain that shall be executed by deputy, and so give over all care of service, and become some sorry book-maker, or a true pioneer in that mine of truth, which (he said) lay so deep. [29]

The nearest Francis Bacon came to office in Elizabeth's reign was when he was proposed for either Solicitor-General or Attorney-General in 1594, at a time when both positions became vacant; but in the end he was bypassed for both offices. It was not until 1607, when King James had been on the throne four years, that Francis was appointed to the high office of Solicitor-General, at the age of forty-six. It is almost certainly because he was so deeply involved with poetry, masques and the writing of plays that he was so blatantly overlooked by Queen Elizabeth, although an extra reason in 1594 may have been that the Queen wanted to punish Francis for his daring stand in parliament against her and Burghley's attempt to usurp the House of Commons' right to raise taxes. Essex, who unsuccessfully tried to help Francis obtain the Attorney-Generalship, reported back to him that the Queen 'did acknowledge that you had a great wit and excellent gifts of speech, and much other good learning. But in law she rather thought you could make show to the utmost of your knowledge than that you were deep.'[30] Some years later (1600), Essex was to write to Francis: 'I am a stranger to all poetical conceits, or else I should say somewhat of your poetical example'.[31]

Burghley, the Queen's closest friend and adviser, and Francis Bacon's uncle who acted *in loco parentis* to both Francis and Anthony when Sir Nicholas died in 1579, clearly had a major role in advising the Queen. We can only guess at his motives. However, Anthony Bacon left a record of how his uncle had acted against his (Anthony's) best interests:. When Anthony returned to England after twelve years' service abroad he discovered that he had been deceived and betrayed by his uncle, who had for all those years taken the whole credit to himself for Anthony's intelligence work abroad. Anthony poured out his anger and disappointment in an interview with his aunt, Lady Russell, of which he made a careful record.[32] Francis, however, appears to have kept his feelings to himself. Or so it seems, because if we take a closer look at *Hamlet* we might see that he satirised his uncle Burghley in the character of Polonius. Moreover, the poisoning not only of Hamlet's father via the ear but also, metaphorically, of the queen's ear by lies and flattery, may be a comment on how Francis perceived his sovereign, Queen Elizabeth, to have been deliberately misled.

Francis Bacon's reputation as a poet was not confined to England. For instance, Jean de la Jessée, private secretary to the Duc d'Alençon, refers to Pallas Athena as being Bacon's Muse in a tribute to Francis Bacon as a poet. Jessée was a friend and correspondent of Francis, and was himself an admired poet. This tribute, which is now in the Lambeth Palace Library among Anthony Bacon's correspondence, is a sonnet in French, addressed to 'Monsieur François Bacon' and signed 'La Jessée'.[33] In this sonnet, La Jessée says that,though men may praise his own Muse, all his admiration is for Bacon's Pallas who made Bacon's clear virtue to shine while his own was in the shade. La Jessée is referring to Pallas Athena, thus equating Francis Bacon's Muse with the supreme Tenth Muse—the Muse of Shakespeare.

In 1610, John Davies of Hereford, the poet and writing-master who wrote the epigram that referred to Shakespeare as 'our English Terence', in the same book addressed a sonnet to Francis Bacon, referring to Bacon and his beloved Muse:

To the royall, ingenious, and all-learned
knight, Sr. Francis Bacon.

Thy Bounty, and the Beauty of thy Witt
Comprised in lists of Law and learned Arts,
Each making thee for great Imployment fitt,
Which now thou hast, (though short of thy deserts,)

Compells my Pen to let fall shining Inke
And to bedew the Baies that deck thy Front;
And to thy Health in Helicon to drinke
As, to her Bellamour, the Muse is wont:
For, thou dost her embozom; and, dost use
Her company for sport twixt grave affaires:
So utterst Law the livelyer through thy Muse:
And for that all thy Notes are sweetest Aires;
 My Muse thus notes thy worth in ev'ry Line,
 With ynke which thus she sugars; so, to shine.

John Davies of Hereford, *Scourge of Folly* (*c* 1610)

Davies not only identifies Francis as a poet but, in a clever turn of phrase with double meaning, he refers to the bays (*i.e.,* the poet's laurel wreath) as decking Francis' 'Front'. *Deck* means 'cover' or 'adorn', and *front* can refer to 'face' as well as 'forehead'. Hence Davies appears to be giving a twofold meaning in his words: firstly, that bays adorn Francis' forehead, and secondly that they cover his face—the latter implying a concealed poet. Moreover, Davies vividly contrasts the two lives of Francis, one as a lawyer dealing with grave affairs and the other as a poet who sports with his Muse. One life is public, the other secret; one is serious, the other fun. Francis always contended that he did not much enjoy the practice of law, whereas he took great pleasure in his literary work and the fountains of Parnassus, for which he felt he was born.

Thomas Campion, a physician, well known for his exquisite songs and lyrics, likewise paid a special tribute to Francis Bacon, when Francis was the Lord Chancellor. Campion addressed a Latin epigram to Lord Bacon, paying tribute both to Francis' love and also to his combination of philosophy and law with the poetry and arts of the Muses:

Ad Ampliss. Totius Angliæ Cancellarium.
FR. BA.
Quantus ades, seu te spinosa Volumina juris
Seu schola, seu dolcis Musa (Bacone) vocat!
Quam super ingenti tua re Prudentia regnat!
Et tota æthereo nectare lingua madens!
Quam bene cum tacita nectis gravitate lepores!
Quam semel admissis stat tuus almus amor.

Tho. Campiani Epigrammatum. Lib II.(1619)

This translates:

To the Most High Chancellor of all England.
FR. BA. [Francis Bacon]

new 'robe'. All this has been accomplished by Francis Bacon, whom Randolph describes as another Apollo. Apollo is Athena's male counterpart. They are god and goddess of the spiritual sun, or of poetry and enlightenment.

In the tribute by John Williams, Francis Bacon is again likened to Apollo, the rarest glory (*i.e.,* Phoebus)[39] of the Muses and chief inspirer of a group of writers, poets and artists who are disciples of the Muses:

> Is it thus falls the rarest glory of the Aonian band? and do we decree to entrust seed to the Aonian fields? Break pens, tear up writings, if the dire goddesses may justly act so. Alas! what a tongue is mute! what eloquence ceases! Whither have departed the nectar and ambrosia of your genius? How is it happened to us, the disciples of the Muses, that Apollo, the leader of our choir, should die?
>
> John Williams, *Manes Verulamiani,* Elegy 12

'Aonian band' refers to the Muses. The word is derived from Aonides, a name for the Muses, whose principal dwelling place, according to the Greeks, was on Mount Helicon in the land of Aones (Boeotia).

The chief of the nine Muses, as we saw, is Pallas Athena, the Tenth Muse. Athena is the one we identified as Shakespeare's Muse. In the tributes acclaiming Francis Bacon as Apollo, the goddess is perceived as his partner or female counterpart. In the following tributes Francis is described as Athena herself:

> If none but the worthy should mourn your death, O Bacon! none, trust me, none will there be. Lament now sincerely, O Clio! and sisters of Clio! Ah, the tenth Muse and glory of the choir has perished. Ah, never before has Apollo himself been truly unhappy!
>
> Anon., *Manes Verulamiani,* Elegy 20

> Bacon … a muse more rare than the nine Muses.
>
> Samuel Collins, *Manes Verulamiani,* Elegy 2

In other words, Francis is equated with Pallas Athena, the Spear-shaker or Shake-speare. This reference is taken further by Thomas Randolph, who links Francis with Quirinus, the Spearman:

> When he [Bacon] perceived that the arts were held by no roots, and like seed scattered on the surface of the soil were withering away, he taught the Pegasean arts to grow, as grew the spear of Quirinus swiftly into a laurel tree.
>
> Thomas Randolph, *Manes Verulamiani,* Elegy 32

The Pegasean arts are the poetic arts in particular, Pegasus being the winged white horse whose hoof struck the side of Mount Helicon and brought forth the Hippocrene, the Muses' stream of poetic inspiration. As we have already seen (see Chapter 5), Quirinus was the title of Romulus, the founder of Rome, whose laurel spear grew into the fragrant laurel or bay tree from which was obtained the wreaths given to the most highly acclaimed heroes, philosophers and poets of ancient Rome.

The Spear-shaker, in the form of two winged Gemini holding spears, is depicted in the headpiece on the title page of the *Manes Verulamiani*. Here the Gemini are portrayed shaking their spears against the dragons of ignorance that can be seen twining their ways along plant stems beneath the twins. The plant itself, with its double stem and exotic flowers, is an amaranth—the fabulous blood-red flower of faith which, according to Pliny, neither withers nor fades and is, as a result, the emblem of immortality. The immortal or ever-living poet, Shake-speare, is thereby cleverly suggested—and not as just one but as two poets.

Shakespeare References

Certain of the elegies in the *Manes Verulamiani* refer directly to the Shakespeare inscription on the Stratford-upon-Avon Shakespeare Monument and to the Shakespeare Folio's eulogies. For instance, the description of the author Shakespeare on the Shakespeare Monument as being like Nestor, King of Pylus, the great statesman and judge, and Virgil, surnamed Maro, the prince of poets, is specifically applied to Francis Bacon by his contemporaries. In addition, they acknowledge that Francis was, in his lifetime, like Socrates in his lifetime, the most renowned orator and celebrated philosopher of his country, famous for his use of the inductive process.

> You have written, O Bacon! the history of the life and death of us all.... Nay, give place, O Greeks! give place, Maro, first in Latin story. Supreme both in eloquence and writing, under every head renowned.
>
> Anon., *Manes Verulamiani,* Elegy 16

> For if venerable Virtue and the wreaths of Wisdom make an Ancient, you [Bacon] were older than Nestor.
>
> Gawen Nash, *Manes Verulamiani,* Elegy 27

The Shakespeare Monument refers to Shakespeare being held in Olympus, the celestial home of the Greek gods and goddesses. Likewise, Francis is said to be a star shining in the rosy heavens of Olympus, being compared to celestial beings such as Zeus, Athena, Apollo and Mercury:

> Think you, foolish traveller, that the leader of the choir of the Muses and of Phoebus is interred in cold marble? Away, you are deceived. The Verulamium star now glitters in ruddy Olympus.
>
> Anon., Manes Verulamiani, Elegy 23

This use of 'Olympus' rather than 'heaven' is not unusual, but the reference to 'traveller' is, especially in the elegy by Thomas Vincent. Resounding like a key note, the strange and, this time, unique inscription ('Stay Passenger, why goest thou by so fast? Read if thou canst...') on the Shakespeare Monument in Stratford-upon-Avon is pointedly alluded to in Thomas Vincent's elegy to Francis Bacon, associating Francis directly and intimately with the Shakespeare Monument, which is specifically called a tomb in its inscription (although it is not a tomb in the normal sense, as no body lies in it):

> Some there are though dead live in marble, and trust all their duration to long lasting columns; others shine in bronze, or are beheld in yellow gold, and deceiving themselves think they deceive the fates. Another division of men surviving in a numerous offspring, like Niobe irreverent, despise the mighty gods; but your fame adheres not to sculptured columns, nor is read on the tomb, 'Stay, traveller, your steps'...
>
> Thomas Vincent, Manes Verulamiani, Elegy 7

The only difference in the specific reference that identifies the tomb is that whereas the Shakespeare Monument uses the word 'passenger' and turns the end of the sentence into a question, Vincent uses 'traveller' and keeps the sentence as a command; but the sense is the same. A passenger is a traveller in this sixteenth- and seventeenth-century context. It refers to a wayfarer of a certain standing and substance rather than a vagabond. It is used as such in *The Two Gentlemen of Verona*, for instance:

> *1st Outlaw.* Fellows, stand fast: I see a passenger.
> *2nd Outlaw.* If there be ten, shrink not, but down with 'em.
> *3rd Outlaw.* Stand, sir, and throw us that you have about ye.
>   If not, we'll make you sit, and rifle you.
> *Speed.* Sir, we are undone; these are the villains
>   That all the travellers do fear so much.
>
> Shakespeare, The Two Gentlemen of Verona, IV, i, 1–6

In his dedicatory poem to the author Shakespeare in the Shakespeare Folio, Ben Jonson refers to Shakespeare's plays as being Shakespeare's progeny, born of his mind. This is almost certainly an allusion to Minerva, who was born from the mind of Jupiter. Minerva is the Roman name for Pallas Athena, who leapt forth from the head of her father, Zeus (Jupiter), fully armed and shaking her spear of light at dark ignorance:

> Looke how the father's face
> Lives in his issue, even so, the race
> Of Shakespeare's minde, and manners brightly shines
> In his well torned, and true filed lines:
> In each of which, he seemes to shake a Lance,
> As brandish't at the eyes of Ignorance.
>
> Ben Jonson, Eulogy, Shakespeare Folio, 1623

Thomas Vincent's tribute to Francis Bacon uses the identical symbolism for Francis and his works, thereby directly associating his own tribute to Francis with Ben Jonson's tribute to Shakespeare—and, of course, by doing this, associating Francis with Shakespeare:

> If any progeny recalls their sire, not of the body is it, but born, so to speak, of the brain, as Minerva's from Jove's.
>
> Thomas Vincent, *Manes Veulamiani*, Elegy 7

Vincent continues his tribute to Francis by stating a philosophy identical to that which underlies the Shakespeare sonnets, one which distinguishes between the higher and lower selves—the higher, better part surviving death while the lower, grosser part dissolves and returns to dust:

> First your virtue provides you with an everlasting monument, your books another not soon to collapse, a third your nobility; let the fates now celebrate their triumphs, who have nothing yours, Francis, but your corpse. Your mind and good report the better parts survive; you have nothing of so little value as to ransom the vile body withal.
>
> Thomas Vincent, *Manes Veulamiani*, Elegy 7

> Oh how thy worth with manners may I singe,
> When thou art all the better part of me?
> What can mine own praise to mine own selfe bringe;
> And what is't but mine owne when I praise thee.
>
> Shakespeare, Sonnet 39

As Bacon writes elsewhere, the mind or genius is the higher self, the better part, and it is this that is to be praised, not the lower self and its body:

they make me ready to cast, by the banks of helicon. May looke,
what a rascally untoward thing this poetrie is; I could teare 'hem
now.

Ovid Junior. Give me, how neere's my father?

Luscus. Hart a'man: get a law-booke in your hande, I will not answer
you else. Why so: now there' some formalitie in you. By Jove,
and three or foure of the gods more, I am right of mine old masters humour for that; this villainous poetrie will undoe you, the
welkin.

Ben Jonson, Poetaster, I, i

With Ovid Senior approaching fast, Luscus does not wish to be found with
his master, who is still engaged with his poetry, so he leaves. Left on his own,
Ovid Junior continues with his poetic and Ovidian studies. In the lines that
follow, Jonson includes the Latin couplet that heads the title page of Shakespeare's *Venus and Adonis* as an epigraph,[42] which, in the persona of Ovid Junior,
he translates as:

> Kneel hindes to trash: me let bright Phoebus swell,
> With cups full flowing from the Muses well.

The evidence is that Jonson is alluding to the poet Shakespeare and associating Shakespeare with Ovid Junior. This association is not without meaning, for Ovid was not only one of the most famous of the Roman poets, but
Venus and Adonis is based on two tales from Ovid's *Metamorphoses*, fused together,
while the epigraph is taken direct from Ovid's *Amores*.

The description of Ovid Junior, who later on is further portrayed as a
younger son who has no wealth of his own, is exactly that of Francis Bacon.
While he was pursuing his law studies at Gray's Inn by command of his uncle
Lord Burghley, who was now his legal guardian, Francis involved himself with
poetry of all kinds—masques, plays, poems, pageants and speeches. He never
wanted to follow the path of a lawyer, desiring rather to pursue his literary
activities full time, but neither his uncle nor the Queen ever allowed this to
happen. In this they were probably following the wishes of Sir Nicholas as
well as their own. It would also have suited the puritanical Lady Ann Bacon,
who was vehemently opposed to either of her sons being involved with
mumming, masking or revelling at the Inns of Court, or with the theatre
elsewhere, and who wrote them letters to that effect.

Luscus, on the other hand, who wears buskins and who is told in the play
that his proper place is among ostlers, matches the character and circumstances of Will Shakespeare—whose first occupation, according to tradition,
was minding horses outside the playhouse.

Further on in the Act, Ovid Senior arrives and castigates his son:

Ovid Senior. … Are these the fruits of all my travaile and expenses? is
this the scope and aim of thy studies? are these the hopeful
courses, wherewith I have so long flattered my expectation from
thee? verses? poetrie? Ovid, whom I thought to see the pleader,
become Ovid the play-maker?

Ovid Junior. No, sir.

Ovid Senior. Yes, sir. I heare of a tragedie of yours coming forth for the
common players there, call'd *Medea*. By my household gods, if I
come to the acting of it, I'le adde one tragick part, more then is
yet expected, to it: believe me when I promise it. What? shall I
have my sonne a stager now?…

Ben Jonson, Poetaster, I, ii, 4–16

Ovid Junior continues in trying to put his father's mind at rest, assuring
him that he is studying law effectively and that he is not known upon the
open stage, nor does he traffic in their theatres, even though he writes plays
(such as *Medea*) for the players:

Ovid Junior. They wrong me, sir, and do abuse you more,
That blow your eaes with these untrue reports.
I am not knowne unto the open stage,
Nor doe I traffique in their theatres.…

Ben Jonson, Poetaster, I, ii, 61–3

All this would seem to constitute a clear inference that Francis Bacon
alias Ovid Junior was writing for the stage under a pseudonym or mask, that
the pseudonym was Shakespeare, and that the actor Will Shakespeare alias
Luscus was involved in making this happen—although, according to Ben
Jonson, Luscus did not appreciate the poetry.

He who hath filled up all numbers

In 1641, some of Ben Jonson's dissertations were printed under the title of *Tim-*
ber or *Discoveries.* Under the heading of 'Dominus Verulamius' Jonson discusses
and highly appraises Francis Bacon as an orator. In the dissertation entitled
'De Augmentis, Lord St. Alban' he discusses Francis as an educationalist. In
the 'Scriptorum Catalogus' he values Francis as a poet and places the deceased

Lord Chancellor at the head of a list of the great thinkers and orators of his time, completely omitting the name of Shakespeare. He carefully uses all the titles that Francis was given when Lord Keeper—as Lord Verulam (*i.e.,* Baron Verulam), Lord St Alban (*i.e.,* Viscount St Alban) and Lord Chancellor—and the words he uses about Francis in all three dissertations are ones of intense personal affection and veneration. His praise of Francis Bacon as quoted here is perhaps one of the finest compliments ever paid by one man of genius to another:

> I have and do reverence him, for the greatness that was only proper to himself, in that he seemed to me ever, by his work, one of the greatest men, and most worthy of admiration, that had been in many ages.
>
> Ben Jonson, Discoveries (1641)

It is very suggestive that Ben Jonson elsewhere praised Francis Bacon's literary talents with the same words and sense as he used to describe the author Shakespeare in the Shakespeare Folio. Using a phrase borrowed from Seneca,[43] Jonson says in his tribute to Shakespeare:

> Or, when thy socks were on,
> Leave thee alone, for the comparison
> Of all, that insolent Greece or haughty *Rome*
> sent forth, or since did from their ashes come.
>
> Ben Jonson, Eulogy, Shakespeare Folio, 1623

Jonson uses the same Senecan description when writing about Francis Bacon:

> ...he who hath filled up all numbers, and performed that in our tongue, which may be compared or preferred either to insolent *Greece*, or haughty *Rome*.
>
> Ben Jonson, Discoveries (1641)

This is the highest praise possible from another scholar–poet and playwright: one who reputed his own works highly, who had produced many plays, masques and poems that many people of the time considered on a par with or even better than the Shakespeare works, who in January 1616 had become Poet Laureate to the King, and who had himself published a carefully-produced folio edition of his own work in that same year.[44]

'He who hath filled up all numbers' is especially noteworthy. Jonson uses the word 'numbers' in the same well-known sense in which Cicero, Virgil, Horace and Ovid all used its Latin original, referring not only to the arts and sciences but also to poetry and drama. This latter sense of 'numbers' is used in the Shakespeare works and was the most common use of the word from the sixteenth century onwards. Milton and Pope, in the seventeenth and eighteenth centuries, continued the use of the word in that same sense.

> If I could write the beauty of your eyes,
> And in fresh numbers number all your graces,
> The age to come would say, 'This poet lies'.

Shakespeare, Sonnet 17

> *Longaville.* I fear these stubborn lines lack power to move;
> O sweet Maria, empress of my love,
> These numbers I will tear, and write in prose.

Love's Labour's Lost, IV. iii. 52—54

Where he writes of him in *Discoveries,* Ben Jonson reveals that Francis Bacon was the star of all the wits, and that in some way they all benefited from him and owed something of their own successes to him. This not only matches Jonson's eulogy to the author Shakespeare in the Shakespeare Folio but it also ties in with the fact that the half-century, *c.* 1576—1626, produced virtually all the great works of the English Renaissance. When Francis died, the situation changed dramatically:

> In short, within his [Bacon's] view, and about his times, were all the wits born that could honour a language, or help study. Now things daily fall: wits grow downward, and *Eloquence* grows backward: so that he [Bacon] may be named and stand as the *mark* and *acme* of our language.

Ben Jonson, *Discoveries* (1641)

Jonson not only considered Francis Bacon to have been one of the greatest men who had ever lived in many ages, but that he maintained that greatness even in times of adversity. Near the end of his life Francis suffered great adversity, a great wrong, to which Ben refers:

> In his adversity I ever prayed that *God* would give him strength: for *Greatness* he could not want. Neither could I condole in a word or syllable for him, as knowing no Accident could do harm to virtue, but rather help to make it manifest.

Ben Jonson, *Discoveries* (1641)

In 1621, at a banquet at York House in honour of Francis Bacon's sixtieth birthday, Ben Jonson read out a twenty-line poem that he had composed in

Not only did Bacon employ teams of secretaries, scholars and writers to assist him, but also his secretaries, trained by him in his own shorthand, used to follow him around, outside and in, as he dictated to them. He had friends by his bedside to record his dreams, which he dictated as soon as he awoke. He often spent time in contemplation, with music being played in an adjoining room to help bring him inspiration, using the music to change his mood and thereby to both enhance and control his imagination. He also used scented herbs and flowers for the same purpose. His imagination was so active that he needed to drink several mugs of home-brewed ale before going to bed, to help him sleep.[2] His knowledge of books was encyclopaedic and his memory stupendous: he would habitually quote from memory and be able to inform his helpers as to where they could find the passage in question. He was not absolutely perfect in this, however, and sometimes misquoted—and some of these misquotations actually appear in the Shakespeare works. He loved nature and was a dedicated naturalist and designer of gardens. He was an equally devoted philanthropist and student of human nature. He was a bold experimenter, who was always looking for practical ways to improve human conditions as well as to raise human consciousness—two things that he believed were interrelated.

As a visionary, Bacon was able to look forward in time as well as back into the past, not only describing in his own fashion many 'mechanical arts and things made by them'[3] that we can recognise as being invented several centuries later (such as the microscope, laser beam, artificial gemstones, airplanes, submarines, nuclear fission and 'sound houses'), with some still to come, but also the stages that human evolution and consciousness would pass through before reaching an enlightened state of being. He foresaw the approaching irreligious, materialistic era, which he nevertheless prayed might never happen, and also the more enlightened ages that would follow. Although his knowledge was highly detailed, panoramic and immense, he always claimed that his greatest knowledge was derived from direct inspiration and revelation from God, for which he continuously gave thanks.

Francis Bacon stated that he was following the path of the Ancients, with the wisdom of Solomon and teachings of Christ as his guide. Of all that he left us, both Baconian and Shakespearean, his only claim for anything new that he offered as his unique gift to humanity was what he called his 'New Method'—an 'Art of Discovery' by which all knowledge (divine, human and natural) might be obtained. He did not intend the method to be used for the sole object of discovering physical laws simply for the material pleasure or profit of humankind, but rather for the upliftment of humanity in body and soul, and the realisation of the more subtle metaphysical and spiritual laws. In particular he intended his method for the discovery of the highest and at the same time profoundest spiritual truth—the Cause of all causes, Love itself.

Bacon believed that all knowledge should be put into practice as charity, for the glory of God and the relief of the human estate. In fact, he could not see how love could be discovered and known without practising it. His method as an idea or philosophy, therefore, is inseparable from the corresponding action: the two go together and evolve together as 'twins'.

> The understanding of man and his will are twins by birth as it were; for the purity of illumination and the liberty of will began together. Nor is there in the universal nature of things so intimate a sympathy as that of truth and goodness.
>
> Francis Bacon, *Advancement of Learning*, V (1640)

> I take Goodness in this sense, the affecting of the weal of men, which is that the Grecians call *Philanthropia*; and the word *humanity* (as it is used) is a little too light to express it. Goodness I call the habit, and Goodness of Nature the inclination. This of all virtues and dignities of the mind is the greatest; being the character of the Deity: and without it man is a busy, mischievous, wretched thing; no better than a kind of vermin. Goodness answers to the theological virtue Charity, and admits no excess, but error. The desire of power in excess caused the angels to fall; the desire of knowledge in excess caused man to fall; but in charity there is no excess; neither can angel or man come in danger by it.
>
> Francis Bacon, 'Of Goodness and Goodness of Nature,' *Essays* (1625)

Drama and Oratory

Drama and speech were important to Bacon. He wrote a profound study on the ethics of the theatre, the uses and abuses of stage-plays, and commended the acting profession as a form of personal training. In fact, drama—or poetry ('poesie'), of which drama is a part—forms the heart of his whole philosophical method. Moreover, Bacon himself was a great orator, admired as such by his contemporaries. Using a quotation from Virgil, Bacon's own description of rhetoric is that it should be like music, and the orator should be like the two celebrated poets and musicians, Orpheus and Arion:

> For the proofs and persuasions of rhetoric ought to differ according to the auditors; so that, like a musician accommodating his skill to different ears, a man should be, *Orpheus in silvis, inter delphinas Arion.*[4] [An Orpheus in the woods, an Arion among the Dolphins.]
>
> Francis Bacon, *Advancement of Learning* (1623), VI, 35

THE SHAKESPEARE ENIGMA

tially the same, that the two together generate form, and that matter, form and motion (spirit) are an indivisible whole (*i.e.,* a Trinity):

> This Love I understand to be the appetite or instinct of primal matter; or to speak more plainly, *the natural motion of the atom*; which is indeed the original and unique force that constitutes and fashions all things out of matter. Now this is entirely without parent; that is, without cause. For the cause is as it were parent of the effect; and of this virtue there can be no cause in nature (God always excepted): there being nothing before it, therefore no efficient; nor anything more original in nature, therefore neither kind nor form. Whatever it be, therefore, it is a thing positive and inexplicable. And even if it were possible to know the method and process of it, yet to know it by way of cause is not possible; it being, next to God, the cause of causes—itself without cause.
>
> <div align="right">Francis Bacon, 'Cupid or the Atom,' <i>Wisdom of the Ancients</i> (1609)[8]</div>

> But one who philosophises rightly and in order, should dissect Nature and not abstract her ... and must by all means consider the first Matter as united to the first Form, and likewise to the first Principle of Motion, as it is found.
>
> <div align="right">Francis Bacon, <i>Principles and Origins.</i>[9]</div>

In terms of humanity, the primary study required, therefore, is into human emotion, and the thoughts and actions derived from and driven by those desires, with the aim of discovering what love is, what it is capable of and what it actually does. Then, beyond human love (or working through human love) we might discover divine love.

> For the principles, fountains, causes, and forms of motions, that is, the appetites and passions of every kind of matter, are the proper objects of philosophy.
>
> <div align="right">Francis Bacon, <i>Thoughts on the Nature of Things</i>[10]</div>

Whereas laboratories of the kind Bacon described in his *New Atlantis*, which we mostly have nowadays, are suitable for enquiry into natural laws, a different kind of laboratory is required for the study of human emotions, which have to be felt, not just seen, in order to understand them. Such a laboratory is the theatre, where the emotions can be experienced and their results seen in a highlighted way, all within a safe environment. Moreover, besides the emotional effect, good drama has an inspirational and educational value, far beyond what can be achieved in a more academic environment. This is in fact an ancient way of learning, having its origins in the classical Mystery schools, as a previous Lord Chancellor of England, Richard de Bury, one of the most learned men of the fourteenth century, pointed out in his *Philobiblon*:

> Accordingly the wisdom of the ancients devised a remedy by which to entice the wanton minds of men by a kind of pious fraud, the delicate Minerva secretly lurking beneath the mask of pleasure.
>
> Richard de Bury, High Chancellor of England, *Philobiblon* (1345)[11]

The greatest sickness of the world has long been recognised as ignorance. The great healers have always been teachers. To teach effectively, the teaching must be pleasurable and able to be received at different levels of understanding and appreciation. For this reason wisdom masked by entertainment has, from ancient times, been known to be one of the best methods to educate people.

As Bacon pointed out, on the stage a history of life can be portrayed 'in a frame' to the human eye or mind. Not only are we then able to see ourselves and life generally as if in a mirror, but we can also perceive the laws of life working and judge what leads to good and what leads to evil. As a result we may draw forth axioms or propositions concerning the laws of life, and derive principles that we can then put into action, to test them out and ultimately do good.

Poetry

Bacon identified three main forms of poetry: Narrative, Dramatic and Allusive Poetry. Narrative poetry 'is a mere imitation of history' and represents historical facts, events and characters in a more heroic vein, which is more appealing and helpful to the human soul. Dramatic poetry 'is as a visible history'—'an image of actions as if they were present'. It is representative poetry shown dramatically on stage, so that our world (and in particular our human world or nature) can be more easily seen in a condensed form, acted out, spotlighted and held up to the eye as if in a frame or mirror: in other words, so that we can see ourselves. Allusive or parabolic poetry, which 'is a narrative applied only to express some special purpose or conceit', is the best or most important of the three, conveying in allegories and parables truths which cannot or should not otherwise be described:

> As for Narrative Poesie, or if you please Heroical ... it seems to be raised altogether from a noble foundation; which makes much for the dignity of man's nature. For seeing this sensible world is in dignity inferior to the soul of man, Poesie seems to endow human nature with that which

History denies... Poesie cheereth and refreshes the soul, chanting things rare, and various, and full of vicissitudes. So as Poesie serveth and conferreth to delectation, magnanimity, and morality; and therefore it may seem deservedly to have some participation of divineness; because it doth raise the mind, and exalt the spirit with high raptures, by proportioning the shews of things to the desires of the mind; and not submitting the mind to things, as Reason and History do. And by these allurements and congruities, whereby it cherisheth the soul of man, joined also with consort of music, whereby it may more sweetly insinuate itself, it hath won such access that it hath been in estimation even in rude times and barbarous nations, when other learning stood excluded.

Dramatical, or Representative Poesie, which brings the world upon the stage, is of excellent use, if it were not abused. For the instructions and corruptions of the stage may be great, but the corruptions in this kind abound; the discipline is altogether neglected in our times. For although in modern commonwealths, stage-plays be but estimed a sport or pastime, unless it draw from the satyr and be mordant, yet the care of the Ancients was that it should instruct the minds of men unto virtue. Nay, wise men and great philosophers have accounted it as the archet or musical bow of the mind. And certainly it is most true, and as it were a secret of nature, that the minds of men are more patent to affections and impressions, congregate, than solitary.

But Poesie Allusive, or Parabolical, exceeds all the rest, and seemeth to be a sacred and venerable thing, especially seeing Religion itself hath allowed it a work of that nature, and by it traffics divine commodities with men.... For it serves for obscuration, and it serveth also for illustration: in this it seems there was sought a way how to teach; in that an art how to conceal. And this way of teaching which conduceth to illustration was much in use in the Ancient times.... Wherefore in those first ages all were full of fables, and of parables, and of enigmas, and of similitudes of all sorts.... So even at this day, and ever, there is and hath been much life and vigour in parables; because arguments cannot be so sensible, nor examples so fit. *There is another use of Parabolical Poesie, opposite to the former, which tendeth to the folding up of those things; the dignity whereof deserves to be retired and distinguished, as with a drawn curtain: that is when the secrets and mysteries of religion, policy and philosophy are veiled, and invested with fables and parables.*

Francis Bacon, *Advancement of Learning* (1640), II, xiii

Poetry, particularly when in the form of drama on stage, is like music: it stirs our emotions as well as appealing to our minds; and this Bacon considered as being vital if we are to discover truth, or even want to discover truth. For truth is warm, not cold: it is vital, not dead. Moreover, it is the emotions, Bacon pointed out, that should be our proper study; for they are the causes, the motivations of all things, with philanthropic love (which is kindness, goodness or mercy) being the greatest of them all. To study them truly, we have to experience them as well as observe them. For this reason, well-designed entertainment provides the greatest form of education, for we should be excited and moved by truth, and enjoy it. What we enjoy, we notice and remember.

More than this, poetry is related to imagination, one of the three principal faculties of the human soul; and without imagination we could conceive of nothing:

> That is the truest Partition of human Learning, which hath reference to the three Faculties of man's soul, which is the seat of learning. History is referred to Memory, Poesie to the Imagination, Philosophy to Reason.
>
> Francis Bacon, *Advancement of Learning* (1640), III, i

Imagination has a primary role in Bacon's philosophy, which means poetry has also. It forms the heart of his method and is, according to Bacon, represented by Janus, the chief of the Roman gods and Doorkeeper of the

He, that concealed things will finde,
Muſt looke before him, and behinde.

49. Janus Illustration IV, page 138, Book 3, from George Wither's Collection of Emblemes (1634)

Mysteries. Janus is usually portrayed with either two or three heads. Three is the most common: one facing to the left, one to the front and one to the right. Since Janus is equivalent to Saturn, the Greek Cronos or Pan, the god of Time, he is said to be looking into the past, the present and the future simultaneously. These are the faces we see. There is also a fourth, hidden face, looking to the rear, signifying that which is beyond time. Bacon, in his *Advancement of Learning*, describes how one face of imagination looks towards reason and the opposite one towards the senses and action, and that therefore imagination is the vital agent between the two, enabling sense to inform the reason, and reason to guide the action.[12] He also points out that in matters of faith and religion the imagination ceases to be just a messenger but becomes greater than reason.[13]

Janus holds the key to the Shakespeare symbolism. He corresponds to the Hindu Brahma, the creator god, whose vehicle or form of manifestation is symbolised by a swan, the emblem of knowledge. His shakti or consort, Saraswati, the creative energy of imagination and invention, is the goddess of eloquence, patroness of the arts and sciences, especially music and rhetoric, and inventress of language: so that, in respect of her attributes, she is analogous to Pallas Athena. 'From the crimson lotus of her hands pours radiance on the implements of writing, and on the books produced by her favour.'[14] Her form is likewise the swan in this symbolism—or, as some would say, she is the swan, the form of Brahma, in which Brahma resides.

As I have mentioned before, Athena (Saraswati) is declared to be the Muse of Bacon, and also of Shakespeare. In both the Bacon and Shakespeare works she shines her attributes brightly. Bacon's whole purpose, which he announced to the world in his writings, was to provide something that would both begin and enable a complete reformation or revolution in the arts and sciences, so as to ultimately restore a state of paradise to the world. For this, Bacon explains that imagination has the key role—and imagination he specifically and

50. *Brahma*

51. *Saraswati*

noticeably relates to poetry. But then, again noticeably, he doesn't publicly or openly explain exactly what poetry he has in mind, which he has provided as his working example of his method. There are just the hints.

The Shakespeare Plays

Francis Bacon seems to have illustrated the use of poetry in his scheme principally by means of the Shakespeare plays, published under the pseudonym of William Shakespeare. These, more than any other, are the expression of his great art.

The Shakespeare plays are examples of all three types of poetry which Bacon identified—narrative, dramatic and allusive—fused as one; for they are heroic in nature, dramatically presented and based on allegorical stories. Moreover, following Bacon's intention (see later, 'Hide and Seek'), they are exoteric, esoteric and acroamatic (enigmatic)—the outer forms veiling many layers of increasingly profound inner truths. This layering leads from the factual, historical or political levels of the play to the moral and psychological levels, then to the higher rational and mathematical levels, and culminates with the spiritual level—a scheme that follows that of the Cabalists and holy Writ, something which, as we have seen and will see further, fits Bacon's grand design well.

In these plays the Franciscan friars, court jesters and suchlike often give away Baconian truths, although they do not hold the absolute monopoly in this. For instance, through the mouth of Jacques in *As You Like It*, Bacon makes his viewpoint and purpose doubly clear:

> *Jacques.* Invest me in my motley. Give me leave
>   To speak my mind, and I will through and through
>   Cleanse the foul body of th' infected world,
>   If they will patiently receive my medicine....
>
>   All the world's a stage,
>   And all the men and women merely players....
>
> Shakespeare, *As You Like It,* II, vii, 57-61, 139—40

In *Pericles*, Simonides, the king of Pentapolis, bluntly states a serious problem of the human mind and will, a problem which Bacon pointed out and which his Great Instauration is designed to avoid:

> *Simonides.* Opinion's but a fool, that makes us scan

Beauty, truth and rarity,
Grace in all simplicity,
Here enclos'd, in cinders lie.

Shakespeare, The Phoenix and Turtle, verse 14

Let not my love be called idolatry,
Nor my belovèd as an idol show,
Since all alike my songs and praises be
To one, of one, still such, and ever so.
Kind is my love today, tomorrow kind,
Still constant in a wondrous excellence;
Therefore my verse, to constancy confined,
One thing expressing, leaves out difference.
'Fair, kind, and true' is all my argument,
'Fair, kind, and true' varying to other words;
And in this change is my invention spent:
Three themes in one, which wondrous scope affords.
    Fair, kind, and true have often lived alone,
    Which three till now never kept seat in one.

Shakespeare, Sonnet 105

Bacon, in his essay on truth, associates truth with light and speaks of truth itself teaching that 'the enquiry of truth, which is the love-making or wooing of it, the knowledge of truth, which is the presence of it, and the belief of truth, which is the enjoying of it, is the sovereign good of human nature'.[18] In his essay on beauty, Bacon associates beauty, in its positive sense, with virtue, and notes elsewhere that 'virtue is nothing but inward beauty; beauty nothing but outward virtue' and that 'beauty makes virtues shine, and vices blush'.[19] As for goodness or kindness, the rare virtue, Bacon speaks of it as the 'top and consummation' of all that is truly human—or greater than human. In his essay on *Goodness and Goodness of Nature* he identifies this with philanthropy or charity, equivalent to the quality of mercy in the Shakespeare plays:

> I take Goodness in this sense, the affecting of the weal of men, which is that the Grecians call *Philanthropia;* and the word humanity (as it is used) is a little too light to express it. Goodness I call the habit, and Goodness of Nature the inclination. This of all virtues and dignities of the mind is the greatest; being the character of the Deity: and without it man is a busy, mischievous, wretched thing; no better than a kind of vermin. Goodness answers to the theological virtue Charity…

> Francis Bacon, 'Of Goodness and Goodness of Nature,' Essays (1625)

A Shakespeare Notebook

Francis Bacon kept a private notebook in which he jotted down various observations and expressions that he thought might come in useful in his literary work. This notebook was called his *Promus of Formularies and Elegancies* and is a source-book of notes for the Shakespeare plays. It consists of a collection of manuscripts, or folios, with 1,655 entries written in Bacon's own hand, which are now kept at the British Museum (Harleian Collection, No. 7017). These folios, numbered from 83 to 132, were written in the years 1594–6,[20] just when the Shakespeare plays were beginning to appear in earnest, and form part of what must have been a much larger collection that was started even earlier and probably continued on further into later years.

This 'Storehouse', which was not published until 1883, contains entries in several languages—English, Greek, Latin, Italian, Spanish and French—of words, similes, phrases, proverbs, apophthegms, colloquialisms, biblical quotations and lines from the Latin poets, and with many words and forms of expression invented by Bacon himself. A great number are used directly in the Shakespeare plays. Some of them appear in print in English uniquely in the plays, and many are used frequently therein. Only a very much smaller number appear in Bacon's own acknowledged works, so that it would appear that Bacon's purpose in such a notebook was particularly for speaking and drama. James Spedding, the principal biographer and editor of Bacon's works, noted that 'this collection (which fills more than forty quarto pages) is of the most miscellaneous character, and seems by various marks in the manuscript to have been afterwards digested into other collections which are lost.'[21] It would seem, also, that other dramatists besides Bacon made use of these collections, which makes sense when Bacon was the acknowledged leader of the poets and employed not a few of them as his own 'good pens'.

Many examples could be given, but I have selected a few that I particularly enjoy and which, I hope, make the point clear. For instance, Bacon appears to have set out not only to furnish the English language with more words but also more phrases and expressions for everyday use, often based on a rich background of foreign languages or deeper esoteric thought. A whole part of one of the folios in the *Promus* is devoted to the subject of salutations such as 'good morrow', 'good soir', 'good matin', 'bon jour', 'good day'. These notes were made in the *Promus* in 1595/6. Some time after the spring of 1596, *Romeo and Juliet* was first performed (and published in quarto the year following), and in it can be found some of these salutations. They appear later in other Shakespeare plays as well—'good morrow' being used one hundred and fifteen times, 'good day' fifteen times, and 'good even' twelve times. Because these particular expressions were utilised a lot, they may not seem so significant to us now;

but a particularly unique and beautiful greeting is 'good dawning', which is noted in the *Promus* as the Spanish word, 'albada,' meaning 'good dawning' and referring to a serenade with which young men salute their lady-loves at the break of day.[22] This expression only appears once in English print, in the play of *King Lear* ('Good dawning to thee, friend'),[23] which was not written until after March 1603 and first published in quarto in 1608.

Bacon's *Promus* note, 'Clavum clavo pellere,' meaning 'To drive out a nail with a nail',[24] coupled with his theories that 'flame doth not mingle with flame'[25] and 'When two heats differ much in degree, one destroys the other',[26] is several times found in the Shakespeare plays; viz. 'As fire drives out fire; so pity, pity' (*Julius Caesar*),[27] 'One fire drives out one fire; one nail, one nail; / Rights by rights falter; strengths by strengths do fail' (*Coriolanus*),[28] and 'Even as one heat another heat expels / Or as one nail by strength drives out another' (*The Two Gentlemen of Verona*).[29] So also are the excellent witticisms that we still use today: 'A fool's bolt is soon shot'[30] and 'Good wine needs no bush'.[31] The former is to be found in *Henry V*,[32] and the latter in the Epilogue of *As You Like It*.[33] Then there is 'All is not gold that glisters',[34] to be found in *The Merchant of Venice* as 'All that glisters is not gold'.[35]

Besides images of fire, Bacon used many beautiful water images in both his poetry and philosophical works. From the *Promus,* I particularly like 'Haile of Perle',[36] which can be found used in *Anthony and Cleopatra* as 'I'll set thee in a shower of gold, and hail rich pearls upon thee',[37] and in Massinger's *Bashful Lover* as 'A shower in April, every drop an orient pearl'.[38] In a profundity of thought, Bacon notes: 'mors omnia solvit' ('Death dissolves all things').[39] It is an alchemical theme, already used in *Venus and Adonis* in 1593 ('By this, the boy that at her side lay kill'd / Was melted like a vapour from her sight...')[40] and probably derived from the works of Hermes Trismegistus, which teaches that 'nothing in the world dies, but compound bodies are dissolved: dissolution is not death'. Peele also used this theme in 1593, in *Edward I* ('O gracious Heavens, dissolve me into clay'),[41] and the idea is found again in 1596, in the anonymous *Edward III* ('Resolv'd to be dissolv'd').[42] The imagery is used in *Hamlet* ('O that this too too solid flesh would melt, thaw, and resolve itself into a dew'),[43] in *Antony and Cleopatra* ('as it determines, so dissolve my life'),[44] and even more famously in *The Tempest* ('The great globe itself, yea all which it inherit, shall dissolve...').[45] In one of the final Shakespeare offerings, it appears in Fletcher's *Two Noble Kinsmen* ('Dissolve my life'),[46] on which Bacon, as Shakespeare, collaborated.

Bacon clearly loved this alchemical theme of the body, or life itself, dissolving into a water or dew, and was noted for it, since it is also to be found in the epitaph on his memorial in St Michael's Church, Gorhambury ('Let compounds be dissolved').[47] It was, moreover, used a century later on the

Shakespeare Memorial in Westminster Abbey, which used the *Tempest* quotation on its scroll (see chapter 14).

Not only did Bacon jot down interesting *bons mots* and coin some useful new words in his *Promus,* but he also noted (*c.* 1594) one of the titles for a Shakespeare play, 'All is well that ends well,'[48] many years before the play was actually written and produced on stage. He also did not miss the chance to comment philosophically on the meaning of his own name, Francis (meaning 'Free'), with his jotting, 'Thought is free,'[49]. This key sentence appears as such in both *Twelfth Night*[50] and *The Tempest,*[51] as well as appearing in a slightly different form in other Shakespeare plays, and is a clue as to the nature of Ariel and what Bacon considered such spirits to be. As for the peculiar phrase, 'numbering not weighing',[52] it is used in the enigmatic 'Address to the Reader' in the Shakespeare Folio:

> From the most able to him that can but spell; there you are number'd.
> We had rather you were weigh'd.

Bacon's *Promus* was first presented in print in 1883 by a Mrs Henry Pott, with translations and cross-references,[53] although Spedding had earlier included parts of the *Promus* in his magnum opus, *The Works of Francis Bacon,* published in 1861. We owe a debt of gratitude to Mrs Pott and other researchers, in her own time and since, researchers who have been courageous enough to brave the prejudice and ridicule often heaped upon them. As a result of their work, it can now be readily seen that not only are the observations and expressions noted down in Bacon's *Promus* used extensively in the Shakespeare plays but also that Bacon's *Essays* and other philosophical writings provide the history and 'tables of invention', together with the philosophical ideas, out of which the Shakespeare plays are constructed. Bacon has done all this so that the life of man can be presented to our eyes, so that we may see ourselves as if in a mirror, dramatically, and learn from the experience:

> *Hamlet.* Come, come, and sit you down, you shall not budge.
> You go not till I set you up a glass
> Where you may see the inmost part of you.

> Shakespeare, *Hamlet,* IV. i. 17–19

Alterations and Mistakes

Alterations in the Shakespeare plays, as time went on, directly reflect Francis Bacon's own changes of opinion; and mistakes in the plays are paralleled by exactly the same mistakes in Bacon's philosophical writings.

For instance, in the second Quarto of *Hamlet*, published in 1604, the tides of the ocean are attributed to the moon's influence, which was the common opinion of that time. But subsequently, Bacon investigated the matter, and in 1616 published a treatise, *De Fluxu et Refluxu Maris*, in which he rejected the lunar theory. In every edition of *Hamlet* after 1616 the reference to the moon's influence on the tides is carefully omitted.

Also, in the same 1604 edition of *Hamlet*, and in the same scene, the ancient doctrine that everything which has motion must also have sense is stated. This is repeated in all subsequent quarto editions:

> *Hamlet*. . . . Sense sure you have
> Else you could not have motion.

Shakespeare, *Hamlet*, III, iv, 71–2

This was a doctrine that Francis Bacon upheld at that time, and which he declared in his 1605 edition of *The Advancement and Proficience of Learning*. But in his revised and much expanded 1623 Latin version of the book (*De Dignitate & Augmentis Scientiarum*) he renounced this theory; and in that same year, in the First Folio of the Shakespeare Plays, the relevant lines and whole concept are edited out.

Art of Discovery

Francis Bacon saw his new method as being a gift to humanity greater than any other invention, since it is a knowledge or 'tool for the mind' that will enable all other knowledges to be discovered. He saw it as helping to fulfil the Christian revelation of love: for, as St John taught, God is love—and particularly love in action, which is mercy or charity. Such is God's glory, which humankind is intended to embody as the 'image' or imitator of God. God is the Creator who creates through mercy, or love in action. Through such love anything and everything good can be created. It is to this aim that Bacon dedicated his life and work.

Intentionally, Bacon partly revealed and partly concealed his method: for it is not just a philosophy, it is an art—an 'Art of Discovery' which, as he said, serves and develops a capacity for divinity, the latter being defined as the light of wisdom imparted to us by prophets and also inspired directly into the human heart: light which enlightens the mind and perfects the body. By partly concealing his method, Bacon provides us with a means of learning it in a practical way: for, in discovering what it is, we learn the method and become practised in it. It is a training school, open to all, with no visible master needed.

Bacon was always at great pains to unite the practical and the philosophical;

therefore he said that he always taught by means of practical examples. His great example for learning the Art of Discovery is his careful concealment of his authorship of the plays he wrote or supervised under the name Shakespeare, but with clues left behind so that the truth can be discovered. This is what Bacon called his example, by which he teaches us his method.

Hide and Seek

Bacon's method for discovering truth is based firmly upon the divine method that King Solomon says God employs: 'It is the glory of God to conceal a thing: but the honour of kings is to search out a matter' (*Proverbs* 25 : 2, Authorised Version). That is to say, truth is hidden from us and we have to find it, little by little. This method is none other than a game of hide and seek, which Bacon refers to many times in various of his writings, such as in his *Advancement of Learning*:

> For of the knowledges which contemplate the works of Nature, the holy philosopher [Solomon] hath said expressly; *that the glory of God is to conceal a thing, but the glory of the king is to find it out:*[54] as if the Divine Nature, according to the innocent and sweet play of children, which hide themselves to the end they may be found, took delight to hide his works, to the end they might be found out; and of his indulgence and goodness to man-kind, had chosen the soul of man to be his play-fellow in this game.
>
> Francis Bacon, *Advancement of Learning* (1640), The Preface[55]

With what might be called an innocent, playful, childlike mind (but not a childish one), and because the Bible says that man was created in the image of God,[56] which he understood to bestow on us a responsibility to fulfil this crea-tive purpose, Bacon set out to imitate the Creator with his own method—a method designed to help us recognise and become proficient in the workings of the divine method. Just as a Shakespeare play encapsulates in microcosm something of life itself, as played out on the macrocosmic stage of the world, so Bacon's method is intended to encapsulate in miniature God's method of enlightenment.

Right at the beginning of the final version of his *Advancement of Learning*, both in the Preface (see the quotation above) and again in Book I, Bacon sets this hide and seek method in context, indicating that it was the method used by King Solomon to acquire wisdom (*i.e.,* truth), for which Solomon was famed; and that, as a result of this acquired wisdom, all power and prosperity were added as an extra bonus. So, although Solomon chose wisdom as the gift for which to ask, rather than material riches and power, he nevertheless acquired all as a result. These blessings, spiritual and material, graced the whole country and nation of Israel throughout Solomon's reign and were only lost later through civil war. The time of Solomon was Israel's golden age.

> So likewise in the person of Solomon the King, we see the endowments of wisdom, both in his petition and God's assent thereunto, preferred before al terrene and temporal felicity. By virtue of which donative and grant, Solomon being singularly furnished and enabled, not only writ those excellent Parables or Aphorisms concerning Divine and Moral Philosophy, but also compiled a Natural History of all verdure or vegetables *From the cedar upon the mountain, to the moss upon the wall;*[57] which is but the rudiment of a plant, between putrefaction and an herb; and *also of all things that breath or move.*
>
> Francis Bacon, *Advancement of Learning*, I, vi (1640)[58]

Solomon was not only known as a great philosopher who wrote parables and aphorisms concerning divine and moral (human) philosophy (*e.g.*, *Proverbs*, *Ecclesiastes* and *Wisdom*), together with a study of nature (*i.e.*, his Natural History), he was also reputed as a supreme poet who wrote the series of allegorical and mystical love poems known as *The Song of Songs*.

During his lifetime Bacon was referred to as 'Solomon', and so this passage from the *Advancement of Learning* reveals Bacon's own aim as well as how others saw him. That is to say, his aim was to be a second Solomon: to inquire or search after truth, to compose great poetry, to study divine, human and natural nature, to write books concerning such matters so as to inspire, assist and inform others, and ultimately to help enable the entire world to discover truth and be blessed with wisdom, power of action and prosperity as a result.[59]

As the *Advancement of Learning* continues, Bacon re-emphasises Solomon's search for truth and also his humility, adding the need to become as a little child, and to play the game, innocently (*i.e.*, not corruptly) and affectionately; and moreover with assistance:

> Nay, the same Solomon the King, although he excelled in treasure and the magnificence of building, of shipping and navigation, of service and attendance, of fame and renown, and the like train of glory, yet of this rich harvest and confluence of glory, he reaps and makes claim to himself of nothing, but only the honour of the inquisition and invention of truth; for so he saith expressly, *The glory of God is to conceal a thing, but the glory of a king is to find it out:*[60] as if according to that innocent and affectionate play of children, the Divine Majesty took delight to hide his works, to the end to have them found out; and as if kings could not obtain a greater

honour than to be God's play-fellows in that game, specially considering the great commandment they have of wits and means, whereby the
investigation of all things may be perfected.

Francis Bacon, *Advancement of Learning* (1640), I, vi[61]

The ultimate concealment is that of God Himself, the supreme Truth.
God is the Author of Authors, who is concealed in and by his own works, and
yet who is at the same time revealed by them: for the works of love reveal
what Love is. This ancient concept is well expressed in the Epistle Dedicatorie
to *The French Academie*, a seminal book with which Bacon was connected:

He [God] cannot be seene of any mortal creature but is notwithstanding
known by his works.

Bacon, as the secret author of the Shakespeare works, imitated God in
this. He was also following biblical injunctions, such as that given by God to
Moses, as well as the example of Jesus, who spoke to the multitudes in parables.

These words shalt thou declare and these shalt thou hide...

Esdras: Exodus II, 14: 5–6

A prudent man concealeth knowledge....

Psalm 12: 23

And the disciples came, and said unto him, 'Why speakest thou unto
them in parables?' He answered and said unto them, 'Because it is given
unto you to know the mysteries of the kingdom of heaven, but to them
it is not given. For whosoever hath, to him shall be given, and he shall
have more abundance: but whosoever hath not, from him shall be taken
away even that he hath. Therefore I speak to them in parables: because
they seeing see not; and hearing they hear not, neither do they understand.'

Matthew 13: 10–13

All this is in fact traditional—the method of the ancient sages, whom
Bacon calls the Ancients. The Cabala, which was considered to be the oral
part of God's revelation to Moses, was consequently so sacred that it could be
explained to none but the most learned and pious of men. Bacon's works are
cabalistic, just as in fact Solomon's are (Solomon is known as one of the great
Cabalists in Jewish tradition), but Bacon does not explain so in his open text,
although the hints are there. The Shakespeare works are also cabalistically

based and are part of the cabalistic scheme of Bacon's Great Instauration.

Certain of the Hermetic texts likewise advocate secrecy, especially in religious matters. Indeed, it is concerning religious matters that Bacon was the most secret or reserved. Pythagoras never committed his philosophy to writing, his school being as much a religious society as it was a philosophical academy. Bacon's more immediate predecessor, Johannes Trithemius, Abbot of Sponheim, one of the great sages of the Renaissance Neoplatonic movement and the friend and teacher of Cornelius Agrippa, admonished Agrippa for publishing the *De Occulta Philosophia*, telling him that he should communicate vulgar secrets to vulgar friends, but higher secrets to higher and secret friends only.[62] Bacon's 'fraternity in learning and illumination', as he referred to it,[63] remained exceptionally well hidden and kept their secrets well; although it should be pointed out that while Bacon did not want to set up any kind of religion, sect or even school as such, he did establish a fraternity or fellowship—a society of poets, philosophers, scientists, artists and others, all seekers after truth.

From the point of view of using these methods, Bacon declared that he was going the way of the Ancients. About the important use of parables, therefore, he says the following in his *Wisdom of the Ancients*:

> Parables have been used in two ways, and (which is strange) for contrary purposes. For they serve to disguise and veil the meaning, and they serve also to clear and throw light upon it.... Nor is there any man of ordinary learning that will object to the reception of it as a thing grave and sober, and free from all vanity; *of prime use to the sciences, and sometimes indispensable*: I mean the employment of parables as a method of teaching, whereby inventions that are new and abstruse and remote from vulgar opinions may find an easier passage to the understanding.... For as hieroglyphs came before letters, so parables came before arguments. And even now if any one wish to let new light on any subject into men's minds, and that without offence or harshness, he must still go the same way and call in the aid of similitudes.

> Francis Bacon, Preface, *Wisdom of the Ancients* (1609), Preface[64]

Secrecy, provided it had a good motive, was to Bacon a virtue, since it was a divine characteristic. 'Therefore, set it down,' he says in his essay *Of Simulation and Dissimulation*, 'that a habit of secrecy is both politic and moral,' and in *Examples of the Antitheta* he says, 'Dissimulation is a compendious wisdom.'[65]

The chief purpose of such secrecy in literature is educational. Besides providing a training course in how the Divine works in nature, there are many other educational benefits. For instance, in the seventh book of the *Advancement of Learning* Francis Bacon observes:

Writings should be such as should make men in love with the lesson, and not with the teacher.

Francis Bacon, Advancement of Learning (1623), VII, i[66]

To hide the teacher certainly helps to focus the mind on the lesson. One of humanity's biggest problems has been the cult of the personality, adoring and serving the human teacher rather than the divine wisdom. Bacon was quite adamant in saying that he had no intention of founding a cult of that nature, but only a culture of the mind and human soul.

Bacon's contemporaries declared that he had filled the world with his writings: but with what writings, unless we include Shakespeare? Those that bear his name of Francis Bacon, although voluminous, do not warrant such a description and are not on a par numerically with writings by many other famous authors. They did not even start appearing until Bacon was in his forties, and the majority of them were written in the last five years of his life.

The nature of what Bacon set up is equivalent to what was once known as a school of the Mysteries, which excludes those who are not either ready or able, but initiates those who are ready and who can 'pierce the veil'. But it is not a school in the usual sense of the word, one which has a particular location, curriculum and board of teachers. Bacon referred to the school that he was talking about as a 'Temple'—a Temple of Solomon that is a temple of knowledge, a temple of light:

> For I am not raising a capitol or pyramid to the pride of men, but laying a foundation in the human understanding for a holy Temple after the model of the World.[67]

The entrance exam is a test of perception, and the training is in whether one can discover the truth. This is done by lifting veil after veil, and entering one court after another, until one reaches the innermost holy of holies and sees truth face to face.

Bacon admitted that he obscured his language and method of delivery intentionally:

> That the discretion anciently observed, though by the precedent of many vain persons and deceivers disgraced, of publishing part, and reserving part to a private succession, and of publishing in a manner whereby it shall not be to the capacity nor taste of all, but shall as it were single and adopt his reader, is not to be laid aside, both for the avoiding of abuse in the excluded, and the strengthening of affection in the admitted.

Francis Bacon, Valerius Terminus, Cap. 18[68]

In this passage he indicates quite clearly the practice that he is following: namely, to publish part of the work and to reserve the rest to a private succession of 'grand possessors' who will look after the material, and students and initiates to study and develop it. Even with the published material, it is to be done in such a manner that it will single out and 'adopt' its reader. Bacon explains it further in a passage from *The Advancement of Learning*:

> Another diversity of Method there is, which in intention has an affinity with the former, but is in reality almost contrary. For both methods agree in aiming to separate the vulgar [dull] among the auditors from the select; but then they are opposed in this, that the former makes use of a way of delivery more open than the common, the latter (of which I am now going to speak) of one more secret. Let the one then be distinguished as the Esoteric method, the other as the Acroamatic; a distinction observed by the ancients principally in the publication of books, but which I transfer to the method of delivery. Indeed this acroamatic or enigmatical method was itself used among the ancients, and employed with judgment and discretion. But in later times it has been disgraced by many, who have made it a false and deceitful light to put forward their counterfeit merchandise. The intention of it however seems to be by obscurity of delivery to exclude the vulgar (that is the profane vulgar) from the secrets of knowledges, and to admit those only who have either received the interpretation of the enigmas through the hands of the teachers, or have wits of such sharpness and discernment as can pierce the veil.
>
> Francis Bacon, *Advancement of Learning* (1623), VI, ii[69]

The idea is to have two methods—the esoteric and the acroamatic (enigmatic). The former is for more ordinary consumption, while the latter is for those who are both deserving of the knowledge and capable of understanding it. Because the ultimate truth is love, to discover and know it means that it has to be experienced and practised; and therefore the search for truth has an ethical basis. Bacon has simply set up a method and treasure trail that attempts to imitate the divine method at work in the universe, whereby self-development and illumination go hand in hand with a moral ethos and loving-kindness. Moreover, Bacon says he has no intention of forcing his doctrine upon anyone, but is simply offering it to anyone who might want it and is ready for it:

> It was said of Borgia of the expedition of the French into Italy, that they came with chalk in their hands to mark out their lodgings, not with arms to force their way in. I in like manner would have my doctrine enter quietly into the minds that are fit and capable of receiving it; for confutations cannot be employed, when the difference is upon first

principles and very notions and even upon forms of demonstration.

Francis Bacon, *Novum Organum* (1620), I, Aph. xxxv[70]

From an early age, Francis Bacon determined to follow a path of secrecy: to play a game of hide-and-seek by obscuring his works and himself in such a way that they were veiled from immediate sight or recognition and yet could be discovered by those who noticed the veil and learned how to lift it. At one stage, he even contemplated masking with pseudonyms not only his poetic but also his philosophical work. For instance, he left notes (*c.*1603) showing that he was intending to publish his philosophical work under the title of *Valerius Terminus or the Interpretation of Nature, with the Annotations of Hermes Stella*—he himself as author being disguised under the pseudonym of Valerius Terminus, and as editor or annotator under the pseudonym of Hermes Stella. Such a design imitates the chief Hermetic texts (the *Corpus Hermeticum*), which involve Poimandres, the *Nous* or Author of all things, speaking to his pupil and scribe, Hermes Trismegistus.

Valerius Terminus is an invented double name which has reference both to the celebrated Roman, Publius Valerius, and the Roman god, Terminus. Publius Valerius, together with Junius Brutus, was renowned for expelling the Tarquins after the rape of Lucrece and founding the Roman commonwealth. Valerius also raised an everlasting monument to the Gemini, as is recorded on an inscription in the Temple of Castor and Pollux in ancient Rome.[71] Terminus is the Roman god of boundaries, represented with a human head and without arms or feet. In this sense he is equated with Janus, the Doorkeeper, who stands on the boundary between earth and heaven, the finite and infinite. The name, Valerius Terminus, thus has a subtle association with Shake-

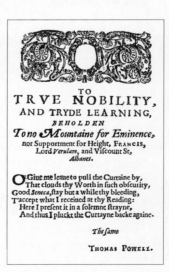

54. *Dedication page, Thomas Powell's Attourney's Academy (1630)*

speare and links directly with the 'Shakespeare' emblems on pages 33 and 34 of Peacham's *Minerva Britanna* (see Chapter 13, 'By the mind I shall be seen').

Hermes Stella is more obvious in its meaning, referring to the great sage Hermes Trismegistus, who was called Mercurius by the Romans. The Star of Hermes/Mercury, referring astronomically to the 'star' or planet Mercury, is known as the Morning Star, herald of the Sun, and is symbolic of Mercury, the god of eloquence and reason. As with the Valerius Terminus pseudonym, Hermes Stella too is intimately linked with the Shakespeare symbolism and design.

After this work, *Valerius Terminus*, however, Bacon rejected the totally-veiled approach and went for the cabalistic design of revealing part and concealing part, in which he used his own name Bacon for his philosophical works and the pseudonym of Shakespeare for his poetic works.

A contemporary of Francis Bacon, Thomas Powell, refers openly to Bacon's secrecy in the Dedication to his *Attourney's Academy* (see illustration 54). The book was published in 1630, four years after Bacon's death, so perhaps by then it was thought to be safer and more expedient to drop hints a little more openly about the treasure trail:

TO

TRUE NOBILITY,
AND TRYDE LEARNING,

BEHOLDEN
To no Mountaine for Eminence,
nor Supportment for Height, FRANCIS,
Lord *Verulam,* and Viscount St,
Albanes.

O Give me leave to pull the Curtaine by
That clouds thy Worth in such obscurity.
Good *Seneca,* stay but a while thy bleeding,
T'accept what I received at thy Reading:
     Here I present it in a solemne strayne,
     And thus I pluckt the Curtayne backe again.

One mighty hint is the reference to pulling back the curtain (*i.e.,* from the discovery place on the stage) and likening Bacon to Seneca. Seneca was a great Roman philosopher who was famed for his oratory and his writings on ethics, as also for his virtue—which he maintained even while living in the imperial Court of Nero. He was also a great tragedian, who wrote ten tragedies. He held a high position in the State and was appointed as a preceptor to the young Nero. During the time that Nero was advised by Seneca, Rome enjoyed relative tranquillity. But once the Emperor began to slide into his violent and debauched behaviour, under the influence of others, Seneca was put aside and forced into retirement on his estate, where he continued to write. Nero eventually commanded the philosopher to take his own life, which he stoically did by cutting his veins and bleeding slowly to death—a tragedy that is referred to in Powell's dedicatory verse in the volume (see above). Seneca was much admired and quoted by Bacon, and in his *Holy War,* Bacon compares himself to the Roman philosopher. There is much of Seneca's influence in the Shakespeare plays, and it has been said about Shakespeare that Plautus and Seneca were his ideals. In the compass of this small verse, Powell actually reveals a good deal about the greatness and the tragedy of Bacon's life.

The Noted Weed

As we saw in Chapter 7, Ben Jonson, in his special poem to honour Bacon on his sixtieth birthday, referred to the Lord Chancellor as standing 'as if some Mystery thou did'st!'[72] In the classical sense, a Mystery is a sacred or allegorical drama, designed to both conceal and reveal truth, which could take place either on the stage of a theatre or the stage of the world. The Baconian Mystery to which Jonson refers has much to do with the 'noted weed', referred to in the Shakespeare Sonnet 76:

> Why is my verse so barren of new pride,
> So far from variation or quick change?
> Why with the time do I not glance aside
> To new-found methods and to compounds strange?
> Why write I still all one, ever the same,
> And keep invention in a noted weed,
> That every word doth almost tell my name,
> Showing their birth and where they did proceed?
> O know, sweet love, I always write of you,
> And you and love are still my argument;
> So all my best is dressing old words new,
> Spending again what is already spent:
>> For as the sun is daily new and old,
>> So is my love still telling what is told.

Shakespeare, Sonnet 76

In Elizabethan English, 'invention' can stand for poetry, which includes drama as well as verse. But what is the 'noted weed' in which this invention is kept? Generally it is taken to mean Shakespeare's motley—his metaphorical garment as a playwright and storyteller, such as is mentioned by Jaques in *As You Like It* ('Invest me in my motley').[73] The motley that Jaques yearns for is otherwise known as fool's weeds, it being the special clothing of a professional or court jester. But such weeds would also constitute Jaques' disguise, as he is not really a professional fool but a lord. That 'weed' means a disguise, witness the use of the word by Bacon in his *History of Henry VII,* where he says:

> This fellow ... clad himself like an Hermite and in that weede wandered about the countrie.
>
> Francis Bacon, *History of Henry VII*

Likewise, Edmund Spenser uses the word to mean disguise. In his *Faerie Queene* he refers to his 'lowly Shepherd's weeds' with which he, at a former time ('whilom'), did mask his Muse:

> Lo, I the man, whose Muse whilom did mask,
>> As time her taught, in lowly Shepherd's weeds,
>> Am now enforc't a far unfitter task,
>> For trumpets stern to change mine other reeds,
>> And sing of Knights and Ladies gentle deeds;
>> Whose praises having slept in silence long,
>> Me, all too mean, the sacred Muse areeds
>> To blazon 'broad, amongst her learned throng:
> Fierce wars, and faithful loves, shall moralize my song.
>
> Spenser, *The Faerie Queene,* Bk 1, Prologue

Spenser is here referring to the style and subject of his early poem, *The Shepheards Calender*, which is masking (*i.e.,* clothing) his Muse's inspiration. But in a more personal sense, he is also referring to his pseudonym of Colin Clout, the shepherd's boy, by which he masked himself as the storyteller and author of the story. Spenser, therefore, uses the word 'weed' to mean both the verses themselves and also the name that describes himself as the poet.

Shakespeare, however, says that he keeps his invention in 'a *noted weed*' (an expression that the printer of the first edition of the sonnets emphasises with italics so that we take note) and continues by pointing out that 'every word doth almost tell my name, showing their birth and where they did proceed'. This refers most obviously to his invention—*i.e.,* his poetry, which includes his plays as well as his sonnets and poems—and is a good reminder to us that we can discover exactly who he really is by a careful study of his poetic work, not his 'portrait' or mask, as the Folio portrait poem states so categorically ('Reader, looke not on his Picture, but his Booke'). However, with *'noted weed'* emphasised as it is, there is a suggestion that it is this expression that almost tells the author's name. So, the question is, what is the 'noted weed'? 'Noted' is surely a clue.

Generally speaking, the word 'weed' as commonly used could mean any herb or small plant, but early on in King James I's reign (*c.*1606) the word became specifically used as a name for tobacco. King James despised tobacco and wrote a treatise against the smoking of it. *The State Calendar* of his time names it as the 'contemptible weed'. That is to say, it was a 'noted weed'—noted in writing by the King as contemptible.

Tobacco was first cultivated by the native tribes of North and South America, who used the weed in their ceremonials, such as in the smoking of the calumet—the peace pipe or medicine pipe. To them it was and still is a sacred plant. It was introduced to Europe in the sixteenth century, one country at a time: France (1556), Portugal (1558), Spain (1559) and England (1565). The introduction of the pipe, with which to smoke the tobacco in native fashion, is generally ascribed to Ralph Lane, the first governor of Virginia, who in 1586 brought an American Indian medicine pipe to Sir Walter Raleigh and taught him how to use it. Raleigh then introduced it to his circle of friends.

Tobacco derives its name from the Spanish *tabaco,* which was the American Indian name for the pipe through which the smoke was inhaled, and for the tubular roll of tobacco leaves they prepared for smoking. Whether the story is true or not, Raleigh's philosophical friends in England, members of the philosophical fraternity (the fraternity of learning and illumination), are supposed to have altered the word slightly so as to provide the salutation, 'To Bacco', which they used when smoking the weed at their meetings, much as we make a salutation when drinking wine. This has a double meaning, *Bacco* being the name of Bacchus, the god of wine, drama and the Orphic Mysteries, and *Bacco* (or *Baco*) also being a form of the surname of the fraternity's overall chief, Francis Bacon, used occasionally by German and Italian philosophers and written on the cover of the Northumberland Manuscript (see Chapter 11). 'Bacco', which was later developed into 'Baccy', was used as an informal name for tobacco: hence Bacco and the noted weed are one and the same, and Bacco is Bacon.

However, there is more to this still. 'To Bacco' carries Bacon's cipher signature thrice over, and in a way that links with the Shakespeare Folio's portrait verse, which begins with 'To'—the first or opening word of the Folio. We will be dealing with this specifically, and with ciphers and their use in the Shakespeare works and memorials by the philosophical fraternity—the Freemasons and Rosicrucians—later on, in chapter 12. But it is worth noting here that 'To' has the Simple Cipher count of 33, which is also the count of 'Bacon'. (The Simple Cipher is a substitution cipher, cabalistic in origin, that uses the Elizabethan twenty-four letter alphabet in which A = 1, B = 2, etc..) 'Bacco' has the count of 23 in the same cipher, which is also the count of 'Fr'. In the gematria of the Simple Cipher, therefore, 'To Bacco' (total count 56) represents 'Bacon, Fr.' or 'Fr. Bacon' (total count 56), which was a normal signature of Francis Bacon. Then, just to make sure that this is clear and definite, in the Reverse Cipher (the Reverse Cipher is the Simple Cipher reversed, such that A = 24, B = 23, etc.) 'To Bacco' counts to 119, which is also the count of 'Fr. Bacon' in the same cipher. Finally, to make it triply clear, in a third cipher, the Kaye Cipher, which is frequently used in conjunction with the other two as an extra validity check, 'To Bacco' counts to 160—and this is also the count of 'Fr. Bacon' in the same cipher. In other words, tobacco is most definitely the noted weed that almost tells Bacon's name.

Bacon's friend, the English antiquarian and Clarencieux king-of-arms, William Camden, in his history of the reign of Queen Elizabeth I, translates Bacco as meaning 'the lame':

Shan O'Neal, bynamed Bacco, that is the lame....

Camden, *Annales* (1615–17)[74]

This is not by chance, for the god Bacchus was said to be lame—his second name Dionysus meaning either 'son of God' or 'the lame god'. Moreover, according to his own sonnets, Shakespeare was lame:

So I, made lame by Fortune's dearest spite

Shakespeare, Sonnet 37

Speak of my lameness, and I straight will halt.

Shakespeare, Sonnet 89

All this helps to makes sense of why Francis Bacon said—in one of his prayers that he left for posterity:

The state and bread of the poor and oppressed have been precious in my eyes: I have hated all cruelty and hardness of heart: I have (though in a despised weed) procured the good of all men.

Francis Bacon's Prayer (c.1621)[75]

This 'despised weed' is Bacon's motley or disguise ('the lowly shepherd's weeds') as a poet–playwright, an occupation that tended to be despised by those in high places. In a more cryptic way it is the 'noted weed' of the Shakespeare sonnet, the despised 'tobacco' that almost tells the author's name.

Chapter 9

Merry Tales

Private Education

Francis Bacon's family background, upbringing, education, friends, colleagues and contacts, as well as his philosophy and life experience generally, not only fit the Shakespeare story but also help to illuminate the story further.

Francis was brought up and educated with his elder brother Anthony, together with Edward Tyrell, a ward of Sir Nicholas Bacon. Besides their parents, Sir Nicholas and Lady Ann Bacon, they had various tutors, including their maternal grandfather, Sir Anthony Cooke.[1] Sir Anthony, reputedly one of the most learned men of his time, had been tutor to the boy king Edward VI. His daughter Ann, Sir Nicholas' second wife,[2] had assisted her father, before her marriage, in the early schooling of both Edward VI and Elizabeth I. She became a friend and confidant of Queen Elizabeth, and one of the Queen's ladies-in-waiting when Sir Nicholas was the Queen's Lord Keeper. Lady Ann was conversant in Greek, Latin, French and Italian, and delighted in translating sermons from Italian into English. She was vehemently Protestant and anti-papist, while Sir Nicholas was far more moderate.

Sir Anthony Cooke, married to Ann Fitzwilliam, was the father of four

56–57. Sir Nicholas Bacon and Lady Anne Bacon. Painted terracotta busts (c.1566), sculptor unknown, at Gorhambury House.

sons and five daughters. Their eldest son, also named Anthony, died in his youth, as did another son. A further Anthony in the Cooke family was the son of Richard, one of the two surviving sons of Sir Anthony. This younger Anthony Cooke, Sir Anthony's grandson and cousin to Francis and Anthony Bacon, was the patron of the poet Drayton, who personified him in poetry under the name of Maecenas.[3] There were, therefore, four Anthonies in the family—three Cookes and one Bacon: so it is not surprising that the name Anthony, Antony or Antonio figures in no less than nine Shakespeare plays, quite apart from the Roman plays, *Julius Caesar* and *Antony and Cleopatra*.[4] Antonio in *Much Ado About Nothing* has his title changed in the fifth act to 'brother Anthony', while the Antonio of *The Merchant of Venice* is largely a caricature of Anthony Bacon, who not only helped his brother generally but also assisted him to finance his attempt to woo the young but wealthy widow, Lady Hatton, his cousin.

Then there is Sir William Cooke. When Shallow refers to his cook in 2 *Henry IV,* Act 5, scene 1, he is called William Cooke. William Cooke was the younger of the two surviving sons of Sir Anthony Cooke and his wife Ann, uncles to Francis and Anthony Bacon. Moreover, that particular 'cook' scene is laid at a seat in Gloucestershire, in which county Sir William Cooke resided.

Sir Anthony Cooke had five daughters—Lady Mildred Burleigh, Lady Ann Bacon, Lady Elizabeth Russell (previously the wife of Sir Thomas Hoby), Lady Margaret Rowlett and Lady Katharine Killigrew. Lady Margaret's husband was Sir Ralph Rowlett of Gorhambury, St Albans, Hertfordshire, whom she married on 27 June 1558, the same day that her sister Elizabeth married Sir Thomas Hoby. Margaret sadly died the next year, after which Sir Ralph wished to sell Gorhambury. Accordingly, Sir Nicholas Bacon purchased the manor house and estate from Sir Ralph in 1561, and two years later set about building a new manor house. When it was finished some years later, complete with white plastered external walls, colourfully painted internal walls portraying myths and wise sayings, a long gallery displaying busts of philosophers and great leaders, and an unusually west-orientated chapel, it was nicknamed 'The Temple'.

58. Anthony Bacon. Painted terracotta bust (c.1566), sculptor unknown, at Gorhambury House.

All the indications are that it was fitted out to be a Platonic or Orphic school of philosophy—*i.e.,* not just a country retreat but also a private academy.[5] Moreover, not far away was Theobalds, one of the two fine country homes[6] of Sir William Cecil, Lord Burghley, which was developed into a palatial Renaissance style home for intellectuals (Burghley patronised scholars rather than poets, much to the latter's chagrin) and a school for young noblemen, some of them being his legal wards, since he was the official Master of Wards.

Of course, the Bacon family did not spend all their time at Gorhambury. It was their country retreat, whereas their London residence was York Place (York House) in the Strand, next to the Queen's rambling palace of Whitehall, her principal residence, a building that stretched along the west bank of the Thames from Charing Cross to Westminster. However, Gorhambury was very important and much loved, and after Sir Nicholas died it became the only Bacon home wholly owned by Lady Anne and her two sons.[7] Here some of the special education of the Bacon brothers certainly took place.

Of all the tutors of Francis and Anthony Bacon, their grandfather Sir Anthony Cooke seems to have been their senior tutor, overseeing their education generally. According to David Lloyd, author of *The Statesmen and Favourites of Queen Elizabeth* (1665), Sir Anthony was preceptor to Francis Bacon prior to Francis taking up residence at Trinity College, Cambridge, in 1573. Presumably this applied to Anthony as well, as the brothers were educated together and both entered Trinity College at the same time. Their other known tutors included Robert Johnson (the household chaplain), who instructed the boys in religion; Amyas Paulet, their French tutor; John Florio, their Italian tutor; Eduardo Donati, their music tutor; and a fencing tutor called Bonetti. At a young age both Anthony and Francis were thoroughly learned in the Classics and could read, write and speak Latin, Greek, Hebrew, French and Italian fluently. They also learnt Spanish and Dutch, played the lute, and were proficient in the art of fencing and horse riding.

Since Sir Nicholas Bacon was the Queen's Lord Keeper of the Great Seal, and also performed the role of Lord Chancellor (without being given that title officially), he and his family attended on the Queen and so were part of the Court. The palaces, gardens, pageants, culture, life and politics of Court were therefore familiar to both Francis and Anthony Bacon, although it did not mean that they were always at Court or were always travelling with the Queen. The usual Court programme for the year was to spend winter (November–January) at York Palace (Whitehall), and in the spring to embark on a circuit of the Greenwich, Richmond and Nonsuch Palaces. This might be broken by a visit to Windsor in April for St George's Day and the Ceremony of the Knights of the Garter, and in some years a return to Whitehall for the Royal Maundy. Occasionally the routine was varied with by-progresses further afield, in which Gorhambury and Theobalds as well as other great houses were included. August and September were usually set aside for major progresses to 'royal' places like Kenilworth Castle, Warwick Castle and Woodstock Palace. Late autumn would be spent at Windsor, Oatlands, Hampton Court or Nonsuch. The Queen's Accession Day tournaments, on 17 November each year, took place at Whitehall.

Francis Bacon was renowned as a child prodigy with a brilliant mind and wit from a young age. David Lloyd wrote about him:

> He had a large mind from his father and great abilities; His parts improved more than his years; his great fixed memory, his solid judgment, his quick fancy, his ready expression, gave assurances of that profound and universal comprehension of things which then rendered him the Observation of Great and Wise.... At twelve his industry was above the capacity and his mind beyond the reach of his contemporaries.
>
> David Lloyd, *The Statesmen and Favourites of England* (1665)

William Rawley, Francis Bacon's private chaplain and confidant in later years, recorded:

> His first, and childish, years, were not without some mark of eminency; at which time he was endued with that pregnancy and towardness of wit; as they were presages of that deep and universal apprehension which was manifest in him afterward: and caused him to be taken notice of by

several persons of worth, and place; and, especially, by the Queen; who,
(as I have been informed,) delighted much, then, to confer with him,
and to prove him with questions.

William Rawley, Life of Francis Bacon (1661)[8]

Anthony Bacon was described as being as great in wit but not so profound
in knowledge as Francis. The two brothers were greatly attached to each other,
sharing the same philanthropic ideals, literary pursuits and passion for life.
Throughout their lives they worked together as partners on Francis' grand
scheme, which they hatched while in their teens at university.[9] In letters Francis
referred to Anthony as his 'comfort' and 'second self', and on a manuscript
belonging to Francis is written, 'Anthony Comfort and consorte'.[10]

University of Cambridge

Thus in April 1573, with a 'new star' (a supernova) in Cassiopeia blazing away
in the heavens, brighter in the sky than Venus and seeming to portend enormous things (the end of the world to some, and the start of the Rosicrucian
work to others), Anthony and Francis Bacon were sent to Trinity College,
Cambridge, accompanied by Edward Tyrell. Anthony was aged fourteen or
fifteen, but Francis was only twelve at this time. They matriculated on 6 April
1573 and were placed under the direct charge of the Master of Trinity, Dr John
Whitgift, one of the Queen's private chaplains, and lodged in a set of rooms
under his roof. (Whitgift afterwards became Archbishop of Canterbury, and
was the one who granted the licence to publish Venus and Adonis in 1593.)
Their contemporaries and friends at Cambridge included John Lyly, William
Clerke, Edmund Spenser, Philemon Holland and Gabriel Harvey.

Francis and Anthony's matriculation into Cambridge University occurred
just three months before the death of Dr Caius, and at the height of the student excitement caused by this choleric, Welsh-hating Master of Gonville and
Caius College, in which the Bacon brothers' uncle, Lord Burghley, was called
upon to mediate. In chapter 6, we saw how Dr Caius was subsequently satirised as the hot-tempered, equally Welsh-hating Dr Caius in The Merry Wives of
Windsor.

Gabriel Harvey, Fellow of Pembroke Hall and Professor of English, was
the tutor of Anthony and Francis in rhetoric and poetry. He was an extreme
classicist, who headed an attempt made in England to force upon a modern
language the metrical system of the Greeks and Romans. In the 1580s he was
one of the members of the English Areopagus of scholar–poets, as also was
'Immerito' (Edmund Spenser)[11] and Sir Philip Sidney, both of whom were
likewise well known to the Bacon brothers.

THE SHAKESPEARE ENIGMA

to Alençon in the spring of 1578, and mentions the tragic story of Hélène de Tournon, one of Marguerite's ladies-in-waiting, who at Liége in 1577 died of love for a young nobleman, the Marquis de Varembon.

After Christmas Francis was in Paris again, where Nicholas Hilliard painted the exquisite miniature portrait of him (see illustration 43, p..159), and it was there that his enjoyable sojourn in France was brought to a painfully abrupt end. On the night of 17/18 February 1579, he dreamt that Gorhambury was plastered all over in black mortar.[21] Two weeks later he received news that his father had died suddenly on 20 February. Shocked, he packed his bags and set off for England as soon as he could, to take part alongside his brother, mother and the rest of the family in the funeral in St Paul's Cathedral on 9 March 1579.[22] A few years later he incorporated this powerful experience into *Love's Labour's Lost* as the shock received by the Princess when brought news of her father's sudden death, which circumstance abruptly ended the festivities at Navarre's Court.

Gray's Inn

In May 1580, nearly a year after Sir Nicholas' funeral and eight months after his brother Anthony had left for the continent on his travels, Francis Bacon took up residence at Gray's Inn. Because his father's chambers were reserved at that time for Edward and Anthony Bacon, he shared chambers with Mr Fulwood in Fulwood House (until November 1587, when the Bacon chambers became free). He was given benefit of 'special admittance' on account of his health, which released him from the obligation of keeping Commons.[23] This meant that he could choose his diet and take meals in his chambers whenever he wanted. In addition, while he had been abroad in France he had been admitted (with all of Sir Nicholas Bacon's sons) to the Grand Company of Ancients, which freed him from all vacations.[24]

Although law was not his main interest, Francis Bacon nevertheless studied it as required of him by his uncle, Lord Burghley, his mother and the Queen. He was called to the Bar and admitted utter barrister on 27 June 1582. Four years later, on 10 February 1586, he was admitted as a Bencher of Gray's Inn. As a Bencher he was allowed a place with the Readers at their table. This was an honour given in recognition of legal talent, and many barristers never became Benchers. Francis, nevertheless, rose to become a Bencher in fewer years than many others took to become barristers.

The following year, on 23 November 1587, he was appointed Reader of Gray's Inn for the term.[25] Two days prior to this (21 November 1587) he had been able to move into the original chambers of Sir Nicholas Bacon, which had been vacated by his half-brother Edward. (Edward was not studying law and had by then taken on the lease of Twickenham Lodge for his residence.) Confirming a grant made nine years earlier, the chambers, together with the whole building containing them, were leased to Anthony and Francis Bacon for a term of fifty years. Because Anthony was still abroad, Francis had the use of his brother's rooms as well. Conveniently, the Great Library was adjacent to and on the same level as these rooms. Servants and secretaries assisting Francis in his great scheme occupied other rooms. The lease gave leave to add additional rooms by building over the others, which Francis accordingly did, and ultimately 'Bacon's Chambers' became an elegant four-storied house.[26]

The Privy Councillors employed Francis as a legal adviser, as an examiner of prisoners and their testimonies, and as a government propagandist. Moreover, the Queen herself used him in various capacities, either for legal advice or for political intelligence. In 1588, she appointed him her Counsel Extraordinary, the first such appointment made. It was seemingly an unpaid position but meant that Francis was at last being acknowledged for the services he had rendered. This brought him 'within the bar' with the judges and sergeants-at-law, and gave him a standing with the sergeants—but without a pension or a regular means for accumulating fees. However, it gave him private access to the Queen, which was an important and much sought-after position. His duties were not clearly defined, except that examining prisoners suspected of treason or other grave offences, protecting the Queen's interests and drawing up official reports were some of the services he was called upon to perform.[27] In 1594 he was given his first Court briefs, which meant that he pleaded before the royal judges in the King's Bench and Exchequer Chamber, but they only amounted to four in number, as far as is known.[28]

In terms of the gathering and assessing of intelligence, Francis Bacon was in constant communication with his brother Anthony, who was acting as an intelligencer abroad, receiving and sending letters, and furnishing to the Queen and her government up-to-date information relevant to policy-making and international dealings. Books were also sent to and fro between the Bacon brothers, as part of their literary endeavours.

Besides serving the Queen and her Councillors in the above-mentioned 'extraordinary' fashion, as a lawyer and an intelligencer, Francis also served on successive parliaments as a Member of Parliament and was very involved with the life of Gray's Inn. His philosophic, poetic and literary endeavours, however, were his real love and, as he saw it, his life's mission. According to his notes he began his 'New Method' in 1587, in which poetry or drama plays a key role. It is at this point in time that the Shakespeare plays began to appear on stage, with *Titus Andronicus* being performed at the Rose by Lord Sussex's Men in 1587, followed by the first history plays—*King John,*

Henry VI (Parts 1, 2 and 3) and *Richard III*—the latter having its first performance in 1592.

By this time Anthony Bacon had returned from the continent. He arrived in England on 4 February 1592 and went to join Francis at Gray's Inn. At the same time, and probably because of this, Francis relinquished his 'suit' to the Queen and Lord Burghley, and made new plans. Except for a visit to Gorhambury made by Anthony in August to see his mother, and a visit that he made to Scotland towards the end of the year, Anthony worked together with Francis in their chambers, with their friends and assistants helping them. Not only did the Shakespeare comedies start appearing, with *The Taming of the Shrew* and *The Two Gentlemen of Verona*, but it was at the end of that year that two further new stars (novae this time, rather than the supernova of 1572–4) appeared like twins in the constellation of Cassiopeia. The following April (1593) 'William Shakespeare' was announced to the world as the author of *Venus and Adonis,* the 'first heir' of the author's invention. Its mate, the second Shakespeare poem, *The Rape of Lucrece,* was registered in May 1594, with both poems displaying the peacock symbol of the Gemini on their title pages (see chapter 5).

In April 1584, just before *Lucrece* was released, Anthony Bacon moved into a house in Bishopsgate Street.[29] It was almost next door to the Bull Inn, where plays were performed, and within easy reach of Shoreditch, where James Burbage's two playhouses, the Theatre and the Curtain, were located.[30] Closed during 1592–3 because of the plague, these theatres had newly reopened when Anthony Bacon arrived in the neighbourhood. At that time Will Shakespeare was one of the actors in James Burbage's company, and Edward Burbage, son of William Burbage of Pinner Park and possibly a relation of James Burbage and his sons, was one of Anthony's servants. William Burbage was well known to the Shakespeares, having been engaged in a dispute with John Shakespeare, Will's father, over a house in Stratford-upon-Avon.

Anthony was not the only one who took on another house. Francis had been using Twickenham Lodge for some years, and in 1595 the Queen granted him the lease of the house, park and woodland in recognition of his services. This gave Francis a valuable and delightful country retreat that was near to London, on the River Thames (a major means of transport) and with the Queen's Palace of Richmond on the other side of the river. He loved being amongst nature, in parks and countryside, and called Twickenham Park his 'earthly paradise'. He usually retreated to it during the law vacations, but sometimes during term as well, together with his lawyer friends and 'good pens'.

This literary activity at Twickenham Lodge seems to have been a mixture of intelligence work and play writing. For instance, in Francis' *Promus* (1594–5) he mentions 'Ye law at Twick'nam for merrie tales';[31] and in a lengthy letter to Anthony, 'from my lodging at Twickenham Park this 25th January, 1594 [1595]', Francis writes:

> I have here an idle pen or two specially one that was cozened, thinking to have got some money this term. I pray you send me somewhat else for them to write out beside your Irish collection which is almost done. There is a collection of Dr James [Dean of Christchurch] of foreign states largeliest of Flanders, which though it be no great matter, yet I would be glad to have it.[32]

Francis further suggests to his brother 'whether it were not a good time to set in strongly with the Queen to draw her to honour your travels', but strangely Anthony never managed to get himself to see the Queen, then or later, even though requested to an audience by her several times. Each time he always fell sick and was unable to travel.[33]

One of the intelligence projects concerned the Lopez Conspiracy. For six months, Anthony Bacon and Essex had been investigating a circle of Spanish and Portuguese plotters, which led to the uncovering of a conspiracy to poison the Queen through the agency of her Portuguese physician, Dr Lopez. Francis Bacon was commissioned in March 1594 to write the government's public advertisement presenting the details of the conspiracy, which pointed the blame directly at King Philip of Spain. Through this and his researches into other cases and possibilities of poisoning, Francis was fairly well informed about the various methods of poisoners and types of poison used. We discover such knowledge in *Hamlet*, where the poison-in-the-ear story is almost certainly based on the murder of Francesco Maria I della Rovere, Duke of Urbino, in October 1538, at the instigation of Luigi Gonzago. The Médicis in France, also, were infamous for their use of poison. Further, knowledge of catatonia and coma-inducing drugs is brought into *Romeo and Juliet*.

In 1594, Francis was appointed as the Deputy-Treasurer (*i.e.*, Deputy-Head) of Gray's Inn for the legal year, which meant that he was co-responsible for the revels that year, including the extra-grand Christmas Revels, *The Prince of Purpoole and the Honourable Order of the Knights of the Helmet*, during which *The Comedy of Errors* was first performed.

It was on 21 March 1595, after he had returned to Gray's Inn from Twickenham Lodge, that Francis Bacon wrote to the Earl of Essex concerning the post that Essex was trying to obtain for him, that of Solicitor-General, pointing out to the Earl that he was not to assume that he (Francis) was greedy to obtain the office, because 'the waters of Parnassus' (*i.e.*, poetic matters) quenched all appetite and desires for such worldly things (see Chapter 7).

In the summer of 1595, Francis was appointed a Member of the Queen's

Counsel Learned in the Law. This rank was reasonably high, next to that of Solicitor, and instituted for the express purpose of protecting the safety of the Queen and realm. At the same time he continued to be employed by Privy Councillors acting for the Queen, as a legal adviser and as an examiner of prisoners (usually with Coke, Fleming and Williams presiding). In this latter role he appeared before the Privy Councillors in the Star Chamber in 1596 and 1597, acting as both Crown Counsel and as an examiner—a role that, with suitable modifications, he put into the hands of Portia in *The Merchant of Venice*.

Anthony, meanwhile, moved into Essex House in August 1595 to assist the Earl of Essex more directly, as a kind of 'secretary of state', complete with his own secretariat. This was at the express request of Francis, who records that he 'knit' his brother's service to the Earl, believing at that time that this was the most profitable course to serve his country—a decision that he bitterly regretted some years later, as things turned out.

> I held at that time, my Lord [Essex] to be the fittest instrument to do good to the state; and therefore I applied myself to him in a manner which I think happeneth rarely among men; for I did not only labour carefully and industriously in that he set me about, whether it were a matter of advice or otherwise; but neglecting the Queen's service, mine own fortune, and in a sort my vocation, I did nothing but advise and ruminate with myself to the best of my understanding, propositions and memorials of anything that might concern his Lordship's honour, fortune, or service. And when, not long after I had entered into this course, my brother, master Anthony Bacon, came from beyond the seas, being a gentleman whose ability the world taketh knowledge of for matters of state especially foreign, I did likewise knit his service to be at my Lord's disposing.
>
> Francis Bacon, *Apology* (1604)

Essex House, previously the Earl of Leicester's House, was well located. It was built on the site of what was once the Outer Temple of the Knights Templar headquarters, on the northern bank of the Thames. Neighbouring it on its east side was the Middle Temple Inn of Court, with its Elizabethan Great Hall where *Twelfth Night* was performed on 2 February 1602 as part of the Inn's Christmas Revels. Next door to Essex House on its west side was Arundel House, with its famous library and collection of antiques, including marble statues, busts and other treasures from Greece and Rome.

Anthony Bacon lived for over four years in Essex House (August 1595 to March 1600), heading an international intelligence network partly inherited from Walsingham and partly built up from his own contacts, which were spread across Europe. Besides Anthony's own secretariat, Essex also had four secretaries

The same year, 1601, as we shall learn in chapter 10, Anthony Bacon tragically died, leaving Francis with Anthony's inherited interest in Gorhambury, which was the reversion of the property to him after Lady Ann Bacon's death. In the following year, on 20 November 1602, Lady Ann surrendered to Francis her life-interest in the manors and estates of Gorhambury, 'in consideration of the natural love and affection' which she bore him. She carried on living there, but her mind was failing with her advancing years and she became 'little better than frantic in her old age'.[38] Francis had to deal with this, so he became somewhat of an expert in the sort of madness that he portrayed in *King Lear*. Lady Ann eventually died in August 1610, enabling Francis to take over the house completely and introduce his new ideas.

Francis redesigned and laid out the park with new vistas, avenues, gardens, woods and summerhouses, as well as building near the river a new mansion, called Verulam House, when the piped water supply to Gorhambury House failed. He linked his new house to Gorhambury House with three parallel roads, running straight and wide enough so that seven coaches could travel abreast along them. Close to and on the north side of Verulam House he designed and constructed what he called 'pond yards', each of the twelve rectangular-shaped ponds being lined with pebbles of varying hues laid in patterns of animals, fishes and other designs. The central pond had an island with a two-storey octagonal banqueting house upon it, floored with black and white marble, covered with Cornish slate and neatly wainscoted inside.

There was also another banqueting house, which stood in a walled orchard behind Gorhambury House. This was reached via an arched gateway, on the top of which was a statue of Orpheus with some verses praising the poet and asking a blessing on the cult of Orpheus that was established there. This banqueting house, which must have also been an octagonal building, had the Seven Liberal Arts and Sciences depicted on seven of its walls, together with descriptions of the benefits that are to be derived from a study of them

60. Verulam House, Gorhambury, St Albans, Hertfordshire. Sketch by Aubrey, 18th century.

plus pictures of such men who had excelled in each. One glaring omission from the list of celebrities was Plato—but then the whole architectural arrangement and symbolism inferred that this was a Platonic Academy that had Plato as its principal. It is not certain whether it was Sir Nicholas Bacon or Sir Francis Bacon who had this banqueting house built, but it was Francis Bacon who was called the 'Third Plato'.[39]

Francis loved Gorhambury and went there often, especially in the spring and summer vacations. He had great walks laid out through avenues of trees and 'delicate groves' of oaks and flowering shrubs. According to Aubrey, 'under every tree there he planted some fine flower—peonies, tulips, violets'. Some of the lawns must have been of camomile, which he liked to walk or lie on, and there were also alleys of burnet, wild-thyme and watermints which, when crushed underfoot, 'perfume the air most delightfully'.[40] He designed his gardens so that 'the breath of flowers, blowing freely or crushed underfoot, should come and go like the warbling of music.' There were oak woods and orchards, walled gardens and 'deserts' (wildernesses). Upon the highest point he built a pyramid-temple, known as 'Bacon's Observatory', which acted as the centre of a vast geometric pattern that Francis laid out across his estate to determine the sites of certain key features.

Even when Verulam House was built, Francis continued to use the Tudor house, which he greatly embellished, as well. The fascinating painted glass windows of the Long Gallery belonging to the Tudor house, depicting all kinds of animals, birds, plants, people and scenes from all over Europe and the Americas, may well have been created by Francis rather than Sir Nicholas Bacon. His table was always strewn with flowers and sweet scented herbs, in order to 'refresh his spirit and his memory'. At the same time he liked to hear music played in an adjoining room while he ate with others or meditated alone.

Not surprisingly Aubrey noted that 'when his lordship was at his country house at Gorhambury, St Albans seemed as if the court was there, so nobly did he live'. As Lord Chancellor, Bacon had to deal with hordes of suitors, knights, noblemen and courtiers, as well as having his own retinue of servants, officers and secretaries. His work did not cease in the vacations, although, as he said, he dedicated the vacations to writing. Whenever he walked through his gardens and groves he often had a secretary at his side, to jot down (in a shorthand which he had invented) his thoughts as they came to him.

Elizabethan Entertainments

To the lawyers of Gray's Inn, and the courtiers and nobles of the Royal Court, Francis Bacon was a noted deviser, director, producer and organiser of masques and entertainments, which included plays. He also wrote speeches for others, and the spring of love. And as it springeth not out of ill, so is it not inter-mixed with ill; it is not like the virtues which by a steep and cragged way conduct us to a plain, and are hard task-masters at first, and after give an honourable hire; but the first aspect of love and all that followeth is gra-cious and pleasant.

Francis Bacon, 'The praise of Love', Of Tribute (1592)[43]

A 'Speach for my Lord of Sussex tilt', also preserved amongst the North-umberland papers, was probably for the 1596 Accession Day Tournament, for which, in Roy Strong's words, Francis was employed by Robert Ratcliffe, the fifth Earl of Sussex, 'to write a doleful story in which as a young knight he makes petition to retire from public life to acquire the virtues of his father'.[44]

Perhaps the most famous Gray's Inn revels in which Francis Bacon was involved were the Christmas Revels of 1594–5, *The Prince of Purpoole and the Order of The Knights of the Helmet* (see Chapter 6). These Gray's Inn Revels were intended to be extra-special that year, and various 'Grand Nights' were designed to be part of the much-extended programme. The Lord Keeper, the Lord Treasurer, the Vice-Chamberlain and others from the Royal Court, plus an 'Embassy' from the 'Templars' (*i.e.,* the Inner Temple Inn of Court), were invited to the Grand Nights, the first of which was on the 27 December, when the *Comedy of Errors* was performed. *The Order of the Knights of the Helmet* followed it on the next Grand Night, 3 January 1595. It is generally agreed, from Spedding onwards, that Francis Bacon was responsible for the fine speeches of the Six Counsellors in this *Knights of the Helmet* entertainment, just as it is generally agreed that the *Comedy of Errors* acted at Gray's Inn was the Shakespeare play of that name. Bacon's style and philosophy pervade the whole Revels, and his authorship of other speeches can be discovered elsewhere in these Revels, including *The Masque of Proteus* with which the Inn entertained the Queen on Shrove Tuesday at Whitehall Palace and which concluded the Revels.

As we learnt in Chapter 6, the theme of these Revels was built around the idea of errors being committed, a trial being held of the 'Sorcerer' responsible, and then the errors being made good and the Sorcerer redeeming himself with something better. The 'Night of Errors', with its *Comedy of Errors,* was there-fore a planned part of the Revels, preparations for which were probably be-gun some months in advance—a usual occurrence for revels and more neces-sary than usual in this case. This was a year when Francis Bacon was co-Treas-urer of Gray's Inn and therefore co-responsible (or perhaps wholly responsi-ble) for the design and planning of the Revels.[45] Bacon, of course, as a recent writer and barrister, Nigel Cockburn, points out, 'would have known of the convention at Gray's Inn whereby the visiting Templarians would walk out on their first visit in a simulated huff after mock disorders'.[46] Cockburn also makes the relevant point that the 'Sorcerer', who would have been played by Francis Bacon if he had designed the Revels, was in all likelihood based partly upon the thirteenth-century Franciscan philosopher and alchemist, Roger Bacon, who was brought to trial by the general of the Franciscan order, Girolamo Masci, as a sorcerer and imprisoned for ten years as a result, and partly upon the fictional character Friar Bacon, a 'real' sorcerer, in the play *Friar Bacon and Friar Bungay* by Robert Greene, which was printed just a few months before the Gray's Inn 1594–5 Revels. The name 'Bacon', therefore, was heavily emphasised![47]

Love's Labour's Lost

Doubtless, Anthony Bacon helped Francis with these Revels, just as he must have done with the Shakespeare plays. He was certainly involved in *Love's Labour's Lost*, which was probably written to conclude the 1594–5 Revels (see Chapter 6). *Love's Labour's Lost,* which was presented before the Queen at Christmas 1597 and published in quarto in 1598, is a play whose theme is essentially a damning comment on the barrenness of an all-male society that deliberately sets itself aside from women and the world in order to discover truth in a purely academic and contemplative way. This theme is pre-eminently Bacon's philosophy—one that follows in Dante's footsteps, wherein truth is recognised as love and in which (for a man) a woman is the awakener, inspiration, focus and teacher of love, and able to lead the man towards an appreciation and experience of divine Love, which manifests itself as charity and a full, loving involvement in life.

The story of the play centres around an academy set up by King Ferdinand of Navarre, consisting of himself and three gentlemen friends who dedicate themselves to living apart from women and worldly things, in austerity and celibacy, in order to study and discover truth. Their vows are broken when the French Princess arrives with her three attractive ladies-in-waiting, with whom the men fall in love. The play culminates with the sudden and dramatic arrival of a messenger announcing the death of the King of France, the Princess' father, and the insistence of the ladies that the men must wait patiently for a year and a day (*i.e.,* a legal year), proving themselves worthy of the women. Berowne in particular is charged to perform deeds of charity in order to claim his lady's hand in marriage.

The King of Navarre begins the play with the words:

> King. Let fame, that all hunt after in their lives,
> Live register'd upon our brazen tombs,
> And then grace us in the disgrace of death;

When, spite of cormorant devouring Time,
Th'endeavour of this present breath may buy
That honour which shall bate his scythe's keen edge,
And make us heirs of all eternity.
Therefore, brave conquerors—for so you are,
That war against your own affections
And the huge army of the world's desires—
Our late edict shall strongly stand in force:
Navarre shall be the wonder of the world;
Our court shall be a little academe,
Still and contemplative in living art.

Shakespeare, Love's Labour's Lost, I, i, 1–14

Berowne, who seems to speak for the author, tries his hardest to point out to his companions that for the men austerely to set themselves apart from women and the world is no way to discover truth:

Berowne. Have at you then, affection's men-at-arms:
Consider what you first did swear unto,
To fast, to study, and to see no woman;
Flat treason 'gainst the kingly state of youth.
Say, can you fast? your stomachs are too young,
And abstinence engenders maladies.
And where that you have vow'd to study, Lords,
In that each of you have forsworn his book,
Can you still dream and pore and thereon look?
For when would you, my Lord, or you, or you,
Have found the ground of study's excellence
Without the beauty of a woman's face?

Shakespeare, Love's Labour's Lost, IV, iii, 286–97

Berowne goes on to associate truth with love and to proclaim not only that love is first learnt in a lady's eyes but also that it is the quintessential emotion, having the motion of all the elements and giving to every power or human faculty a double power, and therefore a double ability to see, hear, feel, taste and thus discover truth:

But love, first learned in a lady's eyes,
Lives not alone immured in the brain,
But, with the motion of all elements,
Courses as swift as thought in every power,
And gives to every power a double power,

Above their functions and their offices.
It adds a precious seeing to the eye;
A lover's eyes will gaze an eagle blind;
A lover's ear will hear the lowest sound,
When the suspicious head of th'eft is stopped:
Love's feeling is more soft and sensible
Than are the tender horns of cockled snails:
Love's tongue proves dainty Bacchus gross in taste.

Shakespeare, Love's Labour's Lost , IV, iii, 323–35

Berowne associates love with the valour or courage of the heart that climbs, like Hercules, the Hesperidean trees, to reach for the golden apples of knowledge. It has the subtlety or intelligence of the Sphinx, which can solve even the most difficult of enigmas, and the musical sweetness of Apollo's lute, strung with light. This love is the divine Love, the 'Word' (*Logos*) or voice of all the gods, which creates harmony whenever it speaks:

For valour, is not Love a Hercules,
Still climbing trees in the Hesperides?
Subtle as Sphinx; as sweet and musical
As bright Apollo's lute, strung with his hair;
And when Love speaks, the voice of all the gods
Make heaven drowsy with the harmony.

Shakespeare, Love's Labour's Lost , IV, iii, 336–41

A poet would not dare to write, Berowne points out, unless he was infused with love's sighs; and then, thus inspired, he would, like Orpheus, transform the world:

Never durst poet touch a pen to write
Until his ink were tempered with Love's sighs;
O! then his lines would ravish savage ears,
And plant in tyrants mild humility.

Shakespeare, Love's Labour's Lost , IV, iii, 342–5

It is from women's eyes, he states, that he has learnt these truths. They are, therefore, the books, arts and academies that reveal, contain and nourish the whole world:

From women's eyes this doctrine I derive:
They sparkle still the right Promethean fire;
They are the books, the arts, the academes,

That show, contain, and nourish all the world;
Else none at all in aught proves excellent.

Shakespeare, Love's Labour's Lost , IV, iii, 346–50

Having made this wonderful argument, Berowne then advises his companions that they are fools to forswear the company of women, as by doing so they will not, of course, be able to discover truth—the very reason for their forming an academy! Since they have already made their oaths, Berowne argues that they should forswear their oaths and that it would be religion, or charity, to do so. Moreover, he points out, it is charity that fulfils the law, and love and charity are one:

Then fools you were these women to forswear,
Or keeping what is sworn, you will prove fools.
For wisdom's sake, a word that all men love,
Or for love's sake, a word that loves all men,
Or for men's sake, the authors of these women,
Or women's sake, by whom we men are men,
Let us once lose our oaths to find ourselves,
Or else we lose ourselves to keep our oaths.
It is religion to be thus forsworn;
For charity itself fulfils the law,
And who can sever love from charity?

Shakespeare, Love's Labour's Lost , IV, iii, 351–61

Such is Bacon's philosophy presented in poetry: Love is the supreme law, which we should strive to know, but we cannot truly know it without experiencing and practising it. He explains the same in his other works, and in different styles to suit the different mediums chosen. One important example is to be found in his *Advancement of Learning*, wherein he declares his opinion that knowledge should only be sought after for the reward and profit of all life and used in charitable ways:

In sum, I would advise all in general, that they would take into serious consideration the true and genuine ends of knowledge; that they seek it not either for pleasure, or contention, or contempt of others, or for profit, or fame, or for honour and promotion, or such like adulterate or inferior ends; but for the merit and emolument of life; and that they regulate and perfect the same in charity. For the desire of power was the fall of angels, the desire of knowledge the fall of man; but in charity there is no excess, neither man nor angels ever incurred danger by it.

Francis Bacon, The Preface, Advancement of Learning (1640)

Bacon's formula, in essence, derived from his various writings, is that God is the All-Good, whose nature or character is Goodness.[48] Good, as an abstract principle, is the unmanifest God; Goodness, as the active condition of being good, is the manifest God. The latter is known as the First-Born or Son of God, whose goodness is love. The Greeks called this First-Born by the name of Eros; the Romans named it Cupid. The Bible refers to it as Light. This love is ever active, ever creative, and is therefore the same as charity. This love is truth. If we are to know truth, we must practice truth.

> I take Goodness in this sense, the affecting of the weal of men, which is that the Grecians call *Philanthropia*; and the word *humanity* (as it is used) is a little too light to express it. Goodness I call the habit, and Goodness of Nature the inclination. This of all virtues and dignities of the mind is the greatest; being the character of the Deity: and without it man is a busy, mischievous, wretched thing; no better than a kind of vermin. Goodness answers to the theological virtue Charity, and admits no excess, but error. The desire of power in excess caused the angels to fall; the desire of knowledge in excess caused man to fall; but in charity there is no excess; neither can angel or man come in danger by it.
>
> Francis Bacon, 'Of Goodness and Goodness of Nature,' Essays (1625)

> Truth, which only doth judge itself, teacheth that the enquiry of truth, which is the love-making or wooing of it, the knowledge of truth, which is the presence of it, and the belief of truth, which is the enjoying of it, is the sovereign good of human nature.
>
> Francis Bacon, 'Of Truth,' Essays (1625)

> For the principles, fountains, causes, and forms of motions, that is, the appetites and passions of every kind of matter, are the proper objects of philosophy.
>
> Francis Bacon, Thoughts on the Nature of Things

It is, in other words, impossible to discover truth without feeling, seeing and being in love, and giving love. To banish all desires or emotions, therefore, besides being an impossible task is also a barrier to the discovery of truth. On the contrary, we should generate, feel, enjoy and study our emotions, especially love, if we wish to find and understand truth.

This viewpoint was one generally held in the Court faction to which Francis and Anthony Bacon belonged. This faction was led by the Earls of Essex, Bedford, Rutland and Southampton, plus Mary Sidney (Countess of Pembroke), Frances Walsingham (Countess of Essex), and Essex's sisters, Penelope (Lady Rich) and Dorothy (Countess of Northumberland). Ideas like this were in direct contrast to those of Sir Walter Raleigh and his circle, which included Gabriel Harvey and John Florio, the poet Matthew Roydon, and the mathematicians Thomas Harriot, Walter Warner and Thomas Hughes. In 1592 this circle was branded 'Sir Walter Rauley's Schoole of Atheism' and in 1594 it was investigated for alleged heresies by a special commission appointed by the Privy Council. The translator of Homer, George Chapman, joined this group. In 1594 he published a poem, *Shadow of Night*, which eulogises a life of contemplation, study and knowledge as opposed to a life of pleasure and practical affairs.

Raleigh's circle was patronised by the Earls of Derby and Northumberland and the Lord Chamberlain, Baron Hunsdon, all friends of Raleigh. Together, these noblemen had opposed and insulted Essex and Essex's circle of family and friends. This insult occurred when the Earl of Northumberland, who married Essex's attractive sister Dorothy in 1594, wrote an essay summing up the philosophy of Raleigh and Chapman's 'School of Atheism' (or 'School of Night' as it is referred to in *Love's Labour's Lost*),[49] to prove to his wife the infinite superiority of the attractions of learning over those of any female whosoever. Previously, in 1585, Lady Penelope Rich (the 'Stella' of Sir Philip Sidney's sonnets) had suffered a similar insult from the hands of the Italian astronomer–academician Giordano Bruno, who bitterly condemned romantic love (and in particular sonnet writing) in an essay, *De gli eroici furori*, dedicated to Sidney, whose own poetry was love poetry inspired by his love for 'Stella' (Penelope Rich). *Love's Labour's Lost* is very much a riposte to Northumberland's insult and Chapman's poem.

Certain characters in *Love's Labour's Lost* are taken from Francis and Anthony Bacon's life-experiences. Anthony Bacon, for instance, was a good friend of Henri de Bourbon, King of Navarre. The two men communicated with each other often. Anthony had lived in Béarn at Henri of Navarre's Court during the summer of 1584, staying with Henri and his sister Catharine de Bourbon. That year, Navarre became the heir to the throne of France,[50] but it was probably in the previous year that he set up his Academy, and 'furnished his Court with principal gentlemen of the Religion [Protestant] and reformed his house'.[51] Both Henri and Catharine are caricatured in *Love's Labour's Lost* as Ferdinand, King of Navarre, and Katharine, one of the ladies attending on the Princess of France. Francis Bacon's connection with Henri of Navarre and Marguerite, Princess of France, has already been discussed.

After his stay at Navarre's Court in 1584, Anthony Bacon remained in France for another eight years, going first to Bourges. Here he remained until January 1585, when he moved to Montauban. Sometime in 1590 he moved to Bordeaux, where he formed a deep friendship with the writer Michel de Montaigne. He remained in Bordeaux until his return to England in February

1592. Navarre had by then become King of France, Henri III having been assassinated on 1 August 1589. Among the papers that Anthony brought home with him to London were some passports that he had been given in 1586 when he must have first contemplated returning home to England.[52] A passport for Anthony's servant Peter Browne, to enable him to travel from Caors (Cahors) to Montauban on his master's affairs, is signed by Geraud de Lomagne, Seigneur de Terride, Seigneur de Serignac, Huguenot Commander of the country between the Garenne and the Pyrenees (26 July 1586).[53] Another passport for Peter Browne, to enable him to travel to Montauban a second time on his master's affairs, is signed by Antoine D'ebrard de St Sulpice, Duke, Baron and Count Bishop of Caors, on behalf of Lord Boyresse (8 August 1586).[54] A passport for Anthony, to enable him and his men, servants, arms and horses to travel safely and unhindered through France to England, is signed by Armand de Goutant, Baron de Biron, Marshal of France (17 September 1586).[55] Anthony also knew the Duc de Longueville, who was a lord-in-waiting on the King of Navarre while Anthony was residing at Navarre's Court. These names are used, slightly altered, as the names of characters in *Love's Labour's Lost*. Dumain, Longaville and Berowne, the three young lords and friends of Navarre in the play, can be seen to be derived from de Lomagne, de Longueville and de Biron, while Boyet, counsellor to the Princess, is derived from the nobleman Boyresse.

The 'fantastical' Spanish character in *Love's Labour's Lost*, Don Adriana de Armado, is, as we saw, modelled on Antonio Perez, the King of Spain's exiled former Secretary of State whom Anthony and Francis Bacon befriended and looked after. Perez escaped from Aragon in 1591 during a dangerous insurrection and, after many adventures, took refuge in Navarre, at the residence of Henri's sister, the Princess Catharine. Perez then came to England in 1593 to live in London, *persona grata*, first at Bishopsgate with Anthony Bacon and then at Essex House, where Essex gave Perez a suite of rooms in return for the intelligence that the Spaniard offered to him (presumably at Anthony's instigation) in December 1594. While living at Essex House, Perez wrote various books and letters in an extravagantly-affected style, for which he became notorious. He published a Spanish book in the summer of 1594, entitled *Les Relaciones* ('Narratives'), under the assumed name of 'Raphael Peregrino', which either gave rise to or was taken from the newly coined word 'peregrinate'. The word is used in *Love's Labour's Lost*. Francis Bacon also used it in the Latin version of his essay 'On Travel'—'De Peregratione in Partos Extremos'.

In August 1595, when Perez went to the French Court, Anthony Bacon moved into Essex House and took over the vacated suite of rooms. In France Perez became a companion of Henri of Navarre, or Henri IV, King of France, as he now was. Perez was treated with almost royal honour and wished to remain there, even though Anthony Bacon and Essex were the ones who were supporting him financially and otherwise. By 1596 Perez had gravely offended the Earl of Essex by his behaviour and ingratitude, as well as exasperating Anthony Bacon who had largely paid Perez's expenses. In the correspondence between Anthony Bacon and his friend Lady Penelope Rich, Essex's sister, each of them refers to Perez as Anthony's 'wandering neighbour'.

Another item of specialist information that Anthony Bacon in particular is most likely to have known concerns the mission of the French Princess in *Love's Labour's Lost,* which occurs in Act II, when she comes on an embassy to the King of Navarre from her father the King of France. Her mission was to demand back the Province of Aquitaine, which was given as surety for a loan, as the full debt of two hundred thousand crowns had been repaid. Navarre quibbles, claiming that the latest payment of one hundred thousand crowns is only half what is owed and that the other one hundred thousand crowns are still to be paid. This plot is taken from an historical event around 1420, described in Monstrelet's *Chronicles,* when Charles of Aragon, King of Navarre, renounced all claim to a certain French territory in consideration that Charles VI, King of France, promised to pay him two hundred thousand gold crowns together with the Duchy of Nemours. In *Love's Labour's Lost* it is Navarre's father who is called Charles, but the arrangement is similar and the sum of money is the same.

Jacobean Entertainments

Francis Bacon was involved in the production of further masques in the reign of King James. One of these was *The Marriage of the Thames and Rhine,* written in celebration of the marriage on 14 February 1613 of King James' daughter, Princess Elizabeth, to the German Prince Frederick, the Elector Palatine. The masque was presented jointly by Gray's Inn and the Inner Temple, and performed before the couple the day after the wedding.[56] The writing of the masque is attributed to Francis Beaumont, but the Lord Chamberlain records that 'the chief contriver' of the masque was Sir Francis Bacon, then Solicitor-General. When the masque was printed the dedication began by acknowledging Bacon as 'You that spared no time nor travail in the setting forth, ordering, and furnishing of this masque.' It continues: 'And you, Sir Francis Bacon, especially, did by your countenance and loving affections advance it'.[57]

At the end of that year Bacon was again involved in the production of a masque, this time to celebrate the marriage of the King's favourite, Robert Carr, Earl of Somerset, to Lady Francis Howard, daughter of the Earl of Suffolk, the Lord Chamberlain. The masque, called *The Masque of Flowers,* was a lavish entertainment, costing 'above £2000' (according to the contemporary writer, John Chamberlain),[58] that was devised, organised and paid for by Francis Bacon, and presented at Court on 26 December 1613 by the gentlemen of Gray's Inn, as a unique wedding gift to the couple.

The four Inns of Court had first proposed to join together in getting up a masque to honour the wedding, but owing to the difficulty of meeting the expenses of a previous masque they could not manage it. Bacon, who had just been made Attorney-General on 27 October, and who was still Treasurer of Gray's Inn, stepped in and offered to undertake the whole cost of the production. At that time all officers of State, along with all courtiers and noblemen, were being expected to present the couple with a wedding gift; and because Somerset claimed to have used his influence with the King to secure Bacon's promotion, Bacon was expected to give in return something substantial. Bacon abhorred the sale of offices for money, one of the great abuses of those times, and appears to have circumvented the difficulty by means of this remarkable present. The masque was a colossal gift financially but was of no monetary value to Somerset whatsoever. It was valuable as a compliment—a splendid compliment—and as a spectacular entertainment for the wedding, but not as anything else. At the same time it conferred great distinction upon Gray's Inn, who rehearsed and put together this elaborate masque all within the space of three weeks.

The masque was published in full shortly after its performance, with a dedication to Bacon as having been 'the Principal, and in effect the only person that did both encourage and warrant the Gentlemen, to show their good affection towards so noble a Conjunction, in a time of such Magnificence', and acknowledging that one Inn of Court by itself, in time of a vacation and in the space of three weeks, could not have performed that which has been performed, were it not that 'every man's exceeding love and respect to you gave him wings to overtake time which is the swiftest of things'.[59] In this tribute to their Treasurer, the gentlemen of Gray's Inn show not only in what high regard they held Bacon, and the love they had for him, but also hint at how he must have inspired, helped and encouraged them in inventing, organising and preparing the masque—something at which he was by then both adept and an old hand.

Chapter 10

Darkness and Light

The Elusive Goal

The internal evidence of the plays, coupled with the various facts concerning the life of Francis Bacon that we have looked at so far, are sufficiently overwhelming, I believe, to justify our assumption, with few reservations, that he was indeed the author of (or the leader of the 'wits' that produced)the literary and dramatic work known to us under the name of 'Shakespeare'. There is far more evidence, yet to be presented, that will confirm the validity of this assumption; but, in order that we may fully understand the Baconian grand design, it will be easier now to continue with the assumption that Francis Bacon was the principal playwright.

The complex and universal nature of the Baconian project, which eventually Francis Bacon called 'The Great Instauration' when he began to publish parts of it in the 1620s, meant that the Bacon brothers' expenses were very high. Yet at no time did they have much wealth of their own; nor, except for one or two notable exceptions, did they receive much support of that nature from others, which made matters very difficult for them. (It was not until Francis married and started to be appointed to official positions in King James' reign that he began to have substantial wealth of his own with which to publish and promote the work more widely.)

Anthony was the wealthier of the two brothers, having inherited various small estates and manors from his father besides the principal interest in Gorhambury as the eldest son of Sir Nicholas and Lady Anne. Francis, by contrast, was left very little—Sir Nicholas having died before he was able to purchase the inheritance that he had planned to pass on to his youngest son. Anthony, therefore, while he was still alive, together with Lady Anne (who was bound by the terms of Sir Nicholas' will to help her sons), was the main financial support for Francis and his project, although Francis must have made some small earnings from legal work and the writing of reports for the Government.

From 1595, as can be discovered from letters, not only did Anthony Bacon run an intelligence network for Essex's benefit but also he and Francis employed a scriptorium of secretaries, writers, cryptologists and translators, some working at Essex House and others working with Francis at Gray's Inn or Twickenham Park. Although Essex promised it, he never managed to pay Anthony Bacon for his service, other than allowing Anthony the use of a wing of his London home, Essex House, in which to live and have his offices. Neither did Lord Burghley, on behalf of the Queen, ever remunerate Anthony for his many years of intelligence work abroad for the Queen and State. Except for some money received from Sir Francis Walsingham in the earlier years of his foreign travel, Anthony seems to have paid for all expenses out of his own pocket, as indeed did Walsingham, who, like Anthony, used up all his wealth in the Queen's service.

It is interesting to note, however, that the eighteenth-century English historian, Thomas Birch, when researching the claim by the poet and dramatist, Sir William Davenant, that Henry Wriothesley, 3rd Earl of Southampton, had given Shakespeare £1,000 in 1597,[1] discovered that it was actually to Anthony Bacon that Southampton had given this sum. That Anthony Bacon was confused with Shakespeare in this matter is very significant to our understanding of where the true authorship lay. If, perhaps, the money was given to Anthony Bacon and then passed on (or some of it passed on) to the actor Shakespeare (which would explain the confusion), we might further deduce how and why the money for buying New Place was acquired and given to the actor Shakespeare, who from the following year onwards had his name, or an adaptation of his name, printed on the title pages of many Shakespeare plays.

First, it is worth reminding ourselves that the first appearance of the Shakespeare name on a published play occurred with the first quarto edition of *Love's Labour's Lost* and the second quarto editions of *Richard II* and *Richard III*, published in 1598 with the names of 'W. Shakespere' (for *Love's Labour's Lost*) and 'William Shake-speare' (for *Richard II and III*) on the title pages.

£1,000 was a very large sum of money in those days, well beyond the normal means of an actor from humble origins, however successful.[2] The same applied to a writer or playwright. In 1597, Will Shakespeare was not yet a sharer in the profits of the playhouse (the Globe not yet having been built), and so his earnings as a hired actor would have been less than the wage of a craftsman. A few years later, when he had become a shareholder and a principal actor in London's most successful theatre company, his theatre earnings for a few years might have topped £50–£100 a year—a high income for those days, but one which was totally dependent on how each acting season went. But in May 1597, when he was still on the low wage of a hired actor and living in relative poverty, Shakespeare suddenly acquired substantial wealth and purchased one of the largest houses in Stratford-upon-Avon, together with two barns and gardens. When he bought New Place it was in a dilapidated state and he had to carry out major renovations, but the house had once been one of the finest houses in Stratford-upon-Avon.

New Place had been built originally by Sir Hugh Clopton, but was owned by William Underhill when Shakespeare purchased it. It may come as a surprise, but the Underhills were not unknown to Francis Bacon. William Underhill was the son of William Underhill senior, an Inner Temple lawyer and clerk of assizes at Warwick. A kinsman of William Underhill, John Underhill of Loxley in Warwickshire, became a gentleman waiter in the service of Francis Bacon, when the latter was Lord Chancellor. John Underhill served at Verulam House from 1618 onwards. He rose to become gentleman-usher to Francis Bacon and steward to Lady Alice, Francis' wife. He became close to her (they were both the same age) and, when Francis died in 1626, he and Alice married. We shall also (see next page) discover a connection through the Hatton family.

Let us return to Anthony Bacon's finances. According to his wealthy uncle, Lord Burghley, Anthony 'lived like a prince', but in fact the records that exist argue against this. Anthony had to live in a small and perpetually damp room in one wing of Essex House, which required a fire to be kept burning every day of the year to make it habitable. However, Anthony did have room for his secretaries and his office (although it is not recorded what the accommodation was), and he chose to stay there, at the 'hub of the wheel' as it were. But the damp conditions played havoc with Anthony's health. He was not only lame from a riding accident in France but in continual pain from gout, which appears to have crippled him. His mother, Lady Anne Bacon, became increasingly worried about his health and several times urged him to move from Essex House to better quarters.

Records show that Anthony paid off many of his brother Francis' debts, mortgaging and selling estates inherited from his father to do so. Yet even so, both brothers had to borrow money from time to time, as the finance from the sale or mortgaging of estates was not always forthcoming in a quick and easy way. Creditors, therefore, were a continual problem. Many times either one or the other brother had to attend court and pay the exorbitant forfeits demanded for late repayment of the loans. Being a lawyer and 'learned in the law', Francis often pleaded his own case. The Shakespeare play, *The Merchant of Venice*, appears to reflect fairly accurately, in a way to suit the play's story, the friendship between the two brothers and the difficulties they endured through being forced year after year to raise loans from usurers.

In the play, Antonio is a good caricature of Anthony, who did trade abroad (but in intelligence rather than merchandise) and who hazarded all for his brother's sake. Bassanio, the friend who is helped by Antonio, is reminiscent of Francis, while the 'Portia' he sought was not only Sophia (Wisdom) on her Mountain of Beauty ('Belmont'), but his second cousin Elizabeth, Lady Hatton. She was the daughter of Sir Thomas Cecil, eldest son of Lord Burghley. Elizabeth's first husband, Sir William Hatton, was stepbrother to William Underhill of Warwickshire, who sold New Place to William Shakespeare. At the request of her family, Elizabeth married Sir William Hatton in 1594, aged seventeen. He was much older than she, but was a very wealthy man, being the heir of his uncle, Sir Christopher Hatton. When he died, in 1597, Lady Hatton inherited his wealth, including Corfe Castle and the Isle of Purbeck, and the imposing Hatton House in Holborn.

Hatton House was previously known as Ely Place, home of the Bishops of Ely, and its gardens were famous for their beauty and design. It was in strolling distance of Gray's Inn, which made it easy for Francis Bacon to visit his vivacious and attractive cousin, which he often did, delighting in her company and in the gardens. It was there, after Sir William's death, that Francis courted his cousin Elizabeth seriously, requesting her hand in marriage (she was then aged twenty, he thirty-six), but in this suit he failed. Instead, under family pressure, Lady Hatton married the Attorney-General, Sir Edward Coke, who had status and wealth.[3] *The Merchant of Venice,* written before it was known that Lady Hatton had accepted Coke's proposal of marriage, can be seen to embody Francis' aspirations while there was still apparent hope, while Hatton House with its beautiful gardens would certainly appear to be the model for Portia's home, Belmont.

During this time, Francis was actually arrested for debt—unjustly, as it happened—because of the malice of a particular creditor, and had to be rescued from the awful possibility of incarceration in the Fleet. His debt was to a goldsmith, a Mr Sympson of Lombard Street, who since the early summer of 1598 had held a bond for a loan to Francis Bacon of £300. Sympson had agreed to wait for the forfeiture of the bond until the Gray's Inn Michaelmas Term began in October. Meanwhile Francis, employed in the Queen's service, was engaged in the examination of a certain John Stanley who was held at the Tower of London, accused of a conspiracy against the Queen. Francis' part in the examination was small, but it entailed him going every day to the Tower to take depositions. While walking homeward from the Tower on 23 September, two weeks before term began and the bond became due, he was suddenly and unexpectedly arrested at the instigation of the goldsmith. He managed to get a message to Sheriff More, a personal friend, and was at once transferred to a house in Coleman Street, from where he sent urgent messages to his friends, including letters to his cousin, Sir Robert Cecil, Secretary of State, and Sir Thomas Egerton, Lord Keeper of the Great Seal. As nothing else is recorded, it is most likely that Francis was released fairly soon afterwards, once his friends had come to his assistance.

In an extraordinarily precise correlation with this incident, Shylock, in *The Merchant of Venice,* gives a fee to an officer of the law to arrest Antonio a fortnight before Antonio's bond is forfeit. This pointed similarity between the stage play and an actual historical event involving Francis suggests that he was either still writing the play in September 1598 (it was registered on 22 July 1598) or, more likely, still improving and adding to it in the final days before its first performance—which must have been in late September, since Francis Meres mentions it in his *Paladis Tamia,* published that month.

The play itself comprises two separate but interlinked tales, one regarding the wooing and winning of a wealthy heiress who is bound by the terms of her father's will as to how and whom she should marry (the Portia story), and the other concerning usury and an old law invoked by a moneylender which is neither humane nor in harmony with later laws (the Shylock story). The first story has its main setting in Belmont, a place of great beauty (as its name declares), whereas the second story has its main setting in Venice. The play as a whole reveals a first-hand knowledge of Venice and its surroundings; while both stories concern legal, political, racial and religious matters centring around the lending or giving of money, either for love or for material gain. The biblical difference between the law of judgment or severity (*i.e.,* 'an eye for an eye'), which Shylock refers to as *the* law, as if it were the only one, and the law of mercy or redemption, is made a primary theme—one that was of great importance to Francis Bacon and which he wrote about many times and in many different ways.

The Belmont story hinges upon a father's will, by which his only daughter and heiress is bound to the terms of a lottery to decide whom she should marry. The Venice story deals with laws concerning usury, with an old Roman law of the 'flesh-bond' which Shylock invokes for the penalty of late repayment of the debt owed, and with laws about harming or murdering, or intending to harm or murder, a citizen of Venice. The old Roman law of the flesh-bond is shown to be not only inhuman but in conflict with the later laws of Venice, and these later laws are shown entirely to negate the Roman law. Moreover, the more humane later laws are not perfect, but are formed out of a racial and religious bias which means, politically, that to be a citizen of Venice necessitates a person to be a Christian.

The situation requires Portia, acting the part of a barrister and counsel to the Duke, to sort out the muddle and prevent several possible miscarriages of justice and a murder. To do this, she has to discover what Shylock's motives really are. This she achieves by her careful line of questioning. She is also the one to urge mercy, pointing out that this is possible to give within the context of the law, and indeed should be given. Portia cannot change the laws of Venice, but she uses everything at her disposal as a lawyer to prevent the murder of Antonio and, at the same time, the possible execution of Shylock and confiscation of his wealth.

Not only is the play thoroughly legal in its reference, but the whole court scene displays an intimate and specialised knowledge of legal affairs in court, adapted for the purposes of the play, with Portia acting a part that combines the examining of prisoners with advising the Doge and his court on the law— a role which, as we have already seen (see chapter 9), Francis Bacon performed in the Star Chamber in 1596 and 1597.

It is also clear that built into the play is Francis Bacon's personal, first-hand knowledge of Venice and its environs, his knowledge of Venetian law and politics, and the help given him by his devoted brother Anthony, whose foreign agents even included two merchants of Venice. As for the matter of old laws, this was an issue which Francis repeatedly championed before Parliament, in an attempt to persuade Parliament of the importance of abolishing obsolete laws as well as making new ones. Humane politics and their associated laws were always of major concern to him.

Like so many of the Shakespeare plays, *The Merchant of Venice* is a true Mystery akin to the Greek Mysteries of initiation as enacted at Eleusis, the emblem of which was a pig. The name Portia means 'pig' or 'sow' (from Latin *porca*, 'sow'), as also 'offering'. In the Eleusinian Mysteries the pig was the offered sacrifice: hence in the play Portia says, 'I stand for sacrifice'.[4] In Celtic mythology the sow was an emblem of the goddess Ceridwen, the Great White Sow, who represented Wisdom, akin to the Greek Sophia. Her piglets signified the disciples and initiates of her Mystery schools. In all probability, Bacon also had in mind his family heraldic crest of a pig or boar when he chose the name for the heroine of his play, who is herself based on the woman he hoped to marry.

In the lottery scene of the Shakespeare play, Portia's suitors have to choose correctly which of three caskets contains her picture. The three caskets of lead, silver and gold refer to alchemy, in which lead is transmuted first into silver and then into gold—a process which is symbolic of the transmutation of the psyche from a leaden baseness to a silver-white purity, followed by the pure or virgin psyche giving birth to the immortal soul, shining like a golden sun. These three metals, therefore, symbolise three successive levels or states of being recognised by the classical Mystery schools and their Hermetic or

Platonic equivalents (including Freemasonry and Rosicrucianism) in the Renaissance. The three levels can be found embodied in many myths, fairy tales and allegorical accounts of world saviours.

At the same time, however, these three metals *in reverse order* can also denote the three successive degrees of initiation[5] that lift a person from one level to the next, wherein gold signifies the testing of a person's desire or will, silver the testing of a person's thoughts, and lead the testing of a person's actions. Loving kindness (as opposed to egoism or self-love), humble understanding (as opposed to arrogant pride), and self-sacrifice (love in action) are the qualities required, corresponding to the Christian formula of faith, hope and charity. As I understand it, faith refers to the intuitive awareness or 'knowing', and the trust in this that comes with being a truly loving and therefore genuinely sensitive person. Hope is the positive vision that develops as a result of understanding that love and its intuitively-sensed wisdom. Charity, which is love in action, is the greatest of the three, but dependent on the other two having been developed first. (This design—of the three degrees and levels—we can find underlying many Shakespeare plays, with perhaps the most complete example being *The Tempest*. Francis Bacon provides a succinct summary of the process, as well as a key to it, in his account of the role of imagination, as previously referred to in chapter 8, wherein sense, will or desire sends to reason via the imagination, and reason or understanding sends to action, also via the imagination.)[6]

Portia has three suitors in the lottery scene. The Prince of Morocco fails at the first test, the Prince of Arragon fails at the second, and only Bassanio passes all three tests. Bassanio is thus the right match for Portia, both of them standing for sacrifice, which itself is based on love and understanding. These are the three degrees of initiation taught in the Mystery schools, the full accomplishment of which leads to a joy excelling all other joys:

> *Bassanio.* And here choose I,—joy be the consequence!
> *Portia.* [Aside.] How all the other passions fleet to air:
>   As doubtful thoughts, and rash-embrac'd despair,
>   And shudd'ring fear, and green-eyed jealousy.
>   O love be moderate, allay thy ecstasy,
>   In measure rain thy joy, scant this excess!
>   I feel too much thy blessing, make it less
>   For fear I surfeit.
>
> Shakespeare, *Merchant of Venice*, III, ii, 107–14

But for Francis himself, this joy through marriage with a woman he loved was an elusive goal: one not yet to be.

Hopeful Aspirations

The next year, 1599, Francis continued with his grand scheme of presenting English history on stage in a dramatised and allegorised form, but choosing this time the 'missing' reign of Henry V. It is described as missing because earlier reigns had already been shown on stage, from King John onwards, and so had some of the later reigns. Shakespeare's *Life and Death of King John* had been presented in 1590. Greene's *Friar Bacon and Friar Bungay*, associated with Henry III's reign, was acted in 1589. Peele's *Edward I* (*c.*1593), Marlowe's *Edward II* (1593) and the anonymous *Edward III* (1596) covered the next three. Shakespeare's *Richard II* and *Henry IV* (Parts 1 and 2) appeared in 1595 and 1596 respectively. The subsequent monarchs Henry VI and Richard III were represented by the four Shakespeare plays, *Henry VI* (Parts 1, 2 and 3) and *Richard III*, which were written and performed as early as 1590–1.

It is thought that *Henry V* was written in the spring of 1599, as it refers very clearly to the Earl of Essex as 'the general of our gracious empress, as in good time he may, from Ireland coming, bringing rebellion broached on his sword'.[7] Against Francis Bacon's advice, Essex had successfully pressured the Queen to appoint him commander-in-chief of a large expeditionary force to be sent to Ireland to crush the Irish rebellion led by the Earl of Tyrone. On 27 March 1599, he set out for Ireland at the head of this army. The expedition was an abject failure, and Essex is reported as having employed most of his time marching around Ireland without making any contact with the rebel army, spending vast amounts of the Exchequer's money, and knighting his friends and companions with undue freedom. This was not, however, to become fully apparent until some time later. Indeed, on his departure, there were great hopes of his success. Essex was at that time the dashing hero of the country.

Francis could see the dangers of Essex leaving the Queen's side and leading such an army, which were first that the power might go to Essex' head, and second that Elizabeth would then learn to fear that power. Nonetheless, Francis' advice to both Queen and Earl fell on deaf ears. Henry V, therefore, can be seen as an attempt to offer advice and encouragement to do the noble thing and be the noble leader, under the mask of a play about one of England's supposed heroes. Francis and Anthony Bacon alike wanted Essex to be successful, but in the right way.

The play, therefore, builds upon the common perception of Henry V and his Agincourt success, and upon the contemporary hero-worship of Essex. As the deputy of the sovereign, Essex could indeed, on Elizabeth's behalf, be likened in their dreams to a victorious Henry V; but it shows King Henry growing step by step in moral and spiritual stature as well as in courage and leadership abilities. Indeed, Henry V is projected as the Renaissance ideal of a king:

one who should be a good Christian and Defender of the Faith; learned, well-versed in theology, just, merciful, self-controlled, without revenge, open to counsel from wise men; familiar with humble people but not corrupted by them; the protector and defender of his kingdom; devoted to the affairs of state, and honourably married.

The play in fact simply continues what had already been started in *Henry IV* three years earlier, when the Bacon brothers threw in their lot with Essex. Prince Hal had been selected from the start to portray the growth and development of the ideal leader, according to the ideas of Francis Bacon's own philosophy—*i.e.,* going deep into dark matter or experience, getting to know all characters, types and qualities of person, and what is good and what not, enjoying life, being friendly with all, dissembling where necessary, yet at the same time remaining untarnished by any real corruption and ready to be 'woken up' to take on responsibility when the time was right. This is what had happened to Francis when his father, Sir Nicholas, died and he had to return to England; and it is what happens to Prince Hal when his father, Henry IV, dies and he has to be king:

> *Cant.* The king is full of grace and fair regard.
> *Ely.* And a true lover of the Holy Church.
> *Cant.* The course of his youth promis'd it not.
>   The breath no sooner left his father's body,
>   But that his wildness, mortified in him,
>   Seem'd to die too; yea, at that very moment,
>   Consideration like an angel came,
>   And whipp'd th' offending Adam out of him,
>   Leaving his body as a Paradise,
>   T'envelop and contain celestial spirits.

Shakespeare, Henry V, I, i, 22—7

There is much of Francis Bacon in the Shakespeare character of Henry V, but also much of Francis' hopes and expectations of Essex. These hopes and expectations were, however, to be utterly dashed.

Forebodings

A few months later, intelligence was received that Essex was not behaving in Ireland according to the charge given him by the Queen and her government. The Queen was both alarmed and incensed, especially as there was in circulation a book referring specifically to the deposition of Richard II and dedicated to Essex, associating the Earl with the popular usurper Henry Bolingbroke and seeming to hint in its dedication that Essex, 'the great expectation of the future', should do as Bolingbroke did. This was a small volume by a young doctor of civil law, John Hayward, entitled *The First Part of the Life and Raigne of King Henrie IIII*, which was published in February 1599, just before Essex left for Ireland. After some copies had been issued, the incriminating dedication page was torn out of the remaining copies before they were circulated. A revised second edition, however, was suppressed, and Hayward was arrested on a charge of treason and of using for that purpose an old story to suit the present times.

The book derived much of its textual material and phrasing from the earlier Shakespeare play, *Richard II*, which since 1597 had been causing great agitation to the Queen because of the deposition scene. Elizabeth was being increasingly likened to King Richard by certain of her courtiers who followed Essex, whereas Essex was being associated by them with Henry Bolingbroke. Even as early as 1578, and again some time before 1588, certain of Queen Elizabeth's courtiers had been hinting at this analogy, but it wasn't until 1597 that this became serious. In 1597, seemingly because of the many performances of Shakespeare's *Richard II* and its popularity, the Queen took this to heart, as she later declared in exasperation to her Keeper of the Records of the Tower, William Lambard:

> *That which passed from the Excellent Majestie of* Queen ELIZABETH *in her Privie Chamber at East Greenwich, 4° Augusti 1601, 43° Reg. sui, towards* WILLIAM LAMBARDE.

> He presented her Majestie with his Pandecta of all her rolls, bundells, membranes, and parcells that be reposed in her Majestie's Tower at London; whereof she had given to him the charge 21st January last past ... she proceeded to further pages, and asked where she found cause of stay ... so her Majestie fell upon the reign of King Richard II, saying, 'I am Richard II. Know ye not that.... He that will forget God, will also forget his benefactors; this tragedy was played 40^tie times in open streets and houses.'

> Queen Elizabeth I to William Lambarde, 4 August 1601[8]

It is not known for certain when the first performance of *Richard II* took place, whether it was as early as 1595 or later, in 1597, when it was first registered for publication, but it evidently contained the deposition scene when first acted.[9] However, when the play was first published in 1597, and again in the next two quartos of 1598, the deposition scene was omitted, almost certainly because of the Queen's and therefore the Privy Council's concern.[10] In addition, the name of William Shakespeare was used in print for the first time in conjunction with plays, on the title pages of the 1598 quartos, *Love's Labour's Lost* ('W. Shakespere'), *Richard II* and *Richard III* ('William Shake-speare'), as already mentioned.

This suggests that it might have been because of the *Richard II* concerns that the Shakespeare mask was made more definite and associated with the plays as well as the poems. It also suggests that that the actor Will Shakespeare, acting as Bacon's mask, might have been paid a large sum of money to enable him to buy New Place, because of the potential risk involved in publicly masking such plays. Notably, no harm ever came to Will Shakespeare and the Lord Chamberlain's company, even though many of his contemporaries associated with other acting companies were thrown into jail for either writing or performing plays that were considered subversive.

The deposition of King Richard II was a historical fact, yet the deposition scene in *Richard II* could suggest not only that the general population had a right to demand the abdication of a sovereign whom they considered unfit to rule, but also that the oath and crowning of a sovereign, which supposedly bestowed a divine right to rule, could be reversed. This was a major point of contention and horror to Queen Elizabeth. In the play the hallowed oath between king and God, between king and people, and between the subject and his king, part of the coronation ceremony, is described graphically as being undone point by point. It is perhaps no wonder that Elizabeth, from her point of view, made the accusation against the author of the play as 'he that will forget God', and then went on to make the point that such a person will 'also forget his benefactors', presumably meaning the Queen herself.

There are many revolutionary ideas expressed in the Shakespeare plays, but this was stepping into particularly dangerous territory. The question of the role of sovereignty within a democracy was always an important one to Francis Bacon, and he had strong ideas about the need for a constructive partnership between sovereign and Parliament. Only a few years previous to the play's publication he had felt the wrath of the Queen after he had stood up in Parliament and, alone, successfully led the Commons in withstanding a coercive and craftily brutal attempt by the Secretary of State, Robert Cecil, on behalf of the Queen and her Ministers, to take away the vitally-important democratic privilege of the House of Commons to deny or grant subsidies to the Crown through the control of taxation. As a result he had suffered eighteen months of royal disgrace, from February 1593 to June 1594.

However, Francis was highly unlikely to have been aiming specifically at the Queen in the play of *Richard II,* as he himself did much to help and support his sovereign. Moreover, he hated armed revolutions and the like, with all the upheaval, suffering and horrors that normally attend them, and without doubt the use of this play to encourage Essex to depose the Queen and install himself as sovereign of England would have appalled him.

But, as the editor David Daniell points out in the Arden *Julius Caesar*, this was a time when the debate in Europe concerning what could best be done about tyranny was intensifying, and in England the 'aristocratic circles were using history, especially Roman history, to express easily decoded criticism of the present Governors, and government'.[11] Besides plays and poems about Pompey and Caesar that were being performed in the mid-1590s,[12] there were various 'closet' plays. Mary Herbert, Countess of Pembroke, for instance, translated Robert Garnier's *Marc Antoine* (1578) and adapted it as *The Tragedy of Antony* (written in 1590 and published in 1592 and 1595), and Samuel Daniel wrote *The Tragedy of Cleopatra* (1595), dedicated to the Countess, his patroness.

This then was the cultural and political climate when the Shakespeare *Tragedy of Julius Caesar* was written and performed. It is believed that this play about the assassination of the great Roman dictator, Caius Julius Caesar, and the civil war that followed, was composed for the opening of the newly-built Globe Theatre on Midsummer's Day 1599. In many respects, Francis Bacon esteemed Caesar highly, but principally for his calendrical reforms and his histories, as also for his ciphers, in which both Francis and his brother Anthony Bacon were specialists. Tyranny, however, Francis hated, and the play is a study in tyranny and what to do, or not do, about it. It also concerns civil liberties. Francis was a great champion of civil liberties and advocate of a strong and equal 'marriage' between the House of Commons and Her Majesty's Government in the House of Lords, for the mutual benefit of each and the overall good of the realm.

Julius Caesar, like *Henry V*, has political overtones which can be related to Essex's expedition to Ireland, in which Francis found himself involved. On the one hand, Francis, as Essex's adviser, had recommended the Earl to take on the then vacant position of Lord Deputyship of Ireland as a suitable position of honour for Essex and in the hope that the proposed treaty with the Irish leader, the Earl of Tyrone, would be concluded peacefully under Essex's supervision. On the other hand, Francis had consistently advised Essex not to get directly involved with matters of war, but to cultivate a more peaceful role and approach. His advice concerning the Deputyship of Ireland was taken, but the rest of his advice went largely unheeded.[13] Essex had already been made the Queen's Earl Marshal in 1597, having gained a great military success in the summer of 1596 when he was General-in-Chief of the expeditionary force that raided the Spanish coast, sacked Cadiz and frustrated Philip II's attempts to fit out a second Armada against England. There were those who suspected that Essex's motives were questionable and his position dangerous, and that even if he was not already secretly plotting to raise a rebellion against the Queen he might be seduced into doing so. However, despite whatever advice he received from Francis and other proponents of more peaceful means, Essex marched off as the Queen's Earl Marshal and Lord Lieutenant of Ireland at the head of the largest army ever sent to Ireland in Queen Elizabeth's reign.[14]

In *Henry V*, by changing history a little, Francis showed what a conquering general might do and be, if he had wisdom and mercy. It was also an obvious attempt to whip up national support for the endeavour, which had to be funded through people's taxes, as well as an attempt to show the legalities that were supposed to lie behind Henry V's claim to the throne of France, and to show why Henry felt he had to do something about it. But in *Julius Caesar,* Francis portrayed what could happen if such a general should impose himself as a dictator, as also what was likely to happen if an existing ruler, even if considered to be a tyrant, should be assassinated. The ageing and increasingly despotic Queen Elizabeth had, like Caesar, finally presented herself as immortal, and the horror of a civil war was always very real. The play can therefore can be seen as a timely warning to the Queen as well as to Essex and his followers.

The association of Essex with Caesar had in fact already been foreshadowed in *Henry V*. In the Prologue to the last Act of *Henry V*, for instance, King Henry is compared to Caesar, and both are likened to the Earl of Essex:

> But now behold,
> In the quick forge and working-house of thought,
> How London doth pour out her citizens!
> The mayor and all his brethren in best sort –
> Like to the senators of th'antique Rome,
> With the plebeians swarming at their heels –
> Go forth and fetch their conqu'ring Caesar in:
> As, by a lower but by loving likelihood,
> Were now the general of our gracious empress,
> As in good time he may, from Ireland coming,
> Bringing rebellion broached on his sword,
> How many would the peaceful city quit
> To welcome him!

Shakespeare, Henry V, v, Chorus, 22–34

Julius Caesar provides a great study in oratory, as also in certain emotions. The prime example of oratory is that of Brutus and Mark Antony in the Roman Forum, speaking to the populace after the assassination of Caesar. Brutus, the noble and stoic politician, delivers a carefully-prepared speech, logical and rhetorically correct according to the classical rules of academia. However, he and his words are emotionally and mentally disengaged from his audience and he is taken by surprise at the unintended effect they have on the plebeians. Antony, by contrast, whose sensual Asiatic life-style is a complete polar opposite to Brutus' austere Roman sobriety, speaks words charged with emotion that are fully engaged with his audience's feelings and thoughts, which he is able to lead and manipulate as he wills. Like an actor, Antony uses stage props and gestures to great effect, which Brutus would never even contemplate in his pure stoicism. Antony, of course, wins the day, 'proving' Francis Bacon's argument that a purely academic approach to life is a dead way, whereas in order to discover and work with truth one has to be fully involved with the emotions and life as it is, not as we think it might be.

The best example of a specific study in emotion is that of anger, which is to be found in the famous quarrel between Brutus and Cassius, a quarrel that takes place in their tent before the battle with Mark Antony's army.[15] In this one scene the stages of their quarrel develop step by step in accordance with that delineated by Francis Bacon in his essay, *Of Anger,* leading up to a final appeasement which is possible and essential before the matter is broken off, lest there be mischief done. The three chief causes and motives,[16] and the corresponding restraints and remedies, are illustrated in detail. The play also presents a good study of envy, dealt with similarly in another of Francis' essays.[17]

Then, in true Baconian brilliance, although the external story of *Julius Caesar* is about the murder of Caesar and the civil war that follows, beneath this outer veil is an inner allegorical story or Mystery concerning the third degree of initiation, in which there are a great many Freemasonic allusions (see my book, *The Wisdom of Shakespeare in Julius Caesar*). Fittingly, Caesar dies from thirty-three stab wounds.

As for the incident of Hayward's book, what is not often realised is that the Queen specifically called for Francis Bacon, who was then one of her Counsel Learned in the Law, to give his opinion on whether there was treason in the book. Of this interview with the Queen, Francis Bacon made a careful report, contained in his lengthy *Apologie concerning the Earl of Essex* that he wrote in 1604 to the Lord Lieutenant of Ireland, the Earl of Devonshire. In it, Francis explains and puts on record the truth of what had happened concerning the Earl of Essex and himself during those troubles:

> About the same time I remember an answer of mine in a matter which had some affinity with my Lord's cause, which though it grew from me, went after about in other's names. For her Majesty being mightily incensed with that book which was dedicated to my Lord of Essex, being a story of the first year of King Henry the fourth, thinking it a seditious prelude to put into the people's heads boldness and faction, said she had good opinion that there was treason in it, and asked me if I could not find any places in it that might be drawn within case of treason: whereto I answered: for treason surely I found none; but for felony very many. And when her Majesty hastily asked me wherein, I told her the author had committed very apparent theft, for he had taken most of the

sentences of Cornelius Tacitus, and translated them into English, and put them into his text.

> Francis Bacon, *Apologie in certaine imputations concerning the late Earle of Essex*
> (1604)[18]

Francis admits to the matter having 'grown from him', and having gone about 'in other's names'. The reference to the author stealing from Tacitus is curious, for in fact Hayward's book does not seem to steal from Tacitus at all, and the source it does steal from, the Shakespeare play of *Richard II,* itself has hardly any borrowings from Tacitus. Francis would have known better than that, and so would the Queen, therefore Francis' meaning must have been something else. He was surely playing a game of wit with the Queen, who was known to appreciate such repartee; for Tacitus was a good synonym for himself, Francis Bacon, as the author of the Shakespeare histories.

Cornelius Tacitus (*c.* 55–120 AD) had been an eminent pleader at the Roman bar and a man of high moral character, who wrote his *Annals* and *Histories* covering the successive reigns of Roman emperors from Tiberius to Domitian. He wrote with a high aim, regarding it as being 'history's highest function to rescue merit from oblivion, and to hold up as a terror to base words and actions the reprobation of posterity'.[19] He was primarily concerned with ethics rather than politics, and the *Annals* and *Histories* are noted for their fine studies of human character.

Bacon considered this interview with the Queen to be so important that he made sure that the event was recorded doubly and publicly by also including the story in his book of *Apophthegms*, published in 1625:

> The book of deposing Richard the second, and the coming in of Henry the fourth, supposed to be written by Dr. Hayward, who was committed to the Tower for it, had much incensed queen Elizabeth. And she asked Mr. Bacon, being then of her learned counsel; *Whether there were any treason contained in it?* Mr. Bacon intending to do him a pleasure, and to take off the Queen's bitterness with a jest, answered; *No, madam, for treason I cannot deliver opinion that there is any, but very much felony.* The Queen, apprehending it gladly, asked; *How? and wherein?* Mr. Bacon answered; *Because he had stolen many of his sentences and conceits out of Cornelius Tacitus.*
>
> Francis Bacon, Apophthegm 58, *Apopthegms New and Old* (1625)[20]

Bacon worked hard with the Queen to save Hayward from being charged as a traitor, which would have culminated with the inevitable and awful death that used to follow a conviction. He also laboured, at the expense of his own personal safety and standing with the Queen, to calm the Queen's rage and allay her suspicions about Essex. Continuing his account, it is clear that Bacon

sort' and 'other self', must have been great. Yet, except for the dedication by Francis of his first edition of *Essays* and *Coulers of Good and Evil* to his 'loving and beloved brother' in 1597, there seems to have been no fitting tribute or remembrance made for Anthony, a much-loved man who gave a lifetime of service to his Queen, his country, his brother Francis, the Earl of Essex and the advancement of learning—unless of course we can count a poem by a foreign poet eulogising Anthony as an 'English Phoenix of celestial origin … the flower of virtue, rare and perfect':

Poeme compose d'un artifice nouveau
Sur le nom, et surnom
Du seigneur
Anthoine Bacon.

A.	Anglois phenix de celeste origine,
N.	Né pour orner et la terre et les cieulx,
T.	Ton renom bruit iusques auz envieux:
H.	Honneur te sert, et vertu te domine:
O.	Ornement seul de sagesse et doctrine,
I.	Iour, et clarité de tout Coeur genereux:
N.	Nous ne scaurions regarder de nos yeux
E.	Eternité qui devant toi chemine.
	Bacone.
B.	Bacon fior di virtu, raro e perfetto
A.	Animo pronto, Angelico intelletto,
C.	Chiaro lume d'honor e caritade
O.	Ornamento e beltà di nostra etade,
N.	Natural real di fideltà pieno
E.	Essempio d'ogni ben sempre sereno.

It is worth noting also that in 1601, the year of Anthony's death, a book by Robert Chester called *Loves Martyr or Rosaline's Complaint* was published. In it was printed the mystical Shakespeare love poem, *The Phoenix and Turtle*, in which a phoenix and turtledove were so united in love that they fled this world in a 'mutual flame' of love.

Light at the End

It took over a year for Anthony Bacon's estate to be sorted out and his debts repaid, with probate being granted on 23 June 1602. It was not until 20 November that year, when his mother signed over her life-interest in Gorhambury to him, that Francis had full control of his inheritance. A few months later, on

24 March 1603, Queen Elizabeth died and James VI of Scotland was proclaimed King James I of England. James' coronation took place on 23 July 1603, at which time Francis was knighted along with three hundred other gentlemen.

From 1589 to 1600 the composition of Shakespeare plays, as far as we know, had averaged about two a year, except for two notable exceptions. The first was the period of the plague years, from summer 1592 to summer 1594, when no plays were forthcoming (instead *Venus and Adonis* and *Lucrece* were published, in 1593 and 1594 respectively). The second was a special burst of three light-hearted plays written at the end of 1594 for the Christmas Revels at Gray's Inn (*Comedy of Errors* and *Love's Labour's Lost*) and the marriage of Elizabeth de Vere and William, Earl of Derby, on 26 January 1595 (*Midsummer Night's Dream*). But during the three years from the start of the Essex troubles to the end of Elizabeth's reign only one play a year was produced—*Hamlet* (1600), *Twelfth Night* (1601/2) and *Troilus and Cressida* (1602/3), the second and third of these being written almost certainly for the Middle Temple and Gray's Inn Christmas Revels respectively. The start of the new reign was also the start of the Shakespeare plays being written again at a rate of approximately two a year (with the exception of 1605, the *Lear* year), until 1607, when Francis was appointed Solicitor-General. From then on, until the last Shakespeare play (*Henry VIII*) in 1613, the plays appeared at the average rate of one a year. They stopped altogether, as far as we know, at the time Francis became Attorney-General in October 1613.

It was, perhaps, with some feeling that, in terms of its title, *All's Well That Ends Well* should be the first to appear in 1603, with Queen Elizabeth solemnly interred in Westminster Abbey and King James safely on the throne. Both Francis and, it would seem, Anthony had laboured hard to ensure that this succession would take place, so as to avert the possibility of civil war or Catholic invasion from abroad: for Elizabeth had repeatedly refused to name her successor. Thus, when James VI of Scotland arrived in England, Francis sought his favour mainly on the grounds of 'the infinite devotion and incessant endeavours (beyond the strength of his body and nature of the times) which appeared in my good brother towards your Majesty's service.... All which endeavour and duties for the most part were common to myself with him though by design (as between brothers) dissembled.'[28] King James listened, and in July 1603 the King appointed Francis Bacon as one of his Counsel Extraordinary, following this in August next year by raising him to King's Counsel Learned and granting Francis a pension of £60 a year in consideration of his brother's 'good, faithful, and acceptable service'.

Measure for Measure followed *All's Well,* and then *Othello* and *Timon of Athens*; while 1605 saw the appearance of *King Lear*. That year also saw the publication of the first version of Francis' *Advancement and Proficience of Learning*, which for the first time publicly laid out his aims. Two further great tragedies, *Macbeth* and *Antony and Cleopatra,* appeared in 1606, the former probably being composed for the performance before King James I and King Christian of Denmark at Hampton Court on 7 August 1606. It was that year, in May 1606, that Francis married Alice Barnham, eldest daughter of Benedict Barnham. Her mother at the time of the marriage was known as Lady Packington, for Alice's father had died when she was five years ten months old and her mother remarried, her new husband being a Knight of the Bath, Sir John Packington of Hampton Lovett in Worcestershire.[29]

Francis and Alice's marriage took place on 10 May 1606 at St Marylebone Chapel in London. His love of drama and splendid costume was on this occasion exceedingly visible, as he was, according to Dudley Carleton, 'clad from top to toe in purple and had made himself and his wife such store of fine raiments of cloth of silver and gold that it draws deep into her portion'.[30] Purple was in fact an extraordinary colour to wear, especially 'top to toe', for the colour was normally reserved for royalty, something incorporated in a still-extant law of 1464 wherein it states that no commoner might wear purple.[31]

The following June, Francis was given his first major appointment in the King's service, as Solicitor-General. Only one Shakespeare play, *Pericles,* appeared that year—the first of the Romances. From then on, the plays averaged one a year—*Coriolanus* (*c.* 1608), *Cymbeline* (*c.* 1609), *The Tempest* (*c.* 1610) *The Winter's Tale* (*c.* 1611) and *Henry VIII* (*c.* 1612–13), with parts of the latter being co-written by John Fletcher. In his legal profession, Francis was elected Treasurer of Gray's Inn and Clerk to the Star Chamber in 1609, Judge of the Marshal's Court and President of the Court of the Verge in 1611, and Attorney-General in October 1613. Coincident with this last and somewhat taxing appointment is a cessation in the appearance of the Shakespeare plays. There are two further plays that can be claimed to form part of the Shakespeare canon, but they are co-authored by Fletcher: *The History of Cardenio,* which is lost, and *The Two Noble Kinsmen,* which was not only co-written by Fletcher but also had only Fletcher's name on the title page. The date given for the writing of these two plays is 1612–13.

After this, Francis went on to become a Privy Councillor in June 1616, Lord Keeper of the Great Seal in March 1617 and Lord High Chancellor in January 1618. He had the title of Baron Verulam of Verulam bestowed on him in July 1618 and that of Viscount St Alban in February 1621. This was the peak of his career, the 'star' of his service to King and country, before his betrayal by the King and impeachment in March 1621. The impeachment was unjust; and yet, as we shall discover, if it had not happened we might not have been left the Folio of the Shakespeare plays.

A Rosicrucian Drama

The play that is traditionally thought of as Shakespeare's 'last play' but which is printed first in the Folio is *The Tempest*. Historically it is not really the last written, as *The Winter's Tale* and *Henry VIII* follow it. However, the matter in it has something to do with the author signing himself off from the performance of his magic—Prospero seeming to represent the author, and his magic the author's poetic ability and stagecraft. Once his project has gathered to a head, Prospero breaks his magic staff and drowns his magic book. Of course, the story is also about far more than this, and Prospero represents many other things.

The story of *The Tempest* is one of initiation and is both complex and beautiful. Of all the Shakespeare plays it is perhaps the most fully-expounded allegory of initiation on all the main levels of being (*i.e.*, as represented by the alchemical elements of earth, water, air, fire and ether). It is one of the three Shakespeare plays that are not based on previously-published stories (*Midsummer Night's Dream* and *Love's Labour's Lost* being the other two). Its first recorded performance took place before King James I at Whitehall on the night of Hallowmas 1611, when it was performed by the King's Men, formerly known as the Lord Chamberlain's Men. It was acted again before the Court during the winter of 1612–13, as part of the grand and prolonged entertainments provided for the visit of Frederick, the Elector Palatine, on his betrothal and subsequent marriage to King James' daughter, the Princess Elizabeth, on St Valentine's Day 1613.

A large proportion of descriptive material for *The Tempest* is derived from the various accounts of the New Found Lands of America. For instance, Shakespeare's dramatic account of the tempest and Prospero's island is largely inspired by the report of the shipwreck of the *Sea-Adventure* upon the Bermuda Islands on the 25 July 1609 and the subsequent experiences of the crew.

The *Sea-Adventure* story began in May 1609 when a fleet of nine ships and five hundred colonists on board set out from England to North America, to strengthen Captain John Smith's Virginian colony at Jamestown. This fleet was sponsored by the Virginia Company, whose principal shareholders and founding Council members included William, Earl of Montgomery, and Philip, Earl of Pembroke (the 'Incomparable Paire' to whom the 1623 Shakespeare Folio is dedicated), the Earl of Southampton (to whom *Venus and Adonis* and *Lucrece* were dedicated), the Earl of Salisbury, Sir George Somers, Sir Thomas Gates and Sir Francis Bacon.

The Virginia Company was first formed as two separate companies in 1606: the Virginia Company of London and the Virginia Company of Plymouth. Both sent ships to the New World, but only the London Virginia Company had early success, in the settling of Jamestown, the first permanent English settlement in North America. It was established on 14 May 1607 by an expedition under the command of Captain John Smith. At Jamestown leadership was a problem, although Smith exerted some sort of control, and so in 1609 the Company obtained a new royal charter establishing a new governing council composed entirely of company members who were empowered to appoint an all-powerful governor or governors in the colony. The new council decided on a single governor and appointed Sir Thomas West, Lord De la Warr, to the post. Sir Henry Hobart and Sir Francis Bacon, the latter being at that time the King's Solicitor-General, prepared the charter for King James' signature. This charter of 1609 and the later one of 1612 were the beginnings of constitutionalism in North America and the germ of the later Constitution of the United States.

In the end, Lord De la Warr was not able to leave England and Sir Thomas Gates was appointed his substitute. Sir Thomas, together with Sir George Somers, sailed in the flagship of the fleet, the *Sea-Adventure*. However, before the fleet had reached the shores of America a storm blew up which separated the *Sea-Adventure* from the rest of the fleet. The wind drove the flagship towards the coast of the Bermudas, where the crew were forced to run their ship ashore. All those on board managed not only to get safely to shore but also to save a large part of the ship's fittings and stores. The other ships of the fleet, with one exception, managed to reach the mainland of America, but in the belief that the *Sea-Adventure* had perished with all aboard her. A report was sent back to England before the end of 1609 giving news of the storm and the supposed foundering of the ship.

The Bermudas had always been held in a mixture of awe and fear by mariners, since the islands, uninhabited at that time, appeared magical, with a constant stormy play of thunder and lightning around their great towering cliffs. No-one went near the islands if they could help it. Some thought they were the abode of 'witches and devils, which grew by reason of accustomed monstrous thunderstorms and tempests',[32] others that they were a remnant of the sacred islands of Atlantis, ruled over by Neptune and Jupiter. The shipwrecked survivors discovered, however, that the interior of the island upon which they were cast was like a demi-paradise, fertile and with plenty of good food and water to sustain life. They continued to live there for a further nine months, managed to refloat and revictual the ship (which was preserved intact) and eventually sailed on to Virginia, reaching the Jamestown colony in May 1610.

The report of this 'miracle' arrived in England in the autumn of that year, together with some of the sailors involved. Various narratives of the wreck were published as a result. However, the official but confidential report on the Bermudas shipwreck and on the state of Virginia generally was a private letter written by William Strachey, Sir Thomas Gates' secretary, to the Council members of the Virginia Company, entitled *The True Reportory of the Wracke and Redemption of Sir Thomas Gates,* dated 15 July 1610. This confidential report was not published until 1625, when it was included in *Purchas His Pilgrimes;*[33] but Bacon, being privy to the report, was in a position to use the story and specific details from it in *The Tempest.* Moreover, when the Virginia Council published their own *True Declaration of the state of the Colonie in Virginia, with a confutation of such scandalous reports as have tended to the disgrace of so worthy an enterprise* (1610), it contained certain important moralisings that can be found in *The Tempest* as basic precepts.

The Tempest actually appears to be a dramatised portrayal of Bacon's scheme for the advancement and proficience of learning; especially what he terms the 'Active Science'—the restoration of the state of Paradise.[34] In this *active* science human beings would, like Prospero, be able to command the very elements of nature through a practical knowledge of the laws of nature, physical and metaphysical, but with everything dedicated to doing good—*i.e.,* to charity or mercy. Prospero, therefore, can be seen as a representation of one of the Rosicrucian philosopher–scientists illustrated in Bacon's *New Atlantis,* known there as the brethren of Salomon's House or College of the Six Days' Work, who are delving into metaphysics and endeavouring to discover and know truth by means of its spiritual form—gradually learning how to release it, direct it, embody it and work with it. Bacon believed that the higher spiritual forms, which are those of love, command and can therefore change the lower forms of nature. The spiritual forms are archetypes or laws, personified as angels or spirits. The spiritual form that Prospero works with in *The Tempest* is called Ariel, a name which in Cabalistic tradition is given to the angel of compassion and love. The *New Atlantis* was written at the same time as *The Tempest* but not published until 1626–7, just after Bacon's death.

One other fascinating source for *The Tempest* is the history of Ludovico Sforza, Duke of Milan, particularly because of its link with Boccalini's *Ragguagli di Parnasso* ('News from Parnassus').[35] This history is given in the *Treasury of Ancient and Modern Times,* translated out of the Spanish of Pedro Mexia and Francesco Sansovino, that was published in London by William Jaggard between 1613–19:

> Ludovic Sforza was brother to Galeas Sforza, duke of Milan, named by some John Andrea, whom he nourished and brought up, and slew in the church of St. Stephen, in Milan, as he was there present at the hearing of mass, albeit they were both sons of the famous warrior, Francis Sforza. By the death of Galeas, a son of his named John, very young in years, remained his successor in the tutelage of Bona, his mother, and of Chico, a native of Calabria, who had been much favoured by his father and grandfather. This Chico immediately banished Ludovic, who wandered as a fugitive through strange countries, and tasted the mutabilities of fortune.

The history continues with an account of how Ludovico (Ludovic), returning from his banishment, forcibly entered Milan and expelled Bona and Chico. He then ruled Milan for the next twenty years with great wisdom and spirit. He married off his nephew, the Duke Ferdinando (Ferdinand), to the daughter of the King of Naples. Taking into account various changes and adaptations, it is possible to see that the names and titles of some characters in *The Tempest* are taken from this history, as well as some of the play's story.[36]

Francesco (Francis) Sforza, father of Ludovico and Galeas, is mentioned in the 53rd Advertisement of Boccalini's *Ragguagli di Parnasso*, published in Venice in 1612. The story or 'Advertisement' relates how Apollo admitted Francesco Sforza into Parnassus. The 77th Advertisement in Boccalini's book is called 'The Universal and General Reformation of the Whole Wide World' and relates how Apollo, concerned about the dreadful state of human affairs, tries to form a society of men famous for wisdom and virtue who could carry out the required reformation. He was, however, unable to find anyone who had even half the qualifications required, so he decided instead to leave the world in the hands of the Seven Wise Men of Greece, plus two Romans and an Italian. The end result was disagreement and confusion, and so the men forthwith abandoned the world as incurable and took to providing for their own safety.

Boccalini's 77th Advertisement was bound together with and used to introduce the *Fama Fraternitatis* of the Rosicrucians. The Rosicrucian fraternity announced their existence with a set of manifestos, the first being the *Fama Fraternitatis, or a Discovery of the Fraternity of the Most Noble Order of the Rosy Cross,* the second being the *Confessio Fraternitatis.* Boccalini's *Universal and General Reformation of the Whole Wide World* supplied the main title of the Rosicrucian manifesto and set the scene for the *Fama,* the latter being the answer to the dilemma posed in the former. That is to say, the aim of the Rosicrucian fraternity was to bring about the required cleansing and reformation of the world, according to a 'perfect Method of all Arts' that their Father, 'Fra. C.R.C.', had devised.

The *General Reformation* and *Fama* were, as far as is known, first published in August 1614, but were circulating in manuscript at the time that *The Tempest* and *New Atlantis* were written. The Palatinate Court of the Elector Frederick and Princess Elizabeth at Heidelberg became a major focus of Rosicrucian thought and development in Germany, and it is significant that *The Tempest* was acted before them immediately prior to their marriage and departure for Germany.

This Rosicrucian association is given further weight by Ben Jonson's masque, *The Fortunate Isles and their Union,* designed for performance at Court on Twelfth Night, 1626. This Jonsonian masque is a parody of *The Tempest* and a cryptic satire on the Rosicrucians. It alludes to certain Rosicrucian matters and influences that are embodied in *The Tempest,* while at the same time providing indications of the esoteric meanings of various characters and events in Shakespeare's play.

Jonson also played his part at the time of the writing of *The Tempest*. He produced a play about a magician and the occult sciences called *The Alchemist* that was performed in 1610 by the King's Men. As he did in *The Fortunate Isles,* in *The Alchemist* Jonson went out of his way to satirise not only magic and magicians but also (seemingly) the whole early-seventeenth century Hermetic-Scientific and Neoplatonic-Cabalistic movement (*i.e.,* the Rosicrucians), which in this instance he does by sketching a portrait of a charlatan magician who, in the company of a whore, deliberately cheats society. *The Alchemist* even parodies the masque scene in *The Tempest* with a fake vision of the Fairy Queen presented by the false magician to one of his weak-minded dupes. But, despite his satire, Jonson was also a proven supporter of the Arthurian and Elizabethan 'Fairie' revival that is based upon the very movement he appears to satirise.

A Finale

Two further Shakespeare plays followed *The Tempest: The Winter's Tale* and *Henry VIII*. *The Winter's Tale* is the last of the great Romances, and is based very much on the story of Demeter and Persephone as acted out in the Eleusinian Mysteries of ancient Greece, just as *The Tempest* is founded upon Virgil's *Æneid,* in particular Book VI, in which Virgil cryptically reveals the classical Mysteries of initiation which allegorically led the candidate, via a tempest and the Underworld of Hades, through the Pillars of Hercules to the Fortunate Isles in the West. Demeter was also known as Hermione (*i.e.,* Harmony), which name is used in *The Winter's Tale* for the Queen of Sicilia, wife of Leontes, Sicilia's King. Persephone became the 'lost one' in the Mystery story, abducted to the Underworld by Hades, and in the version of the Mystery as acted at Cumae, the abduction was said to have taken place in Sicily (Sicilia). Perdita, the daughter of Hermione in the Shakespeare play, means 'the lost one'. But she is found again, both in the play and in the Eleusinian Mysteries, and her mother, seemingly dead through grief, is restored to life. As the embodiment of beauty and love, Perdita represents truth—the truth that was cast away, lost and then found. It is a major classical theme, and one that Francis took up in earnest. A beautiful illustration of this can be seen on the title page of his 1626 *New Atlantis,* where Time brings forth hidden Truth from the Underworld, restoring her to her mother and restoring both to the world (see Chapter 8).

Like all the plays, the esoteric level of meaning is not Francis' only concern, and he invariably incorporates political points of view and details of contemporary life, especially personal ones that are of amusement value and

Into our hands, and to confine yourself
To Asher House, my lord of Winchester's,
Till you hear further from his highness.

Henry VIII, III, ii, 228–32

The two additional lords—the Earl of Surrey, who was also the Earl of Arundel, and the Earl of Pembroke, the Lord Chamberlain—were the ones who, together with the Lord Treasurer and Lord Steward, relieved Francis Bacon of his Great Seal on 1 May 1621.[39]

Chapter 11

The Shakespeare Team

Bacon's Good Pens

The Bacon brothers gathered around themselves teams of scholars, writers and secretaries to assist them in their grand project. As we saw in chapter 7, Francis referred to these helpers as his 'good pens'. These 'good pens' included scholars, lawyers, university wits and poets who acted as secretaries, writers, translators, copyists and cryptographers; and they dealt with correspondence, translations, copying, ciphers, essays, books, plays and masques. Whether they were all employed by either Francis or Anthony Bacon, or simply collaborated voluntarily on certain projects, we don't know, but some of them certainly were directly employed—hence Francis Bacon's note to his brother in January 1595: 'I have here an idle pen or two, specially one that was cozened, thinking to have got some money this term. I pray you send me somewhat else for them to write out.'[1] There were others also, more eminent in their profession, who assisted from time to time.

We know from a number of sources, including the Bacon brothers' correspondence, Rawley's biography and Aubrey's diary, that besides Gray's Inn lawyers these 'good pens' included, at different times, people such as Nicholas Faunt, a good friend of Anthony's who had been secretary and foreign emissary to Sir Francis Walsingham when the latter was the Queen's Secretary of State; Anthony Standen, who was first Walsingham's then Anthony's secret foreign agent; Tom Lawson, Anthony's personal secretary and courier; and Jaques Petit, Anthony's page and courier. There were also lesser-known assistants, such as William Philippes and Edward Jones, all of whom were mainly working with Anthony Bacon on intelligence matters. On other more literary matters there were the poets John Lyly, Ben Jonson, John Florio, John Davies of Hereford, Sir John Davies and George Herbert. There was also the multilingual theologian and scholar, Dr Lancelot Andrewes, Master of Pembroke College, Cambridge, who became Dean of Westminster in 1601, then later Bishop of Chichester, Ely and Winchester respectively, who co-directed the translation of the Bible and who was not only a good friend of long-standing but also Francis' 'inquisitor' during the writing of his *Advancement of Learning*. There was a clergyman and physician, Timothy Bright, who published *Characterie* (1588), the first book on shorthand, and *A Treatise on Melancholy* (1586); the Clarenceux King-of-Arms, William Camden, who had granted John Shakespeare a coat of arms; plus Thomas Hobbes, Thomas Bushell, Peter Böener, Tobie Mathew, a Mr. Young, Sir Thomas Meautys, Doctor Hacket, Bishop of Lichfield, and Dr William Rawley, all of whom I refer to in more detail below.

There were clearly many more, but who they might have been is not certain. Francis Bacon's allusion to 'Ye law at Twick'nam for merrie tales'² obviously suggests that other lawyers from Gray's Inn and possibly other Inns of Court made up this writers' group, at least in the earlier days and maybe throughout the Shakespeare period. Letters show that Gray's Inn men were still assisting Francis in the last years of his life, when he was trying to complete the writing that he had planned for the Great Instauration. Then there were, at the beginning of the 'Shake-scene' era, the university wits of the 1580s whose chief was the author Shakespeare, as suggested by Ben Jonson and Robert Greene (see chapter 3). One of these was Thomas Watson who, as we have seen, was paired with Shakespeare by William Clerke in his *Polimanteia* (see chapter 6).

Besides being a member of the London literary set, Watson was also a lawyer (although he never practised as such) who seems to have spent some time in Italy in the 1570s studying law. Like Chapman, Marlowe and others, Watson was patronised by Sir Francis Walsingham, whom he had met in Paris in 1581, and by Sir Francis' brother, Thomas. Watson wrote both English and Latin verse as well as sonnets and plays. His plays, which were praised for their wit, are unfortunately lost, but his most famous known work is *Hekatompathia*, a collection of one hundred English sonnets that were published in 1582. He also wrote a prose work on memory, and published (in 1590) a collection of Italian madrigals.

Shakespeare scholarship over many years has enabled us to see, or surmise, who in one way or another appears to have collaborated on the Shakespeare plays. This would, of course, make each name part of the same team at some point in time—a team led by their 'Apollo'. This list, if we include those who are closely associated, even if not as collaborators, comprises the following poets and dramatists, who flourished (fl.) in the periods given. Dates in italics are uncertain.

Collaboration took place with:

George Peele	(1558–1596)	Oxford	fl. 1581–1596
Robert Greene	(1560–1592)	Cambridge; Oxford	fl. 1586–1592
Christopher Marlowe	(1564–1593)	Cambridge	fl. 1587–1593
Thomas Heywood	(1574–1641)	Cambridge	fl. 1598–1619
Thomas Middleton	(1580–1627)	Oxford; Gray's Inn	fl. 1598–1627
John Day	(1574–1640)	Cambridge	fl. 1599–1608
George Wilkins	(????–????)	?	fl. 1604–1608
John Fletcher	(1579–1625)	Cambridge	fl. 1606–1625
Philip Massinger	(1583–1640)	Oxford	fl. 1616–1633

Influences from:

Sir Philip Sidney	(1554–1586)	Oxford	fl. 1578–1586
Edmund Spenser	(1552–1599)	Cambridge	fl. 1578–1599
John Lyly	(1554–1606)	Oxford	fl. 1578–1590
Thomas Lodge	(1558–1625)	Oxford; Lincoln's Inn	fl. 1581–1603
Thomas Watson	(1557–1592)	Oxford	fl. 1582–1590
Thomas Nashe	(1567–1601)	Cambridge	fl. 1589–1599
Thomas Kyd	(1558–1594)	Merchant Taylor's School	fl. 1589–1593
Samuel Daniel	(1562–1619)	Oxford	fl. 1592–1615
Francis Beaumont	(1584–1616)	Oxford; Inner Temple	fl. 1600–1613

Association with:

Thomas Sackville	(1536–1608)	Cambridge; In. Temple	fl. 1560–1580
Gabriel Harvey	(1550–1630)	Cambridge	fl. 1574–1593
Edward Dyer	(1543–1607)	Oxford	fl. 1578–1607
Fulke Greville	(1554–1628)	Cambridge	fl. 1578–1628
Mary Sidney	(1561–1621)		fl. 1578–1615
Nicholas Breton	(1545–1626)	Oxford	fl. 1580–1616
Edward de Vere	(1550–1604)	Cambridge; Gray's Inn	fl. 1580–1604
Sir John Davies	(1569–1626)	Oxford; Middle Temple	fl. 1590–1603
Henry Chettle	(1560–1607)		fl. 1592–1607
Thomas Dekker	(1572–1632)		fl. 1592–1612
Michael Drayton	(1563–1631)		fl. 1593–1612
George Chapman	(1559–1634)		fl. 1594–1624
Anthony Munday	(1560–1633)		fl. 1594–1618
Ben Jonson	(1572–1637)	Westminster School	fl. 1597–1631
John Davies of Hereford	(1565–1618)		fl. 1603–1618
John Ford	(1586–1640)	Oxford; Middle Temple	fl. 1613–1634
George Wither	(1588–1667)	Oxford; Lincoln's Inn	fl. 1613–1666
William Browne	(1591–1643)	Oxford; Inner Temple	fl. 1613–1643

A major ongoing work during the time that Anthony Bacon was working at Essex House, in liaison with his brother Francis, was the voluminous correspondence exchanged between Anthony in particular and all the many foreign correspondents—diplomats, noblemen, statesmen, princes, poets, philosophers, and spies. Intelligence of all kinds was gathered and exchanged, and for this many cryptographic methods were employed. The correspondence received had to be both translated and deciphered, and outgoing correspondence suitably encrypted. The Bacon brothers used the intelligence for several purposes. One was to inform the Queen and her ministers of matters pertaining to the security of England, and of political and religious developments abroad. The Earl of Essex was a particular recipient of the appropriate information, Anthony acting as the Earl's friend and private 'secretary of state'. Another purpose was to gather knowledge or 'light'—studies of human nature and the world at large, and of scientific discoveries and philosophical insights. Anthony had correspondents all over Europe, as well as in England, Scotland and Ireland.[3]

Those directly serving Francis acted as his amanuenses, writing down in a shorthand invented by Francis whatever he dictated to them, and then copying it out in full later, ready to be corrected or revised by him. They would often make further copies to send to Anthony or other particular friends, such as Tobie Mathew, for their opinions and criticism of the work before publication.

Next to Anthony, Tobie Mathew (1577–1655) was clearly very important. Francis Bacon refers to two people as his closest friends and confidants—his brother Anthony first and foremost, and Tobie Mathew. Tobie Mathew was the eldest son of Dr Tobie Mathew, Dean of Christ Church, Oxford, later Bishop of Durham and ultimately Archbishop of York. From the age of eighteen Tobie had known Francis, having acted the Squire in Essex's *Device*, written by Francis, on the Anniversary of the Queen's Accession Day in 1595. He was admitted to Gray's Inn on 15 May 1599, aged twenty-two, where he was on intimate terms with both Francis and Anthony Bacon. He became a barrister and a Member of Parliament, first for Newport, Cornwall, then in March 1604 for St Albans, taking over Francis' seat when the latter resigned it in his favour and sat instead for Ipswich. In 1604 Tobie obtained permission to visit France for six months, and on 3 July he set sail for the continent. He returned secretly to London during March–April 1605, and on 1 May 1605 set sail again for France, this time continuing on to Florence where, in June 1606, he became a Roman Catholic. In November 1605, soon after the Gunpowder Plot, Francis sent Tobie a copy of his first edition of *The Advancement of Learning,* which had been published in October 1605.

In the summer of 1607, Mathew returned to England, where he was imprisoned for sixteen months for his Catholic persuasions, until Francis managed to intercede for him and secure his release. But Tobie was then banished from England, and he left for the continent once again in April 1608, where he travelled widely. In 1611 he went to Rome to study for the priesthood. He was ordained in Rome three years later, in May 1614. During all this time he maintained a frequent correspondence with Francis, who sent Tobie various samples of his writings and interchanged various literary ideas. Tobie eventually returned to England in July 1617 and stayed with Francis, who was then Lord Keeper, but was banished for a second time in December 1618 and went to Flanders. Tobie was eventually allowed back to England just after Francis' impeachment in 1621, where he was employed by King James to help forward the proposed marriage of Prince Charles with the Infanta of Spain. He journeyed to Madrid in May 1623 for this purpose, where the Prince and the Marquess of Buckingham joined him. The suit was not successful, but Tobie was knighted for his part in the negotiations. He was banished for the third and final time in 1642, living in exile in Flanders until his death in 1655, during which time he became a Jesuit.

Francis Bacon was known to work fast, quoting from memory, from an enormous store of sources. He usually knew exactly where to find a quotation, often pointing it out to his secretaries for them to check. His mind was so active and his capacity for work was so enormous that he kept his scribes busy day and night. He would have a secretary sit by his bed while he slept, so that he could dictate his dreams as soon as he awoke.

Thomas Hobbes was a particular favourite when Francis was Lord Chancellor, and he would regularly walk with Francis in the gardens and woods of Gorhambury while Francis reflected on nature and dictated his thoughts to him. Hobbes was later to become famous as the author of the work of political theory, *Leviathan*. Aubrey writes that:

> The Lord Chancellor Bacon loved to converse with him [Hobbes]. He assisted his Lordship in translating several of his essays into Latin, one, I well remember, is that *Of the Greatness of Cities*. The rest I have forgotten. His Lordship was a very contemplative person, and was wont to contemplate in his delicious walks at Gorhambury, and dictate to Mr Thomas Bushell, or some other of his gentlemen, that attended him with ink and paper ready to set down presently [at once] his thoughts. His lordship would often say that he liked Mr Hobbe's taking his thoughts, than any of the others, because he understood what he wrote, which the others not understanding, my lord would many times have a hard task to make sense of what they wrote.
>
> John Aubrey, 'Life of Hobbes'. *Brief Lives* (1692)⁴

There was also Peter Böener, who was in Francis' service both as an apothecary and a secretary for many years until the beginning of 1623. Böener later published a translation in Dutch of Bacon's *Essays, Wisdom of Ancients* and *Reli-*

gious Meditations (Leyden, 1646), grouped in one volume, and prefixed the collection with a 'Life of Bacon'.[5] Böener considered Francis Bacon to be 'a phoenix without equal', and records that he 'seldom saw him [Bacon] take up a book. He only ordered his chaplain and me to look in such and such an author for a certain place, and then he dictated to us early in the morning what he had invented and composed during the night'. Böener concludes his testimony to Bacon with a wish that 'a statue in honour of him may be erected in his country as a memorable example to all of virtue, kindness, peacefulness and patience'.[6]

Thomas Bushell served Francis Bacon from 1608 (when aged fifteen) as a gentleman usher, seal-bearer and amanuensis, and stayed with Bacon until Bacon's impeachment, in which, as he later revealed, he was one of the causes of his master being accused of corruption. Francis forgave him, however, and Bushel returned to serve his master until Bacon's death, after which he became a mining engineer in Somerset and Cardigan. He acknowledged that his own knowledge was based on Francis Bacon's knowledge of minerals and mining, for Francis had taken especial care to make Bushell 'the heir to his knowledge in mineral philosophy' and a few other inventions as well.[7]

When he was Lord Chancellor, Francis' chief secretaries were Sir Thomas Meautys and a Mr Young. Meautys became a personal friend of Francis and married the granddaughter of Sir Nicholas Bacon, Francis' half-brother. Francis left the house and estate of Gorhambury to Meautys, and it was Meautys who had the fine memorial statue of Francis, as Viscount St Alban, erected in St Michael's Church, St Albans, over the place where the third-century martyr St Alban was tried and sentenced to death by Geta, the eldest son of the Roman Emperor Severus.

Two other very important friends to Francis Bacon were Dr William Rawley and Dr William Harvey. Rawley was Bacon's private chaplain as well as a secretary. Francis bequeathed most of his manuscripts to Rawley upon his death. Harvey, who announced the discovery of the blood system to the world, was Francis' private physician.

After his impeachment, Francis was deserted by some of his helpers and friends, partly because he could no longer pay them. But there were some whom Francis described as the 'good pens who forsake me not', and they included Ben Jonson, George Herbert, Thomas Hobbes, Peter Böener, Dr William Rawley and Sir Thomas Meautys.

During the post-impeachment years Francis produced the final versions of most of his philosophical works and translated as many of them as he could into Latin, it being the international language. Although Francis himself was well able to write fluently in Latin, French and Italian, he had the assistance of Doctor Hacket, Bishop of Lichfield, together with Ben Jonson and George

Francis Bacon, Baron Verulam, Viscount St Alban, is depicted 'enthroned' in the classic pose of melancholia in its highest expression, that of the great seer, gazing into the heart of the mysterious and invisible presence of God immediately above the high altar. His shoes are crowned with full-blown roses.

Herbert, in translating the final versions of his *Essays, Advancement of Learning* and other works into Latin.[8] Tobie Mathew helped in translating his *Essays* into both Italian and Latin. Ben Jonson also contributed to and probably helped oversee the production of the Shakespeare Folio.

The Final Years

Almost immediately upon receiving the title of Viscount St Alban (the name being taken from the saint, not the place), when Francis was at the height of his public glory, a plot that had been hatched against him by those who envied him and his position came to fruition. It fell upon Francis like a bombshell, even though friends such as Tobie Mathew had tried to warn him that

65. *The Author and Actor. Title page: Francis Bacon's* De Dignitate et Augmentis Scientiarum *(1645)*

FR. BACONIS
De
VERVLAM.
Angliæ Cancellarii
DE
AVGMENTIS
SCIENTIARVM
Lib. IX.

LVGD. BATAVORVM
Apud Franciscum Moiardum,
Et Adrianum Wijngaerde. *Anno 1645.*

With his left hand, Francis Bacon directs an actor clothed in the bacchanalian fawnskin of 'Comedy' towards a temple on an acropolis, while with his right hand he points to a passage in his book of philosophy. On Bacon's cloak is the Sun insignia of Apollo.

The Northumberland Manuscript

A fascinating collection of manuscripts remains, and comes to us direct from Francis Bacon's scrivenery of the 1590s. The collection, which is in the form of an unbound volume, is referred to as the Northumberland Manuscript.[11] It was discovered in 1867 among some papers at Northumberland House, Charing Cross, and is now kept at Alnwick Castle in the possession of the Duke of Northumberland. A contents sheet, much scribbled-over, prefaces the collection and makes clear that some of the original contents were at some point removed (see illustrations 66–67, pp. 301-2).

The original contents included not only philosophical and poetic writings clearly known to be by Francis Bacon but also manuscript copies of two Shakespeare plays, Richard II and Richard III; a Nashe play, The Ile of Dogs; and what sounds like an unknown play, Asmund and Cornelia. Regrettably these plays and Bacon's Essays are among the manuscripts that were removed, the reason for their removal almost certainly being because these works were published in printed form in 1597, thereby making the manuscripts obsolete. The dating of the collection is no later than spring 1597, although it cannot be ascertained with certainty exactly when the collection was made. Some of the works (e.g.,,, Leicester's Commonwealth) go back as far as 1584.

The manuscripts are copies made by several different hands, or scribes. Most of the writing on the contents sheet, which is also its front cover sheet, has been recognised as that of John Davies of Hereford, one of Bacon's 'good pens',[12] who besides being a poet was a professional scrivener and the most skilful penman of his time. His profession was to copy documents for his various employers and also to give instruction in the art of penmanship. One of his sonnets is the one previously quoted, addressed to '*the royall, ingenious and all-learned Knight,* Sr. Francis Bacon', praising Bacon as a lawyer-cum-poet (see chapter 7).

This attribution to John Davies also gives weight to the supposition that the collection was made especially for, or was owned by, some member of the Neville family, since the name *Neville* can be traced in two places on the left-hand corner of the contents page, and nearby is their family motto, *Ne vile velis*. It has been suggested that this was probably Henry Neville, a nephew to Bacon and his junior by just three years, who entered Parliament together with Francis in 1584. John Davies knew Sir Henry well and dedicated one of his sonnets 'To the Noble, discreete and well-beloved Knight, Sir Henry Nevill'. It is known definitely from a letter that Bacon's *Essays* were circulating among his friends for several years prior to January 1597, when they were printed, and the evidence of this 'Northumberland' collection is that the other works represented in the collection were also in circulation in manuscript form, at least

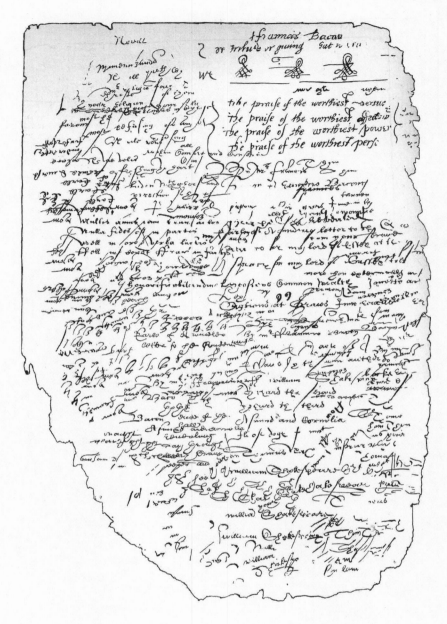

within Bacon's group of friends, being copied for the purpose. It is known
from letters that Bacon's scrivenery of 'good pens' was employed in copying
letters and manuscripts as well as transcribing from dictation Bacon's own
words.

Although heavily overwritten with various notes, names and doodles,
the original index or table of contents can be read as follows:

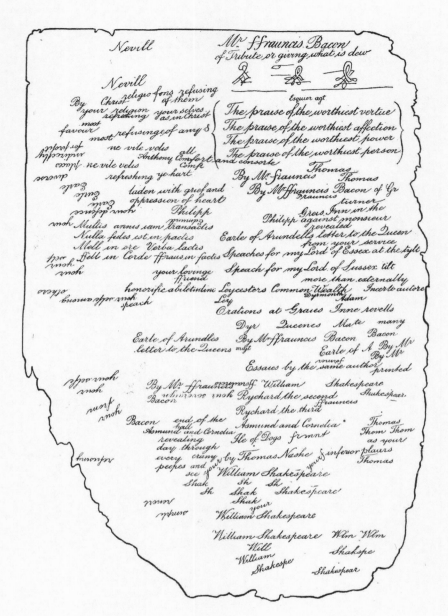

67. Contents
page,
Northumberland
Manuscript:
modern
representation

Mᵣ. ffrauncis Bacon.

Of tribute or giving what is dew.

    The praise of the worthiest vertue.

    The praise of the worthiest affection.

    The praise of the worthiest power.

    The praise of the worthiest person.

introduced romantic literature, a genre of the Italian Renaissance, to England. It helped to inspire many of Shakespeare's plays, notably *The Two Gentlemen of Verona, As You Like it, King Lear*, and the Romances—*Pericles, Cymbeline, The Winter's Tale* and *The Tempest.* Sidney's famous sonnet sequence, *Astrophel and Stella,* written *c.*1583–4 and published in 1591, influenced both Shakespeare's sonnets and *Romeo and Juliet.* Although he died in 1586, Sir Philip Sidney can certainly be counted as a leading light in the early Wilton circle, influencing Francis Bacon before he began to write the Shakespeare plays and poems.

The poets were often entertained at Wilton House. Moreover, Mary Sidney had a 'poetic' retreat in the grounds of Wilton on the banks of the Wiltshire River Avon, so that the 'sweet swan of Avon' could have a reference to this place and to the poets who met there—especially since the swan was associated with both Mary and Philip Sidney. This is because of the phonetic similarity between *Sidney* and the French word *cygne* ('swan'), which the French used jokingly in reference to Mary's brother. In an engraving of Mary Sidney when she was fifty-seven years old (1618), she is shown wearing a beautiful lace collar woven with a halo of swans (see illustration 6, p. 35).

Mary was often at Essex House, and she was staying there when the Queen ordered both her and Anthony Bacon out of the house in March 1600, at the time Essex was placed there under house arrest. When her husband died in 1601, after two years of serious illnesses, she fell in love with a younger man, Dr Matthew Lister, but was not allowed to marry him because of their difference in social status. However, they stayed together for the rest of her life. She eventually retired to the manor of Houghton Conquest, Bedfordshire, granted her by King James I in 1615, where she employed Italian architects to build a new home, Houghton House.

Mary's husband, Henry Herbert (?1538–1601), second Earl of Pembroke, not only supported his wife's patronage of poets but was himself the patron of an acting company, Pembroke's Men. The company was formed about 1577, the year of Pembroke's marriage to Mary Sidney, his third wife. By 1592 the company had in its repertoire several Shakespeare plays. However, the plague years of 1592 and 1593 forced the players to go on tour, but without sufficient success to keep the company going. They disbanded in 1594, selling their plays to other companies. The Shakespeare plays went to the Lord Chamberlain's Men.

William Herbert (1580–1630), who became the third Earl of Pembroke on his father's death in 1601, was educated privately by Samuel Daniel and later at New College, Oxford. Like his mother, he became patron to a group of poets and artists; or, rather, he continued the patronage. They included Shakespeare (whom we believe to be Francis Bacon), Ben Jonson, George Herbert, Philip Massinger, Inigo Jones the architect, and William Brown, author of *Britannia's Pastorals.* William Herbert went to Court in 1597, living in London from 1598 on-

wards. During this period he wrote verse, which was circulated privately among his friends. He was Lord Chamberlain at the time the Shakespeare Folio was printed, and therefore responsible for overseeing the production and publishing of plays and their performance at Court.

Philip Herbert (1584–1650) was created Earl of Montgomery in 1604. On his brother's death in 1630, he became the fourth Earl of Pembroke. He was very different in character to William and in fact had little time for intellectual pursuits. His love was for sport and gambling, but he was also interested in overseas enterprises, being a member of the East India Company and supporting his brother's participation in the Virginia Company. Like his brother William, Francis Bacon knew him well. The Shakespeare Folio is dedicated to both the Herbert brothers, perhaps partly in honour of their mother, Mary, who had died two years previously, but more especially because of their unflinching friendship and support for Francis in his difficult time.

The Earl of Leicester

In the early development of Elizabethan drama and the English Renaissance generally, Robert Dudley, the Earl of Leicester, was pivotal. As the most powerful and influential man in England in Elizabethan England until his death in September 1588, because of his close association with the Queen, who loved him, he made good use of drama and allegory to promote his interests, which ranged from wooing and protecting the Queen (he was known as the 'Shield of Pallas') to politics, education and the development of the arts and sciences. His role should not be underestimated.

For instance, after the Parliamentary Bill against vagabonds[16] had been enacted in 1572, requiring the patronage of actors by either one nobleman or

69. Robert Dudley, Earl of Leicester, aged 44 years. Miniature (1576) by Nicholas Hilliard

two judicial dignitaries, it was Leicester who was the first nobleman to obtain a royal patent for his acting company (in 1574) as an added privilege. This Act of Parliament was the virtual foundation of all professional acting, deliberately creating a distinction between the professional actor, who was patronised by the rich, powerful and learned, and the vagabond. This effectively raised the standard of acting considerably and allowed for the establishment of repertory companies with large financial investments backing them. It also gave such professional actors an entrée to the royal court, where many plays were subsequently performed on a regular basis. The royal patent granted to Leicester's Men, being the first, became the model for all patents granted thereafter.

Leicester, the virtual consort of the Queen, was deeply involved with the scholars, poets, philosophers and scientists of his time, one of the most notable being Dr John Dee. Dee was a renowned scientist, mathematician, Cabalist and astrologer, whose famous books, *Monas Hieroglyphica* (1564) and *General and Rare Memorials pertayning to the Perfect Arte of Navigation* (1577), together with his 'Mathematicall Preface' to the first English edition of *Euclides Elementes* (1570), had a major influence on Queen Elizabeth and Elizabethan society, and helped mould foreign policy. The search for a northern passage to India via America, and the colonisation schemes which followed, were largely inspired by him. Even as early as 1546, while a student at St John's College, Cambridge, Dee was involved with the theatre, designing a mechanical 'flying' device for use in a play performed on stage at Trinity College. Doubtless much influence and knowledge came from Dee via Leicester to the Burbages and their acting company. Indeed, the Act of Parliament concerning the patronage of actors can be seen to have been a deliberate and carefully thought-out action, of great benefit to the realm, and many things point to the Queen and Leicester, together with a particular circle of their friends, as being the inspirers and organisers of this scheme.

In 1575, at the same time as his company of actors were granted a royal

patent, Leicester laid on his famous entertainment for the Queen at Kenilworth Castle, site of Edward III's Arthurian tournaments. The Kenilworth Entertainment was an example of poetry, drama, tournament, pageantry and allegory at its most elaborate and magnificent, and an attempt at a 'modern' revival of the Order of the Round Table. It was followed immediately by the Woodstock Entertainment, laid on by the Queen's champion, Sir Henry Lee, which carried on the theme that was introduced in the Kenilworth Entertainment and introduced the Faerie Queen for the first time. From this fabulous beginning flowed all the subsequent grand entertainments held at Court on Elizabeth's Accession Day Anniversary or other great occasions. The history of the Elizabethan theatre should almost certainly be seen as developing not only in parallel but also in concert with these great Court entertainments.

In such a highly autocratic society, all depended on the Queen's benevolence and where her self-interest lay. By flattering and building up the image of the Queen in this way, something which increased her own power and influence with the people, it encouraged her to continue with her patronage of the arts and sciences. This method of culture-building echoed that in France, where the Valois Court and the *Pléiade* had created a French Renaissance through their *Magnificences* and Courts of Love.

Leicester eventually married Lettice Knollys, the widowed Countess of Essex, which distressed the Queen and caused Leicester's temporary banishment from Court. But in this way he became the stepfather of Robert Devereux, Lettice's son. At the age of ten, after his father's death in 1576, Robert had become the second Earl of Essex. Leicester's sister, Mary Dudley, was married to Sir Henry Sidney, whose children were Sir Philip Sidney and Mary Sidney, Countess of Pembroke. It was during an expedition to help the Dutch Protestant forces in the Netherlands against the Catholic army in 1585–6, when Leicester was commander-in-chief, that his nephew Sir Philip was killed in action. Sir Philip Sidney had been the courtly ideal of the poet–knight and hero of the country, so when he died it was a great loss. Just before he died, in a symbolic act of great significance, he passed his sword on to Robert, Earl of Essex, Leicester's stepson.

In 1569 Leicester acquired the lease of Paget House, the great house once belonging to the bishops of Exeter, built on the site of the Outer Temple of the Knights Templar headquarters. This was adjacent to and on the Westminster side of Middle Temple, close to Temple Bar, the barrier marking the boundary between the City of London and the environs of Westminster. Fleet Street lay on its north side, while to the south the grounds of the house went down to the river Thames, with a water gate and moorings for boats. Leicester transformed the house into a stately mansion, which was his home until his death. It became the meeting place of various poets, writers and artists patronised by the Earl, and was visited often by the Bacon family. When Leicester died, in 1588, Essex took over the lease and renamed the mansion Essex House. This is the house that became the London headquarters for the Essex group, where Anthony Bacon, at the request of his brother Francis, set up his office and home.

The Acting Companies

Leicester's company of players, known as Lord Leicester's Men, was founded by James Burbage, the owner and builder of The Theatre, the first purpose-built public theatre in England. The Theatre was in operation by early1577 and most of the leading acting companies used it for their performances, as well as Leicester's Men. Their amalgamation with Lord Strange's Men took place in September 1588, after the death of Leicester, which in turn was followed by the further amalgamation of this company with the Lord Admiral's Men in 1590. It thus became the predominant acting company in London, performing at Burbage's Theatre.

However, as has been mentioned before (see chapter 2), the following four years were ones of turmoil for the acting companies, with not only the various splits and re-amalgamations, but the two plague years of 1592–4 causing several companies to break up, including Lord Pembroke's Men. The final and perhaps most important split occurred in 1594, when Lord Derby (Strange) died. Most of the members of Strange's company, who were then part of the amalgamated Admiral/Strange's Men, left the Lord Admiral's Men and joined the Lord Chamberlain's Men, under the patronage of the new Lord Chamberlain, Sir Henry Carey, Lord Hunsdon, and led by the Burbages. The newly-formed Lord Chamberlain's Men proved to be the most successful company of all, its only real competitor being the reformed Lord Admiral's Men, led by their great actor Edward Alleyn. These two companies dominated the London scene, being the only ones of any importance to survive the plague. They also became associated with two principal theatres, the Lord Chamberlain's Men being primarily based at The Theatre and the Lord Admiral's Men at The Rose, but both companies performed at either theatre from time to time. The emergence of these two companies in 1594 as the primary acting companies, immediately after the public announcement of the Shake-scene with *Venus and Adonis* and *Lucrece*, is something of which to take note, as we shall discuss below.

From 1594, the Lord Chamberlain's Men were the principal company that performed the Shakespeare plays, with William Kempe as their famous clown and Richard Burbage as the lead actor. The company remained the Lord Chamberlain's Men until 1603, their patron changing to Sir George Carey when he succeeded his father as Lord Hunsdon in 1596 and then as Lord Chamberlain in 1597. (Sir William Brook, Lord Cobham, was Lord Chamberlain for a brief period, July 1596 to March 1597.) In 1603 King James I took over the patronage of the company and they became known as the King's Men, with a new royal patent.

Whereas the Lord Chamberlain's Men won renown through Burbage and the Shakespeare plays, the Lord Admiral's Men, led by their great actor Edward Alleyn, gained fame with plays by Marlowe, Kyd, Dekker, Jonson, Munday, Drayton, Chapman, Peele, Lodge and Chettle. In 1596 the Lord Admiral's Men were formally renamed the Earl of Nottingham's Company when Charles Howard, the Lord High Admiral, was made Earl of Nottingham, although the company continued to be commonly known as the Admiral's Men. After 1603, when the company came under the patronage of the new royal family, it was renamed Prince Henry's Company, finally ending its days as the Elector Palatine's Company or Palsgrave's Company.

In 1598, by decree of the Privy Council, the Lord Chamberlain's Men and the Lord Admiral's Men were the only ones allowed to perform in London for the following twenty-five years, giving these two companies an almost total monopoly of the theatre. In the wake of this decree, the Lord Chamberlain's Men moved their Theatre from Shoreditch on the north side of the City to Bankside on the south side of the river, rebuilding and renaming the playhouse as The Globe, and reopening it in 1599 for public performances. They were followed the next year by the Lord Admiral's Men who moved from The Rose on Bankside and opened in their newly-built playhouse, The Fortune, situated north of the river at Cripplegate, on the northern outskirts of the City. London's two premier acting companies, having been based each side of the River Thames since 1594, north and south of the City of London, polarities to each other, were now switched over in what would seem to be a deliberate design.

The rivalry between the two companies, although real, also appears to have had a helpful purpose, similar perhaps to modern marketing theories, which tell us that if people are given a choice more of each product is sold than if only one was on sale; or perhaps because rivalry and competition tends to promote good value and excellence. Comparisons certainly create interest. That this might have been deliberately planned emerges in the architecture of the Globe and Fortune, for not only were the two playhouses situated on opposite sides of the river, but also they were closely related to each other in design and symbolism, the one being the antithesis or complement of the other.

The builders of the Fortune, who were the same as those of the Globe, were instructed to follow the design and measurements of the Globe in all respects, except that the Fortune was to be square instead of circular. This sounds like nonsense until one realises that the geometric ground-plan of the Fortune was deliberately designed to square the circle of the Globe[17]—a geometric or architectural secret denoting the philosophical 'Mystical Marriage' that occurs when two completely opposite states of being find their balance and harmony together. In addition, the names of the two theatres are intimately linked, for the goddess Fortune is traditionally shown standing on the Globe of the world—the Globe sometimes being represented as a Wheel of Fortune that the goddess turns (see illustration 72, overleaf).

All this would seem to indicate that someone, or some people, knowledgeable about sacred geometry and architecture, and the wisdom enshrined in the ancient myths, were guiding and coordinating the two projects and companies. If so, this was most likely from the 'top', from the two patrons, the Lord High Admiral Charles Howard, Earl of Nottingham, and the Lord Chamberlain George Carey, Baron Hunsdon, who were both relatives of the Queen and high-ranking members of the Queen's Privy Council. They were the ones who controlled both the playhouses and the

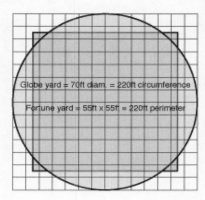

Globe yard = 70ft diam. = 220ft circumference

Fortune yard = 55ft x 55ft = 220ft perimeter

71. Squaring the Circle: The Globe and Fortune Theatres

72. The Goddess
Fortune and the
Globe.
Title page:
Historia Regni
Henrici Septimi
(1642)—Latin
edition of Francis
Bacon's History
of HenryVII

Francis Bacon stands on the platform as President of the Rosicrucian Fraternity, with a knight of the Rosy Cross next to him, supporting and controlling the goddess Fortune. Standing on the ground in front of them is a philosopher with a ('shaking') spear, with which he is trying to control the wheel of fortune. An actor dressed as a knight, with buskins and one spur, holds on to the spear and points to the globe on which Fortune is balanced.

promoted by Sir Nicholas Bacon. Inspired by his experience at the French Court and the new development of drama and pageantry in England, Francis proceeded to develop this programme into something much greater and more universal.

Both Anthony and Francis Bacon were referred to as phoenixes by their contemporaries—a special form of praise but not entirely unique to them— but there may be more in it than one at first supposes. Thomas Tenison (later Archbishop of Canterbury), in the Introduction to his *Baconiana or Certain Genuine Remains of Sir Francis Bacon*, published in 1679, says of Francis Bacon: 'Such great wits are not the common births of time: and they, surely, intended to signify so much who said of the Phoenix (though in hyperbole as well as metaphor) that Nature gives the World that individual species but once in five hundred years'.[5] Tenison signed the Introduction with his initials 'T.T.' (otherwise the book was published anonymously), next to which is the date 'Novemb. 30, 1678'. This particular year, 1678, is 108 years after 1570, when Maier stated that the Rosicrucian fraternity was founded and began its work.

The linking of celestial events to earthly ones, and of bringing the heavens (i.e.,, the realm of spiritual ideas) down to earth and raising the earth to the heavens, is a major feature of the Hermetic work: thus stellar events feature strongly in the planning and timing of the Rosicrucian work. It is interesting, therefore, that Francis Bacon had his first great vision of his future work during his residence at Cambridge University, at the time of the famous Cassiopeia supernova of 1572–4. The birth of new stars (as novae and supernovae were mistakenly called) in the constellation of Cassiopeia, the Heavenly Virgin Queen, were referred to as the birth of her children and said to mark the corresponding birth on earth of some great light, child of the Virgin Queen.

It is significant, then, that a further two novae appeared together in Cassiopeia at the end of 1592. These two new stars shone in the sky like heavenly twins. Just before their appearance Anthony Bacon returned home to join his brother, and almost immediately following their appearance *Venus and Adonis* was published, announcing the author 'William Shakespeare' for the first time and with the sign of the Gemini on the title page (see chapter 5). This was Francis Bacon's thirty-third year.

Cipher Experts & Cabalists

In this unravelling of the Shakespeare enigma we need to look at ciphers and symbolism. Too often these are dismissed as being irrelevant or non-existent in Shakespeare studies, but this is not only to ignore the obvious but also the important. The ciphers, as well as symbolic pictures and emblematic verses, do exist, as can easily be shown, and they are only used because the information they convey was considered sufficiently important to be worth encrypting. With respect to the Rosicrucian, Baconian and Shakespearean works, it is also information that 'marries' heaven and earth, being concerned with both.

The use of ciphers in the Elizabethan and Jacobean eras was widespread, both for encrypting intelligence for personal, governmental or secret society purposes, and also for philosophical study and metaphysical exploration. In terms of the latter, there was a strong tradition of numerology or *arithmomancy* (the Pythagorean term for the oracular use of numbers): passed down, according to tradition, from Orpheus to Pythagoras to Plato, and hence to Platonists and Neoplatonists; and then, combined with the cabalistic tradition of *gematria*, to such Renaissance philosophers as Pico della Mirandola, the Abbot Johannes Trithemius, Henry Cornelius Agrippa, Leon Battista Alberti, Giovanni Baptista della Porta, Girolama Cardano and Dr John Dee.

In terms of state intelligence, the Greeks were probably the first in Europe to use cipher as a means of military communication, followed by the Romans. Julius Caesar developed a famous substitution cipher which he described in his *Gallic Wars*. By the fourteenth century AD, political and diplomatic ciphers were widely used, with the Roman Catholic Church pioneering the way. The science of cryptology begun to make a strong impact in England during the reign of Henry VIII. In Queen Elizabeth I's reign, it became an effective and important part of statecraft. The man chiefly responsible for its high development was Sir Francis Walsingham (?1532–1590), who was the Queen's Secretary of State from 1573 until his death, and who with his brother Thomas organised and ran the Queen's secret service.

The intelligence network consisted of at least fifty spies working abroad in Europe, together with fifteen or more agents at home, and there was a spy school in London where both spies and intelligencers were trained in cryptology. Intelligencers, as distinct from spies, were those who ran sections of the secret service—managing, coordinating and collecting the intelligence, seeing that it reached its intended destination and making important high level contacts. They were usually reasonably high in social standing, well educated, and with friends in high places. Christopher Marlowe and Anthony Standen were members of the network, as spies, as also were Anthony and Francis Bacon, as intelligencers. Walsingham's best cryptanalyst, however, was Thomas Phelippes, a widely travelled and well-educated man who could solve ciphers in five languages. Dr John Dee was another agent, whose code name, '007', has been made famous in our modern era by the author Ian Fleming in his James Bond books and the films based on them. Dee used ciphers both for conveying encrypted messages to Walsingham and the Queen, and also for what was called 'angel magic', in which each angel is believed to correspond to a number and can be invoked or communicated with by means of that number, if one knows how.

Francis Bacon's first mission as an intelligencer seems to have been during his first visit to France. He had a declared interest in cipher and invented cipher systems from his youth onwards. He gives examples in his 1623 Latin edition of *The Advancement and Proficience of Learning.* One of these examples is the Biliteral Cipher, which Francis declares he invented in his youth while in France and which now, in the form of the binary system, is the basis of all computer language. His brother Anthony travelled abroad the year after his father's death and Francis' return, charged by his uncle Lord Burghley with being an agent for Walsingham and the Queen.

Anthony's twelve years abroad as an intelligencer, sometimes in dangerous circumstances, was spent mostly in an area (the South of France) where he could best gather intelligence from Spain and Italy as well as France. Walsingham died in 1590, while Anthony was still abroad, and when Anthony came home and discovered the perfidious behaviour of his uncle, Lord Burghley, and was threatened by Burghley's son, Robert Cecil (*i.e.,* that he held Anthony for his mortal enemy and would make him feel it when he could),6 Anthony readily assented to Francis' request to team up with Essex and provide Essex, rather than Burghley, with intelligence. At that point the secret service became split, with much of Walsingham's network working under Anthony, while Burghley and Robert Cecil developed their own spy ring.

However, this was not the whole story, for the principal work to which the Bacon brothers had devoted themselves was the scheme of the Great Instauration, otherwise known as the Work of the Six Days, by means of which Francis Bacon (and presumably Anthony) believed the whole world could be purified, reformed and brought to the 'Seventh Day' state of illumination and peace. The foundation of this work is biblical or cabalistic, and the Bacon team used cipher in a cabalistic way, embodying it into their published works both as signatures and for other purposes.

Cabala is essentially a science of number or cipher, based on the perception that the laws of the universe are mathematical and that Divinity, as the Absolute Source, Essence and Creator of all things, can be understood as numbers (Hebrew, *Sephiroth*). As in Pythagorean metaphysics concerning the *Tetraktys*,7 these numbers are ten in total (*i.e.,* 1–10), no more and no less, and of these there are the first three (the Holy Trinity) and the seven that are immediately derived from and express the first three. From these divine Ten come everything else—spiritual, psychological and material, including the spiritual 'forms' or angels, human souls and nature. All forms of life are thus ciphers and symbols of truth. As Blaise de Vigènere wrote in his *Traictè des Chiffres*:

> All the things in the world constitute a cipher. All nature is merely a
> cipher and a secret writing. The great name and essence of God and His
> wonders, the very deeds, projects, words, actions, and demeanour of
> mankind—what are they, for the most part, but a cipher?
>
> Blaise de Vigènere, Traictè des Chiffres (1586)

The word 'cipher' comes from the Hebrew word *'saphar',* meaning 'to
number'. What is called 'the Word' in Hebraic, Christian, Greek and Egyptian
religious teachings is essentially number but takes form as a vibration of sound
represented by the alphabet and the spoken or written word. Therefore behind every letter of the alphabet is both a number and a vibration of sound:
hence the idea that words of similar number have similar vibration and therefore similar meaning. From this concept comes a whole science of what is called
gematria, which itself relates to geometry and the idea that God, the Great
Architect of the Universe and Grand Geometrician, geometrises and builds
the universe by means of the Word.

The Word is divine wisdom and its nature is poetic: hence God the Creator is the Great Poet or Bard, whose words and language have number, rhythm,
pattern, beauty of form and sound, and depths of meaning. Man, therefore,
who is made in God's image, can do no better than try to imitate his Creator.
This is the cabalistic viewpoint, which Francis Bacon adopted wholeheartedly—
a viewpoint in which 'man' is understood to be mind or soul, composed entirely of what he/she knows:

> My praise shall be dedicated to the mind itself. The mind is the man and
> the knowledge of the mind. A man is but what he knoweth. The mind
> itself is but an accident [adjunct] to knowledge; for knowledge is a dou-
> ble of that which is; the truth of being and the truth of knowing is all
> one.
>
> Francis Bacon, In Praise of Knowledge[8]

> The essential form of knowledge ... is nothing but a representation of
> truth: for the truth of being and the truth of knowing are one, differing
> no more than the direct beam and the beam reflected.
>
> Francis Bacon, Advancement of Learning (1605), Bk I

'Knowledge' in the Baconian sense is what the Greeks called *Gnosis* and
the Cabalists *Daath*. A modern term for such knowledge is illumination. It is
knowledge of truth, wherein truth is wisdom, the light of God, also known as
the Word of God. Hand in hand with this is the idea that truth (*i.e.,* the Word

or Author of life) is hidden or secret by design—not so that man cannot and neer will find it, but so that he should find it with effort and thereby gain understanding and abilities that he would otherwise not have had. A true cabalist, in other words, not only searches for the truth but also reflects it, imitating it. Just as the truth, which is the Author of the drama of life, is hidden within His works, so the master cabalist likewise takes care to hide his authorship within his (dramatic) works, but in such a way that he can, like divine truth, be found: hence one of the major reasons (if not *the* major reason) for the masking of the authorship of the Shakespeare works.

Francis Bacon considered mathematics to be so important that he dared not speak too openly about the subject in his publicly-acknowledged works. Instead, he provided just one or two cipher examples and a few hints to point the way:

> Nevertheless there remaineth yet another part of Natural Philosophy, which is commonly made a principal part and holdeth rank with Physique special and Metaphysique, which is Mathematique; but I think it more agreeable to the nature of things and to the light of order to place it as a branch of Metaphysique; for ... it appeareth to be one of the essential Forms of things; as that it is causative in Nature of a number of effects; inasmuch as we see, in the schools both of Democritus and of Pythagoras, that the one did ascribe figure to the first seeds of things, and the other did suppose numbers to be the principles and originals of things: and it is true also that of all other Forms, it is the most abstracted and separable from matter, and therefore most proper to Metaphysique; which hath likewise been the cause why it hath been better laboured and inquired than any of the other Forms, which are more immersed in matter.

Francis Bacon, Advancement of Learning (1605), Bk II

Metaphysics, as its name implies, concerns that which exists above or beyond the purely physical state of existence. In cabalistic and Neoplatonic terms, these can be classified, in ascending order, as psychological, spiritual and divine. Number, word and symbol are associated with these three—the symbol or picture expressing the word, and the word or alphabet expressing the number, which number or cipher equates with the divine. Like the Holy Trinity, these three make a unity, and should be considered as such.

The Great Cipher Book

The first great cipher book was *Steganographia*[9] by the Abbot Trithemius. It was circulated in manuscript form from 1499 onwards and eventually printed in Frankfurt in 1606. Della Porta's book, *De Furtivis Literarum Notis,* first published in

Naples in 1563, was probably the next of the great cipher manuals. Then came Blaise de Vigenère's *Traicté des Chiffres ou Secretes Manières d'Escrire*, printed in Paris in 1586 and dedicated to Monsieur Antoine Seguier. The fourth great cipher book was *Cryptomenitices et Cryptographiae* by Gustavus Selenus, published in Germany in 1624, shortly after the publication of Bacon's *De Augmentis Scientiarum* and the Shakespeare Folio. These latter three are linked, for not only were certain cipher methods described in *Cryptomenitices* either invented or adapted by Francis Bacon and used in both the *De Augmentis* and the Shakespeare Folio, but also it is possible that Bacon himself was the primary author of all three works. These three should certainly be considered together.

In the introductory poems of *Cryptomenitices* the author is described as 'Homo Lunae' ('The Man in the Moon'), whereas on the title page the author's name is printed as Gustavus Selenus (see illustration 74, p. 330). 'Gustavus Selenus' is the pseudonym of Augustus, Duke of Luneberg.[10] Gustavus is an anagram of Augustus, while Selenus stands not only for the oldest and wisest of the Satyrs who tutored Dionysus[11] but also for Selene, the Greek goddess of the moon who in Latin is called Luna, thus signifying Luneberg.[12]

Duke Augustus, who was in England at the coronation of King James I and well-known in English Court circles, was a friend of Francis Bacon and the probable leader of the continental group, 'Societas Christiana', associated with the Rosicrucians.[13] The title page states that its 'Steganographiae' is derived from Johannes Trithemius, Abbot of Sponheim. Many of the ciphers in Trithemius' book *Steganographia* are illustrated in *Cryptomenitices*, but there are also examples and details of cipher systems published by Della Porta, Vigenère and others, plus some that were invented and used by Francis Bacon and his group.

The title page of *Cryptomenitices* is itself an example of cryptology of various types, relevant to our story—the anagram of Duke Augustus being one example. Another type shown on this title page is pictorial (or 'hieroglyphic', as such pictorial ciphers were known), as illustrated by the four pictures that surround the central panel of text. Information about these engraved pictures was found in letters sent in May 1620 by Augustus to his literary agent, Philip Hainhofer of Augsberg, in which the Duke gave instructions for the engraving of the title-page plates.[14] The Duke requested that one of the plates was to be of the Abbot Trithemius, and that 'the Abbot should be seen seated at a table writing, with someone who should resemble Gustavus Selenus himself, standing behind him holding his cap, or mitre, a little above his head'. The portrait of Trithemius was to be derived from a recently-published book in the Duke's collection. 'Other pictures,' the Duke suggested, 'should represent the Post, or a Courier carrying letters here, there, on foot, on land, on water, as letters are despatched, and also what is appropriate for sending secret letters.'[15]

74. The
Rosicrucian
Cipher Book.
Title page,
Gustavus Selenus'
Cryptomenitices
et
Cryptographiae
(1624)

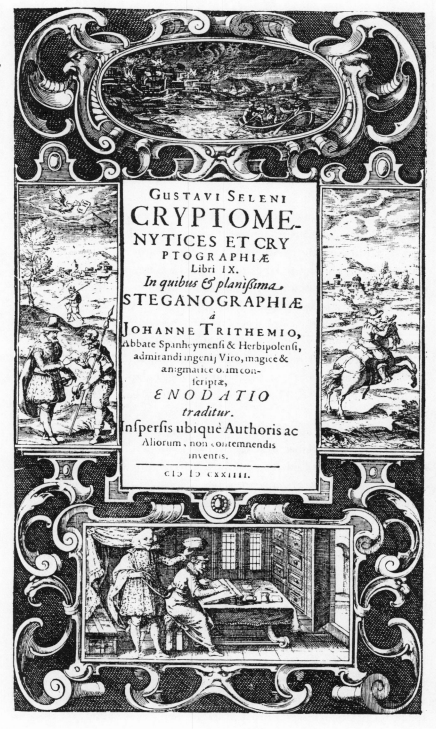

The lower picture on the title page is the one that depicts the Duke Augustus (Gustavus Selenus) standing behind the Abbot Trithemius, who is busy writing at a desk. Only, the depiction of the Abbot does not conform accurately with the portrait of Trithemius mentioned by the Duke. Beneath the monk's habit can be seen the sleeve and ruff of a courtier, and, moreover, the writer's head is not tonsured, as one would have expected of a fifteenth-century abbot of a Roman Catholic monastery. The Duke (Gustavus Selenus) is shown holding an abbot's mitre of unusual appearance above the head of this mysterious 'Trithemius', having just removed it, as he would have done in order to hold the mitre above the Abbot's head. In 1925 an authority on certain cipher methods, Dr H. A. W. Speckman, a professor of mathematics at Arnhem, Holland, noticed that the picture was probably a rebus (*i.e.,* a picture puzzle wherein pictures represent words) coupled with a Trithemius cipher system. Taking the two most extraordinary features of the picture—the courtier-like Trithemius and the mitre that has been removed from his head— as the rebus, Speckman solved the riddle by using one of Trithemius' twenty-two-letter Latin alphabet transposition cipher systems, also known as a 'wheel cipher'. (The Latin cipher alphabet of twenty-two letters is such that I, J and Y are the same, and U, V and W are the same.) He showed that if the letters of 'MITRE' are removed from the name 'TRITHEMIUS', the letters 'THIUS' remain. Using the cipher system and transposing the letters five places to the right (*i.e.,* A becomes F, B becomes G, *etc.*), 'THIUS' becomes 'BNOCA', the anagram of 'BACON'.[16]

The key of '5' is suggested not only by the five letters of 'MITRE' and the five letters ('TSUIH') remaining after 'MITRE' is removed from 'TRITHEMIUS', but also from the five-fold design of the title page, with its five panels, and the five men in the boat (three oarsmen, one helmsman and a courier) who are depicted in the uppermost panel, rowing away from a town at night. Following the Duke's instructions, the right-hand, left-hand and top panels of the title page depict the various ways of despatching a letter, while Trithemius in the lower panel is shown writing one. The right-hand picture (from the heraldic point of view) shows a courier with a spear receiving a letter from a nobleman, while in the distance is another courier (or the same one) hastening away on foot to deliver his message. The left-hand picture portrays the 'Post', riding on horseback and blowing his post-horn. These are the normal ways messages were despatched. The despatching of a secret message, however, and on water, is depicted in the night scene of the top panel. There is no moon shown in this picture, as one might have expected from the association of the author with the moon, but instead the town, the harbour, the sea and the boat carrying the secret message and messengers are lit by four beacons, shown flaming on poles above the town walls. 'Beacon' is not just an anagram

shows the boar's head being presented by the swineherd to a group of three aristocrats, one of whom is a king, seated on a throne behind a table that has an open book on it (see illustration 77). The throne, table and three aristocrats are on a platform that is part of a porch supported by two columns and hung with a curtain behind the throne. In the foreground is a boar rooting the ground, with the motto 'Ulterius' inscribed on its back, as in the Plantin picture, while in the background the sun is rising over a hill in the distance.

The 1549 picture is another clear representation of the Royal Arch Degree, with the three Principals of the Royal Arch receiving the offering of the candidate (the boar) who has given his life in a sacrifice of charity (the Third Degree). The sun, together with the offering, represent the 'exaltation' or rebirth of the Master (Mark) Mason into the higher Royal Arch Degree, which itself is the porch or entrance into the degrees which lie beyond, up to the Thirty-Third Degree.

The 1546 picture, by contrast, is a very simple and direct symbol of the sacrificed life of the Master Mason, as represented by the boar's head, offered to God so as to be raised and exalted into the higher spiritual life. It is a simple symbolism that was in earlier times used at Christmas, when a boar's head was presented at the Christmas feast, signifying the death of the old and the birth of the new—the birth of light.

As an added jest or pointer, Andreas Alciat's initials also form the 'AA' sign, so his initials on the pyramidal keystone of the 1577 Plantin picture are indeed a good mark. In point of fact, Alciat was a highly respected man, a celebrated legal scholar, who was described by the famous German engraver and publisher Theodore de Bry as 'the most noble jurisconsult, but in all liberal learning and especially poetry, so experienced that he could vie with the very highest geniuses'.[24] Alciat was the person who coined the word 'emblem', signifying 'mosaic work' and referring primarily to an epigram in the form of a riddling, moral poem with various levels of meaning, to which was conjoined a motto and a picture. The poems are in large part based upon ancient fables, and the pictures derive from the idea of classical iconography, Egyptian hieroglyphs and European heraldry. Alciat's *Book of Emblems* was immensely popular and had an enormous influence in the sixteenth and seventeenth centuries, being reprinted many times and spawning a whole new industry of emblem writers, artists and books, and affecting the heraldry and pageantry of the Renaissance.

However, it was not Alciat who made the change in the Plantin edition of his book, for he died in 1550, twenty-seven years before Plantin's edition was printed. So, who was responsible for commissioning the 'AA' device, and why?

Almost certainly, the answer lies in the emblem's motto and its key motif—the boar. The boar was, for instance, the chief heraldic motif of the Bacon family crest. Furthermore, although the family motto used on their coat of arms was 'Mediocra firma', meaning 'The middle way is sure' or 'Moderation is strength', the Bacons also used another motto, 'Moniti meliora,' meaning 'Being instructed, to better [things]'. This was painted on the wall overlooking the dining table in the hall of Gorhambury House.[25] This motto is, however, incomplete and should properly read 'Moniti meliora sequamur', which is a quotation from Virgil's *Aeneid*,[26] usually translated as meaning 'Let us, being instructed, strive after better [things]'. Virgil's admonition as it stands is still rather ambiguous, however, but the motto of the Alciat emblem helps to complete it. If we combine the two mottoes, 'Moniti meliora sequamur' and 'In dies meliora', we have 'Moniti in dies meliora sequamur', the full meaning of which is, 'Let us, being instructed, strive after better days', which is a specific allusion to the Golden Age. This was a major theme of Virgil and the Mysteries about which he cryptically wrote, as also of the Renaissance, and it is the particular object of the Baconian work—the Great Instauration referring to the restoration of the Golden Age, the state of Paradise.

The cabalistic title page to the 1640 edition of Francis Bacon's major work, *Of the Advancement and Proficience of Learning*, shows the similar theme of the Great Pillars in another and more detailed way, the 'Moniti meliora' being inscribed on the twin pillars and another well-known Gray's Inn motto, 'Multi pertransibunt & augebitur Scientia' ('Many shall pass through and learning shall be increased')[27] being written between them (see illustration 80). A Masonic handshake appears near the top of the picture, representing the uniting of the two opposite poles or approaches to life as signified by the pillars and the two globes that surmount them. The Great Pillars are also used on the title pages to the Latin versions of his other two major philosophical works, the *Novum Organum* ('New Method') and *Sylva Sylvarum* ('Natural History'), which were published in 1620 and 1626 respectively (see illustrations 81–82, on p. 334). These three title-page pictures cleverly depict the three Craft degrees of Freemasonry that lead up to the Royal Arch Degree, something which is discussed in this book's sequel, *Building Paradise*.[28]

After its appearance in the 1577 *Emblemata*, the next appearance of the 'AA' device was in an emblematic headpiece to Thomas Chaloner's *De Rep. Anglorum Instauranda libri decem*, printed by Thomas Vautrollier in London in 1579, the year Francis Bacon returned from the continent (see headpiece to chapter 1).29 Vautrollier, a French Huguenot who had to leave France because of his religion, set up as a bookbinder and seller in London in 1567, acting as the London agent for Christopher Plantin. He became a printer in 1570, printing books in his printing shop in Blackfriars, London, until his death in 1587—except for a short period when he set up a press in Edinburgh, Scotland (1583–6). While he was in Edinburgh, in 1584, Vautrollier printed *The Essayes of a Prentise in the Divine*

80. The Second Degree Great Pillars. Title page: Francis Bacon's Of the Advancement and Proficience of Learning (1640)

Art of Poesie—an anonymous publication, supposedly written by King James VI of Scotland, and one which carried the 'AA' headpiece. On Vautrollier's death the business was passed on to his apprentice, Richard Field, who mar-

81. The First
Degree Great
Pillars.
Title page: Francis
Bacon's Novum
Organum (1620)

82. The Third
Degree Great
Pillars.
Title page: Francis
Bacon's Sylva
Sylvarum (1626)

ried Vautrollier's widow. Richard Field became the printer of many other famous works published under the heading of the 'Double A', including the second and third editions of Shakespeare's *Venus and Adonis*, printed in 1594 and 1596 respectively (the first edition in 1593 did not carry the 'AA' device).

Alciat's 'In dies meliora' emblem with its 'AA' pyramid appeared again in 1586, on page 53 of Geffrey Whitney's *A Choice of Emblemes*, printed at Leyden by Francis Raphelengius and dedicated to Robert, Earl of Leicester.

From 1585, other printers began to use the 'AA' device in headpieces, with nearly all the books being printed in London and a very few in Edinburgh. A notable one in which the same Vautrollier 'AA' headpiece appeared again was a reprint of Giovanni Baptista della Porta's cipher book, *De Furtivis Literarum Notis, Vulgo De Ziferis,* made by John Wolfe. Although this reprint was made in London in 1591, it retains the publishing date, 1563, of the original book and its reference to being printed in Naples. However, the London reprint adds the 'AA' headpiece, which was not in the original Neapolitan printing.[30] The headpiece shows the two A's each side of a cornucopic vase or 'holy grail', with two birds or phoenixes at either end (see headpiece to chapter 1). It appears only once and is the only headpiece in the book, placed over the dedication to 'Ioanni Soto Philippi Regis'.

Porta's book represents the climax of sixteenth-century Italian cryptography. He and his book had a subtle but profound influence on the Hermetic tradition as it developed in the Italian Renaissance and moved its way through Europe. This was true particularly in the field of bringing magic into the realm of organised science—a magic that had its immediate origins in the *Magia* or

lifetime. On his death, a relative published an English translation naming Bishop Godwin as the original author.[1]

We will see now that the 1623 Shakespeare Folio also contains cipher signatures and other possible messages, confirming Francis Bacon as the author (or primary author) of the plays and associating him intimately with the Rosicrucian fraternity. The ciphers that we shall consider first are referred to as the Simple, Reverse and Kay Ciphers.[2] A more complex and metaphysical version of the Simple Cipher, referred to as the Inquisition Cipher, was published by Archbishop Thomas Tenison in his *Baconiana* of 1679, in which he printed a fragment of a work written in Latin in 1623 by Francis Bacon entitled *Abecedarium Naturæ*.[3]

> For cyphars: they are commonly in Letters or alphabets but may be in Wordes. The Kind of Cyphars (beside the Simple Cyphars with Changes and intermixtures of nulles, and Nonsignificants) are many, according to the Nature or Rule of the infoulding: Wheele Cyphars, Kay Cyphars, etc.
>
> Francis Bacon, *Advancement of Learning* (1605), Bk II

> Let us proceed then to Ciphers. Of these there are many kinds: simple ciphers; ciphers mixed with non-significant characters; ciphers containing two different letters in one character; wheel-ciphers; key-ciphers; word-ciphers; and the like.
>
> Francis Bacon, *De Augmentis* (1623), Bk VI, ch [14]

The Simple Cipher has already been referred to in Chapter 8. An example of it is given in *Cryptomenitices,* Book IV, Chapter 6, page 141 (see illustration 85, p. 342). This is exactly as Francis Bacon and his group employed it, utilising the common twenty-four-letter Elizabethan alphabet wherein the letters I and J are the same, as also the letters U and V. The cipher is a simple substitution cipher, as used in Cabala, whereby A = 1, B = 2, C = 3 and on to Z = 24. Using this system, every word has its own number, and certain words of the same number have an equivalent meaning. Bacon and his group used this system, as well as the Reverse and Kay Ciphers, for the purpose of signing their literary works. There may also be further purposes.

The Reverse Cipher is, quite simply, the Simple Cipher reversed, so that A = 24, B = 23, C = 22 and on to Z = 1.

The Kay or Key Cipher, referred to by Bacon, is just slightly more complex. It uses the letter K, pronounced like 'key' in some Elizabethan English dialects and identified as such in the two versions of his *Advancement of Learning* (see above), as the key letter of the cipher. It is the key in the sense that it is the tenth letter of the Elizabethan alphabet, which begins a series of numbers with two digits rather than the single digit of the numbers 1 to 9. It is the most natural place to start a cipher that uses two-digit numbers, which the Kay Cipher does.

Why do this? Well, it is possible in some circumstances to have a confusion of numerical value when there is a mixture of single and double-digit numbers. For instance, 1223 could be interpreted as representing either ABBC or MY in Simple Cipher. To avoid this kind of confusion, it is necessary to have double-digit numbers throughout the alphabet, and for this the number 10 or letter K is the starting point. From this, the simplest sequence would be K = 10, L = 11, M = 12 on to Z = 24, then returning to the beginning of the alphabet we would have A = 25, B = 26, up to I = 33.

Bacon and his group, however, seem to have rejected using the straightforward Kay Cipher for some reason, and instead extended it slightly. This extended Kay Cipher was first identified by Mr W. E. Clifton, who, while researching the Kay Cipher, fortuitously discovered the solution in two periodical works, *The Repertoire of Records* (1631) and William Rawley's published collection of Bacon's works, *Resuscitatio* (1671).[5] Clifton found that the two common forms of ampersand ('&' and 'e') were included at the end of the alphabet, so that, when the numbering returned to the beginning of the alphabet, it became A = 27, not 25, and I = 35, not 33.

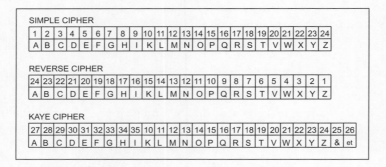

86. *The Simple, Reverse and Kay Ciphers*

By using these three substitution ciphers (Simple, Reverse and Kay), none of them too difficult or complex, not only a double check but also a triple check can be made on the veracity of the cipher message or signature. There are other checks as well, often of a symbolic nature. For instance:

33 = BACON (Simple Cipher)
33 = FREE (Simple Cipher) = the meaning of FRANCIS
67 = FRANCIS (Simple Cipher)
67 = FREE (Reverse Cipher) = the meaning of FRANCIS
100 = FRANCIS BACON (Simple Cipher)
33 (BACON) and 67 (FRANCIS) divide 100 (FRANCIS BACON) into thirds.

33 is a number of major importance, signifying the Thirty-Third Degree, the highest degree of mastery and illumination in Freemasonry, Rosicrucianism and other initiatic Orders, including the Judaic Mysteries and Cabala.[6] Jesus Christ, for instance, was said to have been aged thirty-three when he was crucified and rose from the dead. The number of bones in the spine, through which the kundalini serpent-energy has to be raised, like a fountain of fire, in order to enter the head and produce illumination, is thirty-three. The highest bone of the spine, the thirty-third, is the Atlas, named after the legendary King of Atlantis, who was also known as the Phoenix, or Enoch, 'the Initiate'. Rabbinic literature claims that he was the first human soul to reach the highest heaven both in consciousness and body, to become the Messiah, and that not only do all the wisdom teachings stem from him but that he reappears periodically as the great Teacher to help raise all souls ultimately to the same level of illumination.

The Thirty-Third Degree is sometimes signified by the double-letter 'TT' (employing the Capital Letter Code used by both the Freemasonic and Rosicrucian fraternities, which is still in use today). This 'TT' hieroglyph was used to sign the dedicatory verse to *Shake-speares Sonnets* (see the illustration below) and, as already mentioned, the Introduction to Tenison's *Baconiana*. At the outer, most obvious level of interpretation, the hieroglyph represents the initials of the name of a particular person directly associated with the publication. In the case of the *Sonnets* that person was the printer, Thomas Thorpe, while for *Baconiana* it was the editor, Thomas Tenison. At another level, the 'TT' is a signature carrying a different meaning—a sign that can alert the reader to look for something cryptic.

100 is an extra-special number in the wisdom traditions. It is, for instance, used to denote a thrice-great master, such as Hermes Trismegistus (i.e., Hermes

87. Dedication page: Shake-speares Sonnets (1609)

TO.THE.ONLIE.BEGETTER.OF.
THESE.INSVING.SONNETS.
Mr. W. H. ALL.HAPPINESSE.
AND.THAT.ETERNITIE.
PROMISED.

BY.

OVR.EVER-LIVING.POET.

WISHETH.

THE.WELL-WISHING.
ADVENTVRER.IN.
SETTING.
FORTH.

T. T.

the Thrice-great), who has achieved the Thirty-Third Degree of initiation in terms of the cabalistic holy trinity of power, wisdom and understanding. Francis Bacon described it as:

> ...that triplicity, which in great veneration was ascribed to the ancient Hermes: the power and fortune of a king, the knowledge and illumination of a priest, and the learning and universality of a philosopher.
>
> Francis Bacon, *Advancement of Learning* (1605), Bk I

Since his two names, FRANCIS BACON, not only add to 100 but also divide 100 into one third and two-thirds (*i.e.*, 33 + 67), this triplicity is neatly suggested. It also suggests both the Octave (1 : 2) and Fifth (2 : 3) in music, and the start of the Fibonacci Scale or Golden Mean in geometrical progression (1 : 2 : 3 : 5 : 8, etc.).[7]

In Cabala, 100 is used to denote the spiritual World of Creation, it being 10 x 10 (or 102). 10 is the number of God, the All, as signified by the ten *Sephiroth* and referred to in Cabala as the divine World of Emanation. 10 exists in the single dimension, which modern philosophers might call the unified field that underlies all things. 10 x 10, or 100, is its first extension into space, in a two-dimensional way. 10 x 10 x 10, or 1000 (103), is the third extension, forming three-dimensional space, equated with the psychological or celestial World of Formation.

In sacred architecture and in Freemasonry, which builds the temple, 10 x 10 is the fundamental symbolic measure of the ground plan (or foundation) of the universe. It is represented in the Freemasonic lodge by the chequered floor-cloth, which is composed of an 8 x 8 black-and-white chessboard pattern surrounded by a tessellated border. The border extends the chessboard to the 10 x 10 dimensions.

Modern research has shown that the Globe Theatre in London was based on the same sacred ground plan, its outside circumference being a 100-foot diameter circle that exists, mentally and exactly, within a 10 x 10 square, with each smaller square being 10 ft x 10 ft. The geometric divisions of this determine the ground plan of the rest of the theatre, such as the dimensions of the yard, galleries and stage.

This concept was extended into the organisation of whole societies. One pertinent example is Romulus Quirinus, the Roman spear-shaker and founder of Rome. He divided the people of Rome into three tribes, each tribe having ten curiæ, each curiæ containing ten gentes, and each gentes composed of one hundred people. That is to say, each tribe consisted of ten thousand (100 x 100) people. With three tribes, it meant there were thirty thousand (3 x 100 x 100) Romans. Romulus also instituted a council of one hundred patres or senators. These were the aristocracy who counterbalanced the three-fold power of the king, who was their commander-in-chief, high priest and supreme judge. These one hundred senators were drawn from the three tribes as equally as possible. The numbers 3, 33 or 34, and 100, were thus the ruling numbers or ciphers of the Roman Spear-shaker.

The reason Francis Bacon took his title as Viscount St Alban, after the saint, not the place, has to do with with Freemasonry too. The traditional founder of English Freemasonry is St Alban. By contrast, the Roman city that existed before the medieval town of St Albans was founded was called Verulamium, and Francis' earlier title, Baron Verulam of Verulam, did refer to the place—but to the Roman city rather than the medieval city. Francis therefore adopted for his heraldry a coat of arms depicting two Roman centurions supporting his Bacon family shield (see illustration 48, p. 183). Not only does this depict the Gemini, who were said to be Roman centurions, but also gives a neat double-cipher signature. A centurion was in charge of one hundred men-at-arms, his name being derived from the Latin *centum*, 'one hundred', from which comes our English word 'century'. Whereas 100 is the Simple Cipher for FRANCIS BACON, 200 (*i.e.,* two centuries or 'centurions') is the Reverse Cipher for FRANCIS BACON.

A further cryptograph is that the letter C, the capital letter of 'Centurion', represents the Roman numeral for 100; and C in Simple Cipher is the number 3. Two centurions, therefore, represent the number 33 (i.e., CC = 33). Not only is 33 the Simple Cipher of BACON but also, by inserting the null figure of zero (0), as is allowed and often used in cryptology, we have the number 303. 303 AD is the year given in Freemasonic accounts for the martyrdom of St Alban, even though historically this is not an accurate date (the original St Alban died in 209 AD).[8]

The deliberate association of Francis Bacon with St Alban is of considerable importance, since Masonic historians trace the foundations of modern speculative Freemasonry as being laid in England in the late sixteenth/early seventeenth century. In their legends Freemasons declare that Freemasonry was brought into England from France by St Amphibal and first communicated to St Alban, who 'loved well' the Masons.[9] St Alban (or Albanus), the Masonic history relates, was a knight whose home was at Verulamium and who was appointed by the British Emperor Carausius[10] as the steward of the royal household, chief ruler of the realm and principal superintendent of the Freemasonic assemblies. In 287 AD Carausius granted the Masons a charter and appointed Albanus to preside over them as Grand Master. Albanus set down the Charges and Manners of Masonry, as taught him by his Christian preceptor, Amphibalus (St Amphibal).[11]

The third-century St Alban was adopted as the first patron saint of Britain but was later superseded by the eleventh-century Anglo-Saxon king, Edward the Confessor, who was considered a saint by the English. A century later the crusading Norman king, Richard I, altered this state of affairs and declared England's patron saint to be St George, with the Red Cross and the Rose being the special emblem of the country and nation.

Now, let us see why this is significant. Not only does sixteenth- and seventeenth-century Freemasonry in England seem to be intimately connected with the Rosicrucian Fraternity of that period, but also the cipher numbers 33, 67, 100 and 200 are used frequently and deliberately in the works published under the name of either Francis Bacon or Shakespeare, as also on the Shakespeare memorials. Also used concurrently are the Simple and Kay ciphers for the Fraternity of the Rose Cross, 'FRA ROSI CROSSE', which is 157 in Simple Cipher and 287 in Kay Cipher. To do this, several tricks are employed, some of which are fairly obvious and some not so obvious. The primary cryptograph is the count of words (or sometimes letters) on each key page, with a distinction made between italicised words, normal (Roman) text and, in some special instances, capitals.[12]

Cipher Signatures in the Shakespeare Folio

Portrait verse

The collection of plays in the 1623 Shakespeare Folio is prefaced by nine sheets (eighteen pages), of which all are printed on the front side (recto) but only two are printed on the reverse side (verso), thus giving eleven printed pages that form the introduction to the collection (see illustrations 17–27, pp. 64–75). The two sheets that are printed on their reverse as well as front are the two-page 'Epistle Dedicatorie' signed by John Heminge[s] and Henrie Condell, and the two-page eulogy by Ben Jonson entitled 'To the memory of my beloued, The AUTHOR Mr. WILLIAM SHAKESPEARE: AND what he hath left vs'. Every single one of the printed introductory pages of the 1623 Shakespeare Folio is a key page containing cipher, as also are some other pages in the main volume of the Comedies, Histories and Tragedies, such as the first and last pages of *The Tempest*. But of all these key pages it is perhaps the very first page, containing the portrait verse, which is the key of all the keys (see illustration 17, p. 64). It is, at any rate, the entrance to the mystery—the Alpha of the book.

Not only is the portrait verse cryptic, in the sense previously described, but it also contains cipher that accurately signs the work. In fact, there are various ciphers in this skilfully-constructed verse, but we will just look at the simpler ones, which are perfectly sufficient to make the point. The others (as so far discovered) simply reiterate the same message but in different ways, thereby leaving absolutely nothing to chance. I have rendered the verse below as faithfully to the printed text as possible so as to include its printing anomalies, which in this case, as a key page, are important and allow for the various ciphers to be included. Note that some but not all 'w's are printed as two 'v's, that the single 'v's are printed as 'u's, that some words are capitalised when they are not at the beginning of a line or sentence, and some are not capitalised when they do begin a line:

> To the Reader.
> This Figure, that thou here seest put,
> It was for gentle Shakespeare cut;
> Wherein the Grauer had a strife
> with Nature, to out-doo the life:
> O, could he but haue drawne his wit
> As well in brasse, as he hath hit
> His face; the Print would then surpasse
> All, that vvas euer vvrit in brasse.
> But since he cannot, Reader, looke
> Not on his Picture, but his Booke.
>
> B.I.

After the address, the ten-line verse begins with 'This Figure'. The obvious meaning is that, since the verse is referring to and describing the picture of Shakespeare, the 'Figure' is the picture. However, why use 'Figure' and not the more appropriate word 'Picture' that is used in the last line of the verse? The result is to make the word 'Figure' stand out.

'Picture' can only mean one thing, but another and more usual meaning of 'figure' is number. The words of the verse can therefore be read as meaning that there is a figure or number to be found in the verse, which was 'for gentle Shakespeare cut'. The verse, though, is made up of words, and each word of letters, so where can there be a figure in the verse? But there is one. The very first word ('To') of the whole inscription suggests it, while the opening capitals of the 1st, 3rd and 5th lines, which are made to stand out, spell it. That is to say, it is the figure 2, indicated by the first word 'To' and the opening capitals of the non-indented lines, 'TWO'.

Moreover, the number 2 = B in Simple cipher. If we were to take all five capital letters of the prominent non-indented lines (*i.e.,* lines 1, 3, 5, 7, and 9 of the ten-line verse), we have 'TWOHB'. This gives us 'TWO' plus 'B'—the aspirate 'H', according to normal cipher practice, being a null. So here is a definite emphasis on the number 2 and the letter B.

However, what does 'B' stand for? Using the clue of 'two', we can look to the first and last two letters of the inscription for help—'To' and 'BI'. The Simple Cipher count of the word 'To' is 33 (*i.e.*, T = 19, O = 14), which is also the count of BACON in the same cipher.[13] 'B.I.', on the other hand, has the individual letter values of 2.9. in Simple Cipher. The full stops can sometimes be a sign that the numbers for the letters should be treated separately rather than being added together, and so, if we take them in this way, then 'B.I.' indicates the number 29 which, when reversed, gives 92. This number, 92, is the Reverse Cipher count of BACON.

In this neat way, Bacon has placed his signature at the beginning and the end of the opening inscription of the Shakespeare Folio—an inscription that refers to the author of the Shakespeare plays. With exquisite mastery he uses Simple Cipher at the beginning and Reverse Cipher at the end, with one mirroring the other, and uses two letters in each case to convey his signature, knowing that the number 2 not only equals the letter B in Simple Cipher but also signifies polarity.

Of course, if we had not already discovered, or suspected, that Bacon was the author Shakespeare, we could shrug our shoulders and say that 92 might be the count of another name, and not necessarily Bacon's, as also the number 33; but it would be hard to find a name that began with the letter 'B' and counted 33 in Simple and 92 in Reverse Cipher, and which could be used, therefore, in such a philosophically-beautiful way as in this example. In this kind of situation, the most that cipher can do initially is to confirm what we might suspect or have already discovered using other means, and lead us on to further discoveries: but there are good uses of cipher and bad. The sheer beauty and mastery of this cipher example is that the cipher interplays with and echoes the more esoteric meaning of the text and arrangement of words. The beginning and ending of the verse are its two poles; and the number 2 is pre-eminently the number signifying polarity. In Cabala the holy wisdom and intelligence (*i.e.,* mind) are known as the two poles of creation, with the wisdom being understood as light and the mind being symbolised as a mirror reflecting that light. The reflection of light is the image of light. The Reverse Cipher expresses the image concept, reversing the Simple Cipher that is the object.

To follow this cipher trail to its logical conclusion we should now look for a second way in which the signature is provided, which should complement and confirm the first. Therefore, instead of taking the first and last two letters of the whole inscription, let us take the second word and the second-to-last word of the ten-line verse. The second word is 'Figure', which we already know indicates both the picture of Shakespeare and the number 2, the cipher of 'B', and therefore acts as a key for us. The second to last word of the verse is 'his',

three years. He was rightly denoted under the emblem of the eagle, for his piercing sight into the Divinity; and was a Seraph among the Apostles in respect of his burning Love.

Francis Bacon, *History of Life and Death*

In other words, '93' (or 'IC') is Francis Bacon's cipher for St John the Beloved, the great seer. To say he lived to ninety-three is deliberately to manufacture his age, for tradition asserts that St John lived to be more than one hundred years old. St John's emblem is the eagle, and the *Confession* of the Rosicrucians warns that only those who have received strength borrowed from the eagle may behold the Rosicrucian fraternity and their House of the Holy Spirit. Both St Johns—the Baptist and the Beloved—are taken as the patron saints of Freemasonry, the former associated with midsummer and the latter with midwinter, the two poles of the year. The Craft degrees, however, are more concerned with the Baptist, who purifies, while the higher degrees have a greater link with the meaning of the Beloved, who sees and knows.

In Greek gematria, 93 is the cipher of αγαπε, the ancient Greek word for love in its pure or spiritual form. As Francis Bacon points out, St John the Beloved, who taught that God is love, was known above all as the Apostle of love. His association with Freemasonry and Rosicrucianism can be seen in one key word alone—'free'. 'Free', from Sanskrit *prij*, means 'love' or 'loving'. One of the meanings of the title 'Freemason', therefore, is 'Builder of love', or 'loving builder'. The path of such a labourer, whether belonging to a specific organisation or not, is the path indicated by Jesus when he taught: 'Blessed are the pure in heart: for they shall see God'.[20] First, purify the heart, then one can begin to see God and be illumined.

The number of letters in the wording on the portrait page, which is also the title page, adds up to 157, which is the count of FRA ROSI CROSSE in Simple Cipher.

The Face of Shakespeare

The face of Shakespeare is another of the enigmatic clues to be carefully emphasised in this extraordinary game of hide-and-seek. In the title-page portrait of Shakespeare the face of the author Shakespeare is deliberately veiled or masked by that of the actor; and Ben Jonson's portrait verse fronting the Shakespeare Folio urges us to look at the book of plays, not the engraved picture, if we want to find Shakespeare's wit or mind, the real author; for it is by the mind that he will be seen:

O, could he but have drawne his wit
    As well in brasse, as he hath hit
His face; the Print would then surpasse
    All, that was ever writ in brasse.
But since he cannot, Reader, looke
    Not on his Picture, but his Booke.

The whole sense of Jonson's verse relates exactly to a miniature portrait by Nicholas Hilliard of Francis Bacon, painted for Bacon's eighteenth birthday (25 January 1578, Old Style)[21] at which time both men were residing at the French Court in Paris (see illustration 43, p. 159). The comment painted around the portrait exclaims:

Si tabula daretur digna animum mallem.
['If only a picture deserving of his mind could be made.']

King Duncan, in Shakespeare's *Macbeth,* reiterates the theme:

Duncan. There's no art
    To find the mind's construction in the face...

Shakespeare, Macbeth, I, iv, 11–12

It matches the old English proverb: 'You can't tell a parcel by its wrapping'. To find what's really inside, one has to remove the wrapping and open the parcel—or, in this case, the book.

By the mind I shall be seen

Henry Peacham emphasises this same philosophy in his book *Minerva Britanna,* published in 1612, which is very suggestive of the Shakespeare mystery. Britannia, like Minerva or Pallas Athena, is a Spear-shaker (or was, until a trident replaced her spear). She is the British equivalent of the Greek Pallas Athena or Roman Minerva. Peacham makes this connection abundantly clear in his title, coupling Minerva and Britannia together, as well as using a more unusual form of the name of the British goddess—Britanna.[22]

The title page of *Minerva Britanna* depicts someone concealed behind a theatrical curtain, with the person's right arm reaching in front of the curtain and writing with a quill pen in his right hand on a scroll of parchment. The Latin words that are written on the scroll read, *'Mente Videbor'* ('By the mind I shall be seen'). Entwined in a poet's wreath of bay leaves surrounding the central picture are two further scrolls bearing inscriptions which state the higher/lower self theme: the scroll on the heraldic right of the picture reads *'Vivitur in*

88. Title page,
Minerva Britanna
(1612)

genio' ('One lives in one's genius'), and the other on the heraldic left states *'Caetera mortis erunt'* ('All else passes away'). A further inscription at the top of the page, associated with two candle flames, reads *'Ut aliis me consumo'* ('What else consumes me?'). The presence of the wreath of bay leaves emphasises that the hidden writer is a poet.

Not only does this title page reiterate the Neoplatonic philosophy concerning the higher and lower selves, presenting it in a cabalistic way, but also it vividly depicts the veiling of a poet as well as the veiling of truth. Besides the title, which could be interpreted as 'the British Minerva' or 'the British Spear-shaker', the mottos on the right- and left-hand scrolls strongly suggest that this poet might be Shakespeare because of the higher/lower self theme which matches that of the Shakespeare sonnets. There is, moreover, an obvious invitation to draw the curtain aside, as in a theatre, so as to see the Mystery.

James Arthur, author of *A Royal Romance,* found a particular solution to the puzzle by noticing that certain stanzas from Shakespeare's *Lucrece,* which describe a 'skilful painting, made for Priam's Troy', are illustrated in the emblem on page 33 of Peacham's book, and that these refer, like the title page of *Minerva Britanna,* to a person unseen:

> For much imaginary work was there,—
> Conceit deceiptful, so compact, so kind,
> That for Achilles' image stood his spear
> Gripp'd in an armed hand; himself behind
> Was left unseen, save to the eye of mind:
>> A hand, a foot, a face, a leg, a head
>> Stood for the whole to be imagined.

Shakespeare, Lucrece, lines 1422–8

The picture described in *Lucrece* is of the Greek army and their hero Achilles, drawn up before the walls of Troy in order to revenge the rape of Helen and thereby right the wrong by overthrowing the evildoers. In *Lucrece* it is used as an illustration of Lucrece's dilemma and her hopes for revenge: she being, like Helen, a virtuous wife raped by a man holding royal power and authority. Achilles is represented in the picture solely by his famous spear, so that he is 'left unseen, save to the eye of mind'.

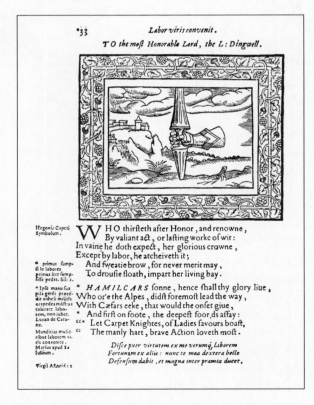

89. Page 33, Minerva Britanna (1612)

The *Minerva Britanna* emblem depicts this same scene and in the same way, presenting itself as the picture described by Shakespeare in his *Lucrece*. It provides two accompanying verses, the second one referring the emblem picture to Hannibal, Hamilcar's son, who crossed the Alps with elephants and defeated the Romans, and the first containing a much finer philosophy: that he who desires honour and renown, either by valiant act or lasting work of wit, can only achieve such laurels of fame through hard labour. There is the suggestion, therefore, that just as the fall of Troy led to the establishment of a new order of society, and the banishment of the rapist Tarquin and his family from Rome brought about a change of government from kings to consuls, so the achievements of chivalric spear-shakers could bring about a new and better era. These are thoughts akin to those developed in several of the Shakespeare tragedies, such as *Macbeth, Cymbeline, King Lear, Romeo and Juliet* and *Hamlet*, whereas the very first line of this *Minerva Britanna* emblem, 'Who thirsteth after Honor, and renowne,' sounds very similar in theme to the first line of Shakespeare's *Love's Labour's Lost,* 'Let Fame, that all hunt after in their lives'.

The page 33 emblem is dedicated to 'the most Honourable Lord, the L: Dingwall'. Lord Dingwall was Sir Richard Preston, whose particular pageant for King James' Accession Day Tilt of 1609 was an elephant with a castle on its

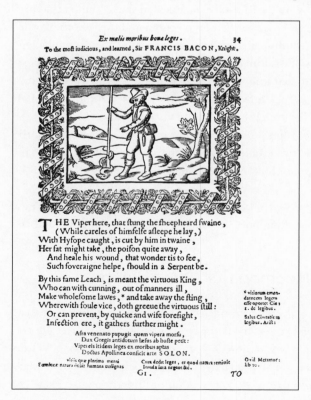

90. Page 34, Minerva Britanna (1612)

back—the Hannibal theme. The emblem, however, which portrays a disembodied, gauntleted hand holding (or shaking) a spear, not only has a direct connection to the Achilles reference in Shakespeare's *Lucrece* but also to the words 'Mente Videbor' being written on the title page scroll by a veiled poet, with the hand holding the spear in the emblem picture equivalent to the hand holding the quill in the title page illustration. It seems, therefore, to be a direct reference to the concealed author of the Shakespeare poems and plays.

Following this clue, James Arthur realised that the words 'himself behind' in the *Lucrece* verse gave the hint that he should look behind the page 33 emblem, and therefore at the following emblem on page 34, in order to discover the veiled spear-shaker or Shakespeare. The page 34 emblem is dedicated to 'the most judicious, and learned, Sir FRANCIS BACON, Knight'. The emblem picture portrays a shepherd with a spear, who is in the process of spearing a poisonous snake that has just bitten him. The shepherd-knight is a typical Arcadian figure used by the Elizabethan poets as a symbol of the courtly or chivalrous poet, such as presented by Sir Philip Sidney in his *Arcadia* and by Edmund Spenser in his *Shepheard's Calendar* and *Faerie Queene*.

The emblem's verses declare that the fat of the viper can provide healing for the wound, neutralising the poison—knowledge that has been confirmed by modern scientists,[23] who have found a chemical in snake's blood that prevents the snakes being poisoned by their own venom and the venom of other species. Following the Apollonian and Athenian myth of the Spear-shakers, who shake their spears of wisdom at the dragons of ignorance and vice in order to generate enlightened knowledge and virtue, this action is likened in the verse to the healing of society by taking away the poison of foul vice through the use of wholesome laws made by a wise and virtuous king.

The page numbers 33 and 34 chosen for the emblems further confirm the direct association of the two emblems with each other as well as their meaning. 33 is the Simple Cipher for BACON. Adding 34 to 33 gives 67, the Simple Cipher for FRANCIS.

When all these factors are taken together, the message for us is that Francis Bacon is the spear-shaking poet or 'Shakespeare' who stands behind the picture or veil.

The Noble and Incomparable Pair of Brethren

The third printed page of the Folio, immediately following the title page with its cryptic portrait, is the first page of the two-page 'Epistle Dedicatorie' (see illustration 20, p. 66). This letter, which is addressed to and dedicates the Folio to William Herbert, Earl of Pembroke, and Philip Herbert, Earl of Montgomery, sons of Mary Sidney, Countess of Pembroke, is also Freemasonic or Rosicrucian in context.

The letter begins: 'To the Most Noble and Incomparable Paire of Brethren'. This form of address, to a 'Pair of Brethren', is highly unusual in normal parlance and is definitely suggestive of two brethren of either the Rosicrucian or Freemasonic fraternity. In fact, since the Rosicrucian fraternity and its degrees seem to have been the higher chivalric degrees of Freemasonry in the sixteenth and seventeenth centuries, the entry to which degrees was the degree of the Royal Arch of Solomon, the 'noble' would seem to indicate a Royal Arch initiate or higher. 'Incomparable', meaning above or beyond compare, would appear to indicate the highest degree, the rulers of the fraternity. William and Philip may indeed have been the two co-Principals (Second and Third), equivalent at a higher Rosicrucian level to the Senior and Junior Grand Wardens in a Craft Grand Lodge, since in the Folio they 'stand behind' the two Great Pillars, Boaz and Jachin ('B.I.'), which is the allotted position of the two Wardens.[24] The expression 'Paire of Brethren' also continues the theme of 'Two' and the Gemini.

The dedicatory letter is carefully composed, and the type it is set in is carefully arranged on the two pages of the Folio on which it is printed. A large part of the text is skilfully based on the dedicatory address to the Emperor Vespasian prefacing Pliny's *Natural History*, and is full of legal terms such as 'arraign', 'tryalls,' 'appeals,' 'quitted by a decree of Court' and 'purchased'. Francis Bacon's familiarity with Pliny's dedicatory address can be seen in his letters to King James I in 1603, to George Villiers (later Earl, Marquis and Duke of Buckingham) in 1616, and to the House of Lords in 1620.

The count of words in italics (including capitalised initials as single words) on the first page of the Epistle Dedicatorie is 157, the Simple Cipher of FRA ROSI CROSSE. The count of italic words on the second page, including the page heading, is 287, the Kay Cipher of FRA ROSI CROSSE (see illustration 21, p. 67). As for the strange but very carefully-arranged spacing, using tricks of the printer's trade and specially-cut characters, it has been demonstrated that the primary reason for this was to enable a cryptogram using the Squared Cipher method, an example of which was printed in *Cryptomenitices* (see illustration 91, p. 363), as well as the Simple and Kay Cipher counts. The specially-cut letters have elongated tails, thereby creating—where required, and without arousing too much suspicion—far wider letter-spacing than normal. These are the only two pages in the Folio where this peculiarity of printing appears. An example of its use is given in *Cryptomenitices*, Book 6, chapter 24, page 336 (see illustration 92, p. 363). This is not the place to go into detail about the Squared Cipher cryptogram in this 'Epistle Dedicatorie', which is far more complex than the Simple, Reverse and Kay Cipher methods, but its likely existence is worth noting.[25]

Hic Versus vario colore diſpar.   Versus Hrabani hi ſunt:

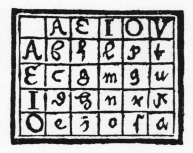

*Litera Lineis incluſa, pergnè aream hinc indè ſparſa, prima, oɛlava,
decimaquinta, vigeſima ſecunda, vigeſima nona & triceſima ſexta, ſive
ultima, tranverſaus Linea prima, oɛlava, decimaquinta, vigeſima ſecunda, vigeſima nona & trigeſima ſexte ſive ultima hujus quadrati,
ſequentia promunt verba.*

Magnentius Hrabanus Maurus hoc Opus fecit.

Baconies

Heading the first Dedication page is a woodcut illustration known as the Cupid, Dionysus or Archer headpiece. Because it is at the top of the page, it is the very first thing that can be seen and read after the portrait of Shakespeare. The headpiece is full of Neoplatonic and alchemical symbolism, and contains a neat Baconian signature in the form of a rebus.

Besides ciphers, which had been rapidly developed into an important science and art during Queen Elizabeth's reign, and formed a vital part of statecraft, the Elizabethans and Jacobeans were very fond of symbols and riddles, both in words and pictures. Emblem books such as Peacham's *Minerva Britanna* were, therefore, very popular, and symbolism was a language in which most people were literate. Rebuses were part of this play of wit, especially when representing a person's name.

A rebus in the general sense is a puzzle consisting of pictures representing syllables or words,[26] while in the more specific sense of a person's name it is a pictorial representation of or a pun on the name of the person, which was used a great deal in heraldry. For instance, the last prior of St Bartholomew's Priory in London used the rebus of a bolt (arrow) piercing a tun (a large beer cask) to represent his name, Bolton. This rebus can still be found carved on a

of roman letters in the same first page of the poem totals 132, the Simple Cipher for FRANCIS ST ALBAN, one of Francis Bacon's signatures when he was Viscount St Alban.

In a slightly different way of counting, the heading of the poem consists of seventeen words and seventy-one letters, totalling 88 (i.e., 17 + 71). 88 is the Simple Cipher for FR ST ALBAN, the shortened form of Bacon's signature as Viscount St Alban.

In another variation of this cipher game, the second page of Jonson's poem has 156 roman letters. This contains a double signature, in that 100 = FRANCIS BACON and 56 = FR BACON in Simple Cipher. The italic words, including Jonson's signature of 'BEN: IONSON' at the end of the poem, amount to 314, the Kay Cipher of FRANCIS ST ALBAN.

By now these cipher signatures have become more of a game, providing confirmations but no more, the definitive ciphers and clues having already been given. This is, perhaps, in keeping with the cabalistic design of the first ten pages, since, in terms of cabalistic symbolism associated with Cabala's 'Tree of Life', we have now passed the 'heart' of the matter and are descending from the more spiritual and ordered into the more chaotic or mortal realms of existence. We shall, therefore, skip on now past the remaining pages of the first ten, which contain the dedicatory poems, to the eleventh page, the list of actors, which starts a new sequence—the sequence of plays.

The First Original

After the dedicatory poems is the list of principal actors, printed on a page that is like a second title page (see illustration 27, p.75). At the top, above the list of principal players, the title of the book is displayed for the second time but in a way that tells a blatant lie: 'The Workes of William Shakespeare, containing all his Comedies, Histories, and Tragedies: Truly set forth, according to their first ORIGINALL'. Allowing for the fact that ultimately *Troilus and Cressida* was included in the Folio (but not *Pericles*, which had to wait for the Third Folio before it was included), the declaration that they are all truly set forth according to their first original is a known untruth, just as the statement in Heminges and Condell's letter to the great Variety of Readers declaring that they 'have scarce received from him [Shakespeare] a blot in his papers' is unbelievable.

However, just as Ben Jonson and those responsible for the Stratford-upon-Avon Shakespeare Monument explained the true meaning of the latter statement, so the former declaration can be understood in another way that is not a lie. That is to say, this 1623 Folio presentation of the plays, as a 'temple of light', with veils hiding mystery after mystery, is truly the first or original such publication of these works. The second sense of the phrase 'according to their first ORIGINALL', with 'ORIGINALL' emphasised as it is, in capitals and an entirely different font (and in the singular rather than the plural that it should have been in if referring to the original manuscripts of the plays), is referring to the Originator of the plays—the Author. That is to say, the Comedies, Histories and Tragedies are truly set forth according to the Author, who is the First Original or Principal, the supreme head of the fraternity.

List of Actors

The list of the principal actors demonstrates a further variation in how the ciphers are counted, continuing the game of wit that is clearly being played. The count of all the letters in the list of principal actors totals 332, which is not one of the cipher signatures. Neither is the count of letters in the list heading ('The Names of the Principall Actors in all these Playes'), which totals 45. But if we deduct 45 from 332 the answer is 287, the Kay Cipher of FRA ROSI CROSSE!

This leaves us with the top heading (the second title of the Folio) and the beautifully illumined and squared 'W' (actually two V's). The latter is in a league of its own, with its two Pan-faced creatures peering out on either side of the interlaced double-V, but the heading contains more of the same type of cipher at which we are looking.

The top heading is made up of two parts: the first three lines and the blatantly unique 'ORIGINAL' on the fourth line, which begs to be numbered separately. The first line has two capital W's, each of which is in fact two V's. The count of the letters of the top three lines, therefore, comes to 111, the Kay Cipher of BACON. Then, in a superlative demonstration of wit, the letter count of 'ORIGINALL' is 9, the Simple Cipher for I. In general terms the first Original is of course the Ego—the 'I'. The First Original of this Folio, though, is the Author—'I, Bacon, Fra Rosi Crosse,' as this second title page declares.

Set Me Free

The Tempest is the first play to be printed in the Shakespeare Folio. Beginnings are always important, just as entrances are to buildings and title pages are to books. In traditional sacred architecture, it is a maxim that the main entrance should either hint at or depict in some way something of the mystery that can be discovered inside the building, like a kind of ground plan or map, so as to prepare and excite the pilgrim. Likewise good title pages may show something similar about the book. As I have mentioned in chapter 12, in Cabala the Beginning is represented by the number 1 and the letter A, which are said to contain everything. All numbers proceed from the number 1 and all letters of the alphabet from the letter A. In the Shakespeare Folio, the preliminary pages act as the doorway to the folio of plays; but in terms of the plays themselves *The Tempest* is the Alpha, the entrance to and beginning of the Mystery.

Why *The Tempest* should have been chosen for this position is obviously important. Possibly equally important is why it is traditionally referred to as the last Shakespeare play. From where did this tradition emanate and why? We have already suggested that *The Tempest* presents in dramatic form Bacon's whole scheme of the Great Instauration, so this is a good reason in itself for it to be the first play in the Folio. It also presents, in the character of Prospero, a personification not only of a Rosicrucian adept but a possible symbolic likeness of the author himself—one who inherited the mantle of Dr John Dee and others, and went one step further—trying to discover what mercy really is, without the loss of justice and true discipline. Having mastered the lesser laws of nature, the final step into true mastery is to give up that mastery and release the spirit of love entirely to perform its own independent will. Hence the very last words of the play, spoken by Prospero to the audience, are: 'As you from crimes would pardon'd be, Let your Indulgence set me free' (see illustration 99, p. 368).

Not only is this a complex theological presentation of divine law, in the sense of how the law of prayer, forgiveness and divine mercy work, but also in the last *two* words is the signature of the Master. For instance, the very last word is 'free'. As I have pointed out earlier, the Simple Cipher count of FREE is 33, which is also the Simple Cipher count of BACON. The Reverse Cipher count of FREE is 67, which is the Simple Cipher count of FRANCIS. The name 'Francis' means 'free'; and the word 'free' has a meaning of 'love'. As for the second to last word, 'Me', it has the count of 33, the Simple Cipher of BACON, as well as referring to the ego—either Prospero or the author Francis Bacon. That is to say, not only does the last word, 'free', represent both 'Francis' and 'Bacon' in a unique way, but also the last two words, 'me free', give the cipher of either 33.33 ('Bacon-Bacon') or 33.67 ('Bacon, Francis'). 33.33 also adds to 66 ('Fra Baconi'), Francis Bacon's Latin signature on books, signifying 'by Francis Bacon', just to make sure we grasp it.[33]

After reading the cryptic signatures and meanings of the Folio's introductory pages, we shouldn't really be surprised by this concluding flourish to *The Tempest*. It is but one further signature of the author Shakespeare, displaying the brilliance of his mind as is so amply vouched for by the plays themselves. It is certainly neat, especially when one considers that the very first word of *The Tempest*, as printed, is 'Master' (see illustration 98). This first word is not spoken, as it is simply the author's identification of the character (the master or captain of the vessel) who speaks the first spoken word of the play. However, taken in the cryptic and cabalistic way, it is noteworthy: for the beginning of the play, as printed, is the unspoken name of the 'Master' while the ending of the play is the spoken name of the Master—'Free' or 'Francis' or 'Francis Bacon', or 'Love'. As Cabala teaches: sound proceeds from silence, light from darkness, and the known from the unknown.

Hang-hog

There are various scenes in many of the Shakespeare plays where the conversation of the more ordinary members of society verges on the ridiculous. Often this is a way of introducing some light-hearted relief into the intense drama, which can give us pause to breathe and take stock, and ground the experience of the play with some earthy humour. However, such scenes often contain remarkable puns and witticisms that are ciphers of another kind that tell the truth. One such example is in *The Merry Wives of Windsor*, Act IV, scene 1. To fully appreciate it, however, one has to read the original text as printed in the Shakespeare Folio, as that is the book with the keys. The important part of the scene in question is printed on the second column of page 53 of the Comedies.

The scene involves a conversation between Mistress Quickly, Mistress Page, her son William and a Welsh parson named Sir Hugh Evans. Evans is asked by Mistress Page to give instruction to her son because the school is closed that day. The instruction, in Latin, then commences, with occasional interjections by the women. The whole object of introducing the Welshman, however, seems to have been that he might mispronounce 'c' as 'g' and thereby say 'hig' and 'hog' instead of 'hic' and 'hoc'. William is also made to say, wrongly, that the accusative case is 'hinc' instead of 'hunc', and Evans, who should have corrected this error, repeats the blunder but with the change of 'c' into 'g' so as to give without confusion the right signature key-words, 'hing, hang, hog'. Mistress Quickly is then able to deliver the cipher sentence, 'Hang-hog is latten for Bacon, I warrant you':

> *Eva.* That is good *William*: what is he (*William*) that do's lend Articles.
> *Will.* Articles are borrowed of the Pronoune; and be thus declined.
>   *Singulariter nominatino hic hac, hoc.*
> *Eva. Nominatino hig, hag, hog*: pray you mark: *genitino huius*: Well, what is
>   your *Accusative-case*?
> *Will. Accusatino hinc.*
> *Eva.* I pray you have your remembrance (childe) *Accusatino hing, hang,*
>   *hog.*
> *Qu.* Hang-hog, is latten for Bacon, I warrant you.
> *Eva.* Leave your prables (o'man)....

THE TEMPEST.

Actus primus, Scena prima.

A tempestuous noise of Thunder and Lightning heard: Enter a Ship-master, and a Botefwaine.

Master.

Ote-fwaine.

Botef. Heere Mafter : What cheere ?

Maft. Good : Speake to th'Mariners : fall too't, yarely, or we run our felues a ground, beftirre, beftirre.   *Exit.*

Enter Mariners.

Botef. Heigh my hearts, cheerely, cheerely my harts ; yare, yare : Take in the toppe-fale : Tend to th'Mafters whiftle : Blow till thou burft thy winde , if roome e-nough.

Enter Alonfo, Sebaftian, Anthonio, Ferdinando, Gonzalo, and others.

Alon. Good Botefwaine haue care : where's the Ma-fter ? Play the men.

Botef. I pray now keepe below.

Anth. Where is the Mafter, Bofon ?

Botef. Do you not heare him ? you marre our labour, Keepe your Cabines : you do afsift the ftorme.

Gonz. Nay, good be patient.

Botef. When the Sea is : hence, what cares thefe roa-rers for the name of King ? to Cabine ; filence : trouble vs not.

Gon. Good, yet remember whom thou haft aboord.

Botef. None that I more loue then my felfe. You are a Counfellor, if you can command thefe Elements to fi-lence, and worke the peace of the prefent, wee will not hand a rope more, vfe your authoritie : If you cannot, giue thankes you haue liu'd fo long, and make your felfe readie in your Cabine for the mifchance of the houre, if it fo hap. Cheerely good hearts : out of our way I fay.   *Exit.*

Gon. I haue great comfort from this fellow : methinks he hath no drowning marke vpon him, his complexion is perfect Gallowes : ftand faft good Fate to his han-ging, make the rope of his deftiny our cable, for our owne doth little aduantage : If he be not borne to bee hang'd, our cafe is miferable.   *Exit.*

Enter Botefwaine.

Botef. Downe with the top-Maft : yare, lower, lower, bring her to Try with Maine-courfe. A plague——

A cry within.   Enter Sebaftian, Anthonio & Gonzalo.

vpon this howling : they are lowder then the weather, or our office : yet againe ? What do you heere. Shal we giue ore and drowne, haue you a minde to finke ?

Sebaf. A poxe o'your throat, you bawling, blafphe-mous incharitable Dog.

Botef. Worke you then.

Anth. Hang cur, hang, you whorefon infolent Noyfe-maker, we are leffe afraid to be drownde, then thou arr.

Gonz. I'le warrant him for drowning, though the Ship were no ftronger then a Nutt-fhell, and as leaky as an vnftanched wench.

Botef. Lay her a hold, a hold , fet her two courfes off to Sea againe, lay her off.

Enter Mariners wet.

Mari. All loft, to prayers, to prayers, all loft.

Botef. What muft our mouths be cold ?

Gonz. The King, and Prince, at prayers, let's affift them, for our cafe is as theirs.

Sebaf. I am out of patience.

An. We are meerly cheated of our liues by drunkards, This wide-chopt-rafcall, would thou mightft lye drow-ning the wafhing of ten Tides.

Gonz. Hee'l be hang'd yet,

Though euery drop of water fweare againft it,

And gape at widft to glut him.   *A confufed noyfe within.*

Mercy on vs.

We fplit, we fplit , Farewell my wife, and children,

Farewell brother : we fplit, we fplit, we fplit.

Anth. Let's all finke with' King

Seb. Let's take leaue of him.   *Exit.*

Gonz. Now would I giue a thoufand furlongs of Sea, for an Acre of barren ground : Long heath, Browne firrs, any thing ; the wills aboue be done, but I would faine dye a dry death.   *Exit.*

Scena Secunda.

Enter Profpero and Miranda.

Mira. If by your Art (my deereft father) you haue Put the wild waters in this Rore ; alay them : The skye it feemes would powre down ftinking pitch, But that the Sea, mounting to th' welkins cheeke, Dafhes the fire out. Oh ! I haue fuffered With thofe that I faw fuffer : A braue veffell

A   (Who

The Tempeſt. 19

And ſeeke for grace : what a thrice double Aſſe
Was I to take this drunkard for a god ?
And worſhip this dull foole?
   Pro. Goe to, away.   *found it.*
   Alo. Hence, and beſtow your luggage where you
Seb. Or ſtole it rather.
   Pro. Sir, I inuite your Highneſſe, and your traine
To my poore Cell : where you ſhall take your reſt
For this onenight, which part of it, Ile waſte
With ſuch diſcourſe, as I not doubt, ſhall make it
Goe quicke away : The ſtory of my life,
And the particular accidents, gon by
Since I came to this Iſle : And in the morne
I'le bring you to your ſhip, and ſo to *Naples,*

Where I haue hope to ſee the nuptiall
Of theſe our deere-belou'd, ſolemnized,
And thence retire me to my *Millaine,* where
Euery third thought ſhall be my graue.
   Alo. I long
To heare the ſtory of your life ; which muſt
Take the eare ſtarngely:
   Pro. I'le deliuer all,
And promiſe you calme Seas, auſpicious gales,
And ſaile, ſo expeditious, that ſhall catch
Your Royall ſteete farre off : My *Ariel* ; chicke
That is thy charge: Then to the Elements
Be free, and fare thou well : pleaſe you draw neere.
              Exeunt omnes.

EPILOGVE,
ſpoken by *Proſpero.*

NOw my *Charmes* are all ore-throwne,
  And what ſtrength I haue's mine owne.
Which is moſt faint : now 'tis true
I muſt be heere confinde by you,
Or ſent to Naples, Let me not ·
Since I haue my Dukedome got ,
And pardon'd the deceiuer, dwell
In this bare Iſland, by your Spell,
But releaſe me from my bands
With the helpe of your good hands :
Gentle breath of yours, my Sailes
Muſt fill, or elſe my proiect failes,
which was to pleaſe : Now I want
Spirits to enforce : Art to inchant,
And my ending is deſpaire,
Vnleſſe I be reliev'd by praier
Which pierces ſo, that it aſſaults
Mercy it ſelfe, and frees all faults.
  As you from crimes would pardon'd be,
  Let your Indulgence ſet me free.   Exit.

The Scene, an vn-inhabited Iſland
Names of the Actors.

Alonſo, K. of Naples:
Sebaſtian his Brother.
Proſpero, the right Duke of Millaine.
Anthonio his brother, the vſurping Duke of Millaine.
Ferdinand, Son to the King of Naples.
Gonzalo, an honeſt old Counceller.
Adrian, & Franciſco, Lords.
Caliban, a ſaluage and deformed ſlaue.
Trincalo, a Ieſter.
Stephano, a drunken Butler.
Maſter of a Ship.
Boate-Swaine.
Marriners.
Miranda, daughter to Proſpero.
Ariell, an ayrie ſpirit.
Iris
Ceres
Iuno   } *Spirits.*
Nymphes
Reapers

FINIS.

THE

THE SHAKESPEARE ENIGMA

Modern editors, completely misunderstanding the meaning, have usually changed the Folio's 'latten' to 'Latin' and reduced 'Bacon' to 'bacon', which kills the intended allusion and hidden meaning. In fact this 'hang-hog' remark relates to a story carefully recorded for posterity by Francis Bacon in one of his apothegms, referring to his father, Sir Nicholas Bacon, Queen Elizabeth's first Lord Keeper, who, as judge, had to sentence a convicted murderer named Hog to be hanged. Hog tried to gain leniency by pleading that he was kin to the Lord Keeper by virtue of his name, but Sir Nicholas replied that 'Hog is not Bacon until it be well hanged'. This was printed as Apophthegm 36 in *Resuscitatio* (1671) published by Dr William Rawley:

> Sir Nicholas Bacon, being appointed a Judge for the Northern Circuit, and having brought his Trials that came before him to such a pass, as the passing of Sentence on the Malefactors, he was by one of the Malefactors mightily importuned for to save his life, which when nothing he had said did avail, he at length desired his mercy on the account of kindred: 'Prethee,' said my Lord Judge, 'how came that in?' 'Why if it please you my Lord, your name is Bacon, and mine is Hog, and in all Ages Hog and Bacon have been so near kindred, that they are not to be separated.' 'I but,' replyed Judge Bacon, 'you and I cannot be kindred, except you be hanged; for Hog is not Bacon until it be well hanged.'
>
> Francis Bacon, Apophthegm 36, *Resuscitatio* (1671)

This story is told by Bacon for its value as a parable, and this is pointed out by Evans in his rejoinder to Mistress Quickly in the next line of the play, where he notes that she has spoken a 'prable' (parable): 'Leave your prables (o'man)'.

'Latten' means a mixture of metals, particularly an alloy resembling or identical to brass. It is used elsewhere in the Shakespeare plays and in Bacon's letters as a wordplay on 'Latin'. This wordplay forms a series of puns, such that 'latten' infers a debased Latin or secret language, confirmed by the Latin word 'latens', meaning concealed.[34]

There is a mystical or mystery context to this story, for the pig—the special emblem of the Eleusinian Mysteries—signified a pupil and son of Apollo, as well as the sacrificial offering to be made. The candidate for initiation was given a pig to look after. When he came to the final initiation he had to sacrifice the pig, which was emblematic of his own self or ego that had to psychologically die in order to enter a higher state of consciousness and expression of life. Death by hanging had reference to initiation, while death by drowning had reference to failure or ordinary death, hence the importance attached to it in *The Tempest* by Gonzalo:

Gonzalo. I have great comfort from this fellow: methinks he hath no drowning mark upon him; his complexion is perfect gallows. Stand fast, good fate, to his hanging: make the rope of his destiny our cable, for our own doth little advantage. If he be not born to be hanged, our case is miserable.'

Shakespeare, The Tempest, I, i, 35

This is a remark that at face value is a straightforward witticism, but actually is chosen carefully by the playwright for its deeper connotation.

Seely Sheep

Another fine example of Francis Bacon's virtuoso wit and love of symbolism, puns, metaphors and enigma mixed with cipher is a comic scene in *Love's Labour's Lost* (V, i) involving Holofernes the schoolmaster or pedant, Sir Nathaniel the curate, Dull the constable, Don Adriano de Armado the braggart knight, Moth the page or boy, and Costard the clown.

The scene begins with Sir Nathaniel, Holofernes and Dull coming out from dinner, where Sir Nathaniel and Holofernes have enjoyed a witty conversation, which they then continue outside the hall. They start talking about Don Adriano de Armado, with whom Sir Nathaniel conversed earlier that day. Don Adriano, let us remember, is a caricature of the King of Spain's ex-minister, Antonio Perez. Holofernes, who says in Latin that he knows the man as well as he knows Sir Nathaniel, describes him accurately and precisely, and includes the newly-created word 'peregrinate' derived from Perez' name:

> *Hol. Novi hominem tanquam te:* His humour is lofty, his discourse peremptory: his tongue filed, his eye ambitious, his gait majestical, and his general behaviour vain, ridiculous, and thrasonical. He is too picked, too spruce, too affected, too odd, as it were, too peregrinate, as I may call it.

Shakespeare, Love's Labour's Lost, V, i

Don Adriano, Moth and Costard soon join them. Costard, hearing the conversation between the pedant and curate, marvels that Holofernes has not swallowed up Moth like he swallows his words, and compares Moth to the famously long word, 'Honorificabilitudinitatibus'. It is Don Adriano, though, who opens up a fascinating game of wit between Moth and his tutor that has more to it than meets the eye:

cipher signature within the long word. Moth (the page) deliberately empha-sises two sets of two vowels, 'ui' and 'ou':

> *Page.* The last of the five Vowles if You repeat them, or the fifth if I.
> *Peda.* I will repeat them: a e I.
> *Page.* The Sheepe, the other two concludes it o u.

There has also been a witty repartee concerning the turning around of a word, or letters, and placing one upon the head of the other (*i.e.,* 'What is Ab speld backward with the horn on his head?'). If we follow this vein of wit and turn *honorificabilitudinitatibus* backwards, and then place it underneath the word spelt normally (*i.e.,* forwards), we can then see what Bacon hoped we would notice:

100. Honorifica-bilitudinitatibus: 'Fr Bacon' Signature

In the forward arrangement the letters of Bacon's name, FR BACON, are spelt out backwards in the third to the eleventh letter, as an anagram, with the two additional I's standing guard on each side of the letter F in the middle of the anagram (i.e., NORIFICAB). In the backward arrangement Ba-con's name is spelt out forwards, in the third to the eleventh letter from the end, likewise as an anagram and with the two I's included (i.e., BACIFIRON).

It should now be possible to see that Moth's two groups of vowels frame the two versions of Bacon's signature, like twin pillars each side of each signa-ture:

101. Honorifica-bilitudinitatibus: Baconian Twin Pillars

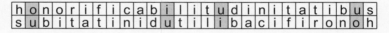

These four columns appear in the diagram as column numbers 2, 12, 16 and 26. The sum of these four numbers is 56, which is the Simple Cipher of FR BACON.

The Perfect Master

As might be expected if Francis Bacon was the author Shakespeare, the name Francis appears many times in the Shakespeare plays. *I Henry IV* has particular fun with the name, drawing attention to it by emphasising it over and over again in Act II, scene iv, in conjunction with the word 'anon'. In this scene there is a short mini-scene of banter between Prince Henry and a 'drawer' (*i.e.,* barman) called Francis. This mini-scene occupies sixty-seven lines of the First Folio, from the first mention of Francis to the last—a number (67) that corre-sponds to the Simple Cipher of 'Francis'. Within it the name Francis occurs twenty-one times (once on page 55 and twenty times on page 56 of the Folio's Histories), and the word 'anon' thirteen times (on page 56).

Most of the mini-scene is printed in the first column of page 56 of the Folio's Histories, and it is in this part of the scene that Francis actually appears, after the Prince has called him, and in which the word 'anon' is used. In quoting this passage I will use the Shakespeare First Folio spelling and italicising, as what it gives is important and often lost with modern editing:

> *Prin.* ...*Anon, Anon sir, Score a Pint of Bastard in the Halfe Moone,* or so. But *Ned,* to drive away the time till *Falstaffe* come, I prythee doe thou stand in some by-roome, while I question my puny Drawer, to what end hee gave me the Sugar, and do never leave calling *Francis,* that his Tale to me may be nothing but, Anon: step aside, and Ile shew thee a President.
>
> *Poines. Francis.*
>
> *Prin.* Thou art perfect.
>
> *Poin. Francis.*
>
> Enter Drawer.
>
> *Fran.* Anon, anon sir; looke downe into the Pomgarnet, *Ralfe.*
>
> *Prince.* Come hither *Francis.*
>
> *Fran.* My Lord.
>
> *Prin.* How long hast thou to serve, Francis?
>
> *Fran.* Forsooth five yeares, and as much as to——
>
> *Poin.* Francis!
>
> *Fran.* Anon, anon sir.
>
> *Prin.* Five yeares: Berlady, a long Lease for the clinking of Pewter. But Francis, darest thou be so valiant as to play the coward with thy Indenture, & show it a fair paire of heeles, and run from it?
>
> *Fran.* O Lord sir, Ile be sworne upon all the Books in England, I could find in my heart.
>
> *Poin.* Francis.
>
> *Fran.* Anon, anon sir.
>
> *Prin.* How old art thou, *Francis?*
>
> *Fran.* Let me see, about Michaelmas next I shal be——
>
> *Poin.* Francis.
>
> *Fran.* Anon sir, pray you stay a little, my Lord.
>
> *Prin.* Nay but harke you Francis, for the Sugar thou gavest me, 'twas a penyworth, was't not?
>
> *Fran.* O Lord sir, I would it had bene two.
>
> *Prin.* I will give thee for it a thousand pound: Aske me when thou wilt, and thou shalt have it.
>
> *Poin.* Francis.

Fran. Anon, anon.

Prin. Anon Francis? No Francis, but tomorrow, Francis: or Francis, on
Thursday: or indeed Francis when thou wilt. But Francis.

Fran. My Lord.

Prin. Wilt thou rob this Leathern Ierkin, Chrystall-button, Not-pated,
Agate ring, Puke stocking, Caddice garter, Smooth tongue Spanish pouch.

Fran. O Lord sir, who do you meane?

Prin. Why then your browne Bastard is your onely drinke: for looke
you Francis, your white Canvas doublet will sulley. In Barbary
sir, it cannot come to so much.

Fran. What, sir?

Poin. Francis.

Prin. Away you Rogue, dost thou heare them call?

'Anon,' on the face of it, means 'in a moment'. Strictly it means 'straight-
way' or 'at once', and is derived from Old English *on ane*, meaning 'in one'.
'Sugar', besides its usual meaning, was also a slang term for poetry, especially
sonnets. Francis Meres speaks of Shakespeare's 'sugared sonnets'.[43]

In this short conversation between Prince Henry and Francis, taking up
fifty lines of speech from the first 'Anon' to the last 'Francis' in the first column of page 56 of the Histories, the name 'Francis' is spoken twenty times and
the word 'anon' is spoken thirteen times. Not only is this an extraordinary
repetition of the two words in such a short mini-scene, but also the total count
of the repetition of the two words (20 + 13) comes to 33, the Simple Cipher of
'Bacon', while the Simple Cipher count of the two words, 'Anon Francis,' comes
to 108, the Reverse Cipher of 'Francis'. Moreover, 56 (the page number) is the
Simple Cipher of 'Fr. Bacon' and of his noted weed, 'Tobacco', as explained at
the end of chapter 8.

Attention is further drawn to what is intended by the careful spelling of
'President' in the Prince's declaration: 'Ile shew thee a President'. Modern editors change the spelling to 'precedent', which matches the vulgar sense of the
conversation, but the Folio reveals openly the hidden or acroamatic sense of
the word. 'President' was not a commonly-used title; but, according to Michael
Maier, the chief or ruler of the Rosicrucian Fraternity bore the title of President.

The Prince declares he will show us this President. Poines immediately
says the name of this President ('Francis'). The Prince confirms it ('Thou art
perfect'). Poins says the name again and Francis enters, on cue, to be seen.
Besides the surface meaning, the expression 'Thou art perfect' can also refer
to a Perfect Master in Rosicrucian terminology, it being the title of the Fifth

Degree of the thirty-three-degree system of the Ancient and Accepted Rite of the Rose Croix, or the Scottish Rite as it was known by when it was reintroduced in the eighteenth century to what had become by then mainstream English Freemasonry.[44] (All initiates above the Fifth Degree continue to be, of course, Perfect Masters, plus whatever else they attain.)

'Seeing' is associated particularly with the Rosicrucians, as already pointed out—St John the Divine (*i.e.,* the Beloved) being the great Seer. That which is called 'second sight'—the visionary capacity to see the truth—is a particular mark of a Rosicrucian. For instance, a seventeenth-century Rosicrucian, Henry Adamson of Perth, wrote, in a poem of 1638:

> For we be brethren of the *Rosie Crosse*;
> We have the *Mason word* and second sight,
> Things for to come we can foretell aright…

Adamson, The Muses Threnodie (1638), p. 32

As for 'Anon', it contains two names (*An* and *On*) for 'The True and Living God Most High' that is a feature of the Third and higher degrees.

The Stratford Monument

The Shakespeare Folio is full of cipher, all of which tells us the real name of the author Shakespeare and that he was not only a Rosicrucian but also the head of the Rosicrucian fraternity, which was Masonic in nature. The Folio, however, is not the only player in this game. Its partner, as we saw in the Shakespeare Trail, is the Shakespeare Monument at Stratford-upon-Avon. As we might expect, and indeed as we have already seen in terms of other kinds of cryptology, this monument is also full of cipher, telling the same story as the Folio.

For instance, the inscription on the Shakespeare Monument tells us that someone's name 'doth deck this tomb' and challenges us to read this name if we can—the name of the person whom envious death has placed within the Shakespeare Monument:

> STAY PASSENGER, WHY GOEST THOV BY SO FAST?
> READ IF THOV CANST, WHOM ENVIOVS DEATH HATH PLAST,
> WITH IN THIS MONVMENT SHAKSPEARE; WITH WHOME,
> QVICK NATVRE DIDE; WHOSE NAME DOTH DECK YS TOMBE,
> FAR MORE THEN COST: SIEH ALL, YT HE HATH WRITT,
> LEAVES LIVING ART, BVT PAGE, TO SERVE HIS WITT.

Whose name decks the tomb? Although a name related to the name 'Shakspeare', it is obviously not actually that name, as that is already given and would not make sense of the challenge if it were the answer. And, moreover, how *does* a name cover or decorate a tomb?

The only words, or letters, on the monument that could spell out a name are those of the inscription. They do, in fact, do so, in different ways. The first two lines, in Latin, liken the author Shakespeare to Nestor, Socrates and Virgil in judgment, genius and art, and conclude with a statement based largely on the Hermetic teachings:

Iudicio Pylium, genio Socratem, arte Maronem:
Terra tegit, populus maeret, Olympus habet.

As we saw eaarlier, Nestor was a king as well as a judge and statesman, Socrates a philosopher renowned for his universality and humanity, and Virgil a poet who was in his writing a 'high priest' of the Mysteries. These three analogies are associated with the triple description of Hermes Trismegistus, the great master and teacher of the Hermetic wisdom tradition. Bacon himself tells us of:

That triplicity, which in great veneration was ascribed to the ancient Hermes; the power and fortune of a king, the knowledge and illumination of a priest, and the learning and universality of a philosopher.

Francis Bacon, *Advancement of Learning* (1605), Bk. I.

Bacon's words tally well with Ben Jonson's dedicatory poem, a poem that likens the author Shakespeare to Mercury, the Latin name for Hermes.

Besides this semi-mystical name of Hermes or Mercury, which is really a title of reverence, a more personal name is encrypted in these two initial lines of the inscription. If we examine the two lines closely, as they are carved in the stone (see illustration 29, p. 80), we should notice that certain letters are formed larger than the others: namely, I P S and M in the first line, and T and O in the second line—six letters in all. In Simple Cipher IPSM = 54 and TO = 33. I have as yet been unable to discover what IPSM signifies, but 33 is the Simple Cipher for BACON. Moreover, if we count the number of small letters in each line, the result is thirty-three for the first line and thirty-three for the second. This, of course, is not by chance and renders the name of the author in a beautiful way: for 6 = F and 33 = BACON in Simple Cipher, while 33 + 33 = 66 = FRA BACONI, also in Simple Cipher, as used at the end of *The Tempest* (see above). 'F Bacon' or 'Fra Baconi', therefore, is the name that decks the tomb. The enciphered name, moreover, confirms the description of the author as a Nestor, Socrates and Virgil, which only fits the one person, Francis Bacon (see Chapter 7).

Further confirmation follows. If we go on to count the larger letters in the main body of the inscription, the six lines in English, we will discover that there are nine such letters (i.e., SPDSTFSHL). 9 = I, the personal pronoun, in Simple Cipher. So, the question 'Who's name doth deck this tomb?' is answered by 'I, F Bacon'. Which F Bacon? In Reverse Cipher the large letters SPDSTFSHL add up to 108, which is FRANCIS. So, the answer is clear: 'I, Francis Bacon'.

The 'tomb' is in fact a monument, not a tomb, and so does not contain a body or the ashes of a body. The body of the actor William Shakespeare of Stratford-upon-Avon, who died on 23 April 1616, is buried beneath the chancel steps of the church, his grave being marked by a stone with no name on it. Francis Bacon, the other 'Shakespeare' (*i.e.,* the author), was alive and well when the Shakespeare monument was erected, *c.*1620–2, and his name certainly decks (*i.e.,* decorates) the 'tomb'.

Chapter 14

Both Your Poets

The Great Assizes

The more we look, unravel the clues, and lift the veils of this mystery, the more we find that Francis Bacon was not just the true author 'Shakespeare' but also the centre, inspirer and head of an organisation or society of poets, philosophers, lawyers, writers, historians, artists, craftsmen, printers, diplomats and intelligencers dedicated to some great aim. Moreover, we find that this society embraced both men and women, and included in its numbers members of the nobility and officers of state as well as knights, gentlemen and others from the more ordinary classes of society. From all appearances, the organisation seems to have been Masonic, or Freemasonic, in nature; but also Rosicrucian in its higher degrees. It pre-existed Francis Bacon in some form or another, and it carried on after Francis' death, as we shall see; but Francis Bacon seems to have been its great 'light'. It is even possible that Francis' birth and subsequent work was prepared for by his elders, if he was, as seems likely, the 'Elias the Artist' foretold by Paracelsus[1]—the one who would not only reveal many things but also bring the world a great gift that would enable all truth to be revealed.

The whole mystery and aim of Francis Bacon and his society is alluded to and almost revealed in the anonymous satirical poem published in 1645, entitled *The Great Assizes holden in Parnassus by Apollo and his Assessours*. The poem is attributed to the poet, satirist and emblem writer, George Wither, who knew Francis Bacon well, having belonged to the group of poets patronised by Southampton and the Pembrokes, and having been one of Bacon's 'good pens'.

The Great Assizes is particularly significant as it relates directly to the four extremely important and influential Rosicrucian manifestos—the *Fama, Confessio, Assertio* and *Report, of the Laudable Order of the Rosy Cross*—that were published in the second decade of the seventeenth century. *The Great Assizes* is a version of the '77th Advertisement' from Traiano Boccalini's *De Ragguagli di*

Parnasso ('News from Parnassus'), which was published at Venice in 1612–13. This was reprinted in 1614, in German translation, as *Allgemeine und General Reformation, der gantzen weiten Welt* ('The Universal and General Reformation of the Whole Wide World'). As mentioned in chapters 10 and 12, it was prefixed to the *Fama*, the first of the published Rosicrucian manifestos.

Boccalini's story is a commentary on the poor state of the world at that time. The setting is the imaginary Court of Apollo on Mount Parnassus. Apollo, lamenting the miserable condition of mortals and the world, determines to cure the world, and for that purpose to found a society of men famous for wisdom and virtue, and to begin a general reformation of the world. Finding it difficult to discover anyone with sufficient qualifications, he decides to leave the reformation in the hands of the Seven Wise Men of Greece, to whom are added two Roman philosophers (Cato and Seneca) and a modern Italian philosopher (Jacopo Mazzoni da Cesena) as Secretary. The sages meet, accompanied by a selection of the most talented of the people, but after much discussion and purifications, none of their suggestions are considered practical and the sages abandon their attempt at the reformation.

The *Fama* then continues the story to show how the world can and will be redeemed by means of a complete reformation of the arts and sciences instigated by a new council of sages—the Fraternity of the Rosy Cross—whose founder and leader is designated by the ciphers 'C.R.', 'R.C.', '*Fra*. R.C.' or '*Fra*. C.R.C.'. Because the founder is referred to as both 'father' of the fraternity and 'brother', the cipher '*Fra*.' is taken to mean brother (*frater*), although we have seen that it can mean Francis as well. 'C.R.C.' is assumed to signify Christian Rosy Cross, a title used in a further Rosicrucian-style publication, *Chymische Hochzeit Christiani Rosencreutz* ('The Chemical Marriage of Christian Rosicross'), written in German by Johann Valentin Andreae and published anonymously at Strasbourg in 1616.

The Great Assizes retells the Universal Reformation story in the form of a new satirical allegory, or jest, with the Rosicrucian Council in place on Mount Parnassus. In the story the author names some real people involved in the Rosicrucian work (see illustrations 8–10, pp. 54–5). The author, George Wither (1588–1667), was no newcomer to the Rosicrucians. Just ten years prior to the publication of *The Great Assizes,* in 1635, he had produced a *Collection of Emblemes, Ancient and Moderne*, with reproductions of Rollenhagen's remarkable set of Rosicrucian emblems (previously published in 1611 and 1613) to which he had added lengthy verses, including a portrait of himself at the beginning which continues the 'face' theme of Bacon–Shakespeare.

The story of the *Great Assizes* concerns Apollo, who wishes to bring about a general reformation of the world, and a group of great authors, poets and playwrights who help him. Enthroned on Mount Parnassus, the Mount of

Poetic Inspiration and place of the Delphic Oracle where he resides with Pallas
Athena, Apollo convenes a High Court, over which he presides with his Chancellor by his side. This Chancellor is portrayed as Francis Bacon. As Apollo's
Chancellor of Parnassus, Francis, Lord Verulam, is second only to Apollo and
the leader of all the rest.

Apollo summons twenty of the great authors as Assessors, of whom Bacon is the chief, plus a jury of twelve lesser poets and dramatists. On trial are
twelve malefactors, who are found to be identified with the twelve jurors. The
malefactors are, in fact, simply job descriptions of the jurors. Bacon heads the
list of great authors, Apollo's Assessors, as Lord Verulam and Chancellor of
Parnassus. Next in order to Bacon comes a trinity of high officers—Sir Philip
Sidney as Lord High Constable of Parnassus, 'William Budeus' as High Treasurer, and 'John Picus, Earl of Mirandula', as High Chamberlain.

'John Picus' refers to the fifteenth-century Italian scholar, Giovanni Pico
della Mirandola (1463–94). He was a chief exponent of Christian Cabala who
worked with Marsilio Ficino at the Medici Court in Florence and helped found
Renaissance Neoplatonism, which developed within a framework of Christi-
anity and included both Hermeticism and Cabala within it.

'William Budeus' was the renowned French scholar and writer, Guillaume
Budé (1467–1540), who was responsible for the foundation by Francis I of the
Collège de France and the library at Fontainebleau which became the French
Bibliothèque National when it moved to Paris. Budé was a humanist whose
writings considerably influenced the revival of interest in Greek language and
literature. His extraordinary memory enabled him to acquire a vast erudition.
He studied law at Orleans, was Secretary to Louis XII, and accompanied Francis I at the Field of the Cloth of Gold in 1520. He corresponded with most of the
learned men of his time, including Erasmus, Sir Thomas More and Rabelais.

Sir Philip Sidney (1554–86) we have met often enough already. He was the
great Elizabethan hero—a courtier, diplomat, soldier, philosopher and scholar-
poet—and was, during the 1580s and until his death on the battlefield, the leader
of the English Areopagus of scholar–poets that laid the foundations for the blos-
soming of serious poetry and Arcadian imagery in the English Renaissance.

Budé and Sidney form a link between Pico and Bacon, spanning a century
of Renaissance Neoplatonism, all of them being pioneering leaders and 'stars'
in the development of Italian, French and English culture—and, indeed, European culture as a whole.

Four others (Julius Caesar, Joseph Scaliger, Ben Jonson and John Taylor),
added to the trinity of high officers, make up a complete list of seven officers
grouped beneath Bacon. Julius Caesar's office is not named, but Joseph Scaliger
is described as the Censor of Manners, Ben Jonson as Keeper of the Trophonian
Den, and John Taylor as Cryer of the Court.

Sir Julius Caesar (1558–1636) was a respected parliamentarian, a judge and, from 1606, Chancellor of the Exchequer. He became Master of the Rolls in 1614 when Sir Fulke Greville took over the position of Chancellor of the Exchequer. He was Master of Rolls when Francis Bacon was Lord Keeper and Lord Chancellor.

Joseph Justus Scaliger (1540–1609) was renowned abroad as the greatest scholar of his day. He studied Greek under Turnebus at the University of Paris and had a critical mastery of both Greek and Latin, plus a respectable knowledge of Hebrew and Arabic (in which he was self-taught). Scaliger also studied jurisprudence under Cujas, the greatest living jurist, at Valence. He founded a new school of historical criticism with sound rules of criticism and emendation, which he transformed into a rational procedure with fixed laws. He revolutionised the traditional ideas of ancient chronology. In 1593 he became Professor at Leyden University, from where he 'ruled the learned world from his throne' until his death.

Ben Jonson (1572–1637), as we already know, was a poet, playwright, essayist and writer of masques, who was ranked with Marlowe and Shakespeare as one of England's three great dramatists.

The last on the list, John Taylor (1580–1653), the 'water poet', was a Thames waterman and London's chief eccentric poet. He wrote poems for state occasions and organised the water pageant for the wedding of Princess Elizabeth and the Elector Palatine in 1613. He made several famous walks and journeys, including one to Scotland and another to Prague, to visit Elizabeth (then Queen of Bohemia), and wrote them up afterwards in book form to sell to subscribers.

These seven, plus Bacon, are all listed in the right-hand column (viewed heraldically) of two columns drawn beneath Apollo, on the first two pages after the title page of the book. The twelve other great authors, who complete the High Council of twenty Assessors, are listed in the left-hand column (viewed heraldically), culminating with Edmund Spenser, who is named as Clerk of the Assizes. These twelve are a mixture of English, French, Dutch, German and Belgian scholars, philosophers and humanists, all but two (Erasmus and Turnebus) being contemporaries of Bacon.

George Wither places himself at the head of the lesser poets and dramatists who comprise the twelve jurors. William Shakespeare is listed eleventh in the list of jurors. However, as the story of the book unfolds, Shakespeare is declared, when examined, to be a mimic or actor pretending to be a poet, not a real poet. All the jurors are English contemporaries of Bacon; and, except for the actor Shakespeare, all are poets or dramatists and most are university graduates. Shakespeare's job description is 'the writer of weekly accounts'.

As one might expect, given Wither's interest in emblems and ciphers, the hierarchical order and numbers given in the story of *The Great Assizes* are significant and based on a cabalistic design. Including Apollo, the total number of characters named amount to thirty-three, the Simple Cipher not only for BACON but also for the total number of degrees in the ancient system of initiation based upon the Cabala, whose Tree of Life has ten Numbers or Principles (*Sephiroth*) and twenty-two paths of wisdom that connect them (see illustration 103, next page). The 33rd degree signifies the unity and source of the whole, which is the Light that is called Apollo. This number thirty-three is disguised in Wither's story by the addition of the twelve malefactors, which would make forty-five characters in all if they were included; but it is made clear in the course of the story that the malefactors are to be identified with the jurors, hence in reality there are only thirty-three characters in total.

Thus Wither, in this scheme of the Parnassian Great Assizes, shows the thirty-two great authors, poets, dramatists and actor William Shakespeare as being manifested aspects of Apollo, who himself is the thirty-third—the representation of Divinity or Unity as Light. Francis Bacon (Lord Verulam) is his Chancellor, right-hand man and second only to Apollo in importance. Bacon's position on the Tree of Life, therefore, is at its head or crown, the Number 1—Apollo's position being everywhere, in the sense of overlighting and being the whole Tree of Life.

Trophonius and Agamedes

In *The Great Assizes* ,Ben Jonson is portrayed as the 'Keeper of the Trophonian Denne'. According to a Greek tradition mentioned by Cicero, Trophonius was the son of Erginus, King of Orchomenus in Boeotia. He and his brother Agamedes were the celebrated architects who designed and built Apollo's temple at Delphi. Having completed the work, the brothers asked Apollo to grant them as a reward whatever was best for men. The priestess of the Delphic Oracle informed them that they should wait eight days and should live during that time with all cheerfulness and pleasure. When the eight days were past, Trophonius and his brother Agamedes were found dead in their bed.[2]

Afterwards, when the country was suffering from a great drought, the Boeotians were directed to apply to the spirit of Trophonius for relief. To do this, they were to seek him at Lebadea in Boeotia, where he gave oracles in a cave. They discovered this cave by means of a swarm of bees, and therein Trophonius told them how to ease their misfortunes—how to find the water which they needed. From that time onwards Trophonius was honoured as a

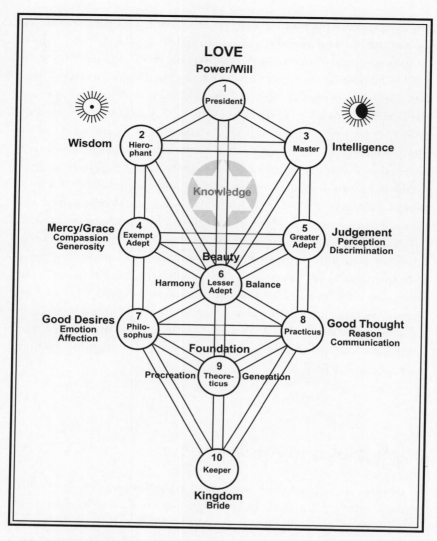

In this diagram, the Tree of Life is viewed from the paneem or face-to-face point of view. This is the viewpoint used in most pictures, emblems and heraldry: i.e., seeing truth face-to-face, as one sees another person face-to-face. All the illustrations in this book are examples of paneem.

The right-hand side or 'pillar' of the Tree is signified by the sun; the left-hand side of the Tree is signified by the moon. There are twenty-two paths and ten principles. Beauty (no. 6) is the heart of the tree, symbolised by the sun-rose. The unnumbered star-circle called 'Knowledge' signifies full knowledge of the whole Tree of Life, comprehending all its paths and principles, which is full illumination, and thus corresponds to the Thirty-Third Degree of initiation, or to the position of Apollo, the Light. This diagram can be used to read many of the cabalistic (Rosicrucian) pictures.

god and considered to be a son of Apollo. A temple and a statue were erected to him, and a pillar was set up at the entrance to the cave.

The cave or den of Trophonius became one of the most celebrated oracles of Greece. Those who consulted the oracle had first to undergo many fasts, ablutions and other solemn ceremonies. Then they were required to sacrifice a ram as an offering to Agamedes and invoke him before entering the cave. Inside they would then be drawn through a narrow entrance into an inner cave by an invisible and irresistible force. After receiving an answer from the oracle they would return backwards from the cave. The recipients of the oracle were always stamped with a melancholic disposition; hence the Trophonian Oracle was associated with the melancholic humour, and the Greek proverbial phrase, καταβαινειν εις Τροφωνιου ('to descend into the cave of Trophonius'), was applied to a melancholy man.

Besides being acknowledged as a son of Apollo, Trophonius was equated with Mercury, or Hermes Trismegistus, whose surname thus became Trophonius (*i.e.,* Mercurius Trophonius). As a son of Apollo, he is imbued with all the attributes of Apollo and sits on Apollo's right hand side as a second Apollo, a Daystar and leader of the choir of Muses.

It seems clear that Wither intended us to equate Bacon with Trophonius. These attributes and titles of Trophonius are precisely the ones applied to Francis Bacon in the *Manes Verulamiani,* and Bacon was referred to even by King James as Apollo:

> I saye with Apollo *'media tutius itur'* ('the middle way is safer') if it may stande with lawe.[3]

By means of denoting Ben Jonson as the Keeper of the Trophonian den, and Francis Bacon as Chancellor of Parnassus, Wither has subtly identified Francis Bacon with Trophonius, the 'son of Apollo' or second Apollo. He has also made clear something else, which is that Anthony Bacon—Francis Bacon's 'comfort', 'consort' and 'second self' as well as brother (*i.e.,* 'Agamedes')—was indeed Francis' partner and co-architect in the design and building of the Rosicrucian 'Temple of Apollo', or 'Temple of Solomon'. Let us, therefore, learn something more about Anthony, to see what this might really mean.

Anthony Bacon

Like his brother Francis, Anthony Bacon was a concealed poet, as is revealed in letters to him and about him. Moreover, when leaving England for France in 1579, his mother's chaplain, Mr Wyborn, wished Anthony Bacon 'success in his chosen profession of literature', revealing (in a letter to Anthony) that

103. Anthony Bacon. Detail from painting by Nicholas Hilliard (1594), at Gorhambury House. Originally labelled as being a portrait of Robert Devereux, Earl of Essex, it is now thought to be of Anthony Bacon.

Anthony's primary purpose was the profession of literature. This helps to put into context Anthony's mission abroad to serve his Queen and country as an intelligencer. He clearly aimed to combine the two things.

Anthony travelled widely in Europe, visiting in particular the kingdoms of France and Navarre, but also Switzerland, Spain, Portugal, Italy, Venice, the Netherlands and Scotland. Not only did he meet and befriend many of the literary and philosophical elite abroad, but also he became and remained the correspondent and friend of spies, scholars, poets, ambassadors, noblemen and women, courtiers, princes and princesses, kings and queens, in many countries. These included Henri IV, King of Navarre and France, the writer Michel de Montaigne, and the great reformed theologians Theodore Beza, leader of the Protestant Reformation centred at Geneva, and Lambert Danaeus, professor of theology in Geneva, all of whom became good friends and paid tribute to Anthony's outstanding intellect and scholarship. He had a good library of his own and in addition was able to use the libraries of the kings, princes and other great noblemen whom he knew and befriended.

Anthony's friends and correspondents not only praised him for his intellect, wit, scholarship and virtue, but they also knew him as a poet and musician. He played the lute and virginals, and sent sonnets home from France from the mid-1580s onwards. After he came home in 1592, he carried on distributing his sonnets privately amongst his friends in England as well as to friends in Europe. Moreover, poets of Europe sent their poems to Anthony for his appraisal and critique, including the French poet Jean de la Jessée (in 1597). As I have already mentioned in Chapter 10, an anonymous continental poet eulogised Anthony as the English Phoenix of celestial origin—a poet of rare and perfect virtue.

Besides being a classical scholar and able to read, write and speak Latin and Greek, Anthony was also able to converse fluently in six to eight different European languages, principally French, Spanish, Italian and German. His fluency was such that he was able to pass for a native of several countries and was even known to correct the language of many people who sent him their writings. He translated into English many letters and works of many kinds in other languages, including Antonio Perez's Spanish letters, and wrote a French translation of the report on the campaign against the city of Cadiz that was circulated on the continent.[4]

Anthony kept a meticulous record of his correspondence, written and received, which still exists, with the exception of his sonnets and all letters pertaining to his Montauban experience (1586–9) and to the Essex rebellion and its aftermath (1600–1), which are either destroyed, lost or unrecognised. He also kept a personal notebook throughout his twelve years abroad in which he jotted down conversations, notes and descriptions of the outstanding men and women of Europe whom he either met or heard of, as well as descriptions of places, together with sonnets and other poems. After his death in May 1601, his brother Francis carefully preserved Anthony's correspondence for posterity, along with many of his own letters. They were entrusted to Thomas Meautys, who eventually placed them in the hands of Archbishop Tenison at Lambeth Palace, where they still rest.[5] In 1754, Thomas Birch published the sixteen volumes of this correspondence, and drew extensively upon them, in his *Memoirs of the Reign of Queen Elizabeth*.

Anthony Bacon's correspondents often used strange, rare and elaborate words, or invented new ones. A high percentage of these words plus many others in Anthony's correspondence are also to be found in the Shakespeare plays, including phrases and expressions unique to Anthony Bacon. That is to say, a large number of words that were either extremely rare or entirely new to the English vocabulary, which were included in the Shakespeare plays, were seemingly used for the first time in Anthony's correspondence, or else derived from it. It appears, therefore, that Anthony and Francis Bacon, with help from their 'good pens', extracted many hundreds of words from Anthony's international correspondence and used them in the Shakespeare works, transforming them by the use of puns and multiple meanings in the plays, and thereby greatly enriching the English language.

One of Anthony's special expressions, like a hallmark, was the manner in which he signed off his letters. He was virtually unique among writers of his time in nearly always doing this with the phrase: 'And so I take my leave', or 'I most humbly take my leave', or 'I humbly take my leave'. This same phrase, or variations of it, is used habitually in the Shakespeare plays.[6]

Anthony suffered greatly physically. He was sick almost continuously from a young age. He had almost gone blind when fourteen years old (which affliction was fortunately only temporary) and inherited a tendency to severe gout, ague or arthritis. In addition, he was injured in France in a riding accident with Henri of Navarre in 1584, and was thereafter lame all through his life. He always walked with a stick, and in later years it seems he could hardly walk at all.

Both Anthony and Francis were deeply religious. Significantly, Anthony adopted Psalms 36 and 37 as his creed, and gave up all worldly ambition and rewards. In a letter to his mother dated 13 July 1596 he wrote:

> For mine own part, the reading and Christian meditation of the 36 and 37 psalms shall, with God's grace, serve me for true preservation to keep me from emulating any worldly prosperity or greatness, or fearing the effects of human power, or malice, so long as it please God to comfort and strengthen the best part of me, as hitherto in his mercy He hath done with extraordinary effects.

This statement may in fact answer the question why Anthony never promoted himself with the Queen for public acknowledgment of what he had done to serve her, or for a position in State, as undoubtedly he could have done, the Queen having shown herself willing.

Psalm 37 contains the key sentence, 'But the righteous showeth mercy, and giveth,' which is the major theme of many of the Shakespeare plays.[7] Psalm 36 refers to God's loving kindness and the shadow of God's wings:

> Thy righteousness is like the great mountains;
> Thy judgements are a great deep:
> O Lord, thou preservest man and beast.
> How excellent is thy loving kindness, O God!
> Therefore the children of men put their trust under the shadow of thy wings.

Psalm 36 : 6—7

This is the source of the Rosicrucian motto 'Sub Umbra Alarum Tuarum, JHVH' ('Beneath the shadow of thy wings, O Lord').

The Other Poet

Armed now with all this information and background to the Shakespeare story, we may be in a better position to answer more fully the question of why Shakespeare refers to 'both your poets' in the last line of Sonnet 83:

verses Shakespeare is forced to admit are filled with the Apollonian light of Adonis and, at least at one moment in time, greater than his own verses. It 'kills' Shakespeare; but as a result he is released from his egoistic desire, possessive love and self-esteem. So, we must ask, who was this other poet, who played such an important part? Is he another aspect of Shakespeare himself, just as in other sonnets Shakespeare splits himself up into a higher and a lower self, the former made of fire and air, and the latter of water and earth? Or is the other poet a historical person, as great in verse writing as Shakespeare himself, and writing similar eulogies to Athena and Adonis, who likewise inspire him?

I think it is possible to acknowledge that both viewpoints may be true, just as the very idea of twinship has many different levels and possibilities of meaning; but the historical viewpoint is definitely most intriguing. We have looked at who the real author Shakespeare really is, as well as his relationship to the actor Shakespeare. We have also briefly looked at those who helped him, who wrote with him or for him. Of these, we must consider Thomas Watson.

There is a school of thought that considers Watson to be the 'rival poet', and one interpretation of William Clerke's reference to Watson in Clerke's *Polimanteia* would seem to point to this (see chapter 6). Clerke's marginal note could even imply that Watson was the author of the Shakespeare poem *Venus and Adonis*, while Francis Bacon was the author of the Shakespeare poem *Lucrece*, with both poems published under the group pseudonym of 'William Shakespeare' and masked by the actor of that name. Watson died in 1592 and *Venus and Adonis* was published the very next year, with the name 'William Shakespeare' attached and announcing the poem as the first heir of Shakespeare's invention. From this point of view, Watson could well have been the 'rival poet' of the sonnets, or even have been the author of the 'rival poet' sequence of sonnets in which he acknowledged the growing eminence of Francis Bacon as an equal and then a better poet who, like Watson himself, wrote verses of praise to their shared Muse, Pallas Athena, and to Apollo. If this is true, then it is also possible that Watson's plays, which he is known to have written but which are 'lost', may have formed the starting-point and inspiration for some or many of the Shakespeare plays, or that he may have been the co-author with Francis Bacon of the Shakespeare plays written before 1592. The publishing of *Venus and Adonis* could have been, therefore, a tribute to Watson as the 'other' Shakespeare—the Shakespeare twin—until Watson's death, and as perhaps the one who more than any other poet–dramatist set in motion the 'Shake-scene' with the poem *Venus and Adonis*, to be followed and matched by Bacon's *Lucrece*.

However, the one outstanding but doubly-veiled person in this story is, I think, Francis Bacon's brother, Anthony. Not only do we know that Anthony was a reputed poet within his circle of friends, and wrote sonnets, but also that he was Francis' brother, 'comfort,' 'second self' and partner in his great scheme—a scheme which has poetry or drama at its heart. Not only was he Francis' brother but, if the association with the story of Trophonius and Agamedes is accurate, Anthony was also co-architect with Francis of the 'temple of light'. We also know from Essex's letter to the Queen in 1594 that Anthony wrote at least one play with Francis, possibly *Henry IV*, and the tone of the letter suggests that it was common for the brothers to write such plays (see chapter 7). Moreover, it shows that the Queen as well as Essex was aware of this. Then, interestingly, Anthony actually was lame. Although the Shakespeare sonnets that refer to the poet as being lame[12] can be readily understood in the metaphorical sense, yet it is also possible that they have a double meaning, just as 'both your poets' could have a double meaning and the story of the Gemini certainly does have a double meaning.

Of course, as far as we know Anthony Bacon died in 1601; so, if this is true, he could not have been involved in writing the Shakespeare plays that appear after that date. Nor is it likely that he collaborated in any of the early plays that were composed before he returned to England in 1592. But he could have co-authored the plays written between 1592 and 1601, which includes virtually all the comedies—and indeed it is a marked fact that the period of the comedies was the same period in which Anthony was in England, helping his brother Francis. As I pointed out earlier, the comedies (with the exception of *All's Well That Ends Well*) more or less ended upon Anthony's death. Likewise, Anthony could well have written some or even many of the Shakespeare sonnets; so that, instead of Anthony's sonnets being lost, his brother Francis preserved them for posterity, in print. In fact, just as a few other writers were contributors to at least some of the Shakespeare plays, so they may also have written a Shakespeare sonnet or two. Mary Sidney is just one of those who has been proposed as a Shakespeare sonneteer.

The Gemini Enigma

The Gemini myth would certainly seem to be a key theme in this whole Shakespeare enigma, so much so that perhaps it should be called the Gemini enigma. It involves a deliberately-created game of hide and seek, in which one man (the actor) masks another man (the author), who in turn is discovered to have been not just the great poet Shakespeare but the head of a philanthropic organisation dedicated to regenerating the arts and sciences so as gradually to raise people out of poverty, ignorance and misery, and bring enlightenment and peace to the world. This man is then discovered to have had a much-loved brother, his co-author and co-architect, who may have been the other poet referred to in the sonnets, thereby forming between them a manifestation of the Gemini myth.

This myth is found to be central to the whole Shakespeare story, embodied in various ways in the sonnets, poems and plays, and portrayed in the headpieces and memorials. The major Shakespeare publications—the poems (*Venus and Adonis* and *Lucrece*), the *Sonnets* and the Folio of *Comedies Histories and Tragedies*—are each headed by a version of the Gemini symbolism. The poems represent the Gemini as two peacocks, the *Sonnets* show them as two naked boys with wings, and the Folio shows them as two naked boys lying on two 'A's, thereby suggesting in this symbolism the spiritual, psychological and physical realms of existence respectively. These realms are known in Cabala as the worlds of creation, formation and action. Indeed, this seems to be more or less the subject matter of those three works: the *Venus and Adonis* myth is an archetypal story about a god and goddess, the sonnets deal with the psychological experiences of the poet (or poets), and the plays portray human behaviour in the physical world. Then there is the Shakespeare Memorial in Trinity Church, Stratford-upon-Avon, which depicts the Gemini as two naked, cherubic boys sitting atop the monument, the one holding a spade in his right hand and resting his left hand on the ground, and the other holding a reversed torch in his left hand and resting his right hand on a skull, the two thereby portraying symbolically (and cabalistically) birth and death (see illustration 2). Finally, to this Gemini theme can be added the allegory of Trophonius and Agamedes, the brothers who were the architects of Apollo's temple. With all this carefully-chosen symbolism, the answer to the Shakespeare enigma seems to be both simple and complex, with multiple levels.

First, at the purely historical level of interpretation, the two 'Gemini' brothers were without doubt Francis and Anthony Bacon, with Francis cast as Trophonius, the Apollonian oracle, and Anthony as Agamedes, who died first. They were the Gemini in an almost literal sense, one could say, the former being more in the light and the latter more in the shadow. Moreover, this is doubly true if the much-propounded theory that Francis was in actuality the son of Queen Elizabeth is correct: for then Francis would have been of royal blood (*i.e.*, the 'immortal') while Anthony was not (*i.e.*, the 'mortal').13 Whether this last point is true or false, they were certainly brought up together as brothers, and loved and helped each other as brothers. Like the Gemini they were twin spear-shakers and Argonauts in search of the Golden Fleece—a theme that Francis used for his 'sons of wisdom' who are in search of truth. The very fact that Francis and Anthony were brothers and worked together as partners on a project that they created together as co-architects, employing others to help them as the metaphoric builders or craftsmen, makes it fitting that they should each be shown associated with the letter 'A', the cipher for the Origin or Architect, on the Shakespeare Folio headpiece.

Then there is the Watson possibility. Thomas Watson and Francis Bacon between them may have been the two poets referred to by the phrase 'both your poets' in Sonnet 83. In this case, Watson and Francis Bacon were the Shakespeare twins, at least during the 1580s and until 1592, when Watson died and Anthony Bacon returned to England to take on the role of twin in terms of creating the Shakespeare plays and announcing the name of Shakespeare to the world with the publication of the 'twin' poems, *Venus and Adonis* and *Lucrece*.

At another historical level of interpretation the Gemini theme refers to the twinship of actor and author, the former masking the latter. The Shakespeare Monument at Stratford-upon-Avon makes this Gemini connection clear in its inscription, with the description of the immortal twin (the author) placed above and the reference to the mortal twin (the actor) placed beneath the central inscription. However, Ben Jonson, George Wither and others make it clear that the actor William Shakespeare was not a poet, and therefore this particular relationship is not one that is referred to by the 'both your poets' phrase in the sonnet.

The actor–author relationship in turn leads to a more symbolic and metaphysical meaning of the Gemini, as also of the term 'both your poets'. Just as the allegory of the Gemini was used in classical times to signify the higher and lower selves—the better and baser parts of the human being—so this is clearly used as a powerful theme in the Shakespeare works. The higher nature is pure and immortal but the lower nature is corrupt and mortal. The Shakespeare Sonnets explain that the earthy, mortal writer wishes to be forgotten, but that the spiritual, immortal author should be eternally praised. Moreover, this higher self is joined in likeness to Apollo and Pallas Athena, the divine Spearshakers or Shakespeares.

The wisdom traditions associate these two selves, higher and lower, with the so-called Twin Pillars or Great Pillars—the Pillars of Enoch, Hercules or Solomon that stand at the entrance to the temple of light. Francis Bacon used them in particular on the title-page of his *Novum Organum* ('New Method'), published in 1620, as a kind of signature. This was the first of the final versions of his philosophical work, carefully translated into Latin, which announced his Great Instauration internationally. His *Sylva Sylvarum* ('Natural History'), which was published on his death in 1626, and the 1640 English translation of his *De Augmentis Scientiarum* ('Advancement of Learning') continued the theme by again using the Great Pillars on their title-pages, but with significant additions and modifications.[14] The right-hand pillar of the two Great Pillars signifies life and im-

106.
*Shakespeare
Memorial,
Westminster*

This publication was followed almost immediately by the design and sculpting of the famous Shakespeare Memorial, which was erected in Westminster Abbey in 1741, and in which Pope was involved. The idea for the statue is said to have originated with the men of the theatre, notably John Rich, manager of Covent Garden, in 1726, the centenary of Francis Bacon's death. Although carved by the famous neo-classical sculptor Peter Scheemakers, the design was by William Kent. The design and making of it was controlled by the four Palladian members of the committee that presided over its birth—notably Richard Boyle, Alexander Pope, Dr Richard Mead and a Mr Martin.

Richard Boyle, the third Earl of Burlington, was a patron of literature and leader of the Palladian group. Alexander Pope, the English poet and satirist, not only published the new edition of Shakespeare's Sonnets but also a whole new edition of Shakespeare's works (1723–5). In the latter he included a 'Life' of Shakespeare that helped perpetuate and strengthen the myth of the actor being the author. Dr Mead was a well-known patron of literature and acknowledged authority on Shakespeare, who had served on the Council of the Royal Society for nearly fifty years and been its Vice-President for a time. He was considered to be one of the greatest authorities on Francis Bacon, and as a result several contemporary editions of Bacon's works, including the 1740 Mallet edition, were dedicated to him. Mr Martin was a member of the Society of Antiquaries.

These four men were responsible for commissioning and erecting a worthy monument on behalf of the nation as a tribute and memorial to the country's greatest poet. Yet they not only allowed but also must have designed and instructed Scheemakers to carve a deliberately-garbled misquotation from The Tempest on the scroll. It is impossible for them not to have known the original text and it cannot be a mistake, since the committee were experts in this matter and there was only one original version of *The Tempest* ever printed—that of the First Folio. It was said that Pope was responsible for the misquotation; yet, in spite of strong criticism, he refused to allow it to be altered. This is really quite extraordinary, and suspicious, so why did he do it?

This misquotation is inscribed on the scroll on which Shakespeare is shown

107. Scroll Inscription, Shakespeare Memorial, Westminster Abbey

THE SHAKESPEARE ENIGMA

leaning and to which he points enigmatically. The inscription on the scroll reads:

> The Cloud capt Tow'rs,
> The Gorgeous Palaces,
> The Solemn Temples,
> The Great Globe itself,
> Yea all which it Inherit,
>   Shall Dissolve;
> And like the baseless Fabrick of a Vision
> Leave not a wreck behind.

Whereas the original version in *The Tempest* reads:

> And like the baseless fabricke of this vision
> The Clowd-capt Towres, the gorgeous Pallaces,
> The solemne Temples, the great Globe it selfe,
> Yea, all which it inherit, shall dissolue,
> And like this insubstantiall Pageant faded
> Leaue not a racke behinde.

The Tempest IV, i, 151–6

Not only is the deliberately-garbled quotation from *The Tempest* clearly cryptic but also the statue of Shakespeare is shown pointing specifically at the word 'Temples' with the forefinger of his left hand, for us to take note. This is a good reminder of the dedication made by Heminges and Condell in their *Epistle Dedicatorie* to the Shakespeare Folio:

> And the most, though meanest, of things are made more precious, when they are dedicated to Temples. In that name therefore, we most humbly consecrate to your H.H. these remaines of your servant Shakespeare....

Heminges and Condell, Epistle Dedicatorie, Shakespeare Folio, 1623

The deliberate left-handedness is once again a pointer to cipher, and there are in fact several ciphers contained within this inscription misquotation. The most obvious is the fact that the whole text has been manipulated so as to contain 157 letters, the Simple Cipher of FRA ROSI CROSSE. Then the word 'Towers' has been shortened to 'Tow'rs', leaving exactly 33 complete words, the Simple Cipher of BACON. The first six lines have been contrived to contain 103 letters, the Simple Cipher of SHAKESPEARE, leaving the last two lines with 54 letters. If the deliberately emphasised two-word inset sixth line is counted again with the last two lines, the result is 67 letters, the Simple Cipher of FRANCIS. This is a clever bit of ciphering, for clearly the division of 157 will not give the ciphers of the two remaining names, FRANCIS (67) and SHAKE-SPEARE (105), but by creating an overlap line of thirteen letters, carefully emphasised to make the decipherer take note, the required result can be obtained. From this simple but clever bit of mathematics, all the necessary signatures have been given to make it clear who Shakespeare really was: Francis Bacon—Shakespeare—Fra Rosi Crosse.

Some years ago, the Baconian researcher, Thomas Bokenham, noticed another strange anomaly in the carved message, which was that the letter 'a' of 'Fabrick' was carved and painted as an 'n'. It has now regrettably been over-painted to make it into an 'a', so its original state can no longer be easily noticed—an entirely forgivable mistake, unlike the modern official graffiti crudely painted a few years ago on the base ('William Shakespeare 1564–1616 buried at Stratford-upon-Avon') that simply makes it harder for anyone to see the original design of the Memorial with its cryptic symbolism. However, taking this 'n' as a clue, Bokenham discovered that if one takes the 'Shall Dissolve' (i.e., the emphasised line) as a starting point, then the 'n' of 'Fnbrick' is the 33rd letter of that final three-line section whose total letter count is 67, thereby giving another neat encipherment of FRANCIS BACON. Moreover, the strange letter 'n', which should be an 'a', has the letters 'F' and 'b' each side of it (i.e., FB—Francis Bacon).

Investigating this further, Bokenham realised that this anomalous letter 'n' has the Simple Cipher number of 13 and that it was probably the key for another Trithemius cipher, in which one counts every thirteenth letter of the open message in order to pick out the letters that will render the cipher message. Taking either the 'F' or the 'b' of 'Fnbrick' as the starting point, the ensuing series of thirteenth letters are either FIRCSA or BNCOHA. With the anomalous 'n' added, the first series is a straightforward anagram of FRANCIS. The second series is an anagram of BACON, the 'H' being counted as a null.

From this we can begin to see why the original Folio text was manipulated in this way. Moving the first line of the original passage ('And like the baseless fabricke of this vision') and substituting it for the fifth line ('Yea, all which it inherit, shall dissolue'), altering 'this' of 'this vision' to 'a' and the word 'racke' to 'wreck', shortening 'Towres' to 'Tow'rs' and modernising the spelling of some other words, enabled the cipher letters to fall into place.

Besides these ciphers, in this blatantly-manipulated verse, the rest of the Memorial is a wonderful example of symbolism. Shakespeare is sculpted standing up but leaning on a plinth, his legs crossed, supporting himself on his right elbow, which rests on top of three books. These in turn are stacked one above the other on a square plinth that is like an altar. A corner of the plinth faces out towards us, rather than a side, and on the three visible corners are sculpted the heads and faces of three sovereigns of England—Elizabeth I, Henry

108. The Three
Heads,
Shakespeare
Memorial,
Westminster
Abbey

V, and Richard III.[23] The scroll is anchored beneath the pile of books, with its main part containing the misquoted text falling over one side of the plinth. This whole composite sculpture is set within but slightly in front of a frame that is carved as a doorway, upon whose threshold Shakespeare and the altar are standing.

That the plinth is actually an altar of a special kind is made clear by the three heads that are made to face in three directions—left, forwards and right. It is typically a Janus altar, an altar of the Mysteries. Janus, after whom the first month of the year is named, is the Alpha of all time-cycles as well as of the pantheon of gods and goddesses. Known alternatively as Saturn or Cronos (Greek), not only is he the Lord of Time and Space, he is also the great Initiator, Hierophant and Oracle who brings Truth out of her hiding-place, or helps us do the same. That is to say, he is the one who reveals Truth. He is the Creator, equated with Brahma in the Hindu tradition, whose emblem is the swan (see Chapter 8). In Cabala, he is associated with the unnumbered Principle of Knowledge—the illumined consciousness or knowledge of the whole Tree of Life. In Neoplatonic thought, he was said to rule the humour of melancholy, the alchemical darkness or *prima materia* ('first matter') out of which light is born. Using Bacon's explanation, we also know that he represents the imagination—the visionary and poetic capacity of the soul.

The posture of Shakespeare, leaning on this Janus altar, confirms this, for it is one of the traditional symbolic postures of melancholy. It can be compared, for instance, with Nicholas Hilliard's miniature portrait of a 'Young Man among Roses', painted about 1587 (see illustration 44, p. 163). In this picture the young man (Essex) is shown leaning against a tree, surrounded by white eglantine roses. The same symbolism is used in the East. In Hinduism, for instance, Krishna is represented in the same way when he is engrossed in playing his flute, with right leg crossed over left and right toe pointed inwards, just like the Shakespeare statue. The effect is to make a figure-of-eight with the legs and feet, symbol of eternity, Mercury and the Holy Spirit. It also makes a *Chi Rho*, the Greek monogram of Christ—the *Chi* signified by the crossed legs and the *Rho* formed by the body plus the curved arm supporting the head.

The Elizabethans fostered the sense of melancholy, which one finds in all

their art, especially music. It can be discovered as a major theme of the Shakespeare plays. It was understood in Elizabethan and Neoplatonic thought as being the essential starting-point for great achievements of the soul. When joined with the jovial humour of Jupiter and raised with enthusiastic passion and ecstasy (*furore*) through three successive developments or degrees (*i.e.,* imagination, reason and intellect), the melancholic person becomes the great seer, of whom St John the Beloved is the exemplar in Christian tradition. Here again is the same theme as in the Shakespeare Folio's 'IC' portrait and 'Beloved' dedicatory verse by Ben Jonson. Moreover, melancholy links us with Trophonius and the Trophonius Oracle.

Crusaders and the Knights Templar also used the crossed legs theme. It was a sign displayed on the memorial of crusader knights to signify that they had been on a crusade to Jerusalem. It was that and something more to the Knights Templar. In the Templar church (Temple Church) in Fleet Street, London, there are nine effigies of knights lying in repose on the floor of the circular nave, their arms and legs disposed in various gestures, plus a stone replica of a closed sarcophagus. It is a series that relates to the Cabala and the degrees of knighthood attainable in the Order. Six of the knights have their legs crossed, each in different ways. One of these six has his legs crossed in a similar way to that of the Shakespeare statue, with his hands held before his heart in a gesture of prayer.

Then there is another important little detail on the Shakespeare Memorial, often overlooked because hard to see. Carved in the stone threshold at the feet of Shakespeare's statue is the signature 'TT 1787'. 'TT', already mentioned in chapter 7, is the Freemasonic and Rosicrucian sigil for the Thirty-Third Degree. They are certainly not the initials of the sculptor, who was Peter Scheemakers, or the designer, William Kent; but it is the signature of the Supreme Council of the Sovereign Grand Inspector Generals—the Thirty-Third Degree initiates of the Rosy Cross, a semblance of which continues to exist in the Thirty-Third Degree of the Ancient and Accepted Scottish Rite of Freemasonry.

The date of 1787, though, seems strange, considering that everything to do with the Shakespeare Memorial (other than the twentieth-century defacements) is highly meaningful. The Memorial was erected in 1741, so why put on it a date of 1787? Or, alternatively, why should someone come along in 1787 and be allowed to carve the sigil and date on the Memorial? What does it mean? The numbers do not correspond to any of the known cipher signatures. However, as a date it is indeed significant, because 108 years prior to 1787, Thomas Tenison had published *Baconiana* (in 1679), which was also signed 'TT'. 108 years back in time from 1679 takes us to 1571, which, allowing for the difference between the Old Style dating used in Elizabeth I's reign and the New Style dating that was adopted later, corresponds to the date given by Michael Maier (1570) for the birth of the Rosicrucian fraternity, as previously mentioned. So it appears that the significance of the 1787 date on the Memorial might be to do

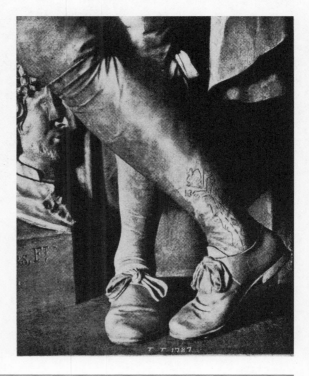

*110. 'TT 1787'
Signature.
Detail:
Shakespeare
Memorial,
Westminster
Abbey*

with the 108-year cycle that the Rosicrucians were working with, and possibly still do.

Wilton House Shakespeare Memorial

A wonder that is not so widely known is that the Westminster Abbey Shakespeare Memorial has a twin. Like human twins, this other memorial is similar but with important differences. Whereas the Westminster Memorial was made for the nation, paid for by public subscription and placed in a public (but holy) place, its twin was created for the Earls of Pembroke and still stands in Wilton House where it was originally placed.

Like the Westminster Memorial, the Wilton Memorial was designed by William Kent and sculpted by Peter Sheemakers. It was completed in 1743 for Henry Herbert, 9th Earl of Pembroke, an architect and lover of the arts, who was a good friend of Lord Burlington and William Kent. Henry's ancestors were the two brothers, William the 3rd Earl and Philip the 4th Earl of Pembroke, to whom the 1623 Shakespeare First Folio had been dedicated, and their parents, Mary Sidney, Countess of Pembroke, and Henry Herbert, 2nd Earl of Pembroke.

Both memorials depict Shakespeare standing with legs crossed, leaning with his right elbow supported on a pile of three books stacked on a plinth and his left arm reaching across his body, pointing with the forefinger of his left hand to a particular word on a scroll that hangs down the front of the plinth. The striking differences between the two memorials are, first, that whereas the Westminster Memorial has a square plinth, the Wilton Memorial has a circular one, and second, that the quotations on the two scrolls are different. Whereas the words on the Westminster Memorial are taken from The Tempest and the particular word pointed to is 'Temples', the quotation on the Wilton Memorial is from Macbeth and the word pointed to is 'Shadow'. Moreover, whereas the quotation used on the Westminster memorial is garbled, the quotation used on the Wilton Memorial is not. The Wilton quotation is also shorter:

> LIFE's but a walking SHADOW
>   a poor PLAYER
> That struts and frets his hour
>   upon the STAGE
> And then is heard no more!

The original version in *Macbeth* reads:

> Life's but a walking Shadow, a poore Player,
> That struts and frets his houre upon the Stage,
> And then is heard no more.

> *Macbeth* V, v, 24–6

The *Tempest* and *Macbeth* quotations are clearly not chosen by chance. For a start, both are from passages that refer to the death or ending of 'actors' and the dissolution of their form into the great 'nothing' or No-thing—the mysterious and awesome 'O' that is referred to so often in the Shakespeare plays.

The lines from *The Tempest* are from a speech by Prospero; those from *Macbeth* are from a speech by Macbeth himself:

> Pro. You doe looke (my son) in a mov'd sort,
>   As if you were dismaid: be cheefull Sir,
>   Our Revels now are ended: These our actors,
>   (As I foretold you) were all Spirits, and
>   Are melted into Ayre, into thin Ayre,
>   And like the baselesse fabricke of this vision
>   The clowd-capt Towres, the gorgeous Pallaces,
>   The solemne Temples, the great Globe it selfe,
>   Yea, all which it inherit, shall dissolve,
>   And like this insubstantiall Pageant faded
>   Leave not a racke behind: we are such stuffe
>   As dreames are made on; and our little life
>   Is rounded with a sleepe.
>
>   *The Tempest* IV, i, 146–58

> Macb. She should have dy'de hereafter;
>   There would have beene a time for such a word:
>   To morrow, and to morrow, and to morrow,
>   Creepes in this petty pace from day to day,
>   To the last Syllable of Recorded time:
>   And all our yesterdayes have lighted Fooles
>   The way to dusty death. Out, out, breefe Candle,
>   Life's but a walking Shadow, a poore Player,
>   That struts and frets his houre upon the Stage,
>   And then is heard no more. It is a Tale
>   Told by an Ideot, full of sound and fury
>   Signifying nothing.
>
>   *Macbeth* V, v, 17–28

The two speeches are complementary. In *The Tempest*, the actors are airy spirits; whereas in *Macbeth* they are human players strutting upon the stage of the world. The *Tempest* speech is full of hope and good cheer concerning a happy conclusion to a work designed to be both just and compassionate. The *Macbeth* speech, by contrast, is full of dismay and despair ensuing from a series of horrific murders done for entirely selfish reasons, and the resulting madness and suicide of Macbeth's wife, the major instigator of the foul deeds.

The Tempest is a story about a magus or white magician, Prospero, who labours to right wrongs, to cleanse his world of evil, to restore law and order, and to raise the consciousness and morality of all the characters, his included, into a better state of being. He achieves this with the essential aid of his spirit, Ariel, whose name denotes the spirit of mercy or love. All that is done is done lovingly, with a strong sense of justice and with no harm done to anyone. The result is one of joy, reunion, justice and redemption. The whole story is one of initiation.

The Tragedy of Macbeth, on the other hand, is a story concerning black magic and horrific deeds of murder, all for the sake of personal, unholy ambition and lust for power. Macbeth and his wife are the joint perpetrators of this horror. It is Macbeth who does the bloody deeds and who speaks the words used for the Wilton quotation when he hears of his wife's suicide, but it is Lady Macbeth who plans the murder of the king, urging on and telling her husband what to do. It is Macbeth who sees and converses with the 'Weird Sisters' or witches, and is tempted by them, but it is Lady Macbeth who consciously and deliberately invokes the dark spirits to fill her 'from the crown to the toe, top-full of direst cruelty'. The result is one of pain, sorrow, injustice, tragedy, madness and violent death.

The Tempest is a comedy; *Macbeth* is a tragedy. *The Tempest* is about good; *Macbeth* is about evil. In Cabalistic terms this relates to the Twin Pillars or Great Pillars of Solomon's Temple, sometimes referred to as the Pillars of Life and Death, or Good and Evil. The Westminster scroll denotes the right-hand pillar of life, light, spirituality, love, mercy, compassion and joy, while the Wilton scroll relates to the left-hand pillar of death, darkness, materialism, severity, cruelty and sorrow. This is further emphasised by the words being pointed to—'Temples' on the Westminster scroll and 'Shadow' on the Wilton scroll—for a temple is a place of light in which God (or Good) resides, while the shadow is a name for the dark side of life that is devoid of light.

Like the messages of the scrolls, the plinths of the two monuments also depict polarity, or complementary opposites, while at the same time being basically similar. They also link in their geometric symbolism with the Globe and Fortune theatres of Shakespeare's time. The Westminster plinth is square in plan like the Fortune Theatre, and the Wilton plinth is circular like the Globe Theatre. To square the circle is the grand philosophical solution to the harmony and union of all life, all worlds, spiritual and material. Only, in this instance of these twin Shakespeare memorials, the spiritual circle is placed in the material left-hand 'pillar' and the material 'square' in the right-hand spiritual 'pillar', thus making a yin-yang arrangement whereby spirit is in matter and matter in spirit.

The twinship is thus complete: for in the story of the Gemini the immortal twin becomes mortal and the mortal twin becomes immortal, each sharing the experiences of both mortality and immortality—and all because of love.

Conclusion

What a treasure trail this is to follow, and what a mystery to unravel! Starting from the initial signposts given in the Shakespeare Folio, and the challenge on the Shakespeare Monument to pause and consider who really is commemorated there, we have found ourselves on an amazing voyage of discovery, guided by the stars of the heavenly twins. Moreover, we find that these twins are, at one level of interpretation, two brothers, both renowned as poets but concealed; while at another level they are actor and author, and at a further metaphysical level they are lower and higher selves, with all that that means.

We have also found that the Shakespeare work is really a group work, led by the group's 'Apollo' or master artist, in the manner of a Renaissance studio, and that they had an extraordinary vision to follow and an unfolding plan to carry out—a plan that was and is somehow in harmony with certain celestial events and time-cycles of the world. This group, it has become plain to see, was dealing with the accumulated wisdom of the ancients and adding wisdom of their own, passing it on to future generations and ages, all for the purpose of helping to make the world a better place—so much so that one day, once we are through the dark crucifying materialism that Bacon himself foresaw the possibility of and prayed would not happen,[24] there might be a golden age or heaven on earth, for everyone and everything.

We discovered that this group adopted the symbols of the rose and cross from their predecessors, who prepared the way for this work, and that the origins of the wisdom and vision of this work go back a long way in time and involve many people from many cultures. We find that this group was networked in some way with other like-minded individuals and groups across the continent of Europe, and, through the Virginia Company and its colonisation schemes, had an interest in and connection with America. It has also become apparent that the group work and vision was passed on privately to some people in successive generations, at least up to the mid-eighteenth century, while publicly some of the ideas (and work done by the group) have inspired the development of modern science and culture, and still do today.

This group, it appears, was actively led by its 'chief' during the high point of the English Renaissance (c.1576–1626). Between them they created works of art, literature, drama and pageantry, and were patronised by certain aristocrats and courtiers close to the Sovereign, and even by the Sovereign her or himself. Their work is passed down to us as a shining jewel in the English heritage; and yet much of it still remains unknown, hidden, waiting to be discovered, partly because they hid it on purpose.

The concealment of so much of their work and knowledge was not so as to keep it secret from anyone else for evermore. On the contrary, great pains were taken by them to ensure that one day much of what they had concealed would be discovered. To this end they set up a treasure trail, with signposts and clues, and ciphers that could be deciphered, all carefully constructed like a giant jigsaw or crossword puzzle. And the aim of it all? To teach and inspire us, it would seem—to teach us the Art of Discovery and the wisdom that waits to be discovered, and to inspire us on to greater things, to create a paradise on earth.

We can see that the Shakespeare enigma is a grand one, and that a phrase like 'both your poets' is a challenge to us to look further and deeper into the mystery of Shakespeare. This is as much the mystery of our selves and of this wonderful world of ours—the stage on which we act our parts—as it is of the historical events and persons who created the mystery.

*

Just as we began this book with a quotation by Ben Jonson, eulogising the author Shakespeare, so it seems fitting to end this book with a quotation by the author himself, eulogising and praying to God:

> May God the Maker, the Preserver, the Renew of the universe, of his love and compassion to man protect and guide this work, both in its ascent to His glory, and in its descent to the good of man, through his only Son, God with us.
>
> Francis Bacon, Prayer at the end of *Abecedarium Naturae*

Notes

Notes to Chapter 1

[1]   To give an example of the encyclopaedic learning of Shakespeare, the following list (compiled by William Theobald and printed in his book, The Classical Element in the Shakespeare Plays) enumerates many of the authors who are sources of classical allusions in the Shakespeare plays. The list includes nearly one hundred different classical authors of works that would have had to have been read in their original by Shakespeare, and twenty-five others (listed in italics) whose works provided quotes or translations from classical sources—and this list is not exhaustive.

Abstemius. Ælian. Æschylus. Æsop. Agard. Alanus. Anacreon. Anaxandrides. Anthologia Græca. Antoninus. Apollonius Rhodius. Appianus. Apuleius. Aristophanes. Aristotle. Artemidorus. Athenaeus. Augustine. Aurelius. Ausonius. Avianus. Avienus. Bacon. Bede. Beza. Bion. Bœthius. Buchanan. Cæsar. Caius. Callimachus. Callistratus. Calpurnius. Camararius. Carcinus. Catullus. Cebes Thebanus. Cicero. Claudianus. Curtius. Dares Phrygius. Democrates. Democritus. Dictys. Dionysius. Empedocles. Ennius. Erasmus. Euclid. Euripides. Valerius Flaccus. Florus. Fracastor. Gellius. Gesner. Giovanni da Genova. Gregorius. Gualtier. Heraclitus. Hermes Trismegistus. Herodotus. Hesiod. Hippocrates. Homer. Horace. Horus Apollo. Isidorus. Juvenal. Lilly. Livy. Lucan. Lucian. Lucretius. Mandeville. Mantuanus. Martial. Menander. Moschus. Muretus. Musæus. Orpheus. Ovid. Palingenius. Paracelsus. Persius. Petronius. Phædrus. Philemon. Philonides. Philostratus. Pindar. Plato. Plautus. Pliny. Plutarch. Pomponius. Posidippus. Priscianus. Propertius. Ptolemy. Sallust. Saxo Grammaticus. Scaliger. Seneca. Silius Italicus. Sophocles. Statius. Strada. Stradanus. Suetonius. Syrus. Tacitus. Terence. Theocritus. Theognis. Tibullus. Tyrtæus. Valerius. Vanini. Varro. Vasari. Velleius. Virgil. Zeno.

[2]   To give some of the more obvious examples, sources for his plots which Shakespeare either had to read or chose to read in either French, Italian or Spanish include:

Spanish sources:

Montemayor's romance, *Diana Enamorada* (1559). No English translation published until 1598. Used in the Shakespeare plays, *The Two Gentlemen of Verona* (1590–5), *A Midsummer Night's Dream* (1595–6), *As You Like It* (1599) and *Twelfth Night* (1601).

French sources:

Two early 15th-century manuscripts, *La Chronique de la Traison et Mort de Richart Deux Roy Dengleterre,* and *Jean Créton's Histoire du Roy d'Angleterre Richard.* Used in the Shakespeare play *Richard II* (1595–6).

Italian sources:

Compilation of 14th-century stories by Ser Giovanni Fiorentino called *Il Pecorane* (1558). No known Elizabethan translation. Used in the Shakespeare plays, *The Merchant of Venice* (1596–8) and *The Merry Wives of Windsor* (1597).

Matteo Bandello, *La Prima Parte de le Novelle, Novella 22* (1554). Translated into French by Belleforest in 1569. Used in the Shakespeare play *Much Ado About Nothing* (1598).

Ariosto's *Orlando Furioso Canto V* (1516/1532). Translated into English by Sir John Harrington in 1591. Used in the Shakespeare plays, *Much Ado About Nothing* (1598) and *As You Like It* (1599).

Ariosto's *I Suppositi* (1509). Translated into English as *Supposes* by George Gascoigne, published 1575. Used

---

in the Shakespeare plays, *As You Like It* (1599) and *The Taming of the Shrew.*

Giraldi Cinthio's *Hecatommithi* (1566) No English translation of *Hecatommithi* is known before 1753. A French translation was published in 1584. Used in the Shakespeare plays, *Measure for Measure* (1604) and *Othello* (1604).

Giraldi Cinthio's *Epitia* (1583). Used in the Shakespeare play *Measure for Measure* (1604).

Boccaccio's *Decameron* (1353). A selection of tales from *Decameron* was translated into English by William Painter in his *Palace of Pleasure*, 1566–7. Used in the Shakespeare plays, *All's Well that Ends Well* (1604), *Cymbeline* (1609–10) and *The Winter's Tale* (1610–11).

3   Philip Sidney, *An Apologie for Poetrie*, para. 16 (c.1579):

> And may not I presume a little farther, to shewe the reasonablenesse of this word Vatis, and say that the holy Davids Psalms are a divine Poeme? …The Greekes named him [David] poieten, which name, hath as the most excellent, gone through other languages, it commeth of this word poiein which is to make: wherein I know not whether by luck or wisedome, we Englishmen have met with the Greekes in calling him a Maker. Which name, how high and incomparable a title it is, I had rather were knowne by marking the scope of other sciences, then by any partial allegation. There is no Art delivered unto mankind that hath not the workes of nature for his principall object, without which they could not consist, and on which they so depend, as they become Actors & Plaiers, as it were of what nature will have set forth.

Greek *poiein* means to make or create, and *poieten* means a maker or creator, from which the English word *poet* is derived.

4   To set the canon of Shakespeare into perspective, let us remember that this beautifully produced book was the combined work of forty–two learned translators, divided into six companies (two each at Oxford and Cambridge Universities, and two at Westminster), helped by 'any learned man in the land', and with the final translations being brought together and polished into shape by an additional board of twelve revisers.

5   William Hazlitt, *Characters of Shakespeare's Plays* (1817).

Notes to Chapter 2

1   Wealthier classes—the gentry and aristocracy—usually did educate their daughters to at least read and write. Will Shakespeare paid to become a gentleman and had wealth enough to educate his daughters if he had wished. It is rather extraordinary, therefore, that if he was the author Shakespeare he did not teach his daughters to at least write.

2   *2 Henry IV,* IV, vii

3   Stratford Register:

'1564, April 26, Gulielmus filius Johannes Shakspere.'

4   Marriage Bond from the Registry of the Diocese of Worcester.

5   The evidence is contained in the writing of Shakespeare's will, which was in all probability penned by Shakespeare himself. The handwriting deteriorates halfway through and at one point it appears he might have suffered a cerebral stroke. According to the handwriting expert, Charles Hamilton, the will has all the appearance of being written by a man who was dying, possibly poisoned with arsenic or suffering with typhoid fever, leading to heart and kidney failure and the

bloated features that are recorded (from Shakespeare's death mask) on the bust of Shakespeare in the Stratford Monument. See Charles Hamilton, *In Search of Shakespeare: A Study of the Poet's Life and Handwriting* (Robert Hale, London, 1985).

⁶ Charles Hamilton, *In Search of Shakespeare: A Study of the Poet's Life and Handwriting* (London: Robert Hale, 1985).

⁷ See Jane Cox, *Shakespeare in the Public Records* (HMSO, 1985).

⁸ For clarity, when using the name Will Shakespeare I shall be referring to the actor Shakespeare from Stratford-upon-Avon.

⁹ Lord Strange's Men became known also as Lord Derby's Men when Henry Stanley, Lord Strange, became the Earl of Derby in 1572. His company was first formed in 1566.

¹⁰ John Aubrey, 'Mary Herbert', *Brief Lives* (The Folio Society edition, 1975), p. 146. The bulk of the *Lives* were written 1679–1680.

Notes to Chapter 3

¹ The list of actors for the performance of *Every Man in His Humour* is given in the Folio of Jonson's work, publ. 1616. Shakespeare's name is shown opposite that of one of the leading roles, that of Mr Knowell. However, this does not necessarily mean that he played that part, as he may have been listed for other reasons, such as being a shareholder of the company, as other cast lists have done.

² Both Mercury and Venus are known as the Morning Star when they are seen rising just before the sun at dawn, thereby heralding the rising of the greater light (the sun or Daystar).

³ *Hamlet*, I, ii, 247.

⁴ Ben Jonson, *Timber: or Discoveries; Made upon Men and Matter* (1641), printed in Ben Jonson, *Workes*, pp. 97–8.

⁵ 'Blotted' in the sense of blotting the lines with blotting paper after they have been written.

⁶ *Julius Caesar*, III, i, 47–8.

⁷ Henry Chettle (*c*.1560–*c*.1607) was writing plays at least by 1598, when he was mentioned by Frances Meres as a fine writer of comedies. He is known to have written or collaborated on at least forty-seven dramas, including the play *Sir Thomas More*, for the Admiral's Men and Phillip Henslowe.

⁸ Shakespeare, *3 Henry VI*, I, iv, III.

⁹ Three years of computer-aided research by Professor Warren B. Austin, of Stephen F. Austin State College of Texas, would seem to validate the opinion that Chettle wrote both pamphlets. His findings were published in a report entitled *A Computer-Aided Technique for Stylistic Discrimination – The Authorship of Greene's Groatsworth of Wit* (1969).

¹⁰ See *The Three Parnassus Plays (1598–1601)*, ed. J. B. Leishman (1949).

¹¹ See especially Ben Jonson's *Every Man out of his Humour* (1599/1600), *The Case is Altered* (1599/1600)

Cynthia's Revels (1600) and *The Poetaster* (1601), Thomas Dekker's *Histriomastix* (1599) and *Satiromatix, or the Untrussing of the Humorous Poet* (1601), and Marston's *Jack Drum's Entertainment* (1600) and *What You Will* (1601).

[12] Up to 1601 Jupiter is mentioned in *The Merry Wives of Windsor, As You Like It* and *Titus Andronicus*. Proserpina does not appear until later, in *The Winter's Tale* and *Troilus and Cressida*. Jupiter appears post-1601 in *The Tempest, The Winter's Tale, Troilus and Cressida, Coriolanus, Anthony and Cleopatra* and *Cymbeline*.

[13] *The Returne from Pernassus or The Scourge of Simony*, V, i. Published in 1616 (London) by John Wright, printed by G. Eld.

[14] Jonson refers especially to the groundlings who stood in the yard. The name is derived from the species of fish that live close to the bottom of a lake or river, who gape with their mouths.

[15] Ref. Public Records: Stratford Court Leet, 29 April 1552 – SC 2/207/82.

[16] This research by C. L'Estrange Ewen was presented in an article, The Name Shakespeare, published in Baconiana No. 84 (1936) p.171.

Notes to Chapter 4

[1] *Pericles Prince of Tyre* was printed in the second issue (1664) of the Third Folio. The two lost plays are *The History of Cardenio* (written c 1613) and *Love's Labour's Won*, first mentioned by Francis Meres in 1598.

[2] The fourteen unregistered plays were *The Tempest, Cymbeline, Twelfth Night, The Winter's Tale, Henry VIII, Julius Caesar, Macbeth, The Two Gentlemen of Verona, Measure for Measure, Comedy of Errors, All's Well That Ends Well, Henry VI Pt 3, Coriolanus, Timon of Athens*. The four registered plays were *As You Like It, Anthony and Cleopatra, Henry VI Pt 1, Henry VI Pt 2*.

[3] *The Merchant of Venice*, IV, i, 301.

[4] The inscription uses the Elizabethan long 's', that looks like an 'f', but we have had to change it to a normal modern 's' wherever it occurs. The Elizabethan use of 'yt' and 'ys' for 'that' and 'this' has been retained, although the 't' was normally placed above the 'y' in the original.

[5] *Service* is originally derived from Sanskrit *seva*, meaning to cherish, honour, worship, particularly in terms of celebration of the divine.

[6] Mark Twain, *Is Shakespeare Dead?* (Harper & Brothers, New York and London, 1909).

[7] In the second verse of Ben Jonson's Tribute to the Author a similar word, *out-shine*, is used in the sense of surpass:—

And tell, how far thou didst our Lily out-shine.

[8] This is recorded in *Anathemata B. Conrado*, issued at Placentia in 1621.

[9] Publius Vergilius Maro (70–19 BC).

[10] Francis Bacon, *Advancement of Learning*.

Notes to Chapter 5

[1] *The Art of English Poesie* (1589), Book 1, ch. 8. (I have modernised the spelling where necessary for clarity.) From as early as 1590 authorship of the book was ascribed to either one or other of two brothers, George Puttenham (*c.*1529–90) or Richard Puttenham (*c.*1520–1601). Nowadays it is usually the former who is thought to have been the author.

[2] In the 16th and 17th centuries 'interludes' meant stage plays, especially of a popular nature, such as comedies. For instance, in 1588, a writer described the full-length play, *Gammer Gurton's Needle,* as 'A proper Enterlude'; and Middleton, in *It's a Mad World* (V, 1), wrote: 'There are certain players come to town, sir, and desire to interlude before your worship.' The familiar 'Pyramus and Thisbe' scene in *Midsummer Night's Dream* is called both a play and an interlude.

[3] These lines are quoted in Ordish's *Early London Theatres* (1894).

[4] Used by Marsden when he published his erotic and satirical poems, *The Metamorphosis of Pygmalion's Image* and *The Scourge of Villainy,* in 1598.

[5] *Sir Thomas More,* III, ii, 219.

[6] Jonson was also jailed in September 1598, when in a duel he killed Gabriel Spencer, a fellow-actor and leading member of Pembroke's Men, and only escaped execution by pleading benefit of clergy. 'Benefit of clergy' was an archaic practice whereby the clergy had the privilege of being outside the jurisdiction of secular courts of law and entitled to trial in ecclesiastical courts. All that was required to 'prove' that one was a member of the clergy was to be able to read in Latin a verse of the Bible, referred to as the 'neck verse'.

[7] The invented name Falstaff is an interesting combination of False and Staff—*i.e.,* the false staff—implying the antithesis of Shake-Spear, the spear of light being the true spear or staff.

[8] The historical 'Falstaff', Sir John Oldcastle (1378–1459), a knight of the Garter, had been one of Henry V's leaders, who fought well at Agincourt and elsewhere. But at Patey he was not so successful and his men fled, and Talbot was captured as a result. After an investigation into the defeat Sir John was exonerated, but 16th century chroniclers chose to follow the story put out by Monstrelet: that Sir John was deprived of the Garter for cowardice. Shakespeare took the basis of his Falstaff character from these chronicle accounts, but built up an entirely different character to the original for the purposes of his drama, as he did with most of his historical characters.

> After the death, on 22 July 1596, of Sir Henry Carey , 1st Lord Hunsdon, who as Lord Chamberlain was the first patron of the Lord Chamberlain's Men, Sir William Brooke, Lord Cobham, was for a short time Lord Chamberlain until his own death on 5 March 1597. The Lord Chamberlain's office reverted to Sir Henry Carey's son, Sir George Carey, 2nd Lord Hunsdon; but Sir William Brooke's son, Sir Henry Brooke, who succeeded as the 8th Lord Cobham, was intent at putting right the slur on his family. Shakespeare changed the Oldcastle name immediately, but the issue went on for three years (1597–1599), with much perturbation, hilarity and gossip, until finally settled with the presentation of the play *The true and honorable historie of the life of Sir John Old–castle,* co-authored by Drayton, Munday, Wilson and Hathaway, acted in 1599 and printed in 1600.

[9] Prof. Brian Vickers, in his book Shakespeare, Co-Author (Oxford University Press, 2002), shows how numerous tests, made by many generations of scholars, seem to demonstrate fairly conclusively that other playwrights contributed substantially to at least five Shakespeare plays: for in-

stance, George Peele wrote almost a third of Titus Andronicus, Thomas Middleton about two-fifths of Timon of Athens, George Wilkins two of the five acts of Pericles, and John Fletcher more than half of Henry VIII and three-fifths of The Two Noble Kinsmen.

[10]   The Earl of Surrey is generally reputed as being the inventor of English blank verse, when he tried to find an English equivalent of the Latin heroic metre for his translation of Virgil. Two forms developed—non-dramatic and dramatic. The latter made use of the iambic line of verse and formed the poetic basis of the entire Elizabethan drama.

[11]   *As You Like It*, III, v, 81–82.

[12]   Quirinus was also a name of Janus, the chief god of the Roman pantheon of gods and goddesses.

[13]   Roma, the goddess of the city whom Mars protected, personified Rome itself as a city. Complementing Mars, she was represented like Minerva (Athena), completely armed, sitting on a rock, holding a spear in her hand, her head covered with a helmet and a trophy set at her feet.

[14]   'The Legend of the Knight of the Red Cross, or Holiness' — Edmund Spenser, Book 1, *The Faerie Queene*.

[15]   In particular the name *George* means 'the Cultivator' or 'Gardener', who looks after the garden (Eden) of the world and helps to promote the culture of humanity. It is a descriptive name of Adam, the generic name of humanity. With his red (or golden) cross, St George is emblematic of the true Christian whose armour is the armour of light and whose goal is to become like Christ, the last Adam or Gardener of the world:

> And so it is written, 'The first man Adam was made a living soul:' the last Adam was made a quickening spirit... And as we have born the image of the earthy, we shall also bear the image of the heavenly. (I Corinthians 15 : 45, 49).

[16]   See Isabel Hill Elder, *George of Lydda* (Covenant Books, 2nd edn., 1980).

[17]   Brit. Mus. Orient MS 686, Fol. 177, Ch. I.

[18]   Mansi. *Concilia* Vol.II, pp. 476–477.

[19]   Elias Ashmole, *Order of the Garter* (1672).

[20]   The Ancient British Pendragon or war leader was an elected man of the garter, leader of the ranks.

[21]   Michael Maier, *Symbola Aureæ Mensæ* (Frankfurt, 1617).

[22]   The cross is either red or gold—gold being the metal and red the colour. In heraldry gold is represented by the colour red. Interestingly, if gold is combined in glass and heated, it imbues the glass with a beautiful rosy red colour.

[23]   Liberal means 'free'. The word 'free' is derived from Sanskrit *priya*, meaning 'loving kindness'. The seven liberal arts and sciences are the arts and sciences of love, which is wise and illuminating.

[24]   Latin, Iu-Pater (Jupiter), meaning 'Father of Light'.

[25]   Athena Promachos (the 'Champion').

[26]   The main central gate was part of the Propylaia, built by Mnesikles in 437–432 BC, which comprised a monumental tripartite entrance to the Acropolis of Athens.

[32] See Ernesto Grillo, *Shakespeare and Italy* (1949); N. B. Cockburn, *The Bacon Shakespeare Question: The Baconian Theory Made Sane* (1998), vii.

[33] *The Taming of the Shrew*, I, i, 10; IV, ii, 95.

[34] *The Taming of the Shrew*, I, i, 42; IV, ii, 81–85.

[35] *The Taming of the Shrew*, IV, iii, 91.

[36] *The Taming of the Shrew*, V, i, 69–70.

[37] *The Two Gentlemen of Verona*, I, i, 53–54, 71–72; II, iii, 33–58.

[38] *The Two Gentlemen of Verona*, IV, ii, 81.

[39] *The Two Gentlemen of Verona*, V, i, 2.

[40] *Romeo and Juliet*, III, v, 114–115.

[41] *The Merchant of Venice*, III, iv, 53–54.

[42] *The Merchant of Venice*, III, iii, 26; III, iv.

[43] *The Merchant of Venice*, III, iii, 27.

[44] *The Merchant of Venice*, III, iv, 49–50; IV, i, 104–109, 119–120, 143–166.

[45] *Othello*, I, i, 183.

[46] *The Winter's Tale*, V, ii, 93–99.

[47] *The Winter's Tale*, V, iii, 63–65.

[48] Introduction, First Arden edition of *Coriolanus* (1922), p. 43.

[49] e.g.,, Dudley Diggs in his *Foure Paradoxes or politique Discourses* (1604), Bodin in his *Six Bookes of a Commonweale* (translated by Knolles in 1606), and Edward Forset in his *Comparative Discourse of the Bodies Natural and Politique* (1606).

[50] Published in English by J A Symonds in the *Fortnightly Review*, Vol XVIII NS, 1875.

[51] See Dr. A A Prins, 'The Learning of Shakespeare', *Baconiana* No. 171 (Dec. 1971).

Notes to Chapter 7

[1] Anthony, whose day and month and place of birth are unknown, was born in 1558.

[2] Robert Naunton, *Fragmenta Regalia,* describes Sir Nicholas Bacon as 'an archpiece of wit and wisdom'. The author of *The Arte of English Poesie* says of Sir Nicholas:

> I have come to the Lord Keeper, Sir Nicholas Bacon, and found him sitting in his gallery alone with the works of Quintillian before him. Indeed, he was a most eloquent man, and of rare learning and wisdom, as ever I knew England to breed, and one that joyed as much in learned men and men of good wits.

> Francis Bacon said of Sir Nicholas that he was 'wiser than he seems'.

[3] Sir Anthony Cooke (1504–76), one of the most learned men of his time, had been tutor to the boy king Edward VI. He was a close friend of Queen Catherine Parr, another lover of learning. He had four sons (two of whom died young) and five daughters by his wife, Lady Anne, daughter of Sir William Fitzwilliam. The eldest son, Anthony, and another son, Edward, died in their youth.

(Edward died in 1576, the same year as his father.) The two surviving sons were Richard and William. Richard's son Anthony was the patron of the poet Michael Drayton. The five daughters of Sir Anthony, all taught by him, were learned and accomplished ladies. These five daughters became through marriage: Lady Mildred Burleigh, Lady Anne Bacon, Lady Margaret Rowlett, Lady Elizabeth Russell (previously the wife of Sir Thomas Hoby), and Lady Katharine Killigrew.

Sir Anthony was a wealthy landowner with estates as far apart as Essex, Warwickshire, Devonshire, and Kent. His family seat was Giddy (or Gidea) Hall near Romford. He had a magnificent library, inherited by his eldest surviving son, Richard—the latter also inheriting Gidea Hall and lands in Essex, and the manor of Hartshill in Warwickshire.

[4] Francis Bacon, *Promus of Formularies and Elegancies,* fol. 103 (written *c.*1594).

[5] *Pléiade* was the name given in Greek literature to seven tragic poets who flourished during the reign of Ptolemy Philadelphus (285–247). The name is derived from the Pleiades, the cluster of 'seven' stars in the constellation of Taurus. In France, during the reign of Henri III (1574–89), another group of seven poets, led by Pierre de Ronsard, took the name of *Pléiade.* Their avowed purpose was to improve the French language and literature by imitation of the classics.

[6] Bodley (the founder of the Bodleian Library at Oxford), himself travelled a great deal. In 1583 he became 'Gentleman-Usher' to the Queen, and in 1588 was appointed by the Queen as Resident Minister at The Hague.

[7] Nicholas Faunt had likewise spent 1581 in France, Germany, Switzerland and the north of Italy gathering political intelligence. Back at the English court in 1582, Faunt collected and arranged the observations he had made abroad. From 1582 onwards Anthony kept in close contact with Faunt, who had become a secretary of Sir Francis Walsingham, the Queen's Secretary of State and head of the intelligence service.

[8] The *Notes on the Present State of Christendom* were transcribed from a collection of Bacon's mss in the care of the Earl of Oxford and printed by Robert Stephens in the supplement to his second collection of Bacon's papers, published in 1734 and reprinted by Mallet in 1760.

[9] Mentioned by Bacon in the French edition/translation of *Sylva Sylvarum,* 1631.

[10] Letter from Essex to the Queen (1594). *Henry IV,* Parts I and II, are estimated to have been written in 1596.

[11] Shakespeare, *Henry V,* Act V, Chorus 30–2.

[12] Sir Philip Sidney, *Astrophel and Stella.*

[13] Anthony Bacon's surviving correspondence was carefully collected by Francis Bacon and bequeathed to his secretary and literary executor, Dr William Rawley, who in turn bequeathed it to Dr Thomas Tenison, Archbishop of Canterbury, who placed it in the Lambeth Palace library, where it still resides.

[14] Spedding VIII, 372. The letter is undated but was probably written in January 1594.

[15] Spedding VIII, 345:

> My singular Good Lord. I may perceive by my Lord Keeper that your Lordship, as the time served, signified unto him an intention to confer with his Lordship at better opportunity; which in regard of your several and weighty occasions, I have thought good to put your Lordship in remembrance of; that now, at his coming to Court, it may be executed; desiring your good Lordship nevertheless not to conceive out

mind by similitude, types, parables, visions, dreams. And again, in all persuasions that are wrought by eloquence, and other impressions of like nature, which do paint and disguise the true appearance of things, the chief recommendation unto Reason is from the Imagination.

[14] *As. Res.* Vol. III. See Edward Moor, *The Hindu Pantheon* (Philosophical Research Society, LA, California, 1976), p. 127.

[15] The 1609 first quarto of *Pericles* prints the sentence as:

> Opinion's but a fool, that makes us scan
> > The outward habit by the inward man.

The use of 'for' in place of the corrupt quarto's 'by' gives a much better sense of what the author intended, which is matched by the corresponding lines in *The Painfull Adventures of Pericles Prince of Tyre* by George Wilkins (1608), a novel which claimed to be 'the True History of the Play of *Pericles,* as it was lately presented by the worthy and ancient poet John Gower':

> The outward habite was the least table of the inward minde.

[16] Spedding, IV, 22–23: transl. of *De Dignitate & Augmentis Scientiarum* (1623).

[17] Spedding, IV, 112: transl. of *Novum Organum* (1620).

[18] Francis Bacon, 'Of Truth,' *Essays* (1625).

[19] Spedding, IV, 473: transl. of 'Examples of Antithesis,' *De Augmentis,* VI (1623).

[20] Folio 85 (the first page of the surviving part of the collection) is dated 5th December 1594, and folio 114 is dated 27th January 1595.

[21] Spedding, VII, 190.

[22] Francis Bacon, *Promus,* fol. 112, front (entry No. 1206).

[23] Shakespeare, *King Lear,* II, ii, 1.

[24] Francis Bacon, *Promus,* fol. 101, back (entry No. 889).

[25] Francis Bacon, *Sylva Sylvarum,* S.31.

[26] Francis Bacon, *De Principiis atque Originibus.*

[27] Shakespeare, *Julius Caesar,* III, i, 171.

[28] Shakespeare, *Coriolanus,* IV, vii, 54–55.

[29] Shakespeare, *The Two Gentlemen of Verona,* II, iv, 188–189.

[30] Francis Bacon, *Promus,* folio 85, front (entry No. 106).

[31] Francis Bacon, *Promus,* folio 93, front (entry No. 517).

[32] Shakespeare, *Henry V,* III, vii, 132.

[33] Shakespeare, *As You Like It,* Epil. 4.

[34] Francis Bacon, *Promus,* folio 92, front (entry No. 477).

[35] Shakespeare, *Merchant of Venice,* II, vii, 65.

[36] Francis Bacon, *Promus,* folio 101, back (entry No. 872).

[37] Shakespeare, *Antony and Cleopatra,* II, v, 45.

[38] Philip Massinger, *Bashful Lover,* IV, i (1636).

[39] Francis Bacon, *Promus,* Fol. 85, back (entry No. 125).

[40] Shakespeare, *Venus and Adonis,* v, 185, 1165–1170.

[41] George Peele, *Edward I* (1593).

[42] Anonymous, *Edward. III,* II, ii (1596).

[43] Shakespeare, *Hamlet,* I, ii, 130.

[44] Shakespeare, *Antony and Cleopatra,* III, ii, 163–4.

[45] Shakespeare, *The Tempest,* IV, i, 154.

[46] John Fletcher, *Two Noble Kinsmen,* III, ii (1613).

[47] The Latin epitaph, composed by Sir Henry Wotton, Provost of Eton, which is inscribed on the memorial, is enigmatic:

> FRANCISCUS BACON BARO DE VERULA STA ALBNI VICMS
> sev notioribus titulis
> Scientiarum Lumen Facundiæ Lex
> sic sedebat
> Qui postquam omnia naturalis sapientiæ
> et civilis arcana evolvisset
> naturæ devretum explevit
> Composita Solvantur
> Ano Dni MDCXXVI
> ætat LXVI
> tanti viri
> mem.
> Thomas Meutys.
> superstitis cultor.
> defuncti admirator
> h.p.

A translation of which reads as follows:

> Francis Bacon, Baron of Verulam, Viscount St. Alban
> or, by more conspicuous titles
> of Science the Light, of Eloquence the Law
> sat thus.
> Who, after all Natural Wisdom
> and Secrets of Civil Life he had unfolded,
> Nature's Law fulfilled—
> Let Compounds be Dissolved!
> In the year of our Lord 1626, aged 66.
> Of such a man, that the memory might remain
> Thomas Meutys
> living his Attendant,
> dead his Admirer
> placed this Monument.

[48] Francis Bacon, *Promus,* fol. 103, front (entry No. 949).

[49] Francis Bacon, *Promus,* folio 96, back (entry No. 653).

[50] Shakespeare, *Twelfth Night,* I, iii, 73

[51] Shakespeare, *The Tempest,* III, ii, 132.

52 Francis Bacon, *Promus*, folio 90, back (entry No. 399).

53 Mrs Henry Pott, *The Promus of Formularies and Elegancies by Francis Bacon* (London, 1883).

54 *Proverbs* 25 : 2.

55 The spelling and punctuation of this quotation from the 1640 *Advancement of Learning* have been slightly modernised to assist reading.

56 *Genesis* i, 28.

57 I Reg. 4.

58 The spelling and punctuation of this quotation from the 1640 *Advancement of Learning* have been slightly modernised to assist reading.

59 But without the heavy taxation and forced labour which Solomon presided over—Bacon's ideas on this were entirely different and based on charity.

⁶0 *Proverbs* xxv, 2.

61 The spelling and punctuation of this quotation from the 1640 *Advancement of Learning* have been slightly modernised to assist reading.

62 Agrippa, *Occult Philosophy*, sig A5.

63 Francis Bacon, *Advancement of Learning*, Part 2 (1605):

> And surely, as nature createth brotherhood in families, and arts mechanical contract brotherhoods in commonalities, and the anointment of God superinduceth a brotherhood in kings and bishops; so in like manner there cannot but be a fraternity in learning and illumination, relating to that paternity which is attributed to God, who is called the Father of illuminations or lights.

64 Spedding, VI, 698: transl. of *De Sapientia Veterum* (1609).

65 Francis Bacon, *Of the Advancement and Proficience of Learning* (1640), page 315.

66 Spedding, V, 4: transl. of *De Dignitate & Augmentis Scientiarum* (1623).

67 Francis Bacon, *Advancement of Learning*, Bk II.

68 Spedding, III, 248.

69 Spedding IV, 450: transl. of *De Dignitate & Augmentis Scientiarum* (1623).

70 Spedding, IV, 53: transl. of *Novum Organum* (1620).

71 See Samuel Pittiscus, 'Castor', *Lexicon Antiquitum Romanorum*. The inscription reads:

CASTORI. ET. POLLUCI. SACRUM
OB. FELICEM. IN. PATRIAM
REDITUM. TOT. SUPERATIS
NAUFRAGII. PERICULIS
...EX. VOTO. CUM
SOCIIS
L. M. P.
C. VALERIUS.   C. F. AGELLUS.

72 Ben Jonson, *Ode for Lord Bacon's Birth-day* (1621).

73 Shakespeare, *As You Like It*, II, vii.

[74] Camden, *Annales rerum Anglicarum et Hibernicarum regnante Elizabetha* (1615–17) Bk I, p. 104 (transl 1675).

[75] Spedding, VII, 229. This prayer was discovered among Bacon's papers (Birch MSS, 4263, f.110). According to Spedding, the prayer was composed 'certainly before the 18th April [1621], and most probably at this very time'. This time was during the period when Bacon's impeachment was being discussed and proposed in the House of Lords, and he had just written his will, dated 10 April 1621. On 18 April Bacon had an interview with the King concerning the charge about to be brought against him.

> Most Gracious Lord God, my merciful Father, from my youth up, my Creator, my Redeemer, my Comforter. Thou (O Lord) soundest and searchest the depths and secrets of all hearts; thou knowledgest the upright of heart, thou judgest the hypocrite, thou ponderest men's thoughts and doings as in a balance, thou measurest their intentions as with a line, vanity and crooked ways cannot be hid from thee.
>
> Remember (O Lord) how thy servant hath walked before thee; remember what I have first sought, and what hath been principal in my intentions. I have loved thy assemblies, I have mourned for the divisions of thy Church, I have delighted in the brightness of thy sanctuary. This vine which thy right hand hath planted in this nation, I have ever prayed unto thee that it might have the first and the latter rain; and that it might stretch her branches to the seas and to the floods. The state and bread of the poor and oppressed have been precious in my eyes: I have hated all cruelty and hardness of heart; I have (though in a despised weed) procured the good of all men. If any have been mine enemies, I thought not of them; neither hath the sun almost set upon my displeasure; but I have been as a dove, free from superfluity of maliciousness. Thy creatures have been my books, but thy Scriptures much more. I have sought thee in the courts, fields, and gardens, but I have found thee in thy temples.
>
> Thousands have been my sins, and ten thousand my transgressions; but thy sanctifications have remained with me, and my heart, through thy grace, hath been an unquenched coal upon thy altar. O Lord, my strength, I have since my youth met with thee in all my ways, by thy fatherly compassions, by thy comfortable chastisements, and by thy most visible providence. As thy favours have increased upon me, so have thy corrections; so as thou hast been always near me, O Lord; and ever as my worldly blessings were exalted, so secret darts from thee have pierced me; and when I have ascended before men, I have descended in humiliation before thee.
>
> And now when I thought most of peace and honour, thy hand is heavy upon me, and hath humbled me, according to thy former loving-kindness, keeping me still in thy fatherly school, not as a bastard, but as a child. Just are thy judgments upon me for my sins, which are more in number than the sands of the sea, but have no proportion to thy mercies; for what are the sands of the sea, to the sea, earth, heavens? and all these are nothing to thy mercies.
>
> Besides my innumerable sins, I confess before thee, that I am debtor to thee for the gracious talent of thy gifts and graces, which I have neither put into a napkin, nor put it (as I ought) to exchangers, where it might have made best profit; but misspent it in things for which I was least fit; so as I may truly say, my soul hath been a stranger in the course of my pilgrimage. Be merciful unto me (O Lord) for my Saviour's sake, and receive me into thy bosom, or guide me in thy ways.

Notes to Chapter 9

[1] An interesting 'Discourse upon the Life of M Francis Bacon' by Pierre Amboise—the first biography of Francis Bacon—is prefixed to the first French edition of Bacon's *Sylva Sylvarum* and

New Atlantis, published in Paris in 1631 by the firm of Antoine de Sommaville and Andre de Soubron under the title of *Histoire Naturelle de Mre Francois Bacon, Baron de Verulan, Vicomte de sainct Alban & Chancelier d'Angleterre*. Pierre Amboise writes:

> Since he was thus born amid the purples[1] and nourished in the hope of a high destiny, his father had him instructed in the arts with such great and exacting care that I do not know to which of the two we are the more indebted for all the fine works he has left us—the mind of the son or the care exerted by the father in its training. Howbeit, our obligation to the father is not slight.

[2] Sir Nicholas Bacon was first married to Jane Fernley, by whom he had three sons—Nicholas, Nathaniel and Edward; and three daughters—Anne, Jane and Elizabeth. Their country home was Redgrave Hall, Suffolk. Jane died in the spring of 1553, and shortly afterwards Sir Nicholas married Anne Cooke, who had helped to nurse Jane in her last year of sickness.

[3] Anthony Cooke married Hawice, daughter of Sir William Waldegrave, by whom he had two sons, Edward and Francis.

[4] The name figures in eight comedies and one tragedy: *The Tempest, The Two Gentlemen of Verona, Much Ado About Nothing, The Merchant of Venice, The Taming of the Shrew, All's Well That Ends Well, Twelfth Night, Love's Labour's Lost,* and *Romeo and Juliet*.

[5] See the author's book, *Dedication to the Light* (1984), 'Gorhambury Platonic Academy'.

[6] The other country home of Lord Burghley was Burghley House in Northamptonshire.

[7] The widowed Lady Anne lived at Gorhambury until her death in August 1610, after which it became Francis' country retreat, Anthony having previously died in May 1601. When Francis died, on Easter Day, 1626, it was in the parish church of Gorhambury (St Michael's) that he was buried, according to his wishes, where Lady Anne had been buried previously.

[8] Published by Rawley in *Resuscitatio* (1661).

[9] Spedding, VIII: *The Letters and the Life of Francis Bacon*, Vol. I, Bk. I, ch. 1, p. 4.

[10] The Northumberland Manuscript.

[11] It is generally assumed that Edmund Spenser was Immerito, the author of the poems published with his name on the title pages, but there are indications that this may be another case of masking.

[12] Spedding, VIII: *The Letters and the Life of Francis Bacon*, Vol. I, Bk. I, ch. 1, pp. 3–4.

[13] Francis Bacon had his degree of Master of Arts conferred upon him in a special congregation, the usual exercises and ceremonies being dispensed with, on 27 July 1594. (Spedding, VIII: *The Letters and the Life of Francis Bacon*, Vol I, Bk I, ch. IX, p. 305.)

[14] Translated from the French by Granville C. Cuningham. See 'A New Life of Lord Bacon', *Baconiana* IV/14 (April 1906).

[15] The Letters Patent dated 30th June 1576 (under the Queen's hand) at the Record Office contain the terms of the licence granted to both Francis Bacon and his half-brother Edward to travel on the Continent for the period of three years, together with their servants, six horses or geldings, baggage and carrying £60 in money, 'for their increase in knowledge and experience'.

[16] According to the *Acts of Privy Council, 1576,* the *Dreadnought* was specially commissioned to convey Paulet and his Embassy to France.

[17]   Edward, son of Sir Nicholas Bacon by his first wife, was the youngest of the three half-brothers of Francis. Edward was educated at Westminster, but does not appear to have gone to Oxford or Cambridge. He was admitted 'ancient' of Gray's Inn, November 1576. Between 1576 and 1593, he was M.P. in succession for Great Yarmouth, Tavistock, Weymouth and Suffolk, becoming Sheriff of Suffolk in 1601. (He followed Francis Bacon in 1584 as Member for Melcombe Regis, both being nominees of the Earl of Bedford who controlled the representation of this Seat.) On 11 May, 1603, he was knighted. His residence was Shrubland Hall, Suffolk. He died on 8 September 1618, and was buried at Banham, Norfolk.

[18]   We know from a letter of John Sturmius to Lord Burghley (State Papers Foreign, 5th December 1577) that Edward Bacon was at Strasburg in December 1577.

[19]   Dr William Rawley, *Life of Sir Francis Bacon.*

[20]   The reunion did not last long, and Marguerite returned to Paris and life at the French Court in 1582.

[21]   This was the very morning that Sir Nicholas was taken ill.

[22]   By express desire of Sir Nicholas Bacon, his body was laid next to that of John of Gaunt in St Paul's Cathedral, London.

[23]   According to Spedding the explanation of Francis Bacon's special admittance was that Francis's mother said that he (Francis) suffered from indigestion caused by untimely going to bed, then musing *'nescio quid,'* when he should sleep, and then in consequence of this rising late from bed.

[24]   By Order of Pension dated 21 November 1576.

[25]   A Reader was appointed for one term only, during which he was expected to lecture for two weeks (later educed to one week) on legal topics. (N. B. Cockburn, *The Bacon Shakespeare Question*, v, 55.).

[26]   Francis Bacon's chambers are now known as No. 1 Gray's Inn Square.

[27]   In 1589 Francis Bacon wrote the *Advertisement* about the Church of England, and a statement of English religious and foreign policy known as 'Sir Francis Walsingham, Secretary, to Monsieur Critoy, Secretary of France'. He was included in several committees of the Parliaments of 1593 and 1597 drafting security and policing legislation, and in 1593 responded to the attack on Queen Elizabeth and English policies made by Robert Parsons. In May 1594 he was appointed Deputy Chief Steward of the Duchy of Lancaster, a lawyer's post devoted largely to adjudicating land and property disputes in the Crown's Lancastrian domains. In June 1594 he assisted the investigation into the 'Walpole Plot'. In August–September 1594 he was examining prisoners in yet another Catholic conspiracy.

[28]   He is known to have argued only four Elizabethan lawsuits in total, all before the royal judges in the King's Bench or the Exchequer Chamber. All were for fundamental issues of law: namely, (1) those concerning the inheritance and conveyance of land, and (2) those concerning contracts and the procedures for suits about them. He pleaded his first case in the King's Bench on 25 January 1594, and his second and third cases followed in February 1595. In April 1594 Francis Bacon took Coke's place in the King's Bench during 'Chudleigh's Case'.

[29] The house had been found for Anthony Bacon by his friend and colleague in the intelligence world, Nicholas Faunt.

[30] James Burbage died in 1594. His son Cuthbert continued as manager and his son Richard as the leading actor of the company. The Lord Chamberlain became their patron.

[31] Francis Bacon, *Promus of Formularies and Elegancies*, Folio 109, Entry 1165 (*c.*1594–1595), ed. and publ. by Mrs Henry Pott (1883).

[32] Spedding, VIII, 321.

[33] The *Promus* entry for 'merrie tales' is not dated but falls into the time period *c.*1594–5. We know that Francis spent some time at Twickenham Lodge in October 1594 (Spedding VIII, 321) even though the Michaelmas law term was in progress (*c.* 9 October–28 November 1594) and that he was back at Gray's Inn by 25 October, where he had a cause to argue (Spedding VIII, 321). The elaborate Gray's Inn Revels, *The Prince of Purpoole and the Order of the Knights of the Helmet,* incorporating the Shakespeare play *Comedy of Errors*, took place that Christmas/New Year (1594/5), in the writing of which Bacon played a major part. He returned to Twickenham Lodge in the new year, spending the Hilary term (*c.* 23 January–12 February 1595) there, from where he wrote the letter dated 25 January 1595 to his brother Anthony.

[34] A statue of Francis Bacon was erected in 1908 by the Benchers of Grays Inn on the Tercenteniary Celebration of his appointment as Treasurer of Gray's Inn. The statue was destroyed in the Second World War, along with the Library and roof of the Hall. The statue was replaced after the war.

[35] This summerhouse was seen by Dodsley (*London and its Environs*) a hundred and fifty years later.

[36] Alice Chambers Bunten, *Francis Bacon and Twickenham Park*, 28; quoted in Alfred Dodd, *Francis Bacon's Personal Life Story* (1949, 1986), vii, 177.

[37] See Alfred Dodd, *Francis Bacon's Personal Life Story* (1949, 1986), vii, 177.

[38] According to Godfrey Goodman, Bishop of Gloucester.

[39] Proclaimed on a plaque above Francis Bacon's head on the title page to the 1640 edition of Bacon's *Advancement and Proficience of Learning*.

[40] Francis Bacon, 'Of Gardens,' *Essays*. See also Norah King, *The Grimstons of Gorhambury* (Phillimore, 1983), 24–29.

[41] E.K. Chambers, *The Elizabethan Stage*, iii, 348.

[42] Spedding, when he published them in his pamphlet in 1580, thought that they were for some festive occasion in 1592 and invented a title for it, *A Conference of Pleasure,* by which this collection of speeches is still generally but erroneously known today. E.K. Chambers, in his *Elizabethan Stage* (III, 212–3), shows that the speeches were almost certainly delivered on 17 November 1595. *The Conference of Pleasure* may, indeed, have been the name of another device that was presented before the Queen in 1592, to which the four 'Of Tribute' speeches, which are also part of the Northumberland Manuscript collection, belong.

[43] Northumberland MS. Folio 10.

[44] Roy Strong, *The Cult of Elizabeth* (Thames & Hudson, 1977), v, 156.

[45] Francis Bacon is referred to as a Treasurer in a record dated 28 January 1594 in the Inn's Pension

Book, and he held that post until 26 November 1594.

[46] N.B. Cockburn, *The Bacon Shakespeare Question,* viii, 113 (privately publ., 1998).

[47] N.B. Cockburn, *The Bacon Shakespeare Question,* viii, 114 (privately publ., 1998).

[48] The words, God and Good, are interchangeable: hence 'goodbye' is derived from 'God be with you'. This derivation is shown gradually developing in the Shakespeare plays, as well as in others:

> I thank your worship. God be Wy you! (Shakespeare, *Love's Labour's Lost,* III, i.)
>
> God b'uy my lord! (Shakespeare, *1 Henry VI,* II, ii.)
>
> Gallants, God buoye all! (Heywood, *2 Edward IV.*)
>
> Farewell, God b'y you Mistress! (Middleton & Dekker, *Roaring Girl.*)

[49] Shakespeare, *Love's Labour's Lost,* IV, iii, 251.

[50] Henri of Navarre became Henri IV, King of France, on 1 August 1589.

[51] We only know of Navarre's Academy because of its being mentioned in an undated letter from Agrippa D'Aubignèe who was a member of Navarre's Palace Academy. D'Aubignèe writes that it was set up in imitation of the one at the French Court and included seven notable gentlemen of Navarre, plus himself and of course the King. A letter in 1583 from Lord Cobham, the English Ambassador, to Sir Francis Walsingham, Queen Elizabeth's Secretary of State, records that the King of Navarre 'has furnished his Court with principal gentlemen of the Religion and reformed his house'. (See Frances Yates, *The French Academies of the 16th Century.*)

[52] In the British Museum of London. Add MSS. 4125, fol. 4; 4126, fols. 3, 4.

[53] The following is a translation of the passport:

> The Seigneur de TERRIDE commanding in these parts for the service of the King under the authority of the King of Navarre.
>
> To all Gentlemen, Governors of towers and places, Captains, Lieutenants, soldiers and other men-at-arms, making profession of the reformed religion and taking the part thereof. We pray all those who to this end must be prayed, and requested, and order and command all those over whom our authority extends to allow *Mr. Peter Brown,* ordinary messenger of the Queen of England now coming from Caors to the town hereafter mentioned to find *Mr. Baccon,* an English gentleman, to pass freely and securely for this voyage only, without delay, obstacle or impediment to the said Brown, and without doing or suffering to be done to him any displeasure or discourtesy whatsoever, but rather all help, favour, support and assistance should it be needed, and requested.
>
> At Montanban the 26th day of July, 1586.
>
> *By order of my said Lord,*
>
> DEGOSSE.
>
> G. LOMAGNE.

[54] The following is a translation of the passport:

> We, ANTOINE D'EBRARD DE SAINCT SUPLICE, Duke, Baron and Count of Caors, Councillor of the King in his Council of State and Privy Council, to all Captains and men-at-arms both cavalry and infantry, Governors of towns, Consuls and Jurats thereof, Wardens of ports, bridges and passes,
>   And to all others whom it may concern, Greeting—Make known that *Master Peter Brown, an Englishman,*

is about to set out for Montaubon upon the affairs of Monsieur Baccon, an English Gentleman at present in the aforesaid town of Montaubon.

Therefore we pray you to suffer him to come and go freely and securely, doing him no wrong nor offering him any impediment, but rather showing him favour and aid should need arise, and he require it of you, offering to do the same in like case.

Given at Caors this eighth day of the month of August one thousand five hundred and eighty-six.

ANTOINE E. DE CAORS,

by command of my said Lord,

D.BOYRESSE.

Endorsed: Passport of Monsieur de Caors for Peter Brown.

8 *August,* 1586.

55 The following is a translation of the passport:

MONSIEUR DE BIRON, Marshal of France, and Lieutenant General for the King in his army of Poitou, Xainctonge, Angoulmois and Aunys.

To all Governors, Captains, Chiefs and Leaders of men-at-arms both cavalry and infantry, Mayors, Sheriffs, Consuls, Jurats of Towns and Keepers of the Gates thereof, Provosts, Judges, and their deputies, Warders of ports, bridges, tolls, passes, jurisdictions and districts, and to all those whom it may concern. We pray those who are to be prayed, order and command those over whom our authority and power extend, to let pass freely and securely through your districts and jurisdictions, Le Sr.de Baccon, who is going to England, with his men, servants, arms and horses, without causing or suffering any to cause him any trouble, obstacle or hindrance, but rather showing him favour, and help if need should be. Given at the Camp at Sanjon the 27th September 1586.

Biron

by my Lord Marshal,

PRADEL.

Endorsed: Pass from the King of France for Mr. Anto. Bacon.

56 King James, unfortunately, rather destroyed the effect of the masque, for as it began he declared that he was far too tired from two days' non-stop celebrations to see the entertainment, and so went to bed. He appointed that the masque should be shown later in the week, but the surprise effect of the costumes and devices and approach by water had by then been lost.

57 Spedding, XI, 343–4.

58 *The Court and Times of James I,* i, 227. Spedding, XI, 343–4.

From 1598 to 1623 John Chamberlain wrote a long series of letters to Dudley Carletoti, which were full of the news of the month: news of the Court, the city, the pulpit, and the bookseller's shop. In these letters each Court masque is described in detail, including the author, actors, plot, performance and how the masque was received.

59 The full text of the dedication, with its original spelling, is as follows:

TO THE VERY HONOURABLE KNIGHT
SIR FRANCIS BACON,

HIS MAJESTIES ATTORNEY GENERAL.

Honourable Sir

This last Maske, presented by Gentlemen of Graies Inne, before his Majestie in honour of the marriage, and happy alliance between two such principall persons of the Kingdome, as are the Earl of Suffoke, and the Earle of Somerset, hath received such grace from his Majestie, the Queen, and Prince, and such approbation from the generall, As may well deserve to be repeated to those that were present and represented to those that were absent, by committing the same to the Presse, as others have been. The dedication of it could not be doubtful, you having been the Principal, and in effect the only person that did both encourage and warrant the Gentlemen, to show their good affection towards so noble a Conjunction, in a time of such Magnificence. Wherein we conceive without giving you false attributes which little neede when so many are true. That you have graced in general the Societies of the Innes of Court, in continuing them still as third persons with the nobility and Court, in doing the King honor, And particularly Graies Inne, which as you have formerly brought to flourish both in the auncienter and younger sort, by countinencing Vertue in every qualitie; So now you have made a notable demonstration thereof in the later and lesse serious kind by this. That one Inne of Court by itselfe, in time of a Vacation, and in the space of three weekes, could performe that which has been performed, which could not have been done, but that every man's exceeding love and respect to you, gave him wings to overtake *Time* which is the Swiftest of Things. This which we alledge for your Honour, we may alledge indifferently for our excuse, if any thing were amiss or wanting, for your time did scarce afford moments, and our experience went not beyond the compasse of some former employment of that nature, which our grave studies mought have made us by this time to have forgotten.

And so wishing you all encrease of honour we rest humbly to do your service.
I G.   W D.   T B.

Notes to Chapter 10

[1]   Nicholas Rowe, 'Some Accounts of the Life, &c. of Mr. William Shakespear', *Shakespeare, Works,* ed. Rowe (1709):

> There is one Instance so singular im Magnificence of this Patron of Shakespear's, that if I had not been assur'd that the Story was handed down by Sir *William D'Avenant*, who was probably well acquainted with his Affairs, I should not have ventur'd to have inserted, that my Lord *Southampton*, at one time, gave him a thousand Pounds, to enable him to go through with a Purchase which he heard he had a mind to.

[2]   The equivalent amount nowadays is hard to calculate, since the relative values of various commodities and skills has changed considerably since four hundred years ago, as well there having been successive devaluations and alterations of the coinage. Calculations of the multiple necessary to discover an equivalent rate at today's values vary from 100 times to 750 times, depending on, for instance, whether one is dealing with the price of a loaf of bread, the value of land or the salary of a grammar school headmaster. Land and property were relatively cheap by today's standards, but food and drink is now approximately 500 times what it was in the 1590s.

> For instance, in Queen Elizabeth I's reign, the master of Stratford-upon-Avon grammar school received a salary of £20 per annum; the first edition of Shakespeare's *Sonnets* and *A Lover's Complaint*, published as one hard bound volume, was sold at 5d (*i.e.,* £0.02) per copy; the quarto edition of a play sold for 6d (*i.e.,* £0.025); the wage of a printer's compositor was 1s (*i.e.,* £0.05) per day; manuscripts of plays

were sold to publishers for between £2 to £10 each play; entrance to the theatre was 1d (standing only) up to 6d for a seat in the gallery; a pint of beer was less than a penny (240 to the pound). In King James I's reign the First Shakespeare Folio sold for £1 a copy.

3   Lady Hatton married the Attorney-General, Sir Edward Coke, on 2 Nov. 1598, secretly by night at Hatton House, the only witnesses being her father and the minister who performed the service. Lady Hatton had insisted on the secret marriage (later legalised and made public), and on keeping her first married name, Lady Hatton. The marriage was not a success.

4   Shakespeare, *Merchant of Venice*, III, ii, 57.

5   *Initiation* means 'entering into' the mystery of life (with its various levels of existence, physical and metaphysical) with conscious awareness, understanding and ability to act therein.

6   Francis Bacon, *Advancement of Learning* (1605), Bk.II:

> The knowledge which respecteth the faculties of the mind of man is of two kinds; the one respecting his Understanding and Reason, and the other his Will, Appetite, and Affection; whereof the former produceth Position or Decree, the latter Action or Execution. It is true that the Imagination is an agent or nuncius in both provinces, both the judicial and the ministerial. For Sense sendeth over to Imagination before Reason hath judged: and Reason sendeth over to Imagination before the decree can be acted: for Imagination preceedeth Voluntary Motion. Saving that this Janus of Imagination hath differing faces: for the face towards Reason hath the print of Truth, but the face towards Action hath the print of Good; which nevertheless are faces....

7   Shakespeare, *Henry V,* Act V, Chorus 30–2.

8   Recorded by Lambarde and first printed by Nichols, iii, 552–553.

9   Shakespeare, *Richard II*, IV, i, 154–318.

10   Not until the play's republication as the fourth quarto in 1608 was the deposition scene replaced in the play, long after Queen Elizabeth had died and King James of Scotland was safely on the English throne.

11   '*Julius Caesar*', The Arden Shakespeare, edited by David Daniell: 'Introduction', p. 11.

12   e.g.,, Thomas Kyd's poem, *Cornelia or Pompey the Great His Fair Cornelia's Tragedy,* published in 1594 and 1595, the two anonymous plays, *1* and *2 Caesar and Pompey*, acted by the Lord Admiral's Men in 1594–5, and *The Tragedy of Caesar and Pompey, or Caesar's Revenge*.

13   Spedding IX, 89–105.

14   The army was 16,000 foot and 1500 horse strong.

15   Shakespeare, *Julius Caesar*, IV, iii.

16   *i.e.,* 'too sensible of hurt'; 'the apprehension and construction of the injury offered to be, in the circumstances thereof, full of contempt'; and 'opinion of the touch of a man's reputation'.

17   Both essays, 'Of Anger' and 'Of Envy', were first published in the 1625 edition of Bacon's *Essays*.

> All the Shakespeare plays are studies in various kinds of emotion, and for these Bacon's *Essays* are an enlightening guide. Bacon developed his *Essays* over the years as a distinctive style of writing, pithy and difficult to write successfully, but which he refined to a high art. Of particular interest in these is the material which he uses and the principles which he defines; for the same material and principles, derived from careful observation, are embodied in the Shakespeare plays.

18   Spedding, X: *Letters and Life of Francis Bacon, III,* iv, 149–50: Francis Bacon, *Apologie in certaine imputa-*

tions concerning the late Earle of Essex (1604).

[19] Cornelius Tacitus, *Annals*, iii, 65.

[20] Also to be found as Apophthegm 22 in *Resuscitatio.*

[21] Hayward remained in prison in the Tower of London until after Elizabeth's death, but was released when King James I came to the throne. He was knighted by James in 1619 and lived until 1627. He was a close friend of William Camden, the Clarenceux King-of-Arms, and Tobie Matthews, two of Francis Bacon's most intimate friends. Hayward wrote the histories of the first three Norman kings, William I, William II and Henry I, the Tudor king, Edward VI, and the early part of Elizabeth I's reign, thus completing the historical series put out under the names of Marlowe, Bacon and Shakespeare.

[22] Spedding, *Letters and Life of Francis Bacon*

[23] As has been well argued by Harold Jenkins in the Arden *Hamlet* (1982), references to Essex's insurrection and the quarrel between Ben Jonson and others ('War of the Theatres') were added in spring/summer 1601.

[24] Order dated 10 March 1600. Lady Leicester, Lord and Lady Southampton, and Fulke Greville, who were also residing in Essex House at that time, were likewise ordered to move.

[25] Spedding, X, i, 7.

[26] This was discovered by Daphne du Maurier, who records it in her book, Golden Lads (Victor Gollancz, 1975), xxv, 259. The church register records:

> May 17th, 1601, Mr Anthonye Bacon buried in the chamber within the vault.

[27] Lambeth Library, Vol. VII, 159.

[28] Spedding, X, ii, 62–3.

[29] A year later Alice's younger sister, Dorothy, married Sir John Constable of Gray's Inn, to whom Francis dedicated the 1612 edition of his *Essays*, addressing him as 'my loving brother, Sir John Constable, knight,' and referring to the 'friendship and society' and 'communication of studies' between them. Bacon ends the dedication by remarking: 'For as my business found rest in my contemplations, so my contemplations ever found rest in your loving conference and judgment.'

[30] Letter from Dudley Carleton to John Chamberlain, 11 May 1606.

[31] This was a bold statement. Since Francis Bacon was not arrested as a result of wearing colours reserved for royalty, the incident may well point to yet another secret concerning Francis Bacon: *i.e.,* that he was really the son of Queen Elizabeth, for which there is some considerable circumstantial evidence and deliberately-made cryptic pointers and allusions. See the author's *Dedication to the Light* (FBRT, 1984).

[32] Stowe's *Annals.*

[33] Part II, Book x.

[34] The Active Science is the sixth and last part of Bacon's *Great Instauration* (*i.e.,* the restoration of the state of paradise, but with knowledge or illumination rather than the initial innocence or naivety).

[35] Trajano Boccali, *Ragguagli di Parnasso,* Vol. 1 (Venice, 1612).

[36] See Peter Dawkins, *The Wisdom of Shakespeare in The Tempest* (IC Media Prod., 2000), xii, 192–200.

[37] The original manuscript of Queen Catharine's divorce speech was recently discovered in the British Library by Maria Perry while researching material for her new book, *Sisters to the King* (London, Andre Deutsch , 2002).

[38] Holinshed, p. 909, mentions only Norfolk and Suffolk as present at this interview. Thomas Howard, the Duke of Norfolk, was also Earl of Surrey: they were not two distinct people, as Shakespeare makes them.

39   Spedding, XIV, vi, 262.

Notes to Chapter 11

[1]   Letter to Anthony Bacon from Francis Bacon, 'from my lodging at Twickenham Park this 25th January, 1594 [1595]'. Spedding, VIII, 321.

[2]   Francis Bacon, *Promus of Formularies and Elegancies*, Folio 109, Entry 1165 (*c.*1594–1595), ed. and publ. by Mrs Henry Pott (1883).

[3]   At times the poetic functions and the intelligence functions were combined in the same persons in the group, such as with Marlowe, who was a poet–dramatist and a spy. Others who were poets earned extra money by copying, translating, deciphering and enciphering intelligence documents, such as those 'idle pens' who were with Francis Bacon at Twickenham, hoping to earn some money that term. Yet it was at Twickenham that Francis Bacon used to write plays and entertainments with his team. It has not been possible to sort them all out, as to who did what, when or where. Poets and playwrights earned virtually nothing by means of their poetry and plays, but by working for the Bacon brothers as part of a team they could be paid for translation and intelligence work. It was, in other words, a type of patronage. I suspect Walsingham helped when he was alive and Secretary of State, as he was a known patron of poets, but in exchange for intelligence work. Dee was one of his spies and beneficiaries, as also Marlowe. So also were Anthony and Francis Bacon, who worked for Walsingham when the latter was Secretary of State and head of the intelligence network that he had set up with his brother.

[4]   *Life of Hobbes*, Aubrey's *Brief Lives* (1692), Vol. ii. Pt. 2. p. 602.

[5]   The only known copy of this book was discovered in 1871.

[6]   Peter Böener, 'Life of Bacon', *De Proef-Stucken van den Franciscus Bacon* (Leyden, 1646).

[7]   Thomas Bushell, *Abridgement of the Lord Chancellor Bacon's Philosophical Theory in Mineral Prosecutions* (1659). See also A. de la Pryme, *Memoirs of Thomas Bushell*, ed. W. Harrison (1878).

[8]   *Baconiana, or, Certain genuine remains of Sr. Francis Bacon, Baron of Verulam, and Viscount of St. Albans in arguments civil and moral, natural, medical, theological, and bibliographica.l...* (London: J. D. for Richard Chiswell, 1679), pp.24–26 & p. 60:

> And, knowing that this Work [the enlarged and final Advancement of Learning] was desired beyond the Seas, and being also aware, that Books written in a modern Language, which receiveth much

change in a few Years, were out of use; he caus'd that part of it which he had written in English, to be translated into the Latine Tongue, by Mr Herbert, and some others, who were esteemed Masters in the Roman Eloquence… The Translation of this Work (that is, of much of the Two Books written by him in English) he first commended to Dr. Playfer, a Professour of Divinity in the University of Cambridge…[but] he sent a Specimen of such superfine Latinity, that the Lord Bacon did not encourage him to labour further in that Work, in the penning of which he desired not so much neat and polite, as clear and Masculine, and apt Expression.

His Lordship wrote them [his Essays] in the English Tongue, and enlarged them as Occasion serv'd, and at last added to them the Colours of Good and Evil, which are likewise found in his Book De Augmentis. The Latine Translation of them was a Work performed by divers hands; by those of Dr Hacket (late Bishop of Lichfield), Mr. Benjamin Johnson (the learned and judicious Poet) and some others whose Names I once heard from Dr. Rawley; but I cannot now recal them

9   Francis Bacon, *Advancement of Learning* (1623), 'Plan of the Work' (Part IV):

And now that we have surrounded the intellect with faithful helps and guards, and got together with most careful selection a regular army of divine works, it may seem that we have no more to do but to proceed to philosophy itself. And yet in a matter so difficult and doubtful there are still some things which it seems necessary to premise, partly for convenience of explanation, partly for present use.

Of these the first is to set forth examples of inquiry and invention according to my method, exhibited by anticipation in some particular subjects; choosing such subjects as are at once the most noble in themselves among those under enquiry, and most different one from another; that there may be an example in every kind. I do not speak of those examples which are joined to the several precepts and rules by way of illustration (for of these I have given plenty in the second part of the work); but I mean actual types and models, by which the entire process of the mind and the whole fabric and order of invention from the beginning to the end, in certain subjects, and those various and remarkable, should be set as it were before the eyes. For I remember that in the mathematics it is easy to follow the demonstration when you have a machine beside you; whereas without that help all appears involved and more subtle than it really is. To examples of this kind—being in fact nothing more than an application of the second part in detail and at large,—the fourth part of the work is devoted.

10   See the author's book, *Building Paradise*, for a fuller explanation of this.

11   See *Collotype Facsimile and Type Transcript of an Elizabethan Manuscript preserved at Alnwick Castle, Northumberland,* transcribed and edited with notes by Frank J. Burgoyne (Longmans, Green and Co, 1904).

12   See *The Northumberland Manuscript,* by T. le Marchant Douse (London, 1904).

13   Shakespeare, *Lucrece*, line 1,086.

14   Tennison MSS, Lambeth Palace Library, vol. 15, folio 110. The Latin words could be translated: 'sweetness in talk and words of milk, but bitter in heart and deceitful in deed'.

15   Francis Bacon, *Essayes. Religious Meditations, Places of persuasion and disswasion* (1597 old style; 1598 new style).

16   The 'Acte for the punishment of Vacabondes', 1572.

17   Whereas the circular yard of the Globe Theatre has been determined to have been delineated by a 70 ft diameter circle, around which the galleries were placed, the square yard of the Fortune Theatre was set out as a 55 ft x 55 ft square. A square of 55 ft x 55 ft will 'square' a circle of 70 ft diameter.

Notes to Chapter 12

[1] Paracelsus Theophrastus von Hohenheim (1493–1541).

[2] *i.e.*, 58 years after Paracelsus' death, which is given as either 1541 or 1544.

[3] Robert Fludd, *Tractatis Apoligetica* (1617).

[4] The *Fama Fraternitatis* (1614) and *Confessio Fraternitatis* (1615).

[5] Thomas Tenison, 'A Discourse by Way of Introduction,' *Baconiana or Certain Genuine Remains of Sir Francis Bacon* (1679), p. 5.

[6] Interview with Lady Russell, in September 1596.

[7] The *Tetraktys*, sometimes referred to as the Pythagorean Triangle, is a triangular arrangement of ten dots or *yods* (Hebrew, *yod*, representing the source or monad) set in four rows, with four *yods* on the bottom row, three on the second, two on the third and one at the top. The top three *yods* represent the Holy Trinity, while the remaining seven signify the seven spirits or rays of light that proceed from the Holy Trinity. The Hebrew *Tetragrammaton* or Holy Name of God (YHVH) is also sometimes shown in this triangular form.

[8] Spedding, VIII, 123.

[9] *Steganographia* is from the Greek, meaning 'Covered Writing'.

[10] Duke Augustus became Duke of Brunswick-Wolfenbuttel in 1634.

[11] Selenus, also spelt Silenus, was reputed to have immense knowledge, knowing both the past and future, and capable of revealing the destiny of anyone who could successfully tie him up during the heavy slumber that followed his heavy bouts of drinking.

[12] *Cryptomenitices* is dedicated to 'Dr. Francisco, Antonio, London, Anglo, Seniori,' a goldsmith's son who became an alchemist and Paracelsist physician, set up business in London in 1600, and published *Apologie of Aurum Potabile* in 1616.

[13] See Frances A. Yates, *The Rosicrucian Enlightenment* (London: Routledge, Kegan & Paul, 1972), xi, 190–196.

[14] In 1910 an illustrated paper was written by C. P. Bowditch describing how J. W. H. Walden, the American who made an English translation of *Cryptomenitices,* visited the Duke's library at Wolfenbattel and there found the Duke's library and original letters to his literary agent concerning cipher book.

[15] See T. D. Bokenham, '*Cryptomenitices* and the Shakespeare Folio of 1623', *Baconiana* Vol. LIII, No. 170.

[16] The 22-letter Latin alphabet is ABCDEFGHIKLMNOPQRSTVXZ. The transposition or 'wheel' cipher, with each letter transposed five letters to the right, can be written thus:

A	B	C	D	E	F	G	H	I	K	L	M	N	O	P	Q	R	S	T	V	XZ
S	T	V	X	Z	A	B	C	D	E	F	G	H	I	K	L	M	N	O	P	QR

The cipher is read on the bottom line (*i.e.,* 'THIUS'), with the top line giving the transposed letters that render the anagram of the enciphered word or message (*i.e.,* 'BNOCA', the anagram of 'BACON').

[17] This is undoubtedly a reference to the uniting of the two kingdoms of Scotland and England, made possible because King James was sovereign of both. When eventually united, they were called 'Great Britain'.

[18] Christophe Plantin's edition of Alciat's *Emblemata* was published in 1577, just a few months after Francis Bacon had left England for France (in September 1576), leaving behind his brother Anthony.

[19] *Andreae Alciati Emblematum Libellus, Nuper in Lucen Editus* ('Andrea Alciato's Little Book of Emblems, Recently Brought Forth to Light' – 1546), published in Venice by the sons of Aldus Manutius. The first edition, with 104 emblems and a text unauthorised by Alciato, was published in 1531 in Augsberg by Heinrich Steiner. The first fully authorised edition was that of 1534, published in Paris by Christian Wechel in 1534, with the 104 emblems expanded to 113. The 1546 Aldine edition was a new collection of 86 previously unpublished emblems, gathered by Petrus Rhosithinus. Other editions followed containing the emblems of all two books, gradually adding more. The 1550 edition, published in Lyons by Guillaume Rouillé and printed by Mathias Bonhomme, was the first to contain the final complete number of 212 emblems (but omitting Emblem 80).

See The Memorial Web Edition of Alciat's *Book of Emblems* on website http://www.mun.ca/alciato and its links to other research sites.

See also W. Lansdown Goldsworthy, *Shake-speare's Heraldic Emblems; their origin and meaning* (London: H. F. & G. Witheby, 1928), chh.1 & 2.

[20] *Emblemes D'Alciat* (Lyon, 1549), published by Ronville/Mace Bonhomme with Barthélemy Aneau's verse-by-verse French translation. This edition contains 201 emblems, 165 of which have an emblem picture (woodcut).

[21] Matthew 21 : 42. Psalm 118 : 22–23. Ephesians 2 : 20–21.

[22] Job 36 : 6; Psalm 144 : 12; Isaiah 28 : 16; 1 Peter 2 : 6.

[23] Hyacinth, the fifteen-year old son of Amilchar, was accidentally slain by a quoit thrown by Apollo during the Spartan games. The quoit hit the ground and bounced up at Hyacinth, who was over-eager to retrieve it, and sliced off the top of his head. Weeping, Apollo changed the slain youth into a flower, his spilt blood determining its colour. Apollo then marked the flower and its leaves with his mourning sighs, 'Ai, Ai', written as the Greek letter *upsilon* (υ), equivalent to the letter u or v, which is like a reversed 'A'. In its capital form (Y) the Greek letter is like the capital letter Y and the glyph for the zodiac sign of Aries. It was used as the symbol of the master. Similarly, in the Druidic alphabet, Y was the symbol for the perfect or holy man.

Ovid, *Metamorphoses*, X, 196:

'Thee my lyre, thee my songs, shall ever celebrate; and, changed to a new flower, thou shalt bear an inscription of my sighs. The time too shall come when a very powerful hero shall be changed into this flower, and his name read upon thy leaves.'

While these things are uttered by Apollo's prophetic mouth, lo, the blood, which faling upon the ground has stained the grass, ceases to be blood, and a flower more bright than Tyrian purple springs up, assuming the same form as the lily, but that in the former is a purple colour, in the latter that of silver. But this is not enough for Phoebus, for he was the author of the honour now bestowed: he marks his own sighs upon the leaves, and the flower has Ai, Ai, drawn upon it in funeral characters.

[24] Theodore de Bry, *Icones Virorum Illustrium* (Frankfurt, 1598), Pt.II, p.134.

[25] This motto was painted on the wall over the dining table in the hall of Sir Nicholas Bacon's

house at Gorhambury, together with a mural of Ceres teaching the sowing of the golden seeds of corn. It was a key reference to the Orphic Mysteries, to which Gorhambury was dedicated (see the author's book, *Dedication to the Light*). It is recorded that the young Francis Bacon used to continually ponder on the meaning of this picture and its motto, and kept inquiring about it.

[26] Virgil, *Aeneid*, iii, 188.

[27] The motto is based on *Daniel* 12, and was used in reference to both Gray's Inn and Lincoln's Inn—the lawyers' Inns of Court in London.

[28] Peter Dawkins, *Building Paradise* (FBRT, 2001), ch. 7, pp. 157–165.

[29] See William T. Smedley, *The Mystery of Francis Bacon* (San Francisco: John Howell, 1910).

[30] Research made by Y. Ledsem revealed that in 1591 John Wolfe re-published Baptista Porta's *De Furtivis Literarum Notis,* first published by Ioa Maria Scotus in Naples in 1563, but according to Spedding not *en vente* until 1568. This reprint was dedicated to Henry Percy, Earl of Northumberland. After the edition had been printed off, the title page was altered to correspond with the 1563 publication, the dedication was taken out and a copy of the original dedication was substituted, but with the difference that over this dedication was placed the AA headpiece that was not in the original 1563 edition of the book. This new 1591 edition was then printed and sold as if it were the original 1563 edition of Porta's great work on ciphers. (See 'A False Dated Book,' *Baconiana*, Vol.VIII, Third Series, Oct. 1910, No. 32.)

 See also William T. Smedley, *The Mystery of Francis Bacon* (San Francisco: John Howell, 1910).

[31] *The Arte of English Poesie* was first published anonymously. Later it was ascribed to 'George Puttenham'.

Notes to Chapter 13

[1] There is at least one example of the cipher being decoded before the translation was published—a copy of the second edition (1628), on the flyleaf of which the original owner had scribbled the decipherment and a description of the exact method used to encipher the message. See Ewen McDuff, 'The Unspeakable Word', *Baconiana*, No. 171.

[2] Other moderately simple cipher systems used by Bacon and the Rosicrucians in the Shakespeare works are the Squared and Caesar (letter substitution) ciphers, the latter being the 'Wheel' ciphers referred to by Bacon.

 An example of squared cipher text is shown on page 140 of *Cryptomenitices* wherein the squared text picks out certain letters, in this instance spaced seven letters apart, which make up an enciphered message. This message reads 'Magnentius Hrabanus Maurus hoc opus fecit', meaning 'Magnentius Maurus Hrabanus made this work'. Hrabanus was an Abbot of Mainz who lived about 850 AD and whose biography was written by the Abbot Trithemius. Hrabanus' cipher work is demonstrated in *Cryptomenitices*. Ewen McDuff and Thomas Bokenham have both done cryptanalytic work on squared ciphers within the Shakespeare text and on the Shakespeare monuments. See Ewen McDuff, *The 67th Inquisition* and *The Dancing Horse Will Tell You* (Private printing, 1973, 1974), and T. D. Bokenham, *A Brief History of the Bacon-Shakespeare Controversy* (FBRT, 1982).

 An example of a Caesar or Wheel cipher used by Bacon is described in Penn Leary's books, *The Cryptographic*

Shakespeare (Omaha: Westchester House, 1987) and *The Second Cryptographic Shakespeare* (Omaha: Westchester House, 1999: http://home.att.net/~tleary/).

Further discussions of ciphers can be found on Mather Walker's web page, http://www.sirbacon.org/Matherpage.htm, provided on Lawrence Gerald's 'Sir Francis Bacon's New Advancement of Learning' web site: http://www.sirbacon.org/; as also on the Francis Bacon Research Trust's web site: http://www.fbrt.org.uk/.

3   See Ewen McDuff, *The 67th Inquisition* (Private printing, 1973).

4   Spedding, IV, 444.

5   A report of Clifton's discovery can be found in Frank Woodward, *Francis Bacon's Cipher Signatures* (London: Grafton & Co, 1923), ii, 7–11.

6   The Thirty-Third Degree is associated with the fact that there are thirty-three bones in the spine, up which the kundalini energy has to be raised, like a fountain of fire, to achieve illumination. The highest bone, the thirty-third, is the Atlas, named after Atlas, King of Atlantis, who was also known either as the Phoenix or as Enoch, the great Initiate. Rabbinic literature claims that he was the first human soul to reach the highest heaven both in consciousness and body, to become the Messiah, and that not only do all the wisdom teachings stem from him but that he reappears periodically as the great Teacher to help raise all souls ultimately to the same level of illumination.

7   The Fibonacci Scale or Golden Mean (Proportion) can be rendered as $1:2:3:5:8:13:21:34:55$ etc.

8   St Alban, or Albanus, was martyred 22 June 209 by Geta, eldest son of the Emperor Severus, when they were in Britain.

9   *Freemason's Guide and Compendium.*

10   Carausius is referred to as a usurper of the throne of Britain. In fact Britain, supposedly under the rule of the Roman Emperor Diocletian at the end of the 3rd century, for a short while declared its independance and its own Emperor, Carausius.

11   *History of Masonry in England.* Records summarised by William Preston, quoted by Manley P. Hall in *The Adepts.*

12   See Frank Woodward, *Francis Bacon's Cipher Signatures* (London: Grafton & Co, 1923).

13   The use of 'To' as a Bacon signature, and its association with the letter 'B', is deliberately confirmed in the thirty-third essay ('Of Plantations') of the 1625 edition of Francis Bacon's *Essays*, where the thirty-third word is 'To'. There are twenty-eight To's in the essay, and 28 = B in Kay Cipher.

14   Michael Maier, *Themis Aurea* (1656).

15   Dr John Wilkins, *Mathematical Magic* (1680), pp. 236–7. The first edition was published in 1642.

16   Spedding, IV, 107.

17   *James* i, 17.

18   In Freemasonic tradition the pillars are said to be hollow, acting as archives to Masonry. In other words, the pillars have both an exoteric (outer) and an esoteric (inner) aspect. In older

---

Masonic tradition the pillars are referred to as the Pillars of Seth, or of Lamech, or of Enoch, or of Noah, or simply the Antediluvian Pillars. One was made of brick and the other of marble, to withstand destruction by fire and water. The Antediluvian Sciences were written in (or on) these Twin Pillars by the three sons of Lamech—Jabal, Jubal and Tubal Cain—so as to preserve the Seven Liberal Arts and Sciences. These Sciences were subsequently recovered by Pythagorus, who found one of the pillars, and Hermes who discovered the other. See Alex Horne, *King Solomon's Temple in the Masonic Tradition* (The Aquarian Press, 1972), xii, 232–238.

[19] 'To the memory of my beloved, the Author, Mr. William Shakespeare,' signed 'Ben: Ionson.'

[20] Matthew, v, 8.

[21] Francis Bacon's recorded birth was on 25 January 1560. In that era the official New Year was on 25 March, which arrangement is known as the Old Style. New Year on 1 January, which was instituted later, is known as New Style. In addition, the calendar used by the Elizabethans was the Julian, which was then ten days behind the Gregorian calendar that we use today. Therefore, to place Bacon's date of birth in a modern context, according to the New Style and Gregorian calendar, he was born on 1 February 1561.

[22] *Brit-Anna* means 'Chosen of Anna', referring to the daughter of Anna. Anna is the Great Goddess or Black Virgin, whose daughter is the White Goddess or Virgin Mary. Britain is still known in Roman Catholic tradition as the 'dowry (or land) of the Virgin Mary'.

[23] Announced in January 1994.

[24] James Anderson, in his *Constitutions of the Freemasons* (1738), made a note of the Grand Masters of Freemasonry in the Elizabethan and Jacobean period in England. From this Kenneth Mackensie made a list of Grand Masters, which he published in his *Royal Mason Cyclopaedia* (London, 1877):

> 1561- Sir Thomas Sackville, Lord Buckhurst.
> 1567 - Francis Russell, Earl of Bedford - Sir Thomas Gresham.
> 1579 - Charles Howard, Earl of Effingham.
> 1588 - George Hastings, 4th Earl of Huntingdon.
> 1603 - King James I.
> 1607 - Inigo Jones, the architect.
> 1618 - William Herbert, 3rd Earl of Pembroke.
> 1630 - Henry Danvers, Earl of Danby.

The first seven all had publications dedicated to them which carried the 'AA' device.

[25] A good account of a decipherment of this cryptogram can be read in Ewen McDuff's *The 67th Inquisition*, in which McDuff also describes the working of Bacon's *Abecedarium Naturæ* or Inquisition Cipher.

[26] Collins English Dictionary.

[27] In the 16th century Islington was still a small village on the top of a hill overlooking London and in the midst of fertile countryside. Canonbury Manor was surrounded by parkland and market gardens, and Londoners would come to Islington for the fresh air and market produce.

[28] *Cony*, or *coney*: from Old French, *conis*; Latin, *cuniculus*.

[29] See *As You Like It*, III, ii, 357; 3 *Henry VI*, I, iv, 62; *Merry Wives*, I, ii, 36; *Taming of the Shrew*, IV, i, 45.

[30] Some students know these Ten *Sephiroth* as represented by the cabalistic diagram known as

'The Tree of Life'.

[31] 1st Version. The pages which had been printed—the first three of *Troilus and Cressida* and the last of *Romeo and Juliet*—were set aside. The Folio was then completed without *Troilus* in it, with a newly printed *Romeo and Juliet* last page now backed onto the first page of *Timon of Athens*, and with the new *Romeo* page numbered 79 instead of 77—*i.e.*, skipping two numbers. Some of these books were then offered for sale, probably in November 1623, as a complete book whose contents matched the Catalogue.

2nd Version. When agreement was eventually obtained, *Troilus and Cressida* was printed from a manuscript on mostly unnumbered sheets and without any prologue, but including the numbered pages of *Troilus and Cressida* (pp 78–80) which had already been printed from the 1609 Quarto version before copyright was bought and the manuscript obtained. The whole of the play was then inserted before the first page of the existing Tragedies. The duplicated last page of *Romeo and Juliet* (p 77) which backed onto the first page of *Troilus* was simply crossed out.

3rd Version. After a few books had been offered for sale in this form as the second version, a prologue to *Troilus,* which was not included in the 1609 Quarto, was obtained and printed on a single leaf, backed by a reprint of the *Troilus* first page (without its number). The earlier leaf (pp 77–78) was cut out and the unnumbered new leaf was inserted in its place, and the Folio was then sold in its third and final version.

See especially Peter W. M. Blayney, *The First Folio of Shakespeare* (Folger Library Publ., 1991), for research on this, and the Introduction by Doug Moston to the Arden facsimile of the 1623 Shakespeare Folio (Applause Books, 1995) for a good summary.

[32] Frank Woodward, *Francis Bacon's Cipher Signatures* (London: Grafton & Co, 1923).

[33] Fr. Baconi de Verulamio — *Sermones fideles* (1644, 1659, 1662, 1685); Francisci Baconi — *De Sapientia Veterum Liber* (1609, 1617, 1633, 1634, 1657, 1680, etc.); and in German version (1654); Fr. Baconi de Verulamio — *Historia Naturalis & Experimentalis de Ventis, &c.* (1648); Franc. Baconi de Verulamio — *Historia Regni Henrici Septimi* (1642, 1647, 1662, 1695); Francisci Baconi — *Operum moralium* (1638); Francisci Baconi — *Scripta in Naturali et Universali Philosophia* (1653, 1685, 1699).

[34] See Arden, 'Latten: Its meaning and Intention', *Baconiana,* Vol. XXXVIII, No. 148 (May 1954).

[35] See note 53, p. 118, The Arden Shakespeare edition of *Love's Labour's Lost*, edited by Richard David (first publ. 1951).

[36] Philip Sidney, *An Apologie for Poetrie* (c.1579). See chapter 1, note 3.

[37] In further support of these cipher signatures, SEELY SHEEP + A HORNE adds in Simple Cipher to 171. This number is the count of FRANCIS in the Kay Cipher. In other words, the metaphoric lamb of God or human creator of the Shakespeare play is Francis Bacon.

[38] The Arden Shakespeare, *Love's Labour's Lost,* ed. by R. W. David (1951/1987), pp. 116–7.

[39] R. L. Eagle, 'The Mystery of Honorificabilitudinitatibus', *Baconiana,* Vol. XLIII, No. 160 (March 1960).

[40] Joan Ham, 'Honorificabilitudinitatibus', *Baconiana,* Vol. LXII, No. 179 (October 1979). See also Martin Pares, 'The Northumberland MS., the Promus, and the Long Word', *Baconiana,* Vol. XLIII, No. 160 (March 1960).

[41] The Fr Bacon' signature can be found in three other arrangements of the group of letters as

well, but the 'I.C.' arrangement seems to be the most significant.

[42]   There is also a further subtle association of *honorificabilitudinitatibus*, referring to the state of being loaded with honours, with the opening line of *Love's Labour's Lost*, 'Let Fame, that all hunt after in their lives,' and the title of the first Rosicrucian manifesto, *The Fame of the Fraternity of the Rosie Cross.* Such fame is equated with honour. *Love's Labour's Lost* was also the first Shakespeare play to carry the Shakespeare name (as 'W. Shakspere') on its title page.

[43]   Francis Meres, *Palladis Tamia* (1598).

[44]   See Michael Baigent and Richard Leigh, *The Temple and the Lodge* (London: Jonathan Cape, 1989).

Notes to Chapter 14

[1]   See chapter 12.

[2]   An alternative tradition states that besides the Temple of Apollo at Delphi the two brother designed and built the treasury of Hyrieus, King of Hyria in Boeotia. They included in the design a secret entrance to the treasury which, when the building was complete and stocked with the King's enormous treasures, the brothers used to enter the building at night and steal some of the treasures, little by little. When the King eventually noticed that his treasure was becoming depleted, he set traps for the thief. Agamedes was caught in one of the traps and Trophonius, unable to rescue his brother and in order to avert discovery, cut off his brother's head. Trophonius was immediately swallowed up by the earth in the grove of Lebadea. He was worshipped there as a hero and the cave became his celebrated oracle. A single pillar was erected outside the cave, where a ram was offered as a sacrifice to Agamedes by those who sought to consult the oracle.

[3]   Apostyle or marginal note made by James I to a 'letter of advice to King James touching the charge against the Somersets' written by Francis Bacon (28th April 1616).

   The motto of the Bacon family was *Mediocria Firma,* which has the same meaning as *media tutius itur.*

[4]   See Joyce Treskunov's PhD thesis at Temple University, *Anthony Bacon and his Work 1558–1601* (publ. 1980, available at the Francis Bacon Library, Claremont, California, USA).

[5]   MSS. 647–662 (Bacon Papers), Lambeth Palace Library.

[6]   Anthony Bacon's first recorded use of the phrase is in 1581, in a letter to his uncle, Lord Burghley.

[7]   Psalm 37 : 21.

[8]   The invisibility presumably refers to psychic invisibility, thereby giving the person some protection from psychic attack. As in the biblical account of the disciples being raised up in a cloud of glory during the transfiguration experience, or Jesus being taken up in clouds of glory at the ascension, the 'glory' or light renders the person invisible from those who are not also in that glory. From this probably comes the saying that masters walk the earth amongst us, yet we see them not.

[9]   Sonnet 20.

[10] Sonnets 53 and 54.

[11] Sonnet 20.

[12] Sonnets 37, 66 and 89 refer to 'lameness'

[13] See the author's book, *Dedication to the Light* (FBRT, 1984).

[14] See the author's book, *Building Paradise* (FBRT, 2001).

[15] *i.e.,* not the chemical compound of that name. The quintessential ether is a name for the primordial, universal substance or matter, which is also symbolised as the 'waters' upon which the Spirit of God moved or hovered in the act of creation. It is the quintessence of the alchemical elements, being both the dark source of the earth, water, air and fire elements, and their ultimate resolution as light. Chaotic ether is dark: perfectly ordered ether is light. The word 'ether' is probably derived from *avir*, the Hebraic name for this primordial matter.

[16] Francis Bacon, 'Proteus, or Matter', *Wisdom of the Ancients.*

[17] Francis Bacon, *Thoughts on the Nature of Things*, iii:

> We should investigate those appetites and inclinations of things by which all that variety of effects and changes which we see in the works of nature and art is made up and brought about. And we should try to enchain Nature, like Proteus; for the right discovery and distinction of the kinds of motions are the true bonds of Proteus. For according as motions, that is, incentives and restraints, can be spurred on or tied up, so follows conversion and transformation of matter itself.

[18] Francis Meres, *Palladis Tamia* (1598).

[19] Francis Bacon comments on Ariosto's poem as follows in his *Advancement and Proficience of Learning* (1640), II, Cap. vii:

> For herein the invention of one of the later poets, by which he has enriched the ancient fiction, is not inelegant. He feigns that at the end of the thread or web of every man's life there hangs a little medal or collar on which his name is stamped; and that Time waits upon the shears of Atropos, and as soon as the thread is cut, snatches the medals, carries them off, and presently throws them into the river Lethe.; and about the river there are many birds flying up and down, who catch the medals, and after carrying them round and round in their beak a little while, let them fall into the river; only there are a few swans, which if they get a medal with a name immediately cary it off to a temple consecrated to immortality. Now this kind of swan is for the most part wanting [rare] in our age.

[20] *In Ed. Allen.* Quoted from Walter Begley, *Bacon's Nova Resuscitatio*, II, p. 182.

[21] Edmund Spenser, *Prothalamion* (1591), lines 37–54. The full verse is as follows:

> With that, I saw two swans of goodly hue
> Come swimming down along the Lee;
> Two fairer birds I yet did never see.
> The snow, which doth the top of Pindus strew,
> Did never whiter shew,
> Nor Jove himself, when he a swan would be
> For love of Leda, whiter did appear:
> Yet Leda was they say as white as he,
> Yet not so white as these, nor nothing near.
> So purely white they were,

That even the gentle stream, the which them bare,

Seemed foul to them, and bade his billows spare

To wet their silken feathers, lest they might

Soil their fair plumes with water not so fair,

And mar their beauties bright,

That shone as heaven's light,

Against their bridal day, which was not long:

Sweet Thames, run softly, till I end my song.

22 Matthew 18 : 3.

23 The sculptures appear to be made from original portraits of the sovereigns: the one of Richard III from the official portrait of him in the Royal Collection (a version of which is in the National Portrait Gallery, NPG 148); the one of Henry V from the cover of the book *De Regemene Principum* ('Of the Regiment of Princes') by Thomas Hoccleve (*c1370–c1450*) in the British Library (the face is the same but the crown and clothes are different); the one of Elizabeth I (who is depicted as a more elderly, wise woman than in most official portraits), possibly from the panel portrait of her in a 'Petrarchan Triumph of Eternity' (*c1620*, artist unknown) in the Menthuen Collection, Corsham Court, or a Nicholas Hilliard woodcut, or the Phoenix Medal. Her death mask image on her tomb may have been an additional influence.

24 Francis Bacon's Prayer, Preface, *De Augmentis* (1623), transl. Spedding & Ellis (1860), IV, p.20:

Wherefore, seeing that these things do not depend upon myself, at the outset of the work I most humbly and fervently pray to God the Father, God the Son, and God the Holy Ghost, that remembering the sorrows of mankind and the pilgrimage of this our life wherein we wear out days few and evil, they will vouchsafe through my hands to endow the human family with new mercies. This likewise I humbly pray, that things human may not interfere with things divine, and that from the opening of the ways of sense and the increase of natural light there may arise in our minds no incredulity or darkness with regard to the divine mysteries; but rather that the understanding being thereby purified and purged of fancies and vanity, and yet not the less subject and entirely submissive to the divine oracles, may give to faith that which is faith's. Lastly, that knowledge being now discharged of that venom which the serpent infused into it, and which makes the mind of man to swell, we may not be wise above measure and sobriety, but cultivate truth in charity.

THE SHAKESPEARE ENIGMA

polair publishing

'the great little publisher for the new age'

THE WORLD IS IN MY GARDEN Chris Maser with Zane Maser
Internationally-acclaimed environmentalist Chris Maser shows how ecological, social, personal and spiritual issues can all be understood through the choices each one of us has to make in our own garden. His wife, Zane, takes us further, into the world of meditation.

ISBN 0-9545389-0-0 · £9.99

YOUR YOGA BODYMAP FOR VITALITY Jenny Beeken
This book has changed the way yoga postures can be taught, because uniquely it works from each area of the body (feet and ankles, sacrum and belly, neck and head, etc.) into a programme of postures. It is particularly suitable for those leading an active life. Sue Peggs' brilliant stop-action photography makes the postures unusually easy to follow.

ISBN 0-9545389-1-9 · £15.99

THE HAMBLIN COURSE IN MYSTICISM
Thirty-six rediscovered lessons by Henry Thomas Hamblin and Joel S. Goldsmith, which with commentary and exercises make a complete course in mysticism. You can indeed heal your life through this positive approach.

ISBN 0-9545389-5-1 · £13.99

IGNITING SOUL FIRE Gaye Mack
Edward Bach, the originator of the famous Bach Flower Remedies, was a true mystic. In his writings there is more about the soul and the lessons it undergoes than has hitherto been realised. Gaye Mack explores the remedies in the light of this, using a knowledge of the chakra system and of basic astrology to illumine for us all how simple flower remedies can help with our deepest problems and … ignite our soul fire!

ISBN 0-9545389-2-7 · £10.99

Forthcoming titles include ROSE ELLIOT'S GLOBAL KITCHEN —a book about ingredients from around the world by Britain's best-known vegetarian cookery writer.

www.polairpublishing.co.uk